The song is notated two ways which are identical in sound. Draw a circle around the dotted notes in version 1 and their tied equivalents in version 2 like this:

D1517644

Clap the song.

30

Clapping response.

Using the blank staff, copy the phrase below changing the tied notes to dotted notes.

A CAPITAL SHIP

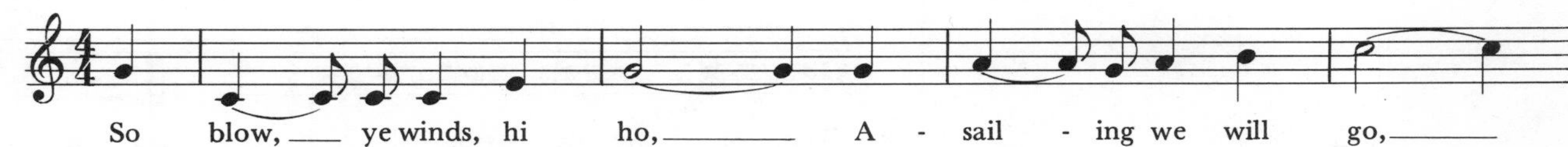
So blow, ye winds, hi ho, A - sail - ing we will go,

From The Fireside Book of Children's Songs. *Copyright © 1966 by Marie Winn and Alan Miller. Reprinted by permission of Simon and Schuster.*

Clap the song as you have written it.

♩‿♪ = what dotted note? ______ 𝅗𝅥‿♩ = what dotted note? ______

30

31

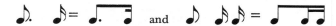

32

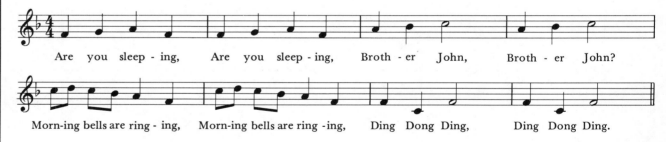

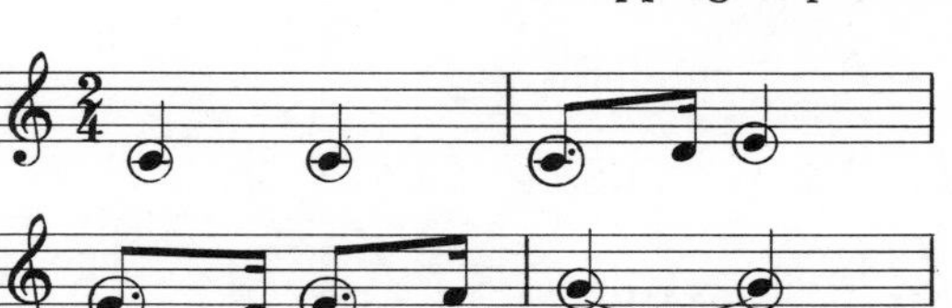

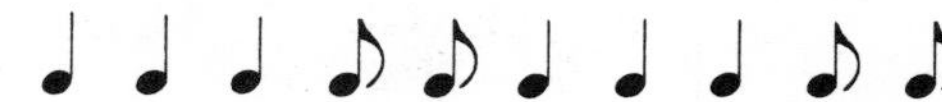

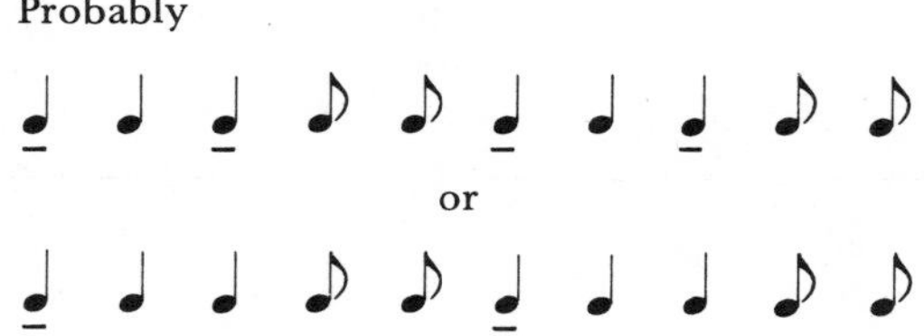

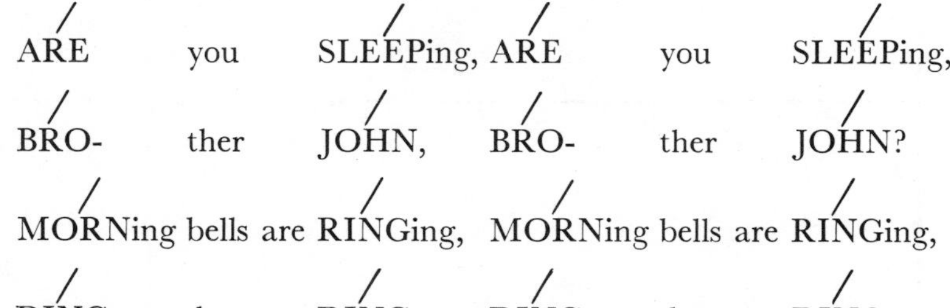

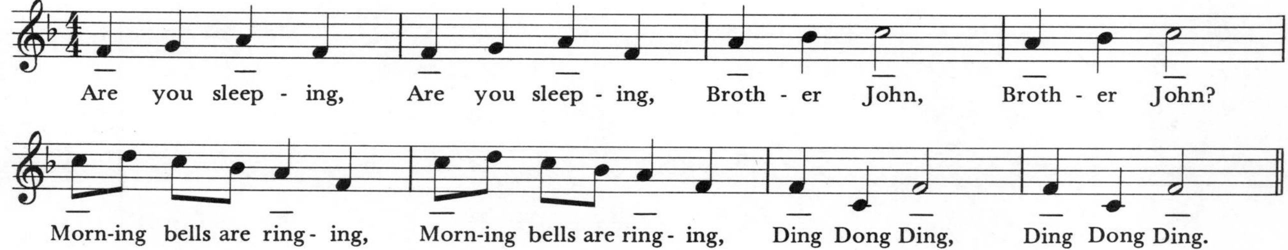

2. 𝄽 𝄽 𝄽

3

Exercise 4: Before you listen to "Four in a Boat," clap the durational pattern. Check your response with the recording.

FOUR IN A BOAT

Four in a boat and the tide rolls high, Four in a boat and the tide rolls high;

Clapping response.

4

Exercise 5: Before listening to the record, clap the durational pattern below. Check your response with the recording. Clap with the repetition of the pattern on the record.

♩ ♪ ♪ ♩ 𝄽 ♩ ♩ 𝅗𝅥

Clapping response.

5

Exercise 6: Follow the music to "Du, Du, Liegst Mir im Herzen" as you listen to the recorded melody. The eighth note is the unit beat. Tap your foot or move your arm to the unit beat as you listen. How many beats does a quarter note receive? ______________ A dotted quarter note? ______________

DU, DU LIEGST MIR IM HERZEN

Du, Du liegst mir im Her - zen, Du, Du liegst mir im Sinn,

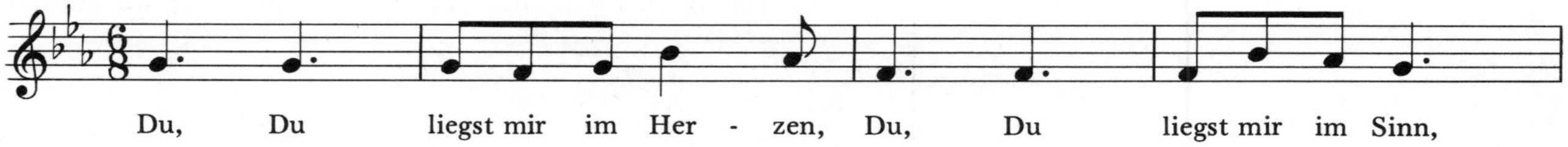

End of Band 2, Side 1

Two, three.

6

Exercise 7: Dotted Notes. Dotted notes whose duration is not a full beat are usually accompanied by a note that completes the beat. For example, the ♩. is usually followed by an ♪ ; when the unit beat is a quarter note, ♩. ♪ equals two complete beats.

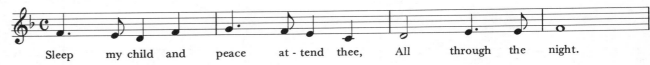

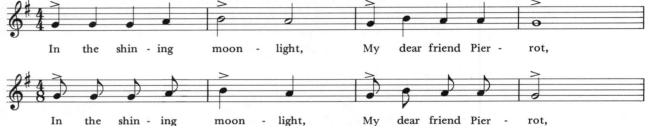

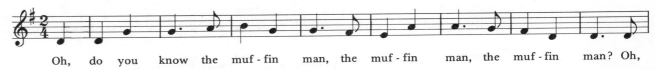

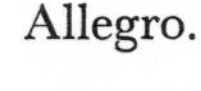

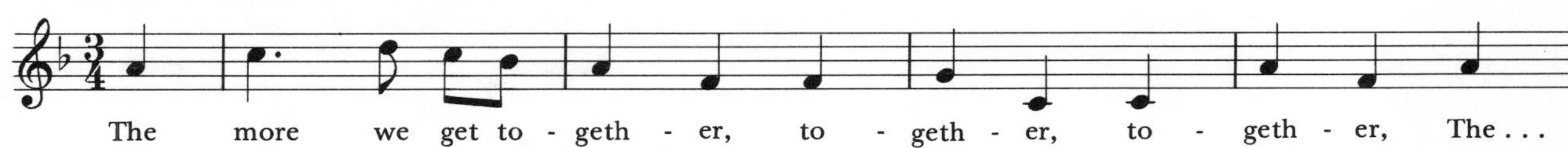

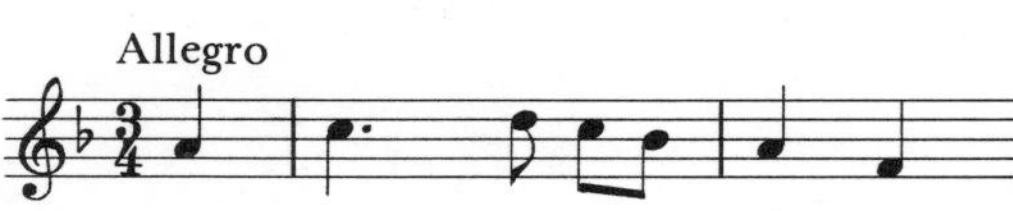

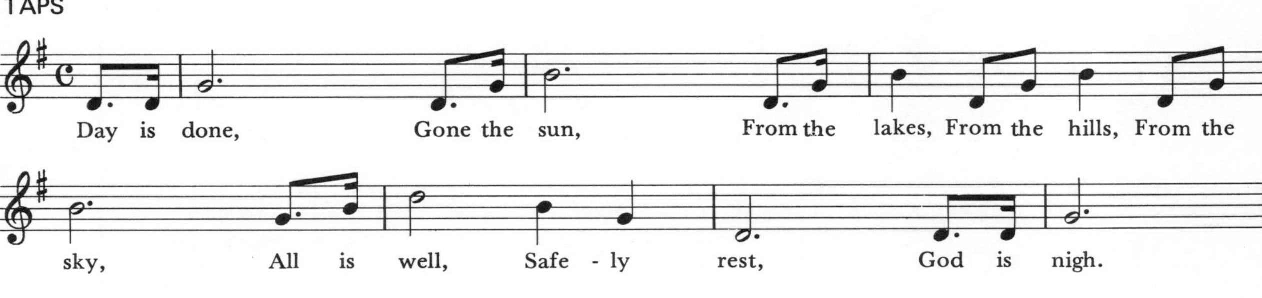

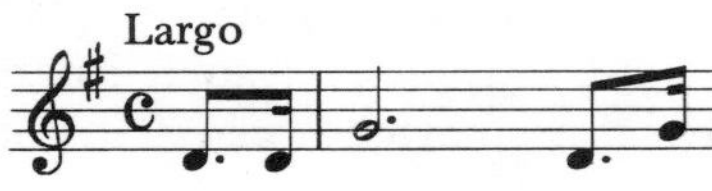

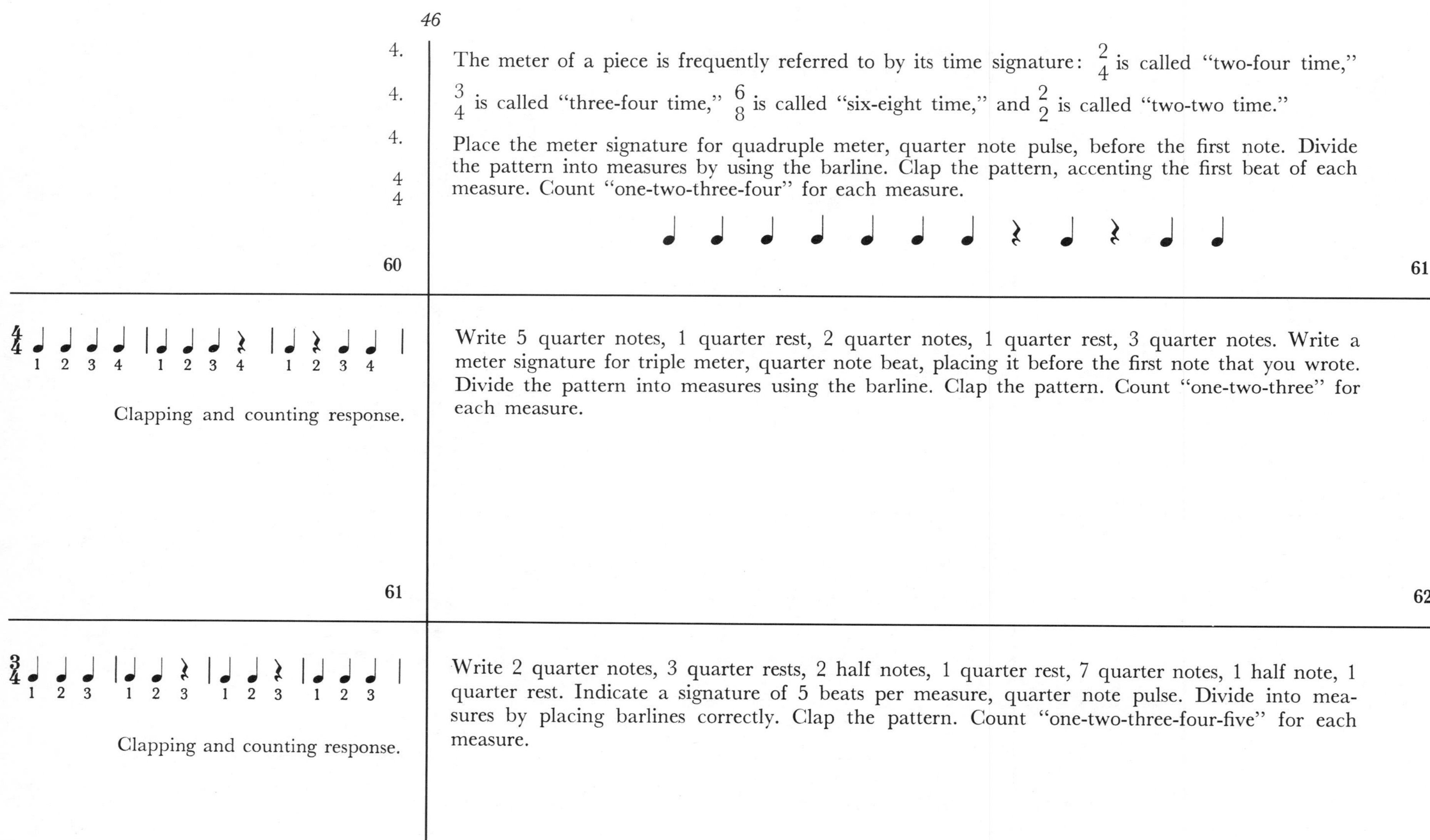

4.

4.

4.

$\frac{4}{4}$

60

The meter of a piece is frequently referred to by its time signature: $\frac{2}{4}$ is called "two-four time," $\frac{3}{4}$ is called "three-four time," $\frac{6}{8}$ is called "six-eight time," and $\frac{2}{2}$ is called "two-two time."

Place the meter signature for quadruple meter, quarter note pulse, before the first note. Divide the pattern into measures by using the barline. Clap the pattern, accenting the first beat of each measure. Count "one-two-three-four" for each measure.

♩ ♩ ♩ ♩ ♩ ♩ ♩ 𝄽 ♩ 𝄽 ♩ ♩

61

$\frac{4}{4}$ ♩ ♩ ♩ ♩ | ♩ ♩ ♩ 𝄽 | ♩ 𝄽 ♩ ♩ |

1 2 3 4 1 2 3 4 1 2 3 4

Clapping and counting response.

61

Write 5 quarter notes, 1 quarter rest, 2 quarter notes, 1 quarter rest, 3 quarter notes. Write a meter signature for triple meter, quarter note beat, placing it before the first note that you wrote. Divide the pattern into measures using the barline. Clap the pattern. Count "one-two-three" for each measure.

62

$\frac{3}{4}$ ♩ ♩ ♩ | ♩ ♩ 𝄽 | ♩ ♩ 𝄽 | ♩ ♩ ♩ |

1 2 3 1 2 3 1 2 3 1 2 3

Clapping and counting response.

62

Write 2 quarter notes, 3 quarter rests, 2 half notes, 1 quarter rest, 7 quarter notes, 1 half note, 1 quarter rest. Indicate a signature of 5 beats per measure, quarter note pulse. Divide into measures by placing barlines correctly. Clap the pattern. Count "one-two-three-four-five" for each measure.

63

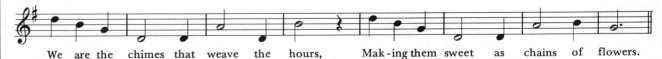

The song is notated two ways which are identical in sound. Draw a circle around the dotted notes in version 1 and their tied equivalents in version 2 like this:

Clap the song.

30

Clapping response.

30

Using the blank staff, copy the phrase below changing the tied notes to dotted notes.

A CAPITAL SHIP

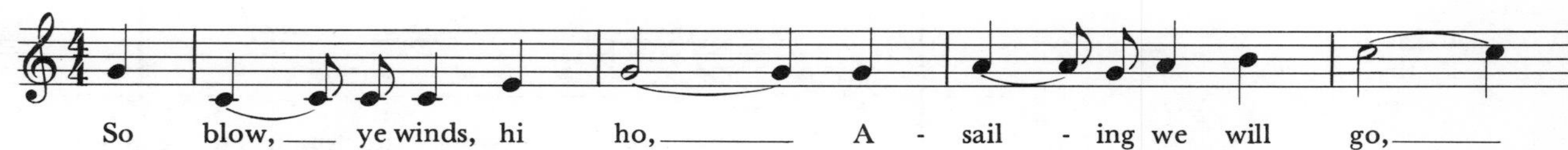
So blow, ___ ye winds, hi ho, ___ A - sail - ing we will go, ___

From The Fireside Book of Children's Songs. *Copyright © 1966 by Marie Winn and Alan Miller. Reprinted by permission of Simon and Schuster.*

Clap the song as you have written it.

= what dotted note? ______
= what dotted note? ______

31

Clapping response.

Notes having flags or tails—eighths, sixteenths, thirty-seconds, and smaller—may be notated two ways. Because the tails can be confusing to read when there are several of these fast notes in a row, two or more notes may be connected by a bar or beam.

Instead of , the notation may be . Similarly, for sixteenth notes, , two bars may be used, , rather than two tails. For thirty-second notes, , three bars, , may be used.

This old English chanty is shown notated with bars and with flags. The versions are identical in sound but version A is generally considered easier to read. The song is on the record, Exercise 13, Application: Duration, Pulse, and Tempo.

WHAT SHALL WE DO WITH THE DRUNKEN SAILOR?

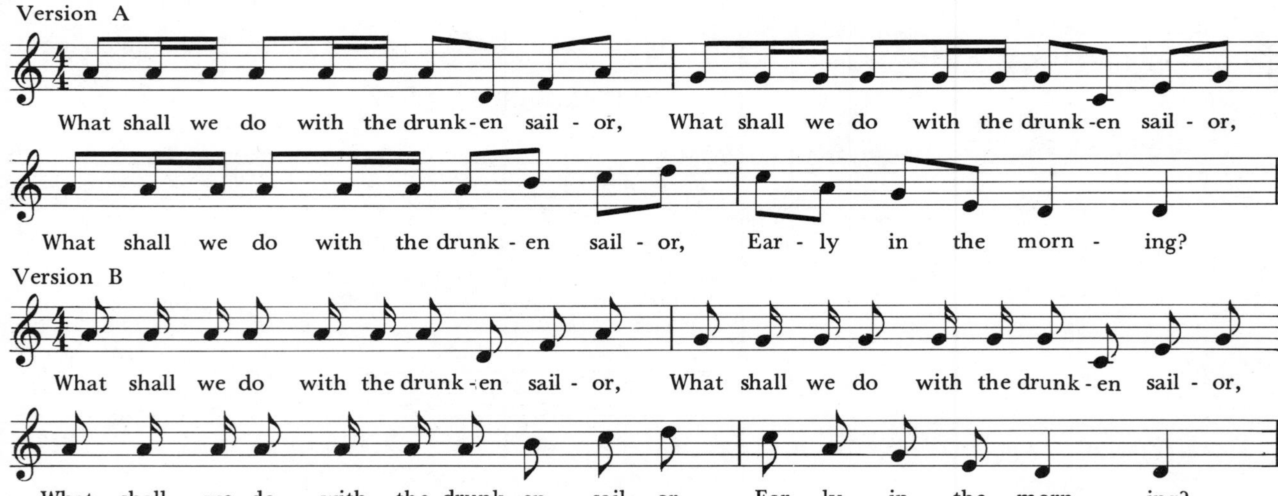
Version A
What shall we do with the drunk-en sail - or, What shall we do with the drunk-en sail - or,
What shall we do with the drunk - en sail - or, Ear - ly in the morn - ing?
Version B
What shall we do with the drunk-en sail - or, What shall we do with the drunk-en sail - or,
What shall we do with the drunk-en sail - or, Ear - ly in the morn - ing?

Bars are also used to connect dotted patterns containing notes of different values when these values are eighth-note values or less:

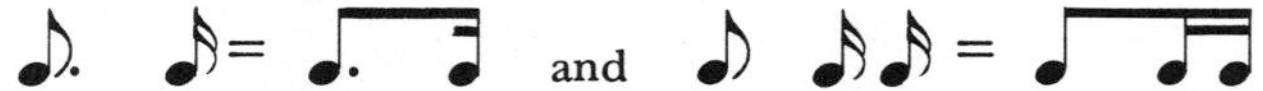
and

Rewrite the following pattern, using bars in place of flags wherever appropriate. (Group the notes in 1-beat patterns with = unit beat.)

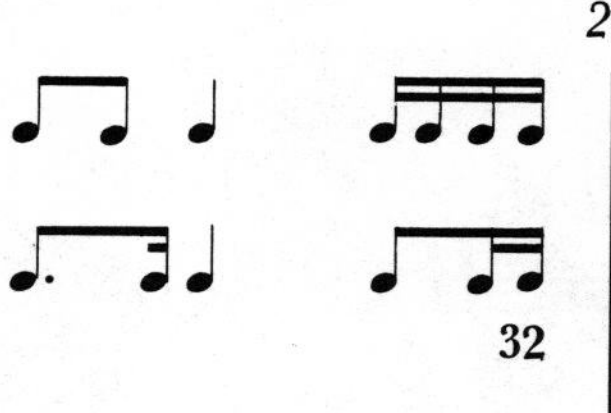
23
32

CHAPTER 3 The Concept of Pulse

In music the notes and rests occur within a steady *pulse,* or *beat,* which we can feel as we listen or perform. Notes and rests can be long or short, but the pulse of a piece of music is usually regular. Inexperienced students often have trouble keeping the musical pulse steady. Walking, marching, clapping, and tapping to music help in strengthening the feeling for steady musical beat. Often one observes a professional musician tapping his foot to assist in feeling the steady beat.

This chapter will (1) help you understand pulse and stress and (2) give you opportunities to experience pulse and stress in musical exercises.

Clap a series of notes at a moderate speed. Keep them even. You have established a beat, or pulse, by clapping steadily. Continue to clap the same pulse while you sing "Row, Row, Row Your Boat." Some notes in the song will be faster than the pulse, but the pulse should remain the same.

Use the ♩ as the unit beat.

ROW, ROW, ROW YOUR BOAT

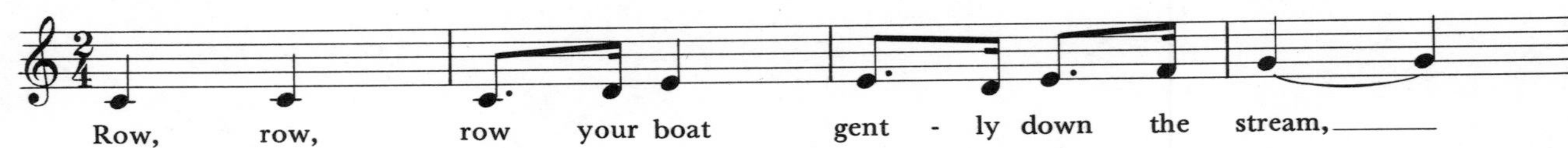

Circle the notes that fall *on* the beat or pulse.

Clapping response.

33

EMPHASIS

Clap this pattern:

Because music is an organized system of sounds and silences, you probably clapped some claps with more emphasis, or more sound, than the others. Patterns of emphasis–nonemphasis provide an organizational system. Emphasis and nonemphasis on certain notes in music organizes music. A steady beat without any emphasis would be uninteresting and meaningless.

Clap the pattern once more. Draw a short line, __, under the notes that you emphasized.

34

Clapping response.

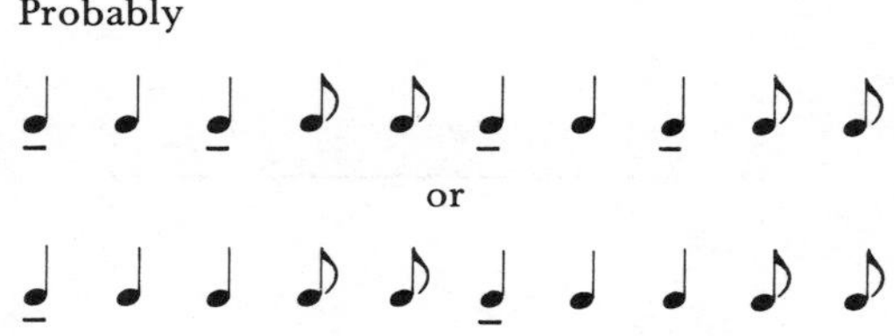
Probably
or

Either would be correct.

34

Language is also organized by patterns of emphasis–nonemphasis, or stress–nonstress. Read the following lines, applying stress (/) as marked.

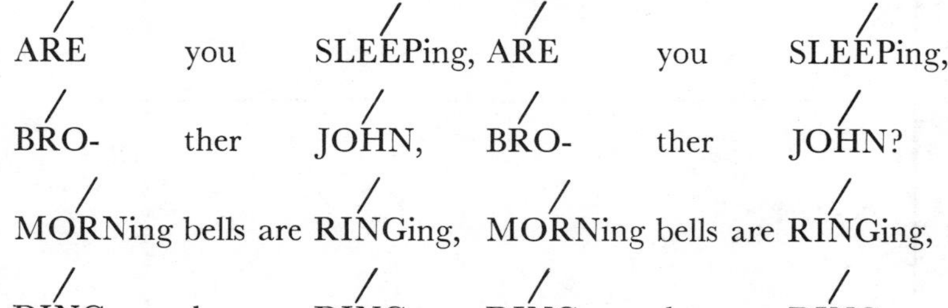
ARE you SLEEPing, ARE you SLEEPing,
BRO- ther JOHN, BRO- ther JOHN?
MORNing bells are RINGing, MORNing bells are RINGing,
DING dong DING, DING dong DING.

Chant or sing "Brother John." Use the same stress as you did in reading, stressing where indicated by "__" under the note.

BROTHER JOHN

Are you sleep - ing, Are you sleep - ing, Broth - er John, Broth - er John?
Morn-ing bells are ring - ing, Morn-ing bells are ring - ing, Ding Dong Ding, Ding Dong Ding.

35

Chanting or singing response.

35

The pattern can be reversed, with the nonstress coming first. Using this emphasis pattern, sing or say the words to "America the Beautiful."

o BEAU- ti- FUL for SPAC- ious SKIES, for AM- ber WAVES of GRAIN,

for PUR- ple MOUN- tain MA- jes- TIES a- BOVE the FRUIT- ed PLAIN.

a- MER- i- CA! a- MER- i- CA! God SHED his GRACE on THEE,

and CROWN thy GOOD with BRO- ther- HOOD from SEA to SHIN- ing SEA.

When a beat or a note is emphasized, a stress is put on it. The term *accent* is used to mean the same thing: stress or emphasis on a note. This sign > above or below a note, , indicates that the note is to be accented; this is usually accomplished by making the note louder.

The use of accent is one device to make music move.

36

Singing or speaking response.

36

CHAPTER 4 The Concept of Tempo

The speed of musical pulse or beat is called the tempo. Often the tempo affects the character or meaning of the music.

When you have completed the exercises in this chapter, you should (1) recognize and understand tempo markings and (2) be aware of the role tempo plays in music.

Whether the tempo of the music is fast, moderate, or slow, the pulse is usually regular. Tap a pulse with your foot or hand, and sing or chant "Brother John" to the pulse you have set using ♩ = unit beat. Keep the tempo steady. Do not speed up or slow down.

BROTHER JOHN

Are you sleep - ing, Are you sleep - ing, Broth - er John, Broth - er John?
Morn-ing bells are ring - ing, Morn-ing bells are ring -ing, Ding Dong Ding, Ding Dong Ding.

37

Tapping and singing or chanting response.

37

A radical change of tempo usually changes the meaning of the music. Therefore, although there is more than one correct tempo for most music, the composer expects the piece to be performed within a certain range of tempos. For example, if you sing "America the Beautiful" at a fast tempo, you will alter the meaning of the music from what the composer intended.

Sing "America" at two different tempi, one fast and one slow. Think of another song and establish the tempo with your foot *before* you sing it by tapping a steady pulse.

38

Singing response.

The composer indicates the tempo he wishes for his music by placing a tempo term, or tempo mark, at the beginning of the number, just above the music. In the music below, "Allegro," meaning "fast," is the tempo mark.

YANKEE DOODLE

Allegro
Fath'r and I went down to camp a - long with Cap - tain Good - in and
there we saw the men and boys as thick as has - ty pud - din'.

The tempo may be given in English or Italian. The tempo terms aid the teacher in determining a proper speed for music with which he is unfamiliar.

Allegro: rapid or fast
Moderato: moderate
Largo: slow

A list of other common tempo terms is found in the glossary.

A rapid tempo may be indicated by the Italian word _______________, a slow tempo by _______________.

38 39

Allegro.

Largo.

Decide if the song below is fast, moderate, or slow. (Notice that the words are humorous; sing the note pattern: ♩ ♪♩ ♪). Fill in an appropriate tempo making.

THE DONKEY

____

Sweet - ly sings the donk - ey at the break of day;

39 40

Allegro.

40

As was seen in frame 40, a tempo indication is helpful and sometimes essential to the teacher and the learners. Deriving tempo from the music alone is extremely difficult. A more exact method of indicating tempo is to state the number of pulses per minute. For example, ♩ = 60 indicates sixty quarter note pulses per minute, or one per second. Tap a pulse you estimate to be about one beat per second (♩ = 60). Sing "America" at this tempo, one quarter note per beat. Does ♩ = 60 seem to be fast, moderate, or slow? ______________ What Italian tempo term would be appropriate? ______________

41

Tapping and singing response.

Slow.

Largo.

41

Frequently, the marking given looks like this: MM = 60. The MM stands for Mälzel's Metronome. The metronome is a mechanical device that gives forth even ticks, like a clock, and can be adjusted to a wide range of speeds. MM = 60 = one pulse per second.

Some guidelines can help one estimate tempo without actually using the metronome. MM = 100, or ♩ = 100, is a moderate tempo. Marches (brisk) are usually played at a tempo between MM = 120 and MM = 132. We have seen that ♩ = 60 is slow.

Using the terms in frame 39, the Italian tempo term most appropriate for MM = 50 is probably ______________ while for MM = 140 it is ______________.

42

Largo.

Allegro.

42

Although the pulse of music is usually steady, *a completely steady beat tends to make music mechanical and unexpressive*. Therefore, composers and performers make slight variations in the tempo. Italian terms are also used to indicate these variations.

Ritard or *ritardando* (abbreviated *rit.*): slow down gradually
Rallentando (abbreviated *rall.*): slow down gradually
Accelerando (abbreviated *accel.*): gradually increase the tempo
A tempo: return to the original tempo

The tempo marking at the beginning of the following song indicates a ______________ tempo. The tempo marking near the end of the song indicates ______________.

SIDEWALKS OF NEW YORK

Allegro — *rit.*

Tripped the light___ fan - tas - tic on the side-walks of New York.

43

30

Fast.

Slow down gradually (ritard.).

43

APPLICATION

This section is designed to assist you in understanding the concepts introduced in the preceding chapters. Since music is an aural art, hearing examples of the concepts is essential to full understanding. Use of the record is strongly recommended as a review of the material in order to show the relation of cognitive concepts to musical sound and to supplement classroom activities.

How to Use the Records

The records are divided into bands, each of which contains several learning exercises. The exercises are clearly printed on the label and are announced on the record. Before listening to the record, read through the entire group of questions included in a single band. Answer all of the questions that can be answered without listening to the record. Then listen to the record and answer as many additional questions as you are able the first time. A second and a third hearing are recommended, not only to answer the questions but also to reinforce your understanding of the concepts being dealt with in the exercise and to learn some musical materials.

APPLICATION: Duration, Pulse, and Tempo

Exercise 1: Long and Short Duration. Three patterns will be played, each repeated immediately. Listen to the pattern, then clap, tap, or chant "long" "short" with repetition.

Clapping, tapping, and chanting response.

1

Exercise 2: Line Notation for Long and Short Duration. Listen to three patterns. Each will be played twice. Using line (sausage) notation, write each in the space below. Write as you listen both times. The record is banded in order to allow for additional listenings.

1.

2.

3.

---

1. ____ __ __ ____ __ __.
2. __ __ __ __ ____ ____ __ __.
3. __ __ ____ __ __ ____ __ __ __ __ ____.

2

Exercise 3: Rests. Listen to the melody of "Sugar Bush." Tap the quarter note beat and count the number of quarter rests that occur at each break in the melody, after the words "me," "be," and "merrily." Circle the correct answer.

1. 𝄽 2. 𝄽 𝄽 𝄽 3. 𝄽 𝄽 𝄽 𝄽

End of Band 1, Side 1

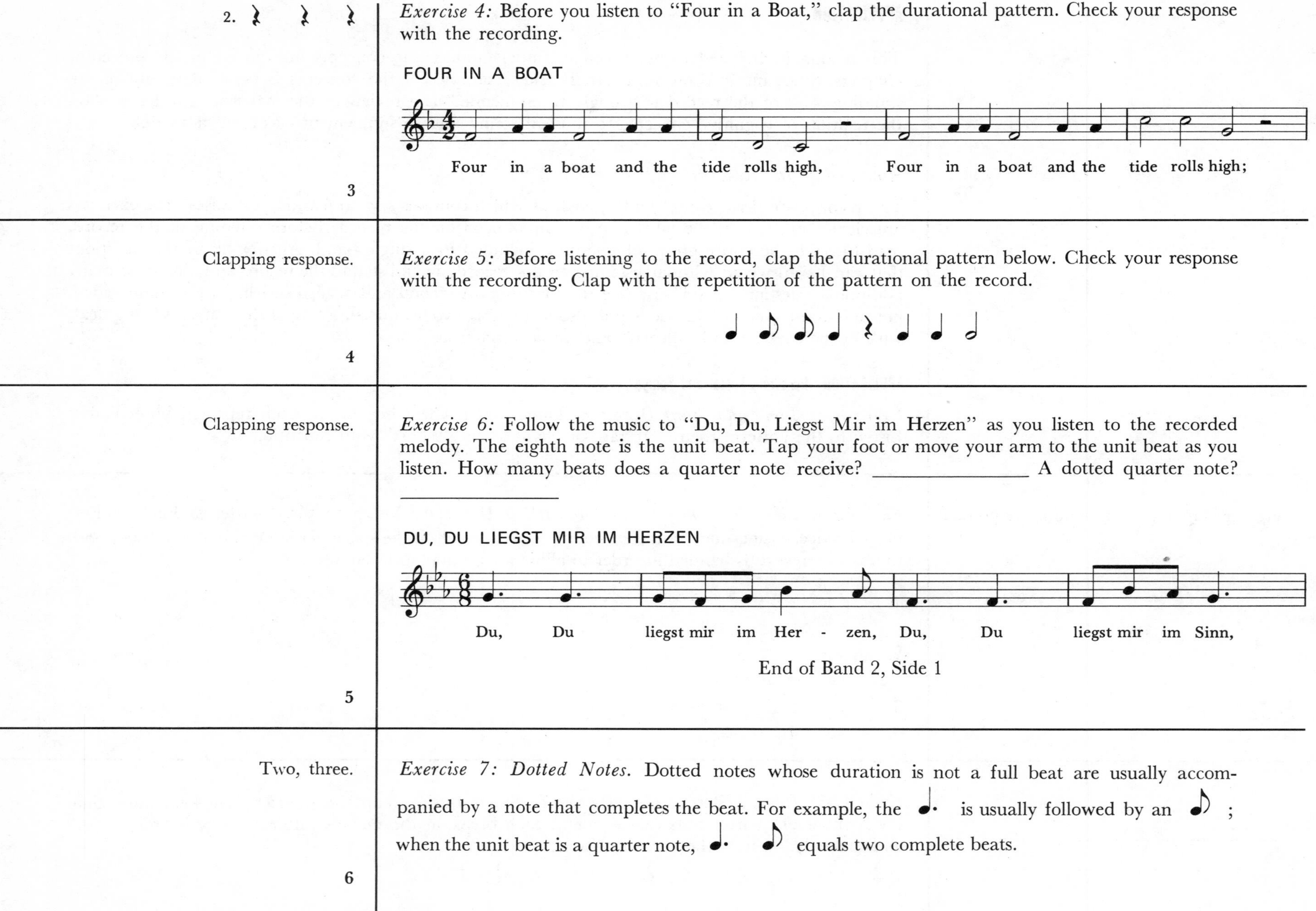

2. 𝄽 𝄽 𝄽

3

Exercise 4: Before you listen to "Four in a Boat," clap the durational pattern. Check your response with the recording.

FOUR IN A BOAT

Four in a boat and the tide rolls high, Four in a boat and the tide rolls high;

Clapping response.

4

Exercise 5: Before listening to the record, clap the durational pattern below. Check your response with the recording. Clap with the repetition of the pattern on the record.

♩ ♪ ♪ ♩ 𝄽 ♩ ♩ 𝅗𝅥

Clapping response.

5

Exercise 6: Follow the music to "Du, Du, Liegst Mir im Herzen" as you listen to the recorded melody. The eighth note is the unit beat. Tap your foot or move your arm to the unit beat as you listen. How many beats does a quarter note receive? ______________ A dotted quarter note? ______________

DU, DU LIEGST MIR IM HERZEN

Du, Du liegst mir im Her - zen, Du, Du liegst mir im Sinn,

End of Band 2, Side 1

Two, three.

6

Exercise 7: Dotted Notes. Dotted notes whose duration is not a full beat are usually accompanied by a note that completes the beat. For example, the ♩. is usually followed by an ♪; when the unit beat is a quarter note, ♩. ♪ equals two complete beats.

Mark the places in the music where the dotted quarter is followed by an eighth note to complete two full beats. Tap the steady quarter note pulse as you listen to the melody on the record. Notice that the eighth note falls *between* two pulses.

MUFFIN MAN

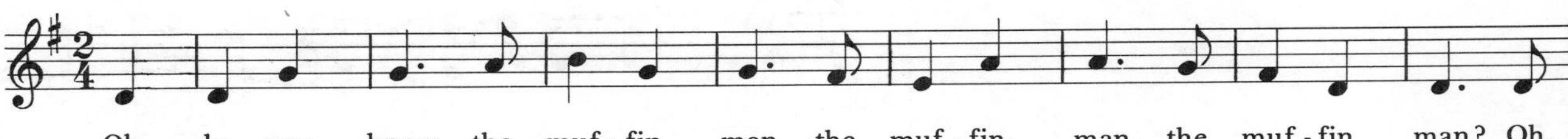
Oh, do you know the muf - fin man, the muf - fin man, the muf - fin man? Oh,

do you know the muf - fin man who lives in Drur - y Lane?

Tapping response.

7

Exercise 8: Dotted Notes. Sing the phrase below with the record, tapping the steady quarter note pulse. There will be two taps (pulses) on the dotted quarter note, the eighth note falling between two taps. Beneath the music, write "1" for each pulse, "&" for the eighth note on the partial pulse.

1 1 & etc.

ALL THROUGH THE NIGHT

Sleep my child and peace at - tend thee, All through the night.

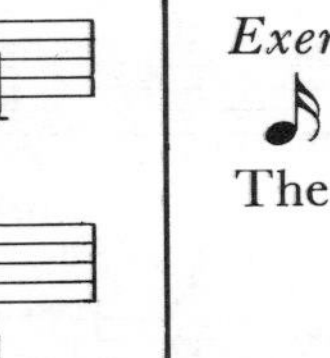

1 1 & 1 1 1 1 & 1 1

1 1 1 1 & 1 1 1 1

8

Exercise 9: Dotted Notes. The dotted eighth note, , is usually followed by a sixteenth note, , like this: . With a quarter note unit beat this pattern fills one complete pulse. The pattern below is often referred to as the "skipping pattern."

Count the dotted patterns ( ) in the verse to "Battle Hymn of the Republic," below. There are ______ patterns. Tap the pulse as you listen to the record.

BATTLE HYMN OF THE REPUBLIC

20.

Tapping response.

Exercise 10: Dotted Notes. The refrain to "Battle Hymn" contains examples of both common dotted patterns, and . Mark the places where the dotted quarter–eighth note pattern occurs. Tap the pulse as you listen.

9

Tapping response.

Exercise 11: Dotted Notes. The song below contains dotted patterns, dotted quarter notes *not* followed by completing eighth note, and a dotted rest. Tap the pulse as you listen. Be sure to tap steadily during the rests.

RAINDROPS KEEP FALLIN' ON MY HEAD

10

rain - drops are fall - in' on my head. They keep fall-in'

Tapping response.

Exercise 12: The system for dotted rests is identical to that for dotted notes. However, the use of dotted rests is not common. Instead, two rests are written (𝄽 𝄾) rather than making use of the dot (𝄽.). The song below has two places where a dotted rest might be used, but two rests are used instead. Mark the two places. Tap the pulse as you listen, tapping steadily during the rests. Check your response with the repetition.

GOD BLESS ALL

God bless all good friends here, A mer-ry, mer-ry Christ-mas and a hap-py new year!

11

Exercise 13: The following song contains many fast-moving notes that are smaller than the unit beat. The unit beat is the quarter note (♩ = 1); eighth notes and sixteenth notes are faster than the unit beat and fall between the pulses. Clap the pulse as you listen to the song. Then mark a line under the notes on which the beat or pulse falls.

WHAT SHALL WE DO WITH THE DRUNKEN SAILOR?

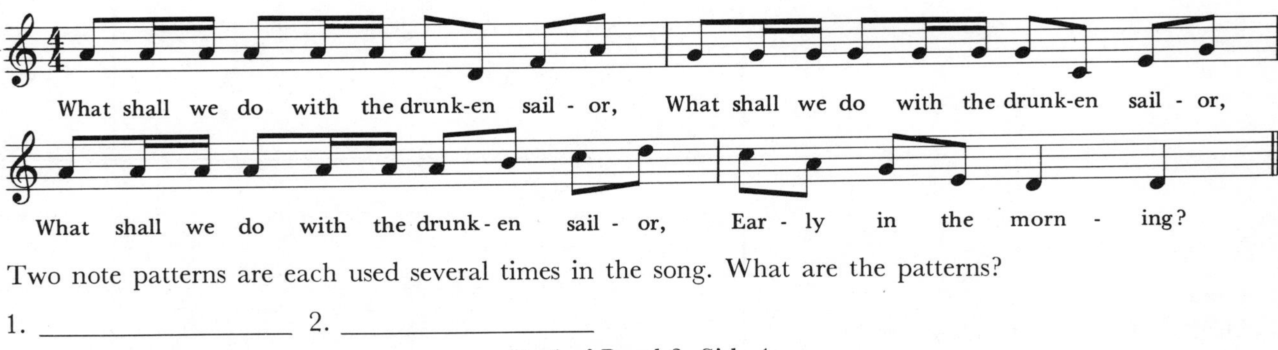
What shall we do with the drunk-en sail - or, What shall we do with the drunk-en sail - or,
What shall we do with the drunk - en sail - or, Ear - ly in the morn - ing?

Two note patterns are each used several times in the song. What are the patterns?

1. ________________ 2. ________________

End of Band 3, Side 1

12

1.
2.

13

The directions for many of the following exercises are given only in the book. Use the book with the record.

Exercise 14: Tempo. Below is a musical phrase written two ways. Sing and clap phrase #1 with the record, counting one count to each ♩. Observe the accents. Do the same for phrase #2, counting one count to each ♪ .

IN THE SHINING MOONLIGHT

In the shin - ing moon - light, My dear friend Pier - rot,
In the shin - ing moon - light, My dear friend Pier - rot,

Are the tempos for the two phrases the same, or different? ______________ The speed of the unit beat, or pulse, is *not* determined by the kind of note used for the unit beat.

End of Band 1, Side 2

Singing and clapping response.

Same.

14

Exercise 15: Two versions of "Brother John" are sung. Which version is "Allegro"? ____________

Which version is "Moderato"? ______________

Which tempo is more appropriate for the song? ______________

End of Band 2, Side 2 (A STOP BAND)

Second.

First.

Allegro is probably more appropriate for a "wake up" song.

15

Exercise 16: The metronome will be heard at two different speeds. Determine if the speed is MM = 60 (Largo), MM = 100 (Moderato), or MM = 132 (Allegro).
Tempo 1 is ______________. Tempo 2 is ______________.

Allegro.

Largo.

16

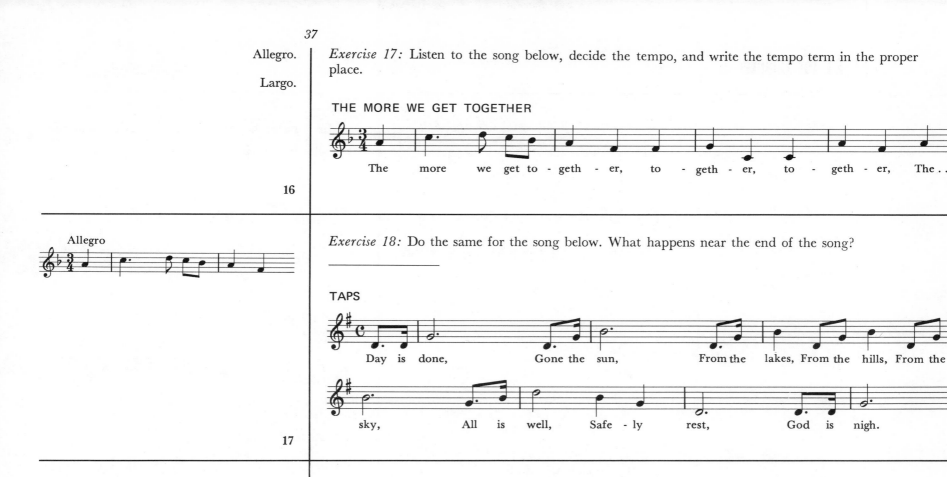

Exercise 17: Listen to the song below, decide the tempo, and write the tempo term in the proper place.

THE MORE WE GET TOGETHER

The more we get to - geth - er, to - geth - er, to - geth - er, The . . .

Allegro

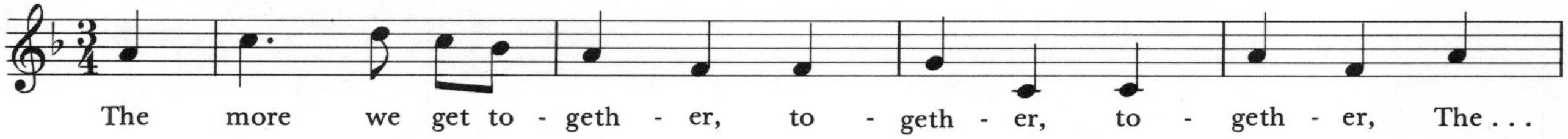

17

Exercise 18: Do the same for the song below. What happens near the end of the song?

____

TAPS

Day is done, Gone the sun, From the lakes, From the hills, From the sky, All is well, Safe - ly rest, God is nigh.

Slows down (rall, or rit.).

18

End of Band 3, Side 2
End of Application Section 1

PRETEST for Chapter 5: Meter

Mark the answer or *answers that are correct.*

1. In most music the stress occurs on the:

   —— a. first beat of the measure
   —— b. second beat of the measure
   —— c. either the first or second beat of the measure
   —— d. first and last beats of the measure

2. An accent mark is written:

   —— a. >
   —— b. + R
   —— c. •
   —— d. —

3. The time signature is also called the:

   —— a. meter signature
   —— b. tempo signature
   —— c. pulse indicator
   —— d. metronome marking

4. The time signature consists of two numbers. The bottom number indicates:

   —— a. the number of pulses in each measure
   —— b. the tempo of the number
   —— c. the number of counts a quarter note receives
   —— d. the kind of note that receives one beat

5. In $\frac{2}{2}$ meter how many beats does each of the following receive?

   a. 𝅝 ____
   b. ♩ ____
   c. ♩. ____
   d. 𝅗𝅥. ____
   e. 𝅗𝅥 ____

6. Mark an X through the incorrect measures in meter.

7. Write 2 quarter notes, a dotted eighth, a sixteenth note, a quarter note, a quarter rest, a quarter note, a quarter rest, a quarter note, 2 eighth rests, 3 quarter notes, 2 eighth notes, a half rest.

   Indicate triple meter, quarter note beat. Divide into measures by use of the barline.

8. If 8 is the bottom number of the meter signature, the top number is ______.

9. Complete the second measure using only one rest.

10. Insert the correct meter signatures for the following patterns, quarter note pulse.

a.

b.

11. Bar the following song correctly.

12. Which of the following is (are) compound meter(s)?

—— a. $\frac{2}{4}$

—— b. $\frac{3}{4}$

—— c. $\frac{5}{4}$

—— d. $\frac{6}{4}$

13. Bar the following song.

14. The sign **C** for the meter signature indicates:

—— a. $\frac{2}{4}$

—— b. $\frac{3}{4}$

—— c. $\frac{4}{4}$

—— d. $\frac{6}{8}$

15. Another way to indicate alla breve is:

—— a.

—— b. ♩ = 120

—— c.

—— d. ¢

16. Cut time is another way of saying:

—— a. $\frac{2}{4}$

—— b. $\frac{6}{8}$

—— c. $\frac{2}{2}$

—— d. $\frac{4}{4}$

Answers

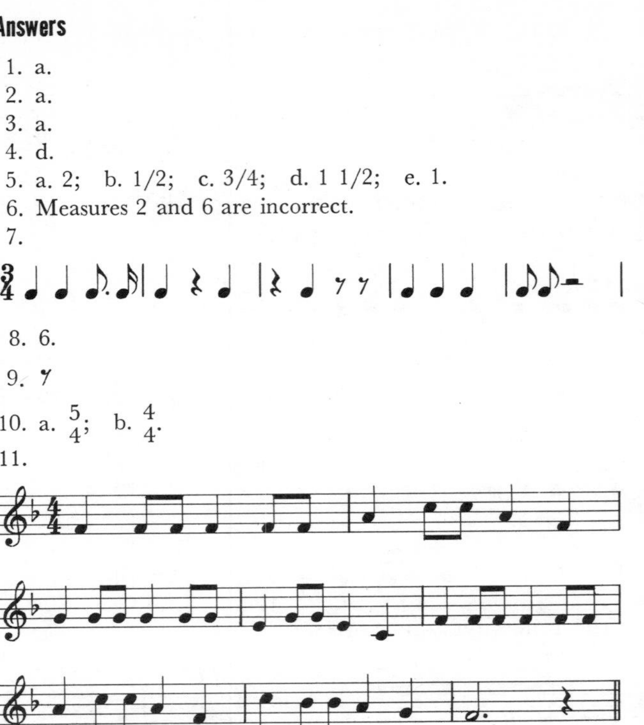

1. a.
2. a.
3. a.
4. d.
5. a. 2; b. 1/2; c. 3/4; d. 1 1/2; e. 1.
6. Measures 2 and 6 are incorrect.
7. (see notation)
8. 6.
9. 𝄾
10. a. $\frac{5}{4}$; b. $\frac{4}{4}$.
11. (see notation)

12. d.
13. (see notation)
14. c.
15. d.
16. c.

From your score determine if you can omit sections of the text.

CHAPTER 5 The Concept of Meter

Meter is the division of music into groups of regularly accented and unaccented pulses. Because much of the music of the Western world has a metrical basis, it is an essential concept to master. When you have completed this chapter, you should have accomplished the following objectives: (1) an understanding of the meter signature and its use; (2) a knowledge of duple, triple, quadruple, compound, and other meters; (3) ability to count note–rest values and note–rest patterns in various meters; and (4) ability to recognize various meters when listening to music.

As stated in Chapter 3, a steady beat without any emphasis is uninteresting and meaningless. Clap these quarter notes with equal stress. Make each note exactly like the others.

♩ ♩ ♩ ♩ ♩ ♩ ♩ ♩ ♩ ♩ ♩ ♩

Without stress–nonstress we have nothing more than a group of similar sounds. Emphasis–nonemphasis provides organization to aid you in following the sounds, and it helps to make the group of sounds musical.

44

Clapping response.

44

Using the accent mark (>), mark the stress on every fourth note.

1 2 3 4 1 2 3 4 1 2 3 4

♩ ♩ ♩ ♩ ♩ ♩ ♩ ♩ ♩ ♩ ♩ ♩

Clap the pattern with the accents you have marked.

45

♩ ♩ ♩ ♩ ♩ ♩ ♩ ♩ ♩ ♩ ♩ ♩
> > >

Clapping response.

45

By using accents you have organized the pulses or beats into groups of four. Organizing unit beats into groups is the basis for *meter*. In the previous frame, the quarter note received one beat, and there were four beats in each group. This regular grouping of beats constitutes a *measure*. Measures are separated by a vertical line called a *barline*. The number of beats in a measure can be 4 as shown below, 2 as in the song "San Sereni," or some other quantity.

SAN SERENI

San Se - re - ni de la bue - na, bue - na vi - da, Ha - cen a - si, a -
si, los za - pa - te - ros A - si, a - si, a - si, a - si, me gus - ta a - mi.

Notice how the barlines divide the song into measures.

The first beat of the measure is usually emphasized and does not need the accent mark. Accent marks are therefore reserved for unusual stress or stress on some other pulse of the measure.

Use barlines to divide the first pattern into measures with four beats in every measure. Make the quarter note equivalent to one beat. Clap it, counting "one-two-three-four" for each measure.

Do the same for the second pattern.

46

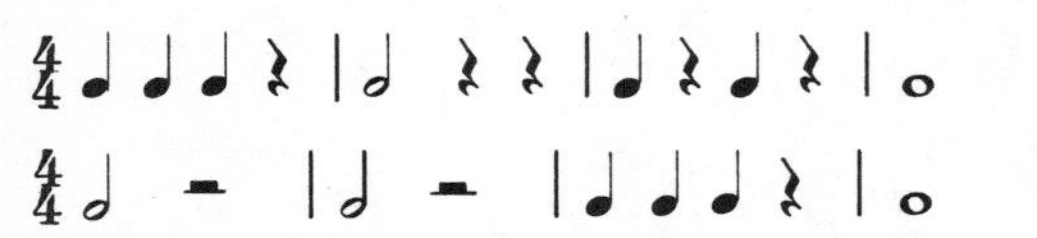

Clapping response.

46

METER SIGNATURE

A meter signature is placed at the beginning of a piece of music to indicate how the pulses are organized. The meter signature, consisting of two numbers, i.e., $\frac{2}{4}$ $\frac{3}{4}$ $\frac{6}{8}$, and so on, provides information on the number of beats in a measure and the unit beat. The bottom number indicates the unit beat—what kind of a note receives one beat; the top number indicates the number of beats in each measure. In this case a quarter note (quarter = 1/4) gets one beat.

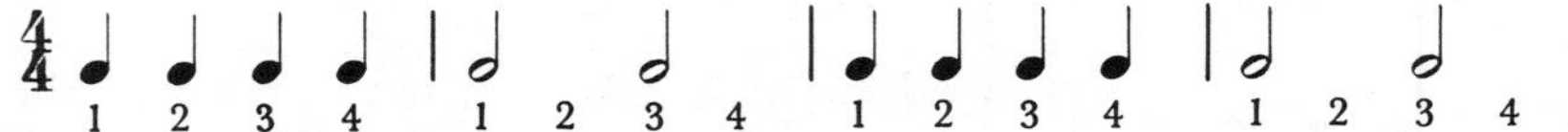
1 2 3 4 1 2 3 4 1 2 3 4 1 2 3 4

Clap the pattern and count aloud.

47

Clapping and counting response. 47	If the meter signature is $\frac{3}{4}$, there are ______ beats in each measure and the ______________ note is the unit beat. 48
3. Quarter. 48	Remember that the meter is the pattern of stress–nonstressed pulses into which the music is organized. This pattern is usually "ONE-two," "ONE-two-three," "ONE-two-three-four," or perhaps another such as "ONE-two-three-four-five." The meter signature is the sign that indicates the meter. It tells how many pulses in the measure and what kind of note gets one pulse. The meter signature is also called the time signature. If the meter signature is $\frac{6}{8}$, the ______________ note receives one beat and there are ______ pulses in each measure. A meter signature of $\frac{2}{2}$ means that the ______________ note receives one beat and that there are ______ beats in the measure. 49
Eighth, 6. Half, 2. 49	If the bottom number of the meter signature is 4, what would be the top number for this measure? 50
3. 50	If the bottom number of the meter signature is 8, what is the correct top number? 51
6. 51	Using only one note or rest, complete the following measure. 52

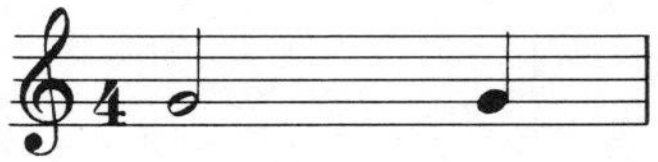

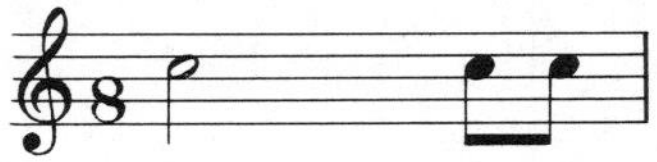

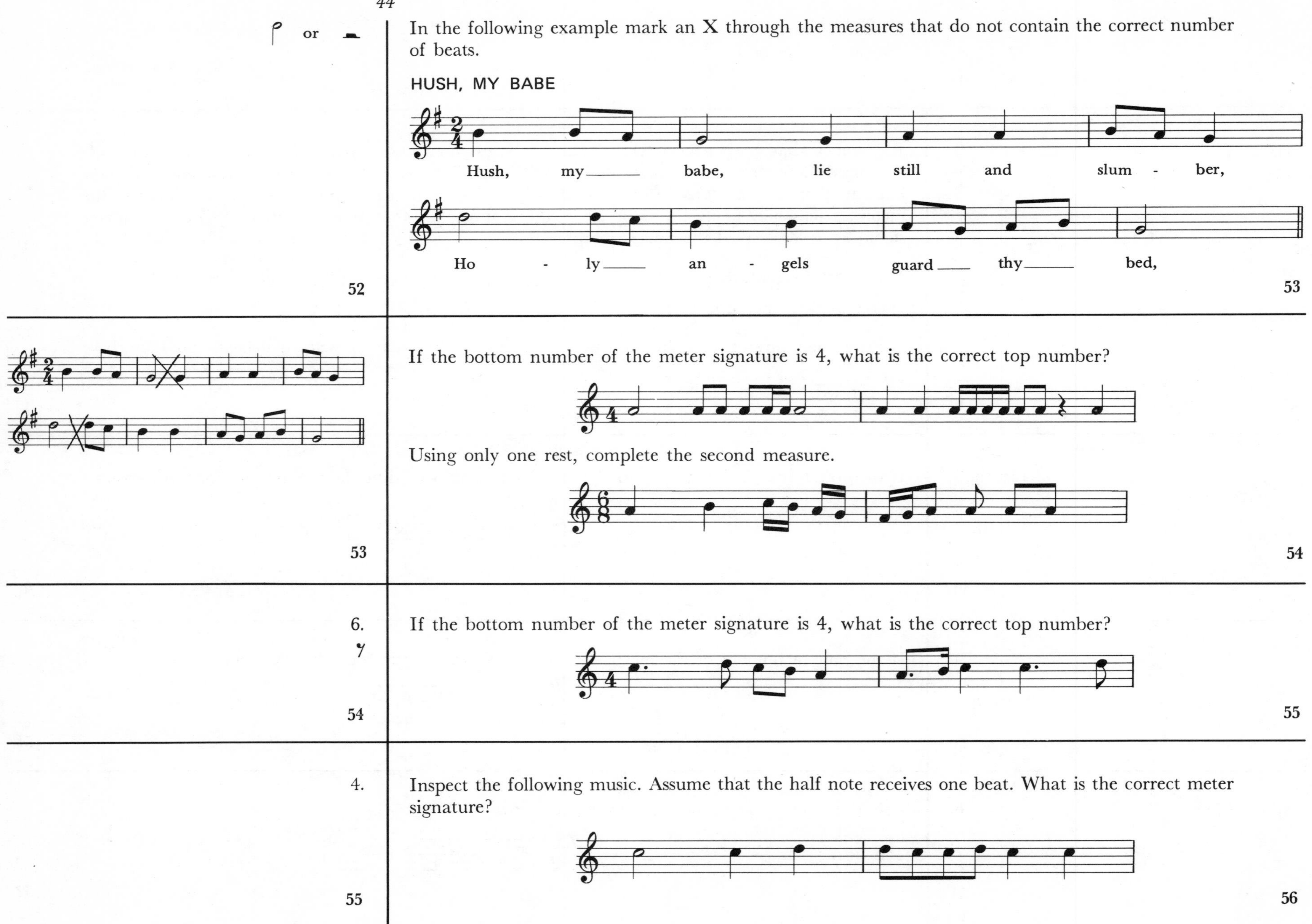

or

52

In the following example mark an X through the measures that do not contain the correct number of beats.

HUSH, MY BABE

Hush, my babe, lie still and slum - ber,
Ho - ly an - gels guard thy bed,

53

53

If the bottom number of the meter signature is 4, what is the correct top number?

Using only one rest, complete the second measure.

54

6.

54

If the bottom number of the meter signature is 4, what is the correct top number?

55

4.

55

Inspect the following music. Assume that the half note receives one beat. What is the correct meter signature?

56

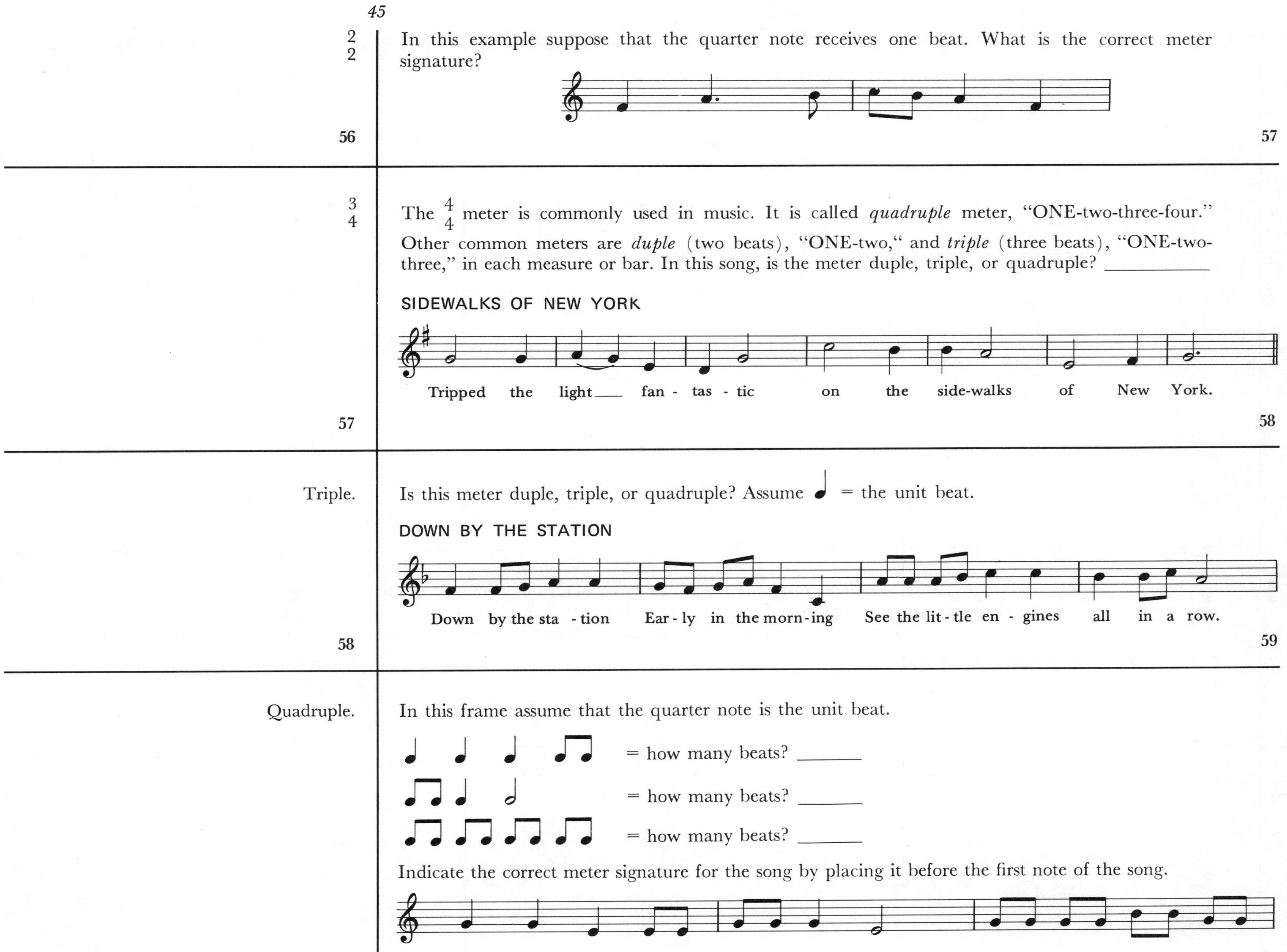

$\frac{2}{2}$

In this example suppose that the quarter note receives one beat. What is the correct meter signature?

56 — 57

$\frac{3}{4}$

The $\frac{4}{4}$ meter is commonly used in music. It is called *quadruple* meter, "ONE-two-three-four." Other common meters are *duple* (two beats), "ONE-two," and *triple* (three beats), "ONE-two-three," in each measure or bar. In this song, is the meter duple, triple, or quadruple? ________

SIDEWALKS OF NEW YORK

Tripped the light___ fan - tas - tic on the side-walks of New York.

57 — 58

Triple.

Is this meter duple, triple, or quadruple? Assume ♩ = the unit beat.

DOWN BY THE STATION

Down by the sta - tion Ear - ly in the morn - ing See the lit - tle en - gines all in a row.

58 — 59

Quadruple.

In this frame assume that the quarter note is the unit beat.

♩ ♩ ♩ ♫ = how many beats? ______

♫ ♩ 𝅗𝅥 = how many beats? ______

♫ ♫ ♫ ♫ = how many beats? ______

Indicate the correct meter signature for the song by placing it before the first note of the song.

59 — 60

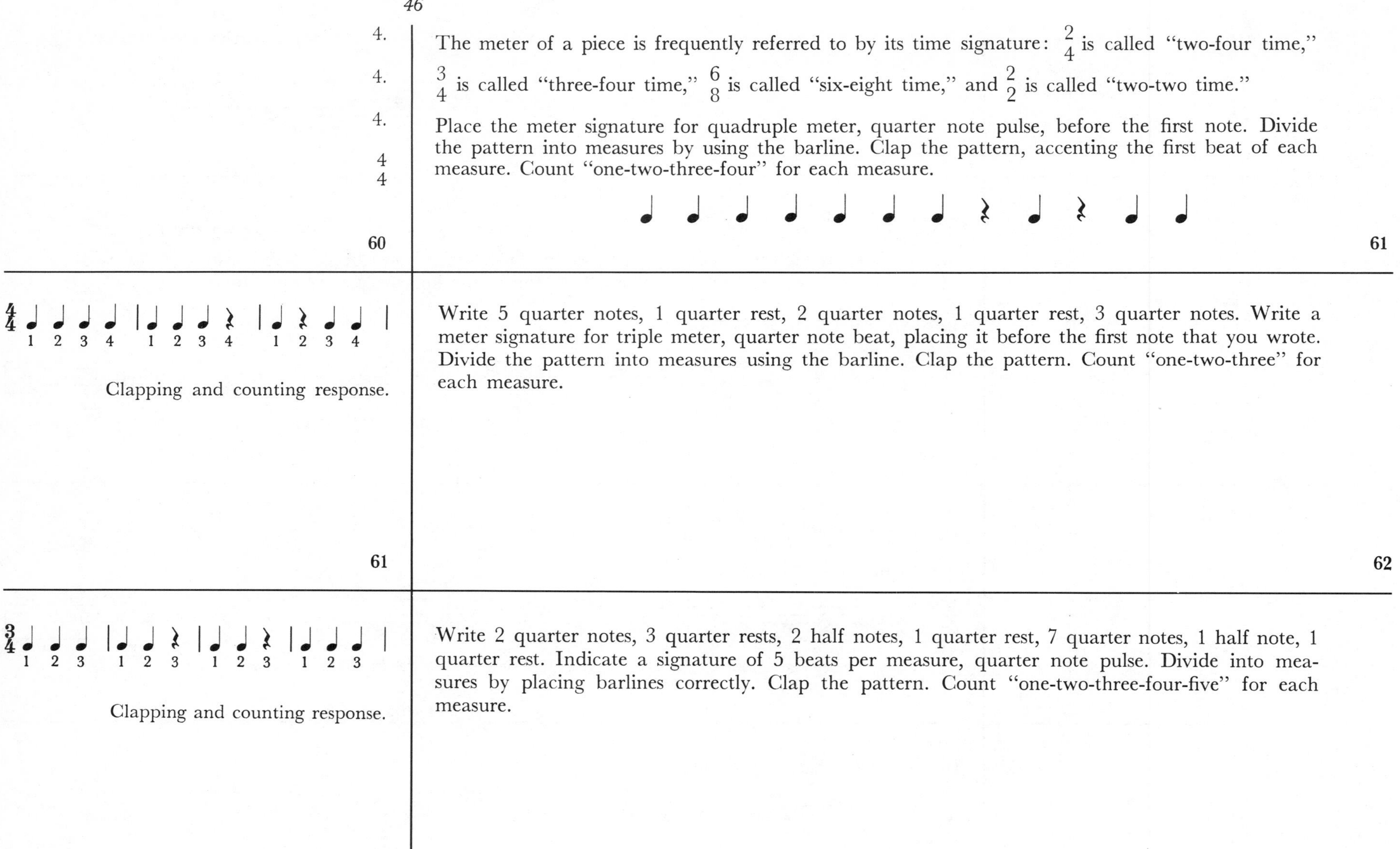

4.

4.

4.

$\frac{4}{4}$

60

The meter of a piece is frequently referred to by its time signature: $\frac{2}{4}$ is called "two-four time," $\frac{3}{4}$ is called "three-four time," $\frac{6}{8}$ is called "six-eight time," and $\frac{2}{2}$ is called "two-two time."

Place the meter signature for quadruple meter, quarter note pulse, before the first note. Divide the pattern into measures by using the barline. Clap the pattern, accenting the first beat of each measure. Count "one-two-three-four" for each measure.

61

Clapping and counting response.

61

Write 5 quarter notes, 1 quarter rest, 2 quarter notes, 1 quarter rest, 3 quarter notes. Write a meter signature for triple meter, quarter note beat, placing it before the first note that you wrote. Divide the pattern into measures using the barline. Clap the pattern. Count "one-two-three" for each measure.

62

Clapping and counting response.

62

Write 2 quarter notes, 3 quarter rests, 2 half notes, 1 quarter rest, 7 quarter notes, 1 half note, 1 quarter rest. Indicate a signature of 5 beats per measure, quarter note pulse. Divide into measures by placing barlines correctly. Clap the pattern. Count "one-two-three-four-five" for each measure.

63

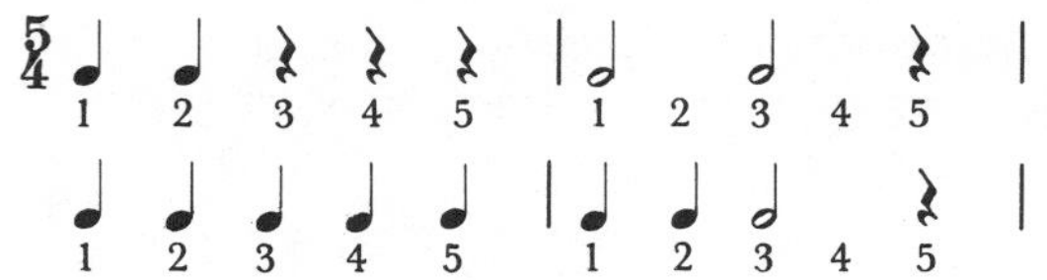

Clapping and counting response.

63

Some of the preceding frames have required counting the number of pulses in a measure. Musical counting is an important aid in establishing and feeling a steady pulse. With 4 beats to a measure, the counting is ONE-two-three-four, ONE-two-three-four, etc. With 3 beats to a measure it is ONE-two-three, etc. Rests and notes are counted alike, for the pulses are still present. Counting must be steady because the musical pulse is generally steady.

Special counting systems are used for notes of less than one pulse. These are introduced later.

Place the correct meter signature before each of the following patterns. The pulse is the quarter note. Clap or tap the patterns, resting on the rests. Count aloud.

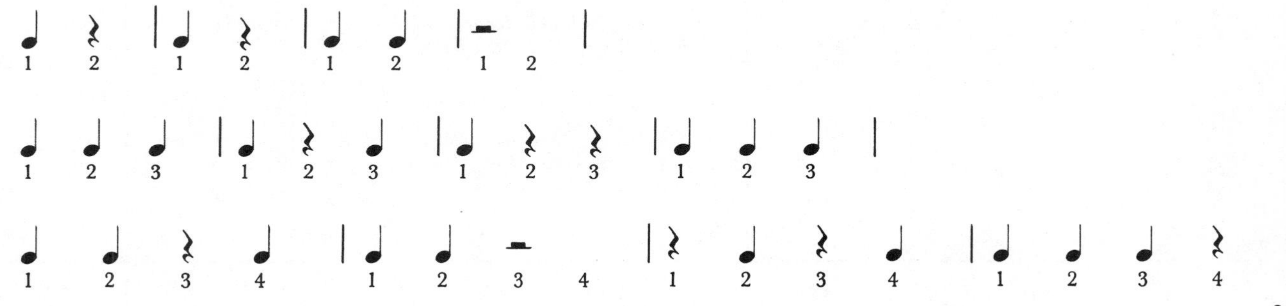

64

2
4

3
4

4
4

Clapping or tapping and counting response.

64

Insert the meter signature in the song below. The quarter note receives one pulse. First establish a steady pulse and then tap the pattern of the song. How many counts does each of the following receive?

𝅗𝅥 = ____ ; ♩ = ____ ; 𝅗𝅥. = ____ ; 𝄽 = ____ .

WE ARE THE CHIMES

Sing the song.

65

3
4

Tapping response.

𝅗𝅥 = 2; ♩ = 1; 𝅗𝅥. = 3; 𝄽 = 1.

Singing response.

65

In much folk and contemporary music, other meters are used besides duple, triple, or quadruple. Five-beat meter and seven-beat meter are frequently found. Look carefully at the time signature; then correctly draw in the barlines.

MISTRESS VANGELIO

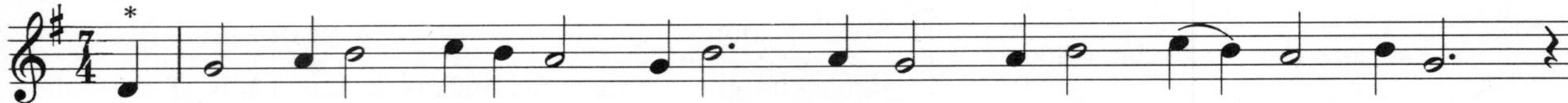

From the Juilliard Repertory Library. © *Copyright 1970 by Canyon Press, Inc. Used by permission.*

Clap and chant the song.

* This single note by itself, called a "pick-up," occupies only part of a measure. The first full measure begins with the next note.

66

Clapping and chanting response.

66

Contemporary music also makes frequent use of irregular meters; that is, a pattern of duple meter may be followed by a pattern of quadruple followed by a pattern of triple, and so forth. Sometimes different performers play different meters in the same piece.

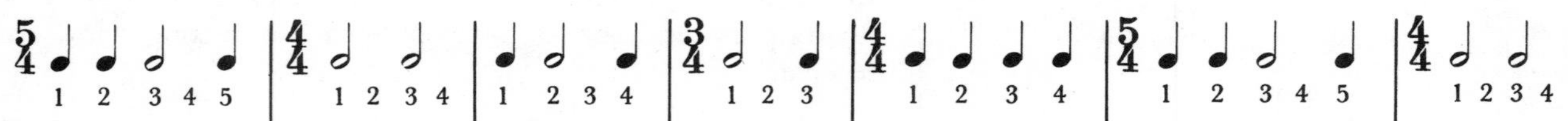

Set a steady quarter-note pulse; then clap or tap the rhythm pattern above, counting the number of beats given in each meter signature. Begin slowly. Do not stop between measures. Increase the speed when the pattern becomes easier.

67

Clapping or tapping and counting response.

67

This song is by the twentieth-century composer Béla Bartók. The note pattern is identical to the one you clapped in the preceding frame. The song is presented on the recording for the next Application section.

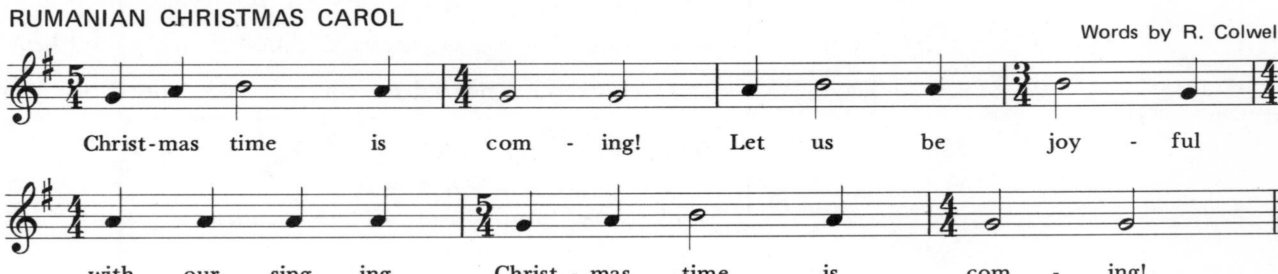

Copyright 1918 by Universal Edition, Renewed 1945. Copyright and Renewal assigned to Boosey & Hawkes, Inc. for U.S.A.

Used by permission of Boosey & Hawkes, Inc. and Editio Musica Budapest.

Some music has little metrical pulse, for example this plainsong. Notice that the musical example has no meter signature and no barlines. Chant it, giving all the ♪ 's the same value and the ♩ 's twice the value of the ♪ 's.

From the Juilliard Repertory Library. © Copyright 1970 by Canyon Press, Inc. Used by permission.

68

Chanting response.

68

To be enjoyed, music must be felt as well as heard. Teachers want their students to respond to the beat and stay with it, to feel the pulse and meter of music. Counting and clapping can be done to any song. Larger movements are often used on count ONE to emphasize the meter. Contemporary popular music is excellent for feeling the beat.

When notes that are of shorter duration than the unit beat occur, they are referred to as a divided beat. A method is needed for counting the divided beat correctly. If the ♩ = unit beat, ♪'s are counted using "and" (&): 3/4 ♫ ♫ ♫
1 & 2 & 3 & .

Similarly, 𝅗𝅥 = unit beat, ♩ are counted ♩ ♩ ♩ ♩ , etc; ♪ = unit beat, 𝅘𝅥𝅯𝅘𝅥𝅯 𝅘𝅥𝅯𝅘𝅥𝅯.
1 & 2 & (quarter notes); 1 & 2 & (sixteenth notes)

Write the counting under the patterns below.

69

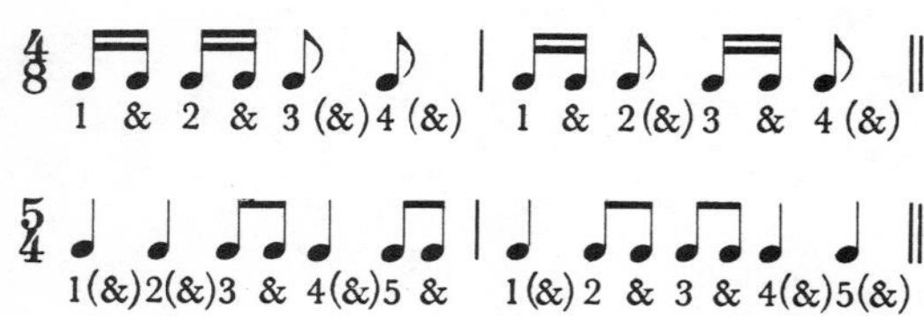

69

Write the counting below each of the two melodies below, using "&" for the divided beat.

SWEETLY SINGS THE DONKEY

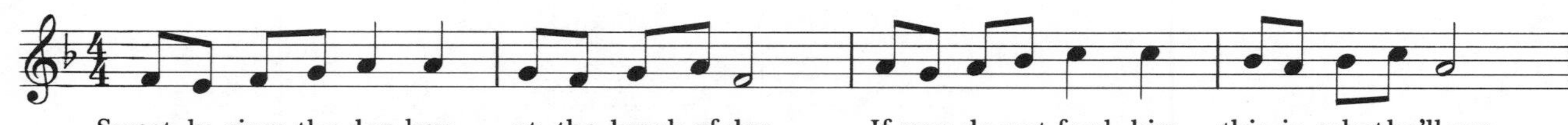

70

1 & 2 & 3(&) 4 (&) 1 & 2 & 3(&) 4(&)

1 & 2 & 3 (&) 4 (&) 1 & 2 & 3 (&) 4 (&)

70

Write the counting below the melody. Remember that ♩. = ♩ + ♪ .

ALL THROUGH THE NIGHT

Sleep, my child, and peace at-tend thee, All through the night.

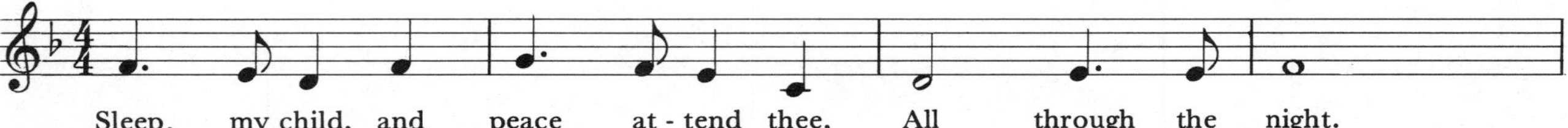

71

1(&)2 & 3(&)4(&) 1(&)2 & 3(&)4(&)
1(&)2(&)3(&)4 & 1(&)2(&)3(&)4(&)

71

Place a three-four meter signature in front of the first note and divide the music into measures, using barlines. Underline each note that comes on count one. Place an asterisk under the pick-up.

THE MORE WE GET TOGETHER

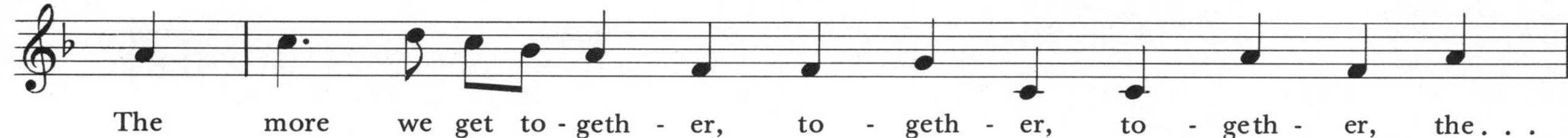
The more we get to - geth - er, to - geth - er, to - geth - er, the. . .

72

72

Initially, a child may be able to move to a steady pulse but not be able to keep in time with the music or with other children. Fitting movement to music or to one another's movements is a more advanced skill and can be postponed. Large motions, which the child can see and follow, will help both in the beginning stages of establishing a steady beat and in the later stages of beating time to music.

Moving to music helps establish a feeling for pulse and meter. This can be done by walking (stepping) to the pulse and using some other bodily motion to give the stress to count ONE. Stamping, bowing, swinging, and so forth can be used to show accent. Moving to music is one of the activities recommended by Jaques-Dalcroze, who developed a method "to create by the help of rhythm a rapid and regular current of communication between brain and body, and to make feeling for rhythm a physical experience." Small children should begin with larger body movements and work toward smaller, more refined movements as they mature and gain experience.

In moving to music, small children should use large body movements to assist them in feeling the ________________.

73

Beat or pulse.

73

With children (and with adults) developing the feeling for meter is more important than intellectualizing the mathematical relationships. Chanting familiar rhymes is one good way to help children feel duple, triple, and so forth. "Are you Sleeping, Brother John?" is a good example of quadruple meter. Write the counting (1, 2, 3, 4) beneath the words and think "one, two, three, four" as you chant or sing.

BROTHER JOHN

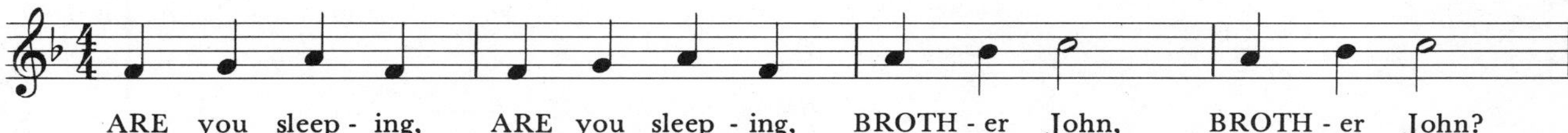
ARE you sleep - ing, ARE you sleep - ing, BROTH - er John, BROTH - er John?

74

74

Chant the rhyme below with strong accents to help establish the feeling for meter. The capitalized syllables are to be accented.

PUS-sy cat, PUS-sy cat, WHERE have you BEEN? I'VE been to LON-don to VIS-it the QUEEN.

PUS-sy cat, PUS-sy cat, WHAT did you THERE? I FRIGHT-ened a LIT-tle mouse UN-der her CHAIR.

"Pussy Cat, Pussy Cat" is in $\frac{?}{4}$ meter. ______

Write the counting under the first line of the rhyme.

75

Chanting response.

3.

PUS -	sy	cat	PUS -	sy	cat
1	2	3	1	2	3
WHERE	have	you	BEEN?		
1	2	3	1	2	3
I'VE	been	to	LON -	don	to
1	2	3	1	2	3
VIS -	it	the	QUEEN		
1	2	3	1	2	3

75

As you chant "Simple Simon," notice that it can fit either into duple or quadruple meter:

Duple: SIM-ple SI-mon MET a PIE-man, etc.
1 2 1 2 1 2 1 2

Quadruple: SIM-ple Si-mon MET a Pie-man.
1 2 3 4 1 2 3 4

This is true since four is a multiple of two.

SIM-ple Simon MET a pie-man GO-ing to the FAIR. said
SIM-ple Si-mon TO the pie-man LET me taste your WARE.

76

Chanting response.

76

The top number of the time signature tells the number of ______________ in a measure.

The lower number of the time signature tells the kind of ______________ that gets one pulse or beat.

The time signature is also called the ______________ signature.

We have now considered note values, rest values, pulse, and meter. The following frames provide the opportunity to practice what you have learned.

77

Beats.

Note.

Meter.

77

Omit the next 19 frames if you do not need the practice. Begin again with frame 97.

Place the time signature for quadruple meter in front of each of the two patterns below, quarter note pulse. Draw in the barlines. Clap and count the patterns.

78

Clapping and counting response.

78

In duple meter each measure contains ______ beats.

In quintuple meter each measure contains ______ beats.

In quadruple meter each measure contains ______ beats.

79

2.

5.

4.

79

Bar the following musical patterns. Clap or tap them. Count, using 1 & 2 &, etc., if necessary to help make the divided beats.

80

Clapping or tapping response.

$\frac{3}{4}$ 1 2 & 3 | 1 2 3 |

1 2 & 3 | 1 2 3 |

$\frac{4}{4}$ 1 2 & 3 4 | 1 2 3 4 & |

1 2 3 4 | 1 2 3 4 |

80

Below are the words and durational values to "Skip to My Lou." Sing or chant the song, looking at the note pattern as you sing. Bar the pattern correctly.

Flies in the but-ter-milk, shoo fly, shoo, Flies in the but-ter-milk, shoo fly, shoo

81

Singing or chanting response.

81

In moving to music, the addition of rests may increase the difficulty both of feeling the pulse and of moving to the pattern. If there is a rest on count "four" of each measure, the clapping is not so simple, and the marching is noticeably more difficult than if a note were on count "four."

March in place, or if seated, move your feet to the notes. Say "rest" on count four. Substitute a clap, tap, or nod for "rest" (count four).

82

Physical response.

82

Below, a durational pattern is presented twice. For A, write a $\frac{5}{4}$ signature, bar it, clap it, counting aloud, accenting the first beat. For B, write a $\frac{2}{4}$ signature, bar it, clap it, counting aloud, accenting the first beat.

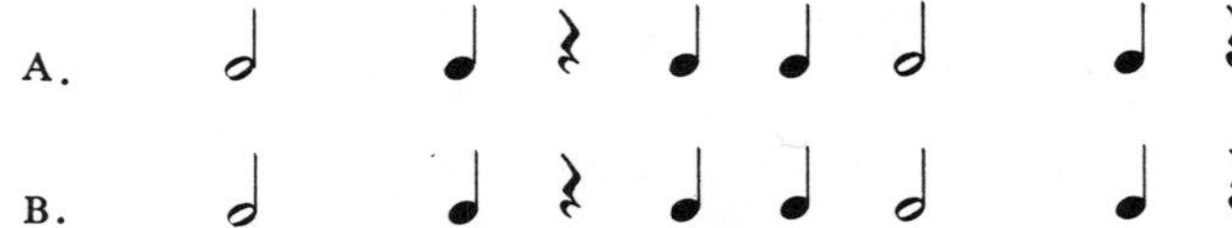
A.
B.

The patterns should sound and feel different.

83

Clapping and counting response.

83

THIS OLD MAN

This old man, He played one, He played nick - nack on my thumb,
Nick- nack, pad-dy - whack, Give a dog a bone, This old man came roll - ing home.

Assume a quarter note pulse, put in the meter signature (two counts to each measure), bar it, clap, and sing or chant it.

84

2
4

Clapping and singing or chanting response.

84

Draw barlines for the following patterns. Clap, tap, and count aloud.

85

Clapping, tapping, and counting response.

85

Sing the song below, looking at the music as you sing. Bar the music.

The ♪ gets______ beat(s), the ♩ ______ beat(s), the ♩. ______ beat(s).

OATS, PEAS, BEANS

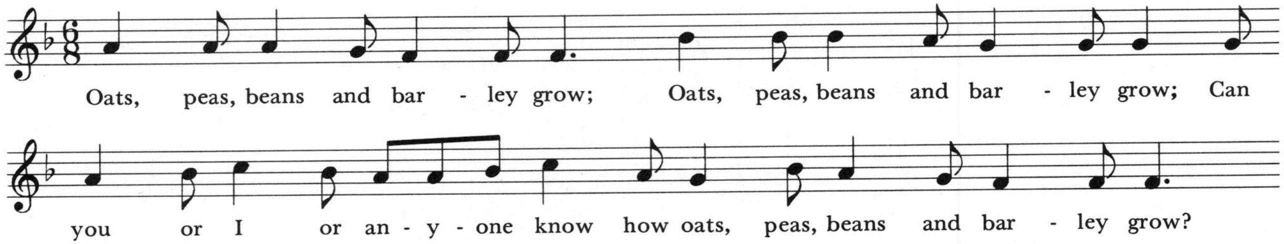

Oats, peas, beans and bar - ley grow; Oats, peas, beans and bar - ley grow; Can

you or I or an - y - one know how oats, peas, beans and bar - ley grow?

86

Singing response.

1.

2.

3.

86

The half note may be used as the basic unit of beat.

$\frac{5}{2}$ = five pulses to each measure
= half note receives one beat (two quarter notes equal one beat, one quarter note receives 1/2 beat)

$\frac{3}{2}$ = three pulses to each measure
= half-note pulse (half note receives one beat)

$\frac{2}{2}$ = two beats in a measure
= half-note pulse

In $\frac{5}{2}$ time, a quarter note receives ______ beat(s).

87

1/2.

87

Bar the following examples. Clap, tap, and count aloud.

88

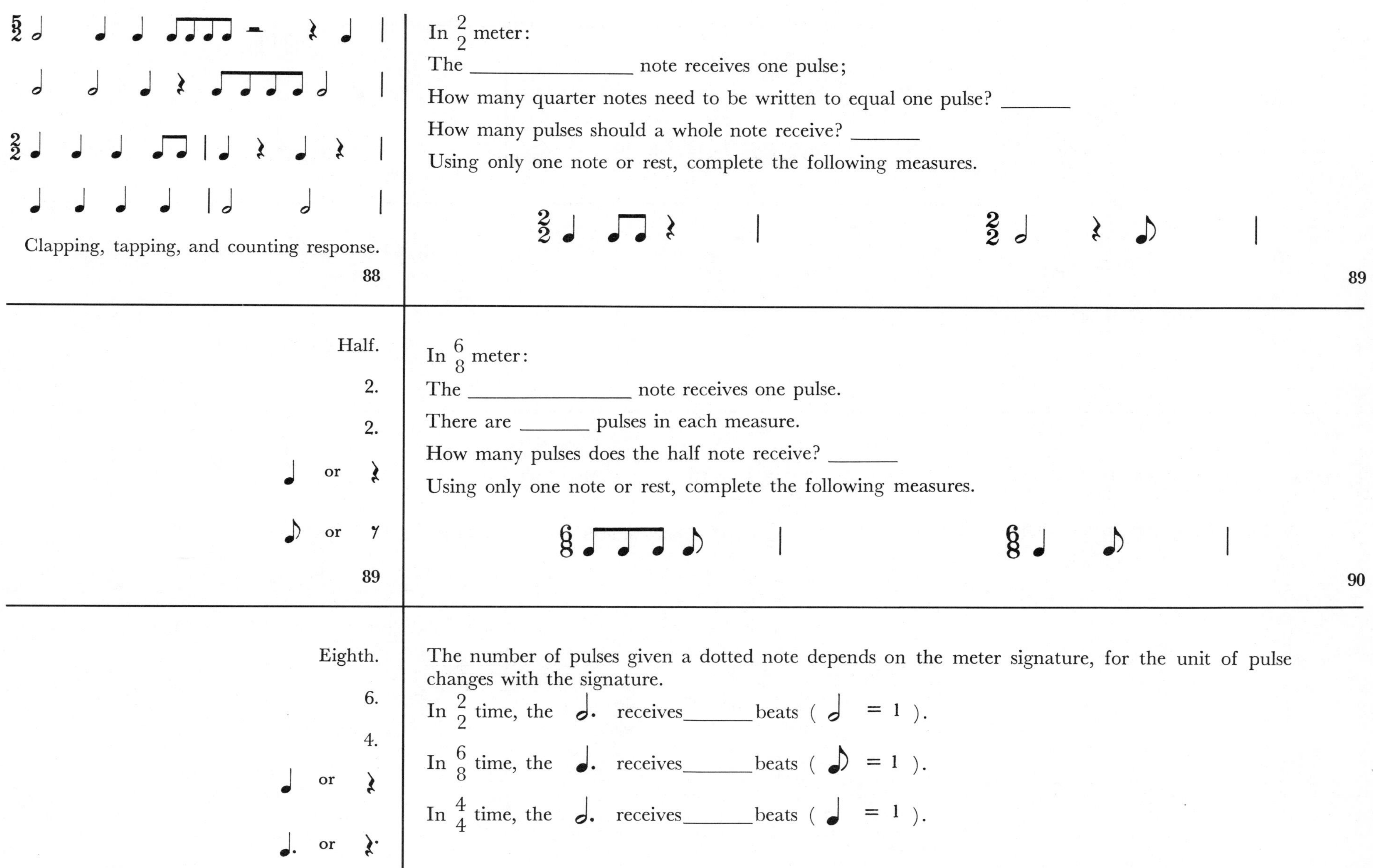

Clapping, tapping, and counting response.

88

In $\frac{2}{2}$ meter:

The ______________ note receives one pulse;

How many quarter notes need to be written to equal one pulse? ______

How many pulses should a whole note receive? ______

Using only one note or rest, complete the following measures.

89

Half.

2.

2.

♩ or 𝄽

♪ or 𝄾

89

In $\frac{6}{8}$ meter:

The ______________ note receives one pulse.

There are ______ pulses in each measure.

How many pulses does the half note receive? ______

Using only one note or rest, complete the following measures.

90

Eighth.

6.

4.

♩ or 𝄽

♩. or 𝄽.

90

The number of pulses given a dotted note depends on the meter signature, for the unit of pulse changes with the signature.

In $\frac{2}{2}$ time, the 𝅗𝅥. receives______beats (𝅗𝅥 = 1).

In $\frac{6}{8}$ time, the ♩. receives______beats (♪ = 1).

In $\frac{4}{4}$ time, the 𝅗𝅥. receives______beats (♩ = 1).

91

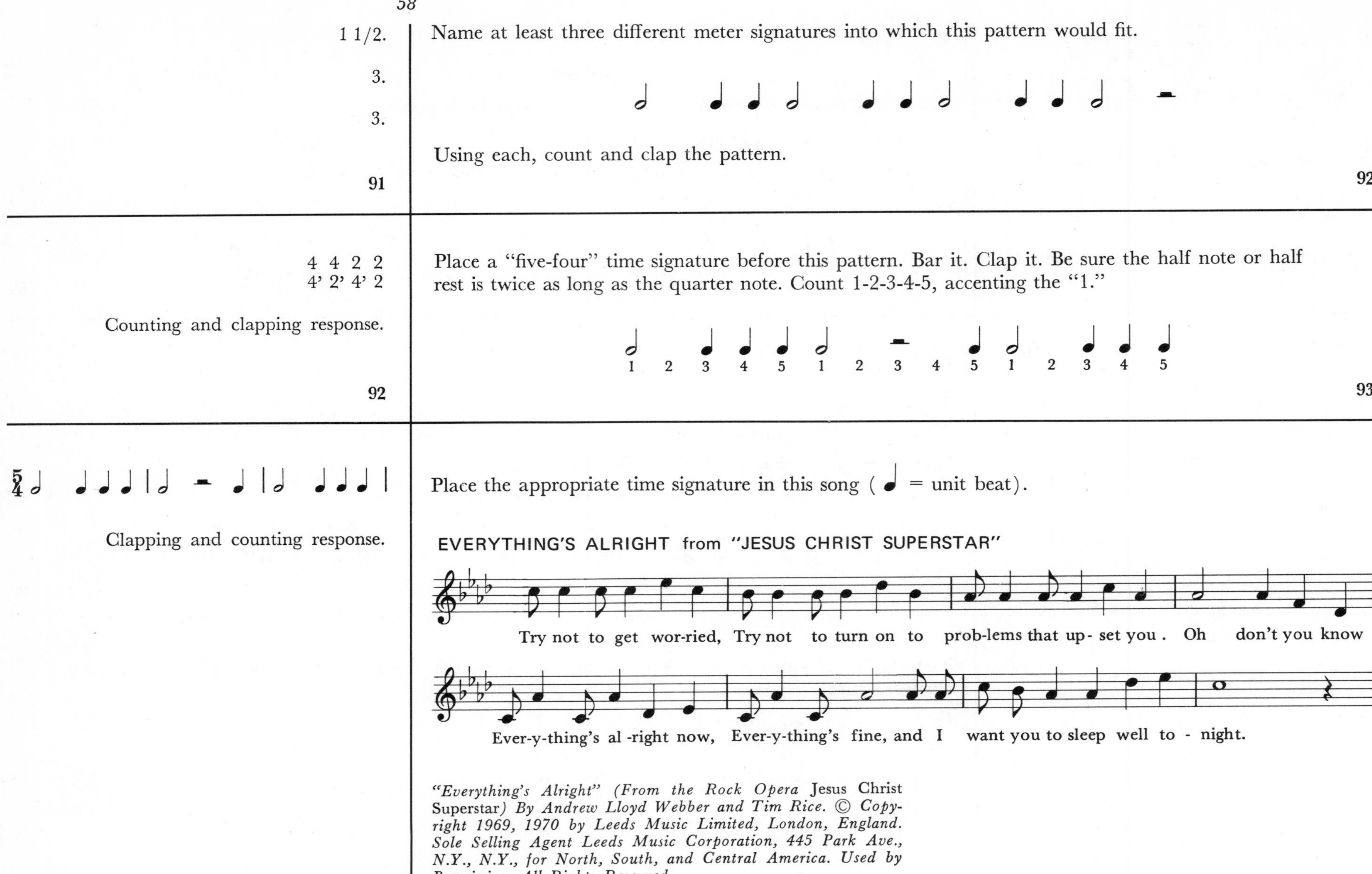

1 1/2.

3.

3.

91

Name at least three different meter signatures into which this pattern would fit.

Using each, count and clap the pattern.

92

---

4 4 2 2
4' 2' 4' 2

Counting and clapping response.

92

Place a "five-four" time signature before this pattern. Bar it. Clap it. Be sure the half note or half rest is twice as long as the quarter note. Count 1-2-3-4-5, accenting the "1."

1 2 3 4 5 1 2 3 4 5 1 2 3 4 5

93

5
4

Clapping and counting response.

93

Place the appropriate time signature in this song (♩ = unit beat).

EVERYTHING'S ALRIGHT from "JESUS CHRIST SUPERSTAR"

Try not to get wor-ried, Try not to turn on to prob-lems that up- set you . Oh don't you know
Ever-y-thing's al -right now, Ever-y-thing's fine, and I want you to sleep well to - night.

94

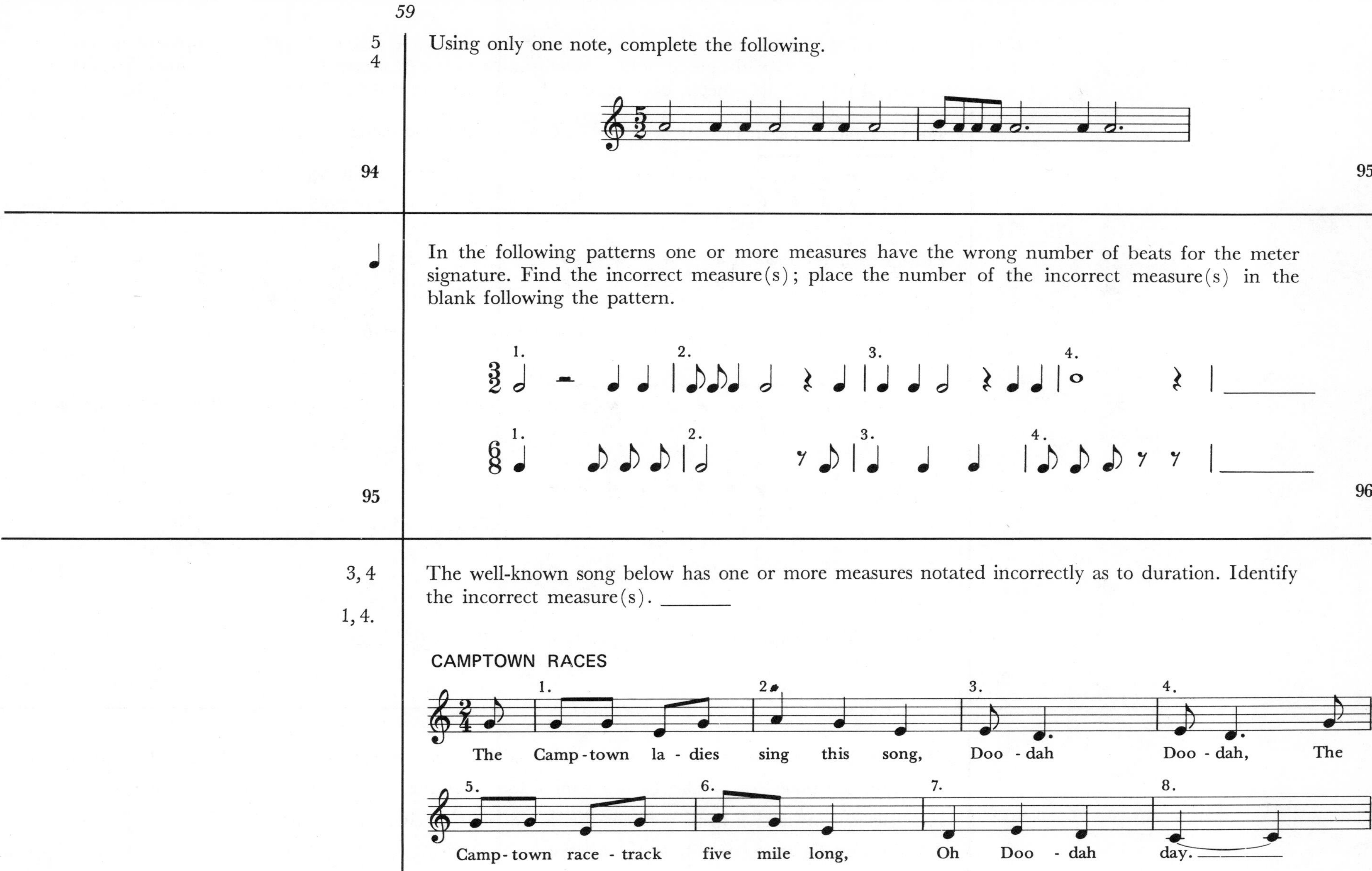

5
4

94

Using only one note, complete the following. 95

♩

95

In the following patterns one or more measures have the wrong number of beats for the meter signature. Find the incorrect measure(s); place the number of the incorrect measure(s) in the blank following the pattern.

96

3, 4

1, 4.

96

The well-known song below has one or more measures notated incorrectly as to duration. Identify the incorrect measure(s). ______

CAMPTOWN RACES

97

2, 4, 7.

Several other terms related to meter are important. The first of these terms is compound meter. Duple, triple, and quadruple are often called simple meters. *Compound meters* are simple meters combined with a triple meter, each main pulse divided into three rather than two.

For example, duple meters are $\frac{2}{8}$, $\frac{2}{4}$, and $\frac{2}{2}$. Compound duple meter has two main beats,

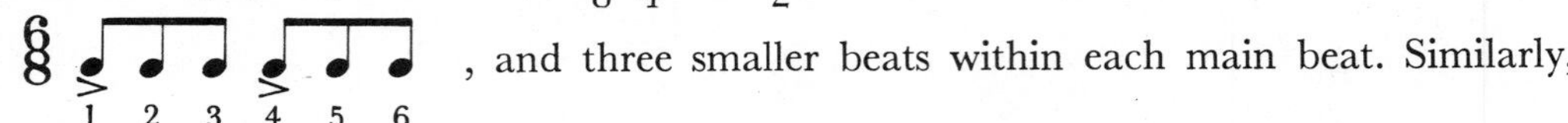

1 2 3 4 5 6

, and three smaller beats within each main beat. Similarly,

with $\frac{6}{4}$:

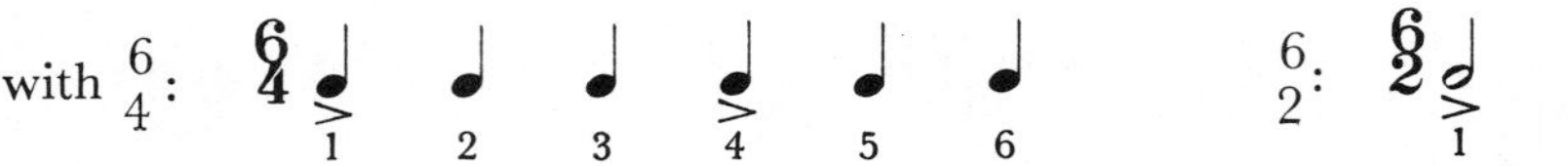

1 2 3 4 5 6

$\frac{6}{2}$:

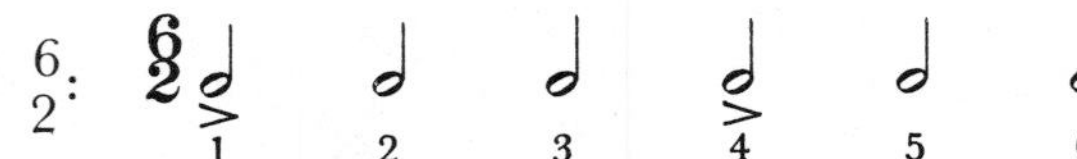

1 2 3 4 5 6

Simple triple meters are $\frac{3}{8}$, $\frac{3}{4}$, and $\frac{3}{2}$. Compound meters derived from these would be:

$\frac{9}{8}\left(\frac{3}{8}+\frac{3}{8}+\frac{3}{8}\right)$ 1 2 3 4 5 6 7 8 9 Three main beats, each subdivided into 3 smaller beats.

$\frac{9}{4}\left(\frac{3}{4}+\frac{3}{4}+\frac{3}{4}\right)$ 1 2 3 4 5 6 7 8 9

$\frac{9}{2}\left(\frac{3}{2}+\frac{3}{2}+\frac{3}{2}\right)$ 1 2 3 4 5 6 7 8 9

How would a compound meter derived from $\frac{4}{8}$ be indicated? ______ From $\frac{4}{4}$? ______

97 98

$\frac{12}{8}$

$\frac{12}{4}$

Occasionally, the meter signature is not indicated by numbers but by a **C** or **₵**. The **C** stands for "common time," or $\frac{4}{4}$. The **₵** is a symbol for "cut time," or $\frac{2}{2}$, meaning that "common time" has been cut in half: 2 beats per measure, a half note receiving one beat.

Cut time, or **₵**, is referred to as "alla breve."

In cut time (**₵**, $\frac{2}{2}$):

♩ = ______ beat(s)

𝅗𝅥 = ______ beat(s)

𝅝 = ______ beat(s)

Another expression for cut time ($\frac{2}{2}$) is ______________.

98 99

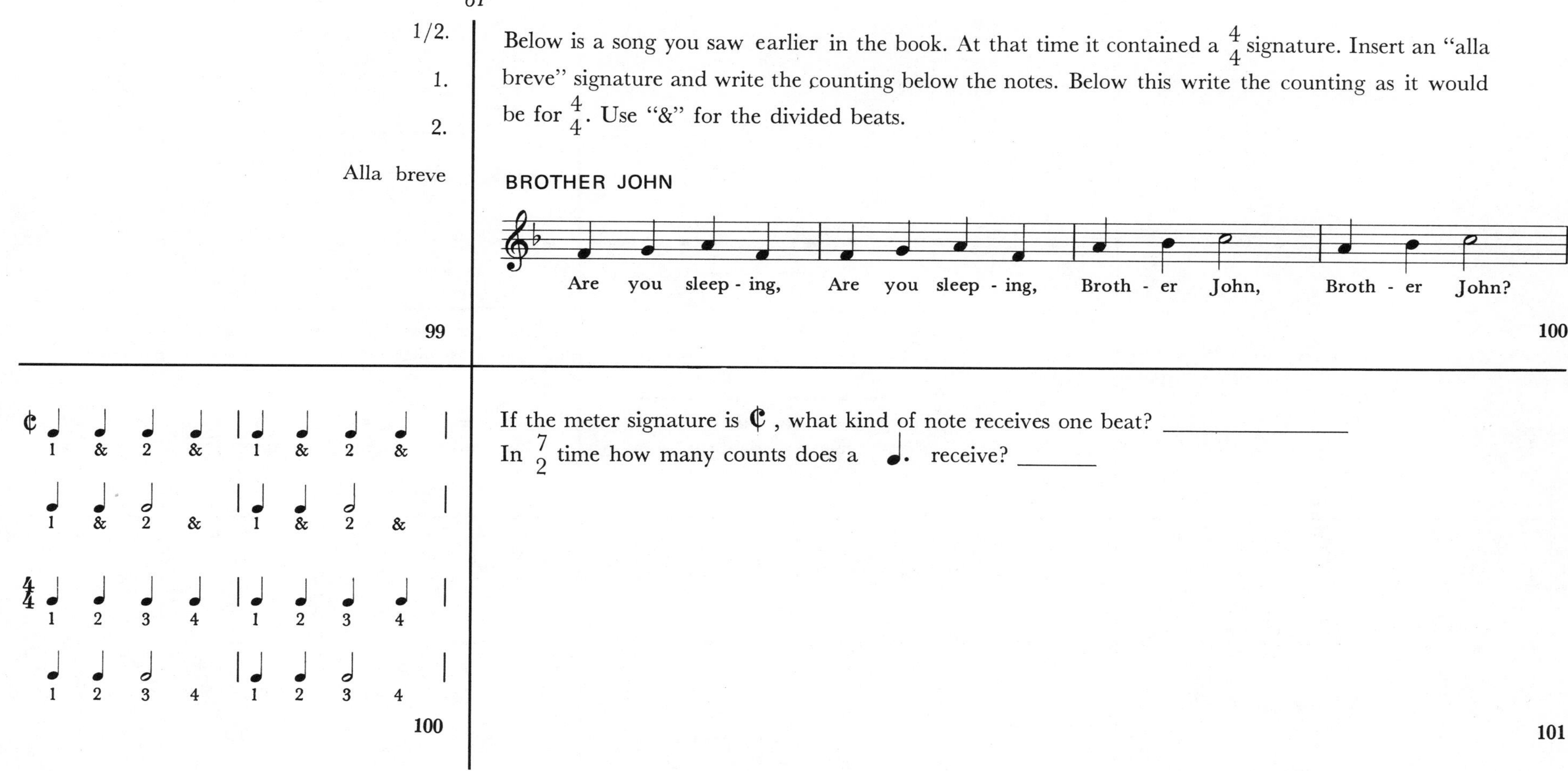

1/2.

1.

2.

Alla breve

99

Below is a song you saw earlier in the book. At that time it contained a $\frac{4}{4}$ signature. Insert an "alla breve" signature and write the counting below the notes. Below this write the counting as it would be for $\frac{4}{4}$. Use "&" for the divided beats.

BROTHER JOHN

100

100

If the meter signature is ¢, what kind of note receives one beat? ________________

In $\frac{7}{2}$ time how many counts does a ♩. receive? _______

101

Half.

3/4.

101

Bar this song. Sing it.

THREE BLIND MICE

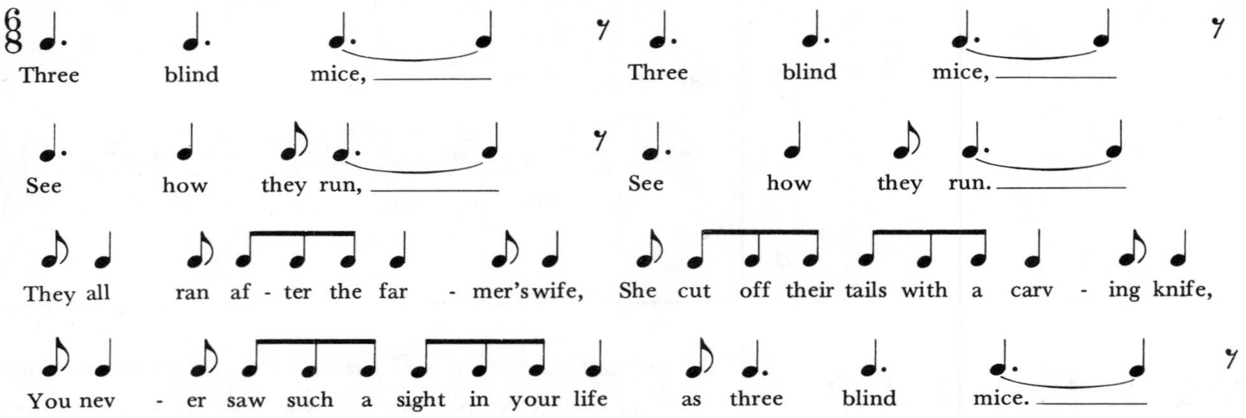

Three blind mice, Three blind mice,
See how they run, See how they run.
They all ran af - ter the far - mer's wife, She cut off their tails with a carv - ing knife,
You nev - er saw such a sight in your life as three blind mice.

102

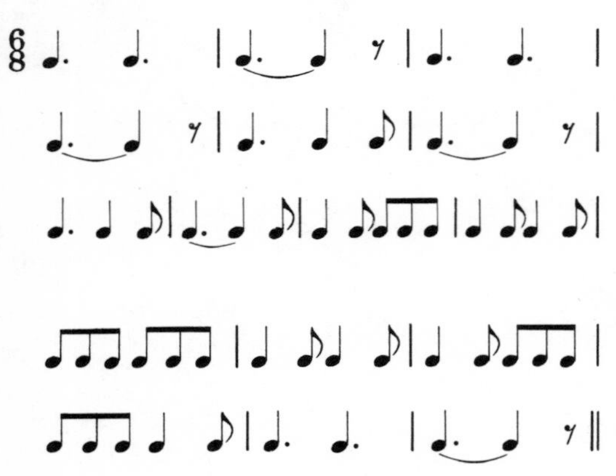

Singing response.

102

Which are the incorrect measures in this song? ________________.

1.
2.
3.
4.
Lon - don Bridge is fall - ing down, fall - ing down, fall - ing down,
5.
6.
7.
8.
Lon - don Bridge is fall - ing down, My fair la - dy.

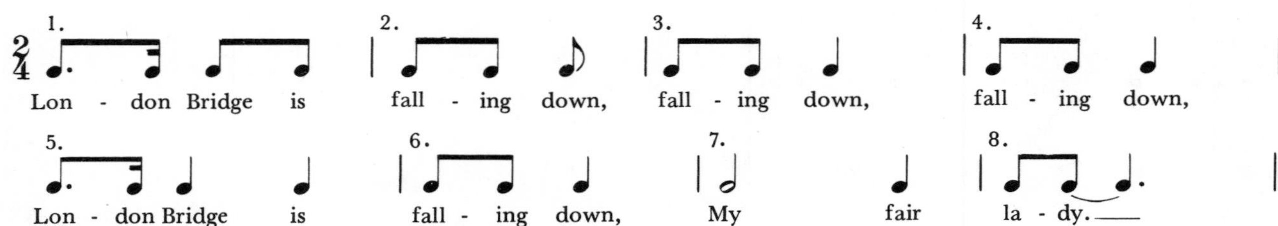

103

2, 5, 7, 8.

103

Below are the first few measures of "America." Many of the barlines are misplaced. Copy the notes on the blank staff, putting in the barlines correctly so that each measure has 3 beats and the accent falls on count "1."

104

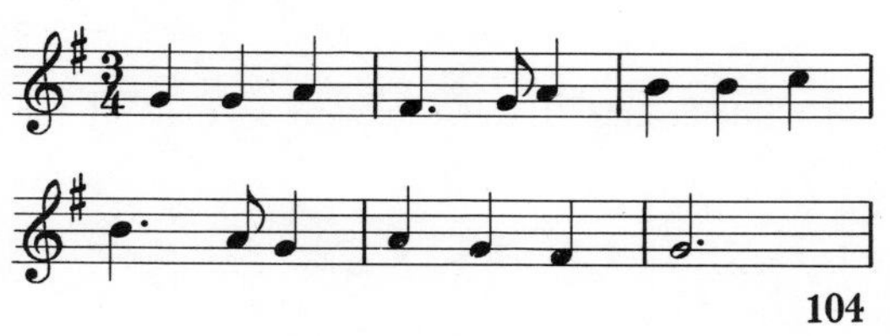

104

PRETEST for Chapters 6–7: Rhythm and Amplitude

Mark the correct answer or *answers.*

1. The pick-up or anacrusis is:

    —— a. a partial measure

    —— b. usually accented

    —— c. usually not accented

    —— d. a part of the song without words

2. Match items in the left column with the appropriate term in the right column.

a. crescendo	1. pick-up
b.  ♩ ♫	2. dotted rhythm
	3. very loud
c. fortissimo	4. "ta ti-ti"
d.  2/4 ♪ | ♩ ♩	5. soft
	6. triplet
e. piano	7. gradually increase volume
f. mf	8. gradually increase tempo
g.  (diminuendo sign)	9. very soft
h.  ♩. ♬ ♩. ♬	10. moderately loud
	11. mixed meters
i. 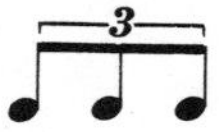 (triplet eighth notes, 3)	12. diminuendo

Answers

1. a, c.
2. a. 7.
   b. 4.
   c. 3.
   d. 1.
   e. 5.
   f. 10.
   g. 12.
   h. 2.
   i. 6.

From your score determine if you can omit sections of the text.

CHAPTER 6 The Concept of Rhythm

The objectives of this chapter include providing information that will allow you to clap and count more complex rhythm patterns such as the triplet, sixteenth note, and other combinations; to introduce you to several different systems of rhythmic notation and counting; and to have you understand the meaning and use of the pick-up and the terminology used to designate amplitude. We have already used rhythm in the preceding pages. Whenever we clapped, tapped, or moved to note patterns, we were using rhythm. Rhythm simply means the pattern made by two or more notes grouped in time. Regular rhythm is the pattern made when all the notes are of equal duration: or . When we beat the pulse or the meter of these and similar patterns using stress–nonstress, we are beating a regular rhythm pattern.

Although we respond to regular rhythm, we take greater pleasure in patterns created by grouping notes and rests of different duration. Clap the pattern below. Count, using "&" for the divided beats. This pattern is more interesting than a group of notes all of equal duration, and such a pattern is more typical of our conventional definition of rhythm.

105

Clapping and counting response.

Rhythm is felt by the performer and the listener; often it need not be intellectualized. Very young children can learn complex rhythms by rote. Inspection of kindergarten and first-grade music books will indicate that selection of the music is not limited by the complexity of the rhythm.

If the teacher must learn the rhythm from the notation, establishing the pulse and using some system of counting are essential in determining correct rhythm.

The *triplet* is a common rhythm pattern. The triplet in music is similar to the usual definition of the word, three things just alike. Triplets are three equal notes performed to a single pulse, 3 ,

105

or performed to two pulses, [triplet quarter notes]. When we perform triplets, care must be taken that the three notes are equal and that they fit into the duration of the pulse or pulses.

Set a steady beat and then chant "merry merry" to feel the normal eighth-note division of the beat. Keeping the same pulse, chant "Mer-ri-ly mer-ri-ly" to feel the triplet division of the beat. You may wish to make up your own words, such as "hearty" and "beautiful," etc.

106

Chanting response.

106

When the beat is divided into two eighth notes, we count "One-and-Two-and-Three-and," etc. to help us make the eighth notes even. This is exactly like saying "mer-ry mer-ry mer-ry." To help in performing triplets evenly, we count "One-and-a Two-and-a Three-and-a," keeping the counting steady as if we were saying "mer-ri-ly mer-ri-ly mer-ri-ly."

Write the counting beneath the rhythm patterns; then count aloud and clap. Use 1& 2& or 1 & a 2 & a.

107

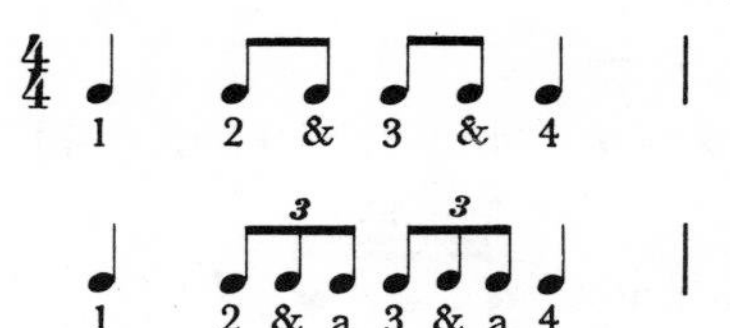

Counting and clapping response.

107

Triplets are indicated by a small "3" placed above or below the group to show that the normal two-division has been replaced by a three-division.

Whenever possible, the notes are grouped together by a beam. Often there is a curved line above or below the notes; this indicates grouping and is not a tie. Measures 1 and 5 contain triplets.

1. 2. 3. 4. 5. 6.
3
3

BAIZHAN BOY

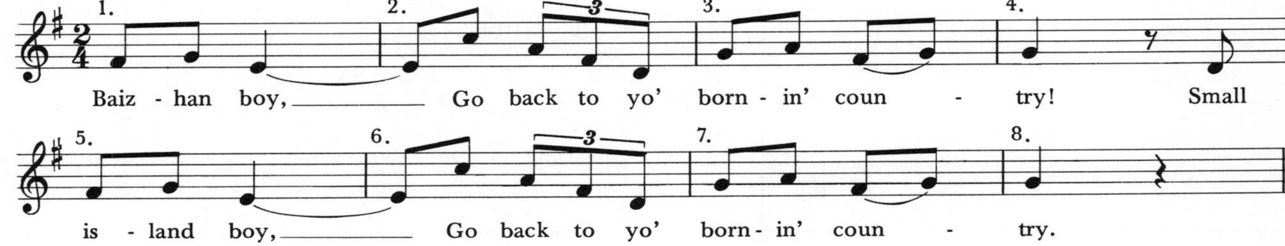

1. 2. 3. 4.
3
Baiz - han boy, Go back to yo' born - in' coun - try! Small
5. 6. 7. 8.
3
is - land boy, Go back to yo' born - in' coun - try.

In which measure(s) do triplets occur? ______

What kind of note is used for the triplets? ______________

How many counts or beats does each triplet receive? ______________

108

2, 6.

Eighth note.

One count (1/3 count for each note).

108

In this song how many times does the triplet occur? ______ It falls on what beat of the measure? ______ Chant or sing the song after you have tapped the rhythm.

JUANITA

3
Ni - ta, Jua ni - ta, Ask thy soul if we should part.
3
Ni - ta, Jua ni - ta, Lean thou on my heart.

109

2.

3.

Tapping and chanting or singing response.

109

Triplet eighth notes are the most common triplet figure, [triplet eighth notes] but triplets may also be quarter notes, [triplet quarter notes], half notes, [triplet half notes], or sixteenth notes, [triplet sixteenth notes].
In the song below, measures _______ and _______ contain triplet patterns. Each of these triplets occupies how many beats? _______. How many ♩ notes would *usually* occupy the space taken up by [triplet quarter notes]?

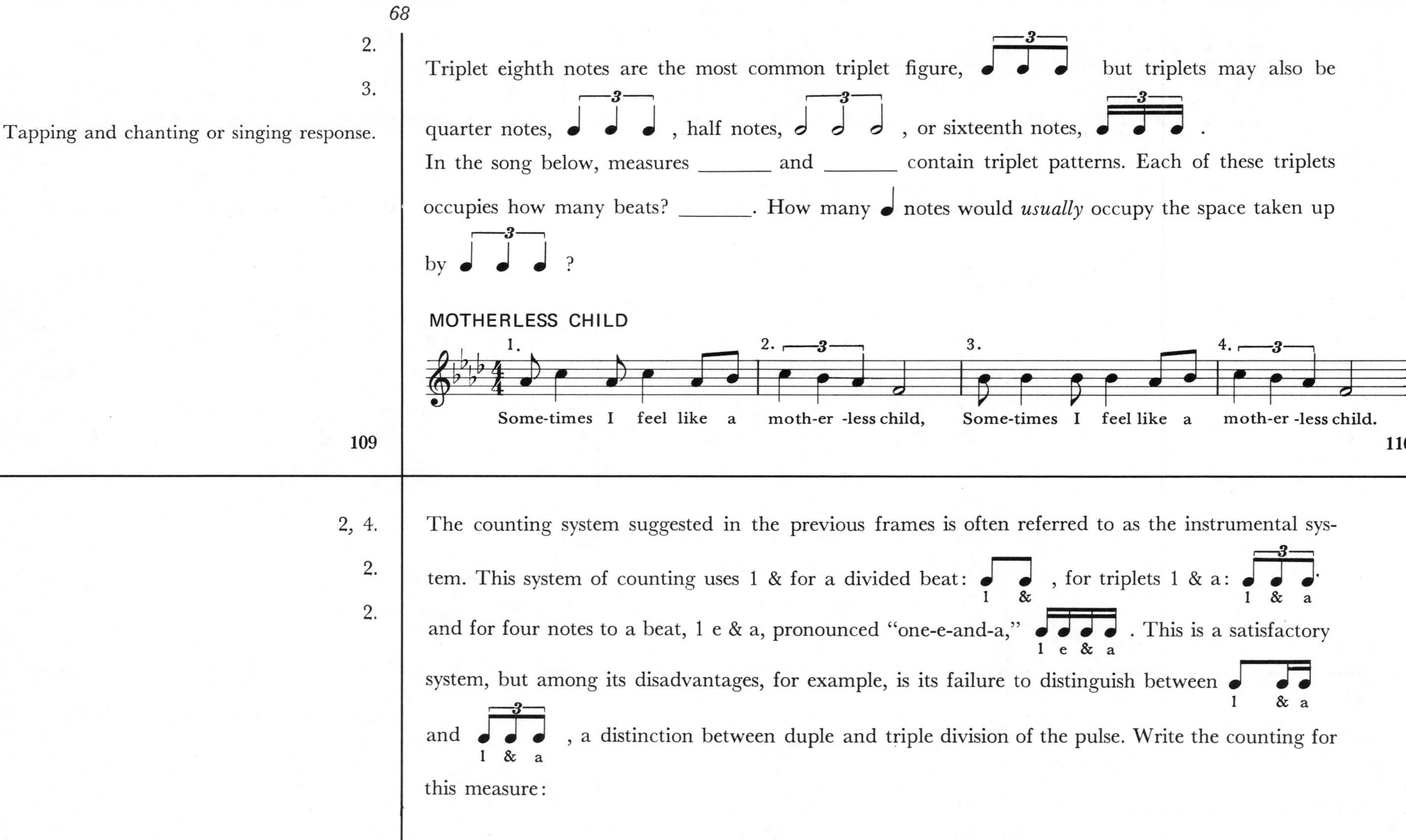

MOTHERLESS CHILD
1.
2.
3.
4.
3
Some-times I feel like a moth-er -less child, Some-times I feel like a moth-er -less child.

110

2, 4.

2.

2.

110

The counting system suggested in the previous frames is often referred to as the instrumental system. This system of counting uses 1 & for a divided beat: [eighth notes: 1 &], for triplets 1 & a: [triplet: 1 & a]. and for four notes to a beat, 1 e & a, pronounced "one-e-and-a," [sixteenth notes: 1 e & a]. This is a satisfactory system, but among its disadvantages, for example, is its failure to distinguish between [eighth and two sixteenths: 1 & a] and [triplet: 1 & a], a distinction between duple and triple division of the pulse. Write the counting for this measure:

4/4 [eighth notes] [sixteenth notes] [triplet] [quarter note]
_ _ _ _ _ _ _ _ _ _

111

111

Counting to music, like most things, takes practice. Two additional rhythm patterns are somewhat common:

counted 1 & a and counted 1 e &.

1 & a   1 e &

Write the counting under the pattern, and tap it, counting aloud.

112

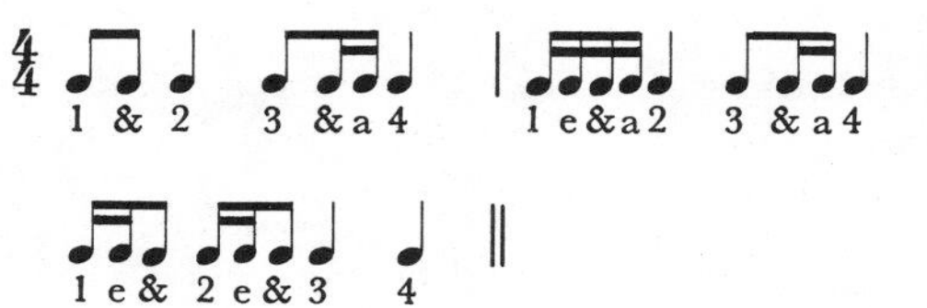

Tapping and counting response.

112

Counting helps make rhythm exact. For example, if half notes are not counted, (1 2), their duration is only guessed at, and they are often rushed.

DOWN IN THE VALLEY

Write in the counting. The pick-up begins on count 7.

* Pick-up. Explained in frame 119.

113

113

Write in the counting and sing "This Old Man" using the counting pattern rather than the words.

THIS OLD MAN

114

114

The rhythm patterns would constitute an entire measure in, ______ time.
4

The mark for identifying stress in music is an ______________ mark and the symbol for it is ______.

115

2.

Accent, >

115

The Hungarian system of counting is often called the Kodály or Richards system, after two people who have used it successfully. The system can be used before notes are introduced. Simple visual symbols are used to designate different durations and pulse.

The is used to designate a quarter note duration. Two eighths are designated by either or , 4 sixteenths by or . Simple syllables are used for chanting: is "tah tah," is "ti ti," and "ti di ti di."

This system also has drawbacks, one being that the syllable "ti" is used for both rhythm and pitch and another being that duple and triple meter are not differentiated clearly.

Wee Willie Winkle

Runs through the town

Upstairs and downstairs

in his nightgown

Rapping at the window

Crying at the lock

Are the children in their beds

Now its eight o'clock

The symbol for a rest remains the same. Chant the words and then the rhythmic syllables "tah" and "ti ti" as you look at the symbols.

116

Chanting response.

The Richards symbols are often made in the air by the students. The symbols for Wee Willie Winkle are right hand symbols; if made with the left hand, they might be | ⊔ with no change of meaning.

Triplets are notated ⊓⊓ (3), a single eighth note ♪, all in preparation for the introduction of notation. This rhythm pattern | ⊓ ⊓ | would be sung ta ti ti ti ti ta.

Draw the rhythmic notation symbols for the following:

POLLY WOLLY DOODLE

Oh I went down South for to see my Sal, Sing pol-ly wol-ly doo-dle all the day.

Using "ta" and "ti," sing it.

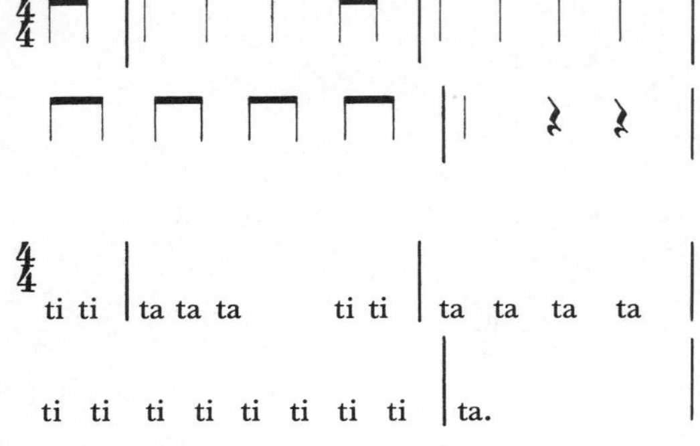

Singing response.

Gordon has adopted a French system for counting that has the advantage of distinguishing between duple and triple.

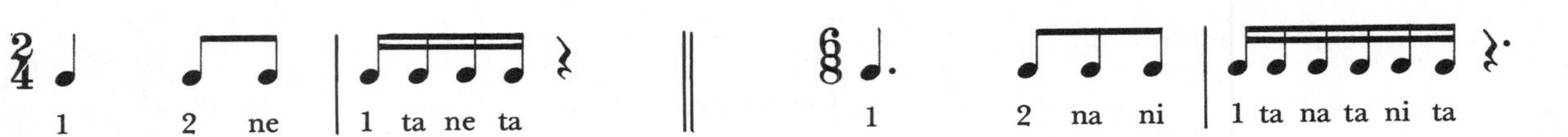

This more complex system emphasizes the importance of melodic rhythm, a rhythm that corresponds more closely with the text of a song and is the rhythm that organizes the tones into a musical context. It does not use any of the sounds that are used for pitch syllables in the "do, re, mi" system.

In his book Gordon* illustrates the difference between his system and that of Mary Helen Richards as follows:

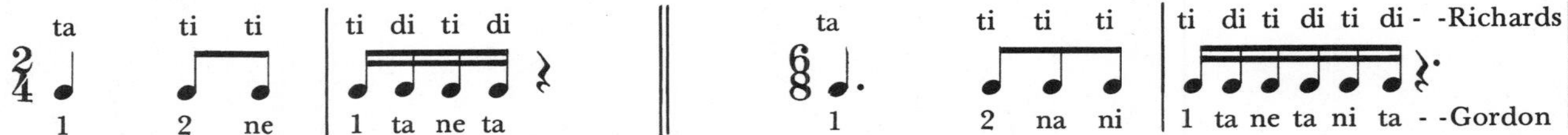

Sing the rhythm of this song using the Kodály method.

THIS OLD MAN

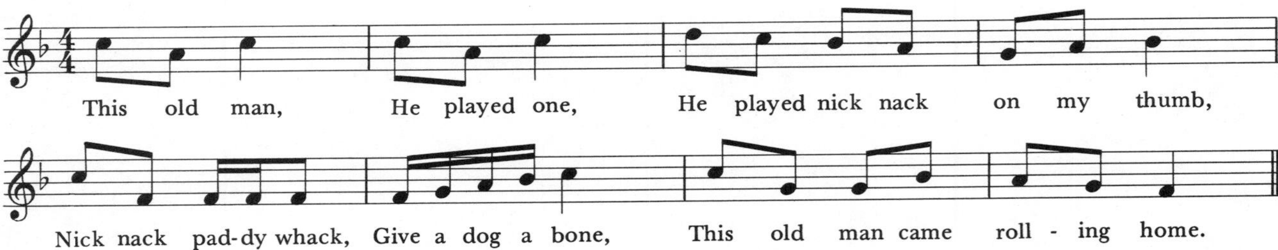

* Edwin Gordon, *The Psychology of Music Teaching* (Englewood Cliffs, N.J.: Prentice-Hall, Inc., 1971), p. 74.

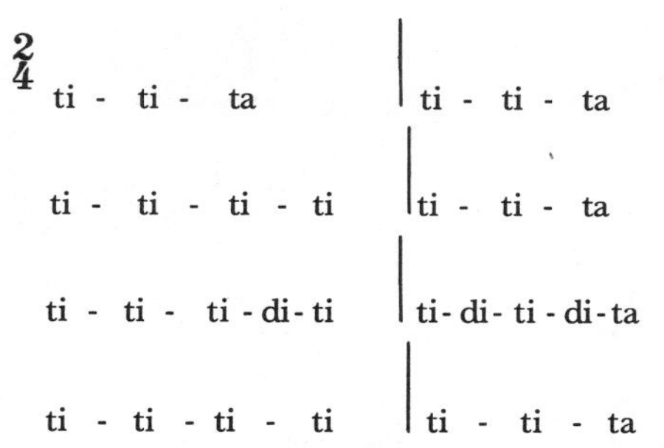

118

Variety may be added by the use of a pick-up note, also called an upbeat or anacrusis. Music need not always begin on the downbeat (count ONE), of the measure. It may begin with a partial measure, often only the final beat of a measure. This is called the pick-up and is not stressed. In "America the Beautiful" the word "Oh" is a pick-up, with the stress on BEAU-, the downbeat.

AMERICA THE BEAUTIFUL

Chant the first phrase of "The Star-Spangled Banner,"watching the notated rhythm.

THE STAR-SPANGLED BANNER

How many notes constitute the pick-up for "The Star-Spangled Banner"?______

119

Chanting response.

2.

119

Write the notation for the pick-ups in the two songs below. Chant or sing the songs; notice that the pick-up note or notes are unaccented.

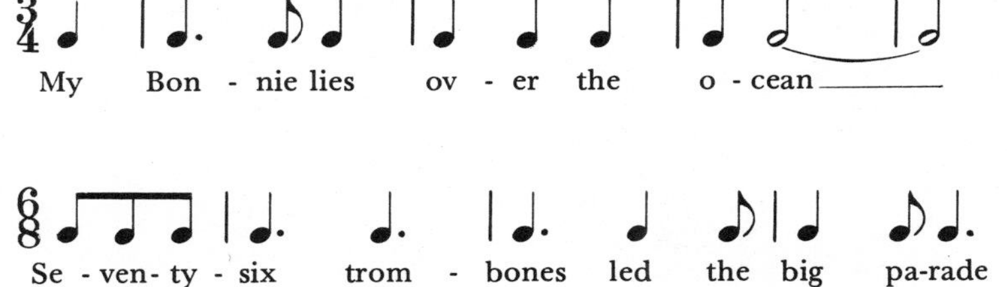

120

𝅗𝅥

♩♩♩

120

DURATION AND METER REVIEW, Frames 121-125

With the quarter note as the basic pulse (♩ equals one beat), give the number of pulses for each of the following notes: 𝅝 = __ 𝅗𝅥 = __ ♩ = __ ♪ = __ 𝅗𝅥. = __ ♩. = __

In $\frac{6}{8}$ meter there would be ______ pulses in each measure, the _______________ note would receive one beat.

If the quarter note is the basic pulse, how many notes or rests of the following type occupy the duration of one beat?

♪ = __ 𝅘𝅥𝅯 = __ 𝄾 = __ 𝅀 = __ 𝄿 = __

With the half note as the basic beat, how many notes of the following type occupy the duration of one beat?

𝅘𝅥𝅰 = __ ♩ = __ ♪ = __ 𝄿 = __

121

4, 2, 1, 1/2, 3, 1 1/2.

6, eighth.

2, 4, 2, 8, 4.

16, 2, 4, 8.

121

Assume that the quarter note is the unit beat. Draw a meter signature and construct a complete measure of whole notes, then one of quarter notes, and so forth.

Quadruple meter:

$\frac{4}{\ }$ 𝅝 ________ | ♩ ________ | 𝅘𝅥𝅯 ____________________ |

♪ ______________ | 𝅗𝅥 _______ ‖

With the eighth note as the unit beat, construct measures consisting of each of the following notes:

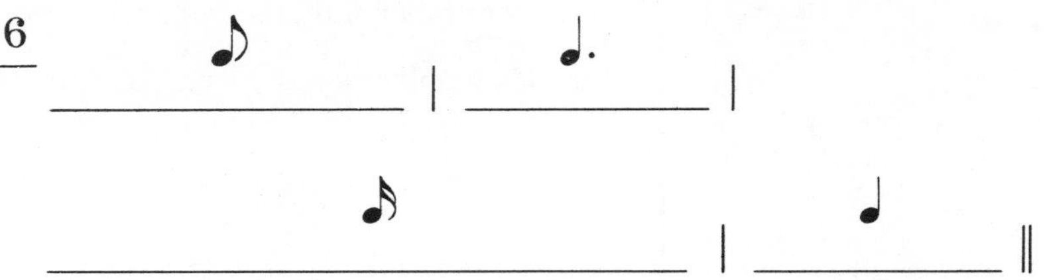

Find the rhythmic errors. Circle them.

THE FIRST NOEL

The primary stress in "The First Noel" should be on the

___ first note
___ second note
___ third note

The dotted note in the first full measure receives _______ counts

The rit. at the end of the song means ________________

Third note.

1 1/2.

Slow down (ritard).

123

The top number in the meter signature indicates how many ______________ in a measure; the bottom number indicates what kind of a note gets ______________ beat.

The **C** in place of the numerical meter signature indicates $\frac{\quad}{4}$ meter, or common time.

124

Beats.

One.

4.

124

Music is divided into measures by a ______________ line.

♩ = 60 is a ______________ marking.

The Italian word meaning to gradually increase the tempo is ______________.

The Italian word indicating to gradually decrease the tempo is ______________ or ______________.

The organization of duration into accented and unaccented pulses constitutes ______________.

Two or more notes may constitute a ______________ pattern.

125

Bar.

Tempo.

Accelerando.

Rallentando, ritard.

Meter.

Rhythm.

125

CHAPTER 7 The Concept of Amplitude

The concept of amplitude is not difficult to understand. We are aware of loud and soft sounds in our everyday life. They add interest and variety, as well as meaning, to the sounds we hear. A sound that remains at the same degree of loudness or softness is distracting and not very expressive, like a person speaking without a change of inflection. Musical sound, like all sound, ranges from extremely soft to extremely loud. Usually there are changes in amplitude in the use of stress–nonstress and accent–nonaccent.

The concept of amplitude, like that of duration, is relative. How long is long? How loud is loud? Exact tempo can be established by using the metronome, although almost all musicians do not adhere to an exact, mechanical tempo. The measuring device for amplitude is a complicated scientific machine and is not a classroom device. When listening to music or performing it, each person forms his own standards of loud and soft. Dynamic markings are terms and signs that the composer uses to indicate amplitude in the composition.

The most familiar dynamic markings are given below. Like the tempo marks, these terms are also Italian.

pianissimo	pp	very soft
piano	p	soft
mezzo piano	mp	medium soft
mezzo forte	mf	medium loud
forte	f	loud
fortissimo	ff	very loud

Compare the terms and their definitions to discover the meaning of "mezzo" and the "issimo" ending. Mezzo means _______________. The ending "issimo" means _______________.

126

Medium.

Very.

126

Look at the following song. What amplitude or volume is desired?

_______________ meaning _______________.
Italian English

LIEBES MÄDCHEN

Andante
p

Lie - bes mäd - chen, hör mir zu, öff - ne leis das Git - ter;

127

Piano.

Soft.

127

In this song two dynamic markings are given. What amplitudes are indicated?

_______________ and _______________.
English English

O LORD MOST HOLY

piano

O Lord most ho - ly, O Lord most might - y,

mezzo forte

O lov - ing Fa - ther, We sing praise to thee al - way.

128

Soft.

Moderately loud.

128

For many centuries musicians have used and delighted in contrasting dynamic levels. However, it was not until the seventeenth century that markings were used to indicate a gradual change of dynamics.

- crescendo, abbreviated cresc. = gradually get louder
- decrescendo, abbreviated decresc. = gradually get softer
- diminuendo, abbreviated dim. = gradually get softer

Note that decrescendo and diminuendo are two terms that have the same meaning.

79

Much music of our time just fades away instead of having a forceful and definite ending. In the song "Row, Row, Your Boat," show how this gradually getting softer might be indicated in the music.

ROW, ROW, ROW YOUR BOAT

129

129

APPLICATION: Meter, Rhythm, and Amplitude

Exercise 19: You will hear three songs played, with the first beat of each measure counted "ONE." Decide the meter for each. Then listen to the songs again as each is counted metrically.

Meter for song 1: duple triple quadruple quintuple ________________

song 2: duple triple quadruple quintuple ________________

song 3: duple triple quadruple quintuple ________________

End of Band 4, Side 2

Quadruple

Duple.

Triple.

Exercise 20: Listen to these songs and determine if the meter is duple or triple.

1. ________________
2. ________________
3. ________________

End of Band 5, Side 2

19

Duple.

Triple.

Triple.

Duple.

Exercise 21: Use of body motions with the music is helpful in feeling pulse and meter. Sing "The More We Get Together" with the record. Repeat it clapping or tapping your foot with the pulse. On the third hearing, add a second bodily motion only on count one, such as nodding your head or using the other hand or foot. Practice the two motions with the music until you have mastered them.

THE MORE WE GET TOGETHER

The more we get to - geth - er, to - geth - er, to - geth - er, The

more we get to - geth - er the hap - pi - er are we.

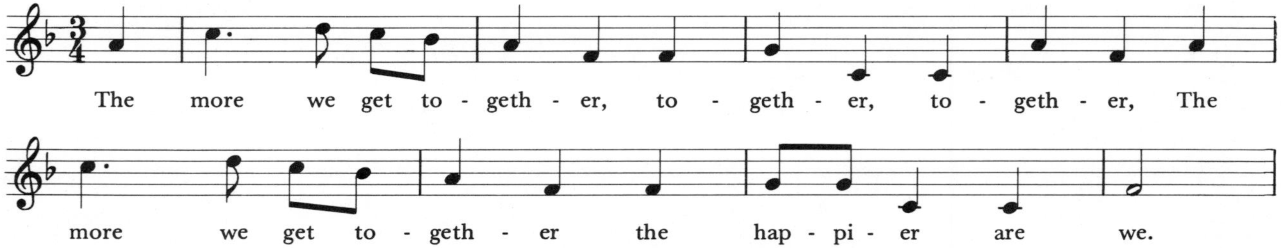

For your friends are my friends and my friends are
your friends,
The more we get together the happier are we.

End of Band 6, Side 2

20

Clapping or tapping and moving response.

21

Exercise 22: Determine the meter, quarter note pulse, for the following song. Write the correct meter signature.

WE ARE THE CHIMES

We are the chimes that weave the hours, Mak-ing them sweet as chains of flowers,

Count the rhythm as you sing the song; check your answer with the record.

End of Band 1, Side 3

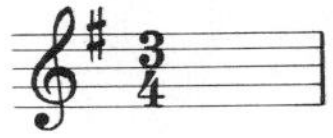

Counting response.

22

Exercise 23: Examine the song below. The unit beat is the eighth note. Write in the correct meter signature. Check you answer by listening as the song is counted on the record.

MY ISLAND HOME

End of Band 2, Side 3 (A STOP BAND)

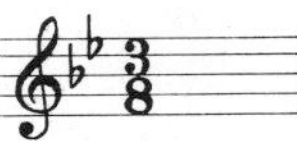

23

Exercise 24: Listen to the record and select the rhythm pattern from those given below that you hear repeated frequently.

a.
b.
c.

a.

24

Exercise 25: Listen to the recording and select the rhythm pattern that you hear repeated frequently.

25

Exercise 26: Quick changes in meter provide a different feeling to music from that of a regular metrical pattern. Listen to the changes of meter as you follow the music.

RUMANIAN CHRISTMAS CAROL NO. 2

Christ - mas time is com - ing! Let us be joy - ful with our sing - ing.
Christ - mas time is com - ing!

"Rumanian Christmas Carol #2" by Béla Bartók. Copyright 1918 by Universal Edition, Renewed 1945. Copyright & Renewal assigned to Boosey & Hawkes, Inc., for U.S.A. Used by permission of Boosey & Hawkes, Inc. and Editio Musica Budapest.

Sing with the recording.

Singing response.

Exercise 27: An absence of almost any metrical feeling is found in some music. Listen to the following song which has little stress and no discernible meter. Follow the music as you listen.

CONDITOR ALME SIDERUM

From the Juilliard Repertory Library.

26

Listening response.

Exercise 28: Hearing with your eyes takes extensive practice. One begins very early, however, to try to determine what music might sound like while looking at the notation. This rhythm pattern is rather complex. Follow the notation as you listen to it. Clap to the repetition.

End of Band 3, Side 3

27

Listening and clapping response.

Exercise 29: In Exercises 29–31, follow the music as you listen to the recording. Place an X through every measure in which the rhythm is different from that played.

BLOW THE MAN DOWN
1.
2.
3.
4.
Come all ye young fel - lows that fol - low the sea, Yeo - ho, Blow the man down! And
5.
6.
7.
8.
please pay at - ten - tion and lis - ten to me, Give us some time to blow the man down!

28

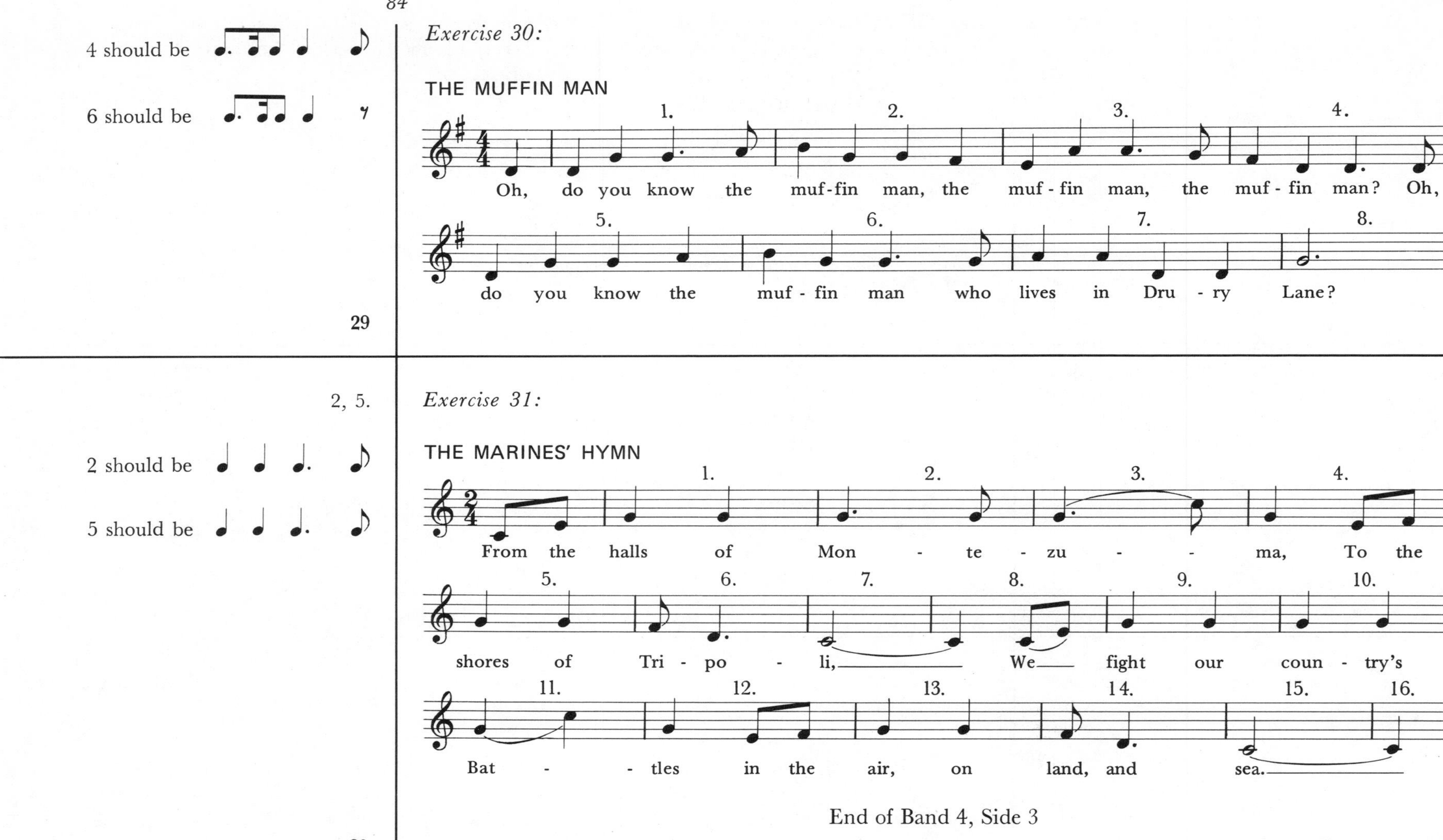
4 should be
6 should be
29
Exercise 30:
THE MUFFIN MAN
1. 2. 3. 4.
Oh, do you know the muf-fin man, the muf - fin man, the muf - fin man? Oh,
5. 6. 7. 8.
do you know the muf - fin man who lives in Dru - ry Lane?
2, 5.
2 should be
5 should be
30
Exercise 31:
THE MARINES' HYMN
1. 2. 3. 4.
From the halls of Mon - te - zu - - ma, To the
5. 6. 7. 8. 9. 10.
shores of Tri - po - li, We fight our coun - try's
11. 12. 13. 14. 15. 16.
Bat - - tles in the air, on land, and sea.
End of Band 4, Side 3

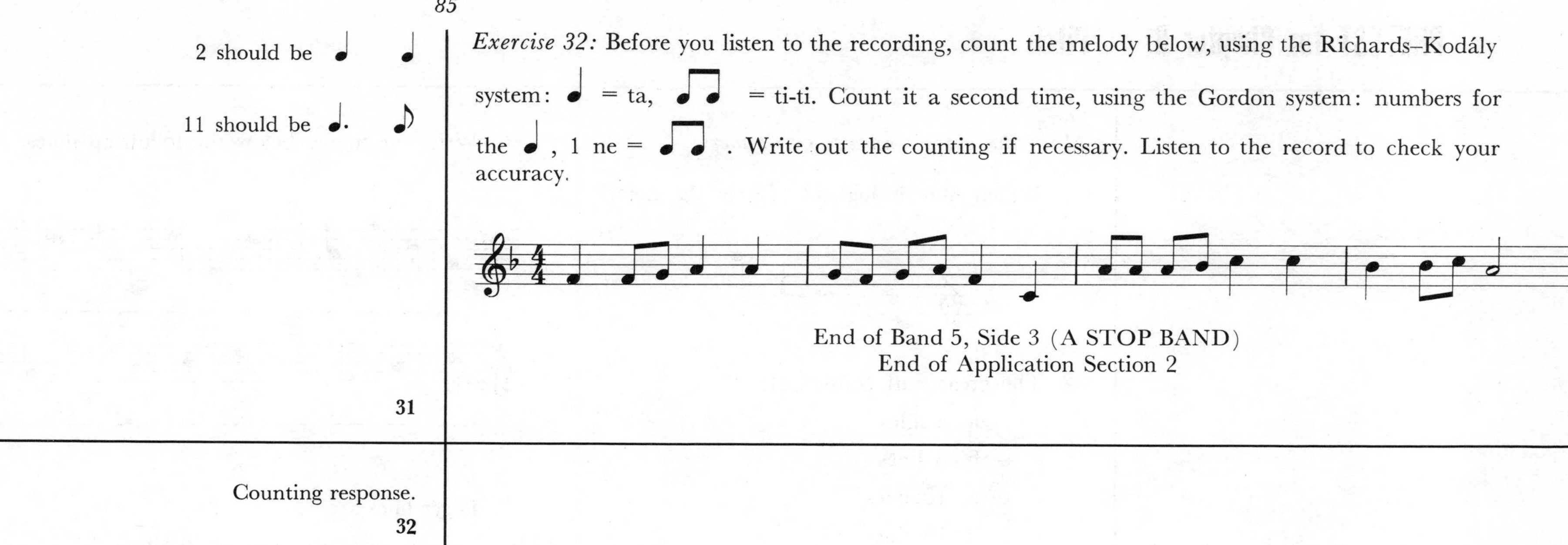

2 should be ♩ ♩

11 should be ♩. ♪

31

Exercise 32: Before you listen to the recording, count the melody below, using the Richards–Kodály system: ♩ = ta, ♫ = ti-ti. Count it a second time, using the Gordon system: numbers for the ♩, 1 ne = ♫. Write out the counting if necessary. Listen to the record to check your accuracy.

End of Band 5, Side 3 (A STOP BAND)
End of Application Section 2

Counting response.

32

PRETEST for Chapter 8: Pitch

Mark the correct answer or *answers.*

1. Which note is higher? (Circle the note.)

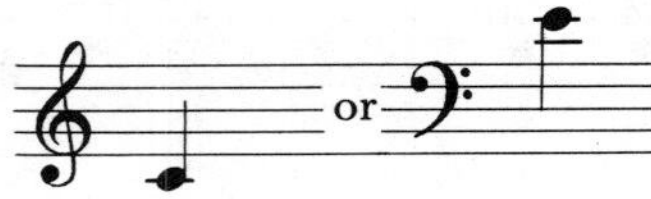

2. The great staff consists of:

   —— a. 5 lines
   —— b. 8 lines
   —— c. 10 lines
   —— d. 15 lines

3. The two dots in the bass clef signature are centered around the:

   —— a. G line
   —— b. F line
   —— c. D line
   —— d. A line

4. The treble clef is also known as the:

   —— a. G clef
   —— b. F clef
   —— c. D clef
   —— d. B clef

5. Notes on or within the bass clef range from:

   —— a. e–f
   —— b. d–g
   —— c. f–b
   —— d. g–a

6. Write the names below the following notes.

7. Leger lines are:

   —— a. another name for barlines
   —— b. another name for stems on notes
   —— c. lines in the repeat sign
   —— d. added lines above or below the staff

8. Middle C is so named because it is the:

   —— a. middle of the singing range
   —— b. middle of the range of Western music
   —— c. middle of the great staff
   —— d. middle of the piano keyboard

9. Name the lines of the bass clef. ____ ____ ____ ____ ____

10. An octave is:

    —— a. a type of scale
    —— b. a high note
    —— c. an interval of an eighth
    —— d. the notes played by the fingers of each hand

Answers

1.

2. c.
3. b.
4. a.
5. d.
6. a e b c f f g g c a f d c a f c d b a b g.
7. d.
8. c.
9. G B D F A.
10. c.

From your score determine if you can omit sections of the text.

CHAPTER 8 The Concept of Pitch

The concepts of duration, meter, and rhythm have been discussed. Although these concepts can be used to create interesting and exciting musical patterns, they are limited. A drummer uses these but he also uses instrumental color and sometimes pitch. Even if he is playing only a single snare drum, he can strike his sticks together, strike the rim of the drum, or play on different parts of the drum to vary the sound, thus using instrumental color and sometimes pitch.

The concept of pitch is as basic as the concept of duration, for pitch is the basis of melody, and music depends on melody. Pitch is not a concept that all children instinctively know. It exists in varying degrees of sophistication in children, and it must be taught to children regularly and over a long period of time if they are to become skillful in perceiving this concept.

This chapter on pitch is designed to help the learner achieve the following objectives: (1) an understanding of "high" and "low"; (2) familiarity with the G clef, the F clef, and the great staff; and (3) knowledge of the pitch names of the clefs.

The concept of pitch—higher, lower, and the same—is one that children must understand if they are to "hear with their eyes" or "see with their ears." Children may be able to sing melodies accurately without realizing what is meant by "high" and "low" in music. High pitches do not occupy some high position in space such as the top of a ladder or above the rooftops. In music, the word "higher" means that these pitches contain more vibrations per second—a higher (greater) number of vibrations. Low pitches have fewer, or a lower number of, vibrations per second. The term is really a numerical one rather than a spatial one. Pitches can be close together or far apart. A low pitch on a large pipe organ has approximately 16 vibrations per second. This is slow enough that the vibrations are identifiable and can almost be counted.

Higher pitches have a greater number of ______________ per second than do lower pitches.

130

Vibrations.

130

When pitches are pictured by symbols on a music staff, the high notes are actually higher than the low notes, so that looking at music can help a child understand how the terms "high" and "low" are used in relation to pitch.

The *great staff* is used to designate specific pitches; it is made up of ten written lines with an unwritten line dividing the ten in half. Notes are symbols for duration; when placed on the staff, on a specific line or space, a note becomes also a symbol for ______________.

131

Pitch.

131

The unwritten line stands for a specific pitch, referred to as "middle C." Either set of five lines may be used alone. The upper five lines—those above the middle C line—are called the treble clef or treble staff. The treble clef is designated by this symbol: 𝄞

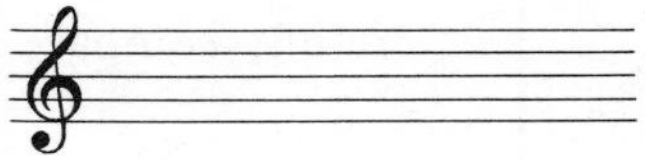

Pitches having a greater number of vibrations per second will be written ______________ middle C. (above) (below)

132

Above.

132

The treble clef sign winds around the second line, which is named the G line. For this reason, the treble clef is also referred to as the G clef.

Draw a few G clef signs on the blank staff below. First draw the straight line.

Then, beginning at the top, draw the curved line, curling it around the second line. G

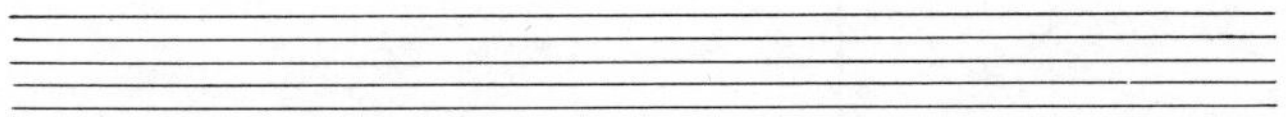

Carefully compare your drawings with the model answer. Students will expect their teacher's clef signs to look like those printed on their music.

133

Each one of the treble clefs should look like

this: G

Top of the treble clef sign extends above staff; bottom of curve lies on bottom line of staff.

133

The lower five lines of the great staff—those below the middle-C line—are called the bass clef or bass staff.

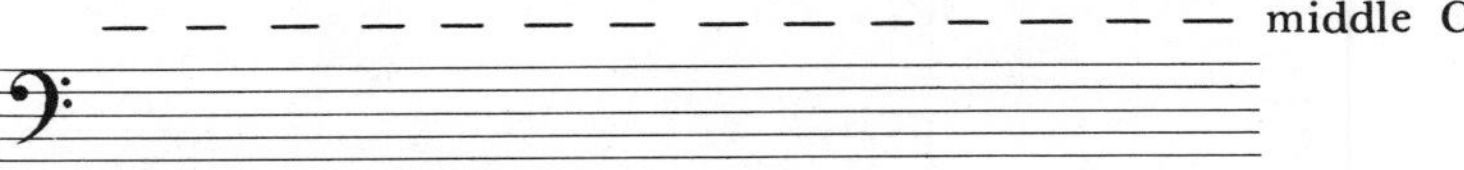

The bass clef sign has two dots, one on either side of the fourth line, which in the bass clef is named the F line. Thus, the bass clef is also referred to as the *F clef*. F

Draw a few F clef signs on the blank staff below. Start the curl around the F line, go up to the top line, curve around to end just at the bottom line. Place a dot on either side of the F line (fourth line from bottom).

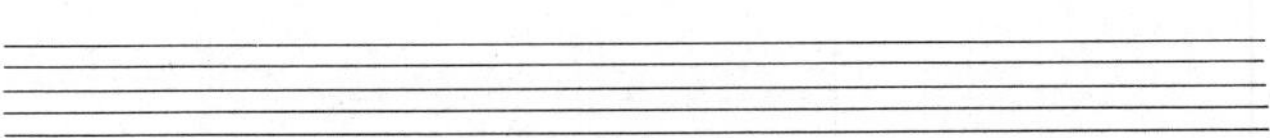

Carefully compare your drawings with that of the model answer.

134

Each one of the bass clefs should look

like this: F

Top of the staff touches the top line curving around and extending *almost* to the bottom line.

134

When a note is placed on the staff, it is placed either on a line or on a space. The note on a space occupies the complete space but does not cover the adjacent lines.

The notes occupying the lines are placed so that the line goes through the middle of the note. This note is the same size as the note that fills the space—it goes half way up to the next line and half way down to the lower line.

Each line and space of the great staff stands for a different pitch, the lowest pitch on the lowest line. Each line and space has a letter name, following the alphabetical order A through G, then starting over again. The lowest line in the bass clef is G; the top line of the treble clef is F.

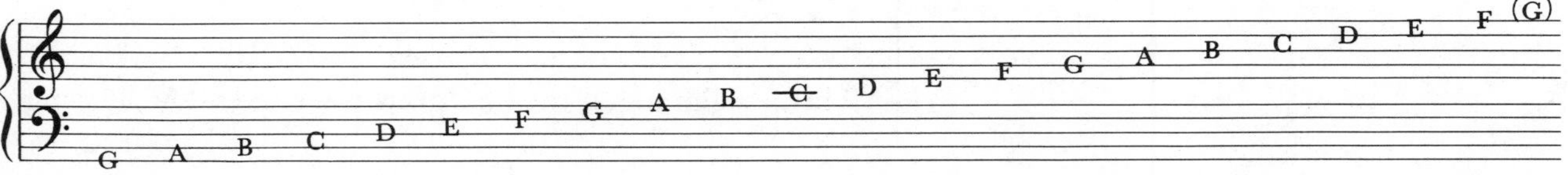

What pitch lies on the unwritten center line? ______________, on the second space, bass clef? ______________, on the third space, treble clef? ______________

135

Middle C.

C.

C.

135

In order to identify the notes written on the two staffs, one must learn the names of the lines and spaces. Can you determine a system for remembering the names of the lines and/or spaces?

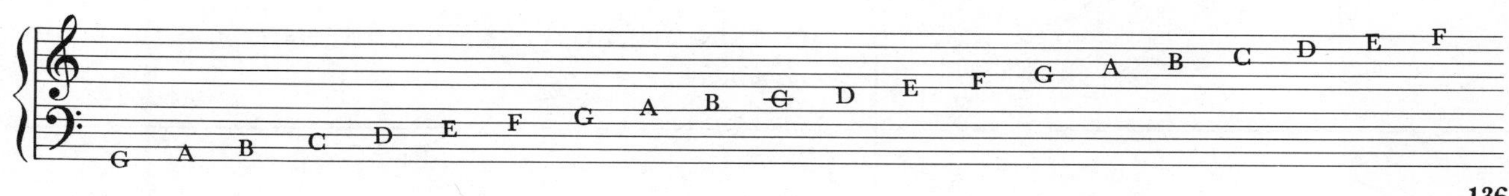

136

Varied response: mnemonic devises; reference to alphabetical order for line–space–line–space, etc.

136

Write the correct letter name beneath each note.

137

137

A method for remembering the treble clef space names was illustrated: from bottom to top the letter names of the spaces are F A C E, face.

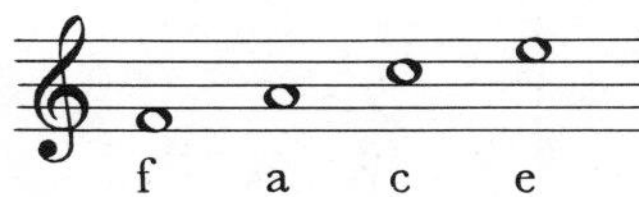

Many teachers use mnemonic devices to help students learn the pitches of one or both staffs. For instance, the spaces in the bass clef can be remembered by the little phrase, "All Cows Eat Grass" (first letter of each word), or "All Cars Eat Gas."

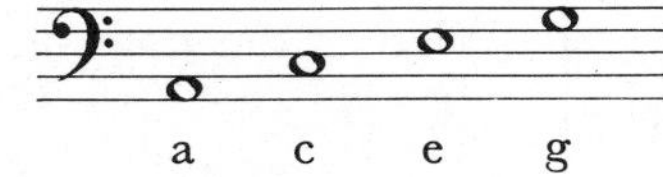

Students should make up their own mnemonics to aid in learning.

Similar mnemonics can be used to aid in remembering the names of the lines:

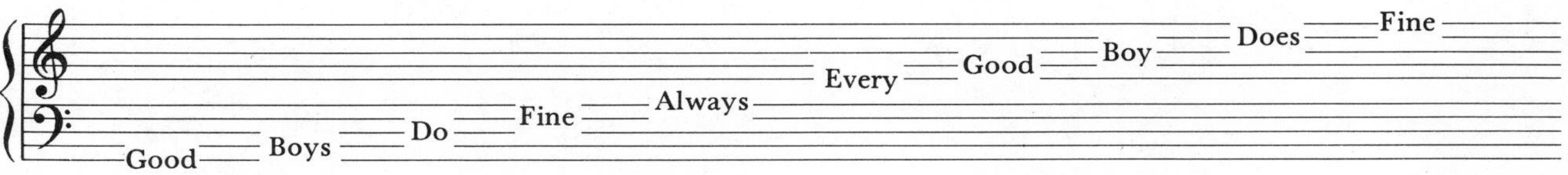

Cover the staff with your hand or a piece of paper.

Name the bass clef *lines,* in order, starting at the bottom. ________________

Name the treble clef *lines,* in order, starting at the bottom. ________________

138

G B D F A.

E G B D F.

138

Write the letter names on the spaces in the great staff.

139

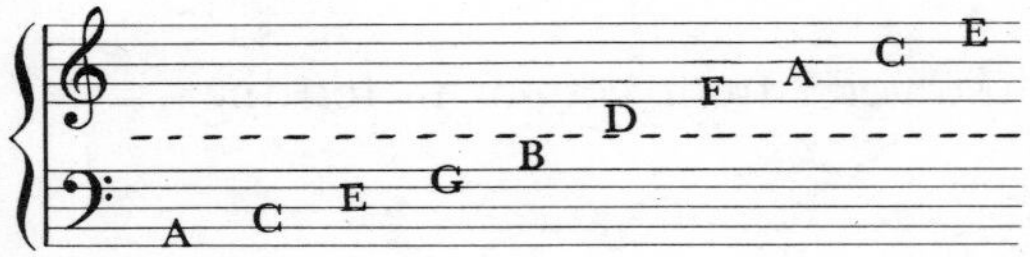

E C A F D B G E C A

139

Notice that the names of the lines and spaces are not the same for the bass clef as for the treble clef but they do go in an alphabetical order.

This note is E. This note is G:

Each note is in the same position on the staff, but each has a different clef sign.

What is the note on the first space of the treble clef? _______

What is the note on the first space of the bass clef? _______

140

F.

A.

140

Using whatever system you wish, identify these notes:

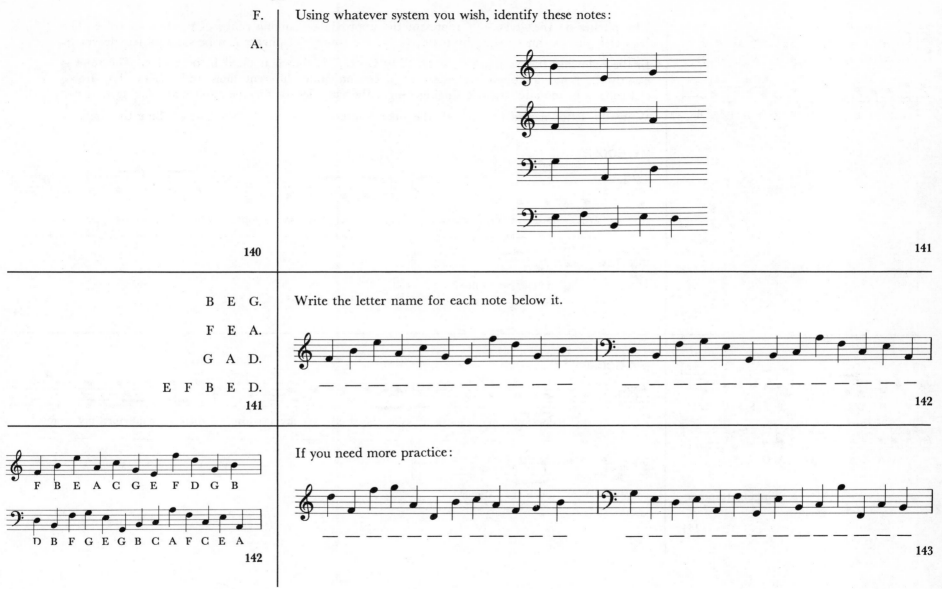

141

B E G.

F E A.

G A D.

E F B E D.

141

Write the letter name for each note below it.

— — — — — — — — — — —

— — — — — — — — — — — — — —

142

F B E A C G E F D G B

D B F G E G B C A F C E A

142

If you need more practice:

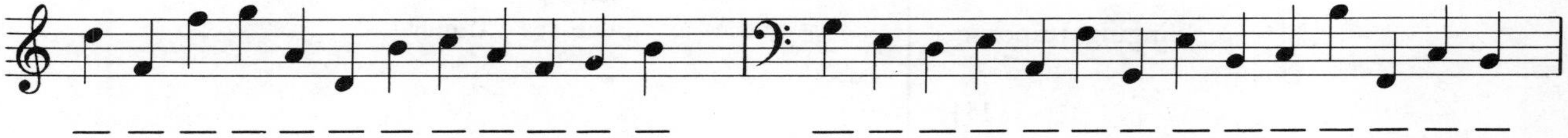

— — — — — — — — — — — —

— — — — — — — — — — — — — —

143

143

The pitches on the great staff represent the approximate singing range of the human voice. The bass clef pitches can be sung by male voices; the treble clef pitches can be sung by female voices.

In the following frames the little song, "My Goose," is shown notated in both clefs. The tune is exactly the same, although the notes are placed on quite different lines and spaces. The treble clef song is in the adult female singing range; the bass clef song in the adult male singing range.

Write the letter names underneath the notes for both versions of "My Goose." Sing the song.

MY GOOSE

144

Singing response.

144

MY GOOSE

Why does - n't my goose sing as well as thy goose, When I paid for my goose

twice as much as thine?

145

145

The distance between any pitch and the next higher or lower repetition of that letter name, for example, E to E, is called an octave. In the preceding frames, "My Goose" in the treble clef is one octave higher than "My Goose" in the bass clef.

The distance from F to F is called an ________________.

The distance from to is called an octave.

146

Octave.

146

Write the note an octave above each note.

Write the note an octave below each note.

147

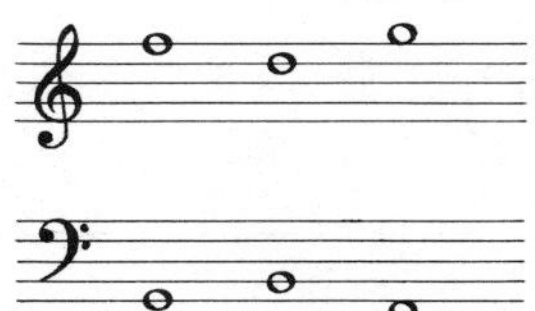

147

Placement of the stem of the note is important for legibility. Notes on the bottom two spaces and lines are written with their stems up . Notes on the top two lines or spaces are written with their stems down . The middle line is optional, the stems may go either up or down. This rule applies to both treble and bass clefs.

Draw a line through the incorrectly written notes.

148

148

LONDON BRIDGE

Lon - don Bridge is fall - ing down, fall - ing down, fall - ing down,

Write "London Bridge" in the bass clef, also starting on D.

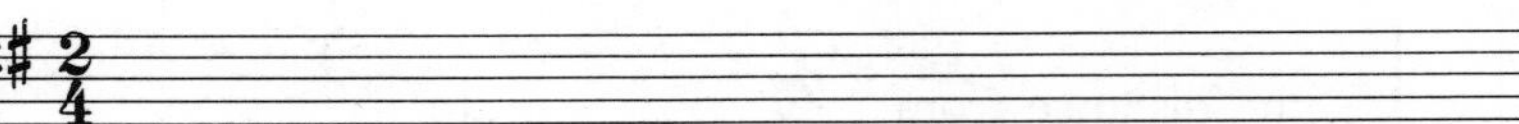

Examine the time signature, then draw barlines to separate the notes into measures.

149

149

The musical instruments used in band and orchestra usually have a range extending beyond that of the clefs; they play pitches higher or lower than those of the great staff. Rather than using other clefs for a few very high or low notes, leger lines can be added to the staff to indicate these notes. The notes A, B, and C have been indicated by the use of leger lines above the treble clef and B below. (The pronunciation is "ledger" and some texts now call the lines ledger lines.)

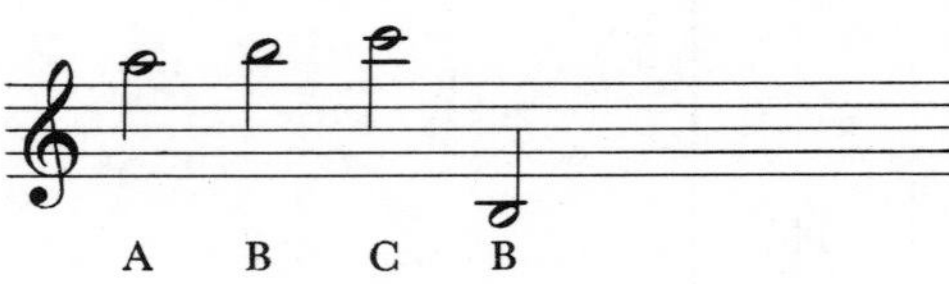
A B C B

Lines added above or below a staff are called ______________ lines.

Is middle C a leger line? ______________

150

Leger.

Yes.

150

In the example below, which note is lower? ______________

1 2

The second pitch is named ______________.

151

2.

Middle C.

151

Write out "Poor Wayfarin' Stranger" by following these directions. Draw the treble clef sign on the staff; the meter is 3 beats to a measure; a half note gets 1 count. Write the following notes: D quarter note, D quarter note, A quarter note; put in a barline, A dotted half, G quarter note, 2 A quarter notes, G and F eighth notes, D half note, 2 D quarter notes, A quarter note. (The first three notes are pick-up notes.) Place the other barlines correctly. Make sure the stems go in the proper direction.

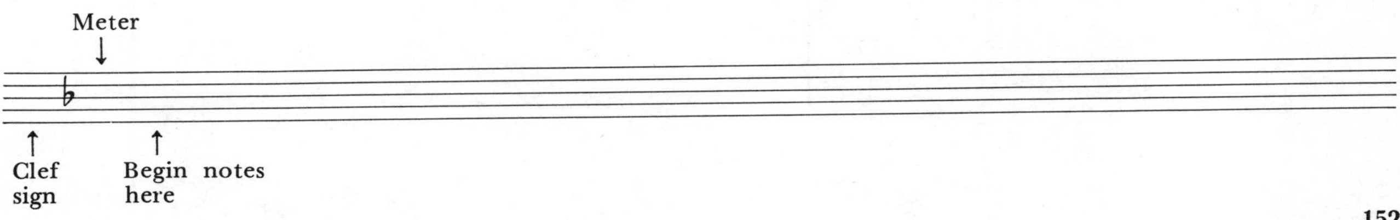

152

152

Write this song an octave higher; use leger lines whenever necessary.

ON TOP OF OLD SMOKY

153

98

PRETEST for Chapter 9: Keyboard

Mark the correct answer or *answers.*

1. The piano keyboard is arranged with:
   —— a. one black key next to every two white keys
   —— b. one white key between every two black keys
   —— c. black keys in groups of twos and threes
   —— d. white keys in groups of twos and threes

2. B is located:
   —— a. between two black keys
   —— b. just above two black keys
   —— c. just above three black keys
   —— d. just above a white key

3. If one plays only white keys on a piano keyboard, he will play:
   —— a. all half steps
   —— b. all whole steps
   —— c. nearly an equal number of whole steps and half steps
   —— d. mostly whole steps with a few half steps.

4. Enharmonic notation is illustrated by:
   —— a. F-sharp and E-flat
   —— b. B-flat and A-sharp
   —— c. F-flat and E
   —— d. G-sharp and A

5. Mark the number on the keyboard that corresponds to the notes:

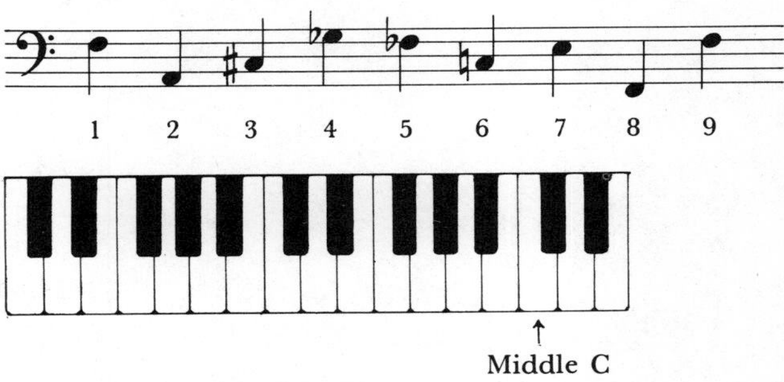

6. Mark with an X on the keyboard the first five notes of "The Star-Spangled Banner." Make the first note G.

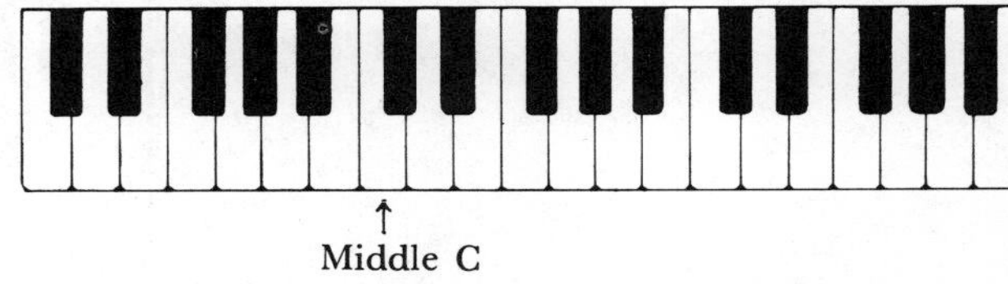

7. On the keyboard mark with an X all of the notes you would have to use to play this song.

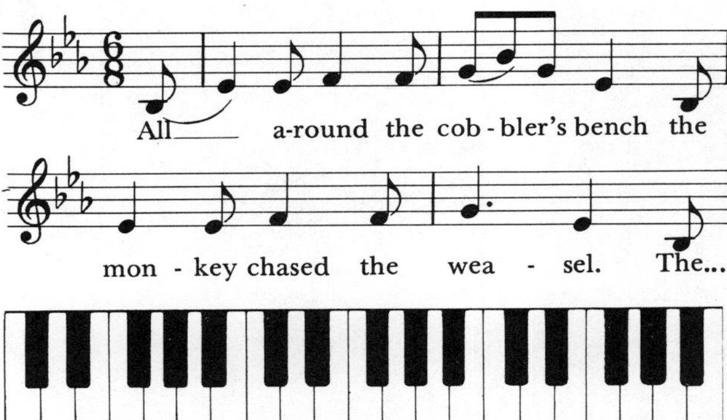

8. Mark in order (using numbers) the notes you would depress to play a d natural minor scale.

Middle C

9. Write the names of a descending chromatic scale beginning on C.

Answers

1. c.
2. c.
3. d.
4. b, c.
5.

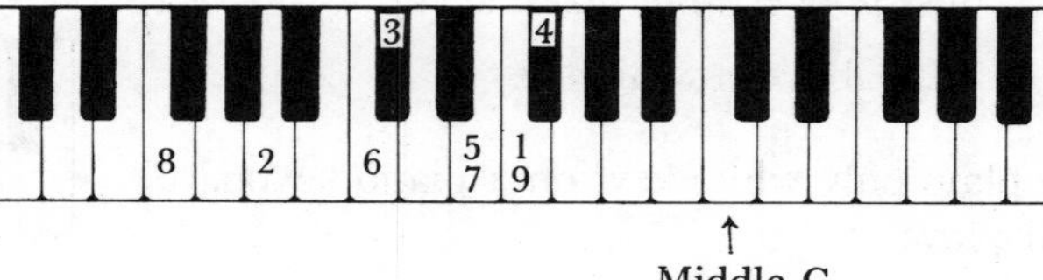

Middle C

6.

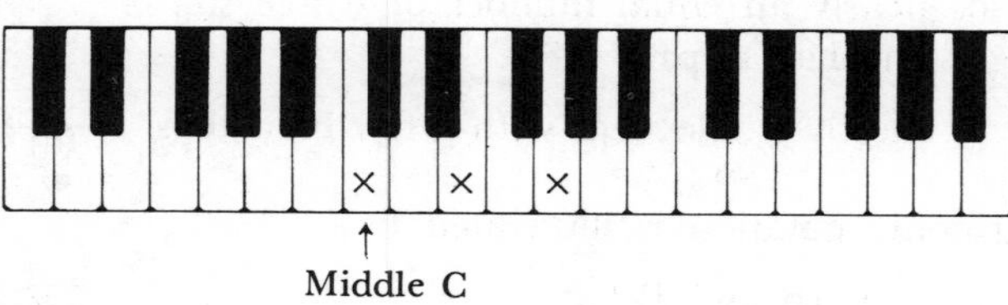

Middle C

7.

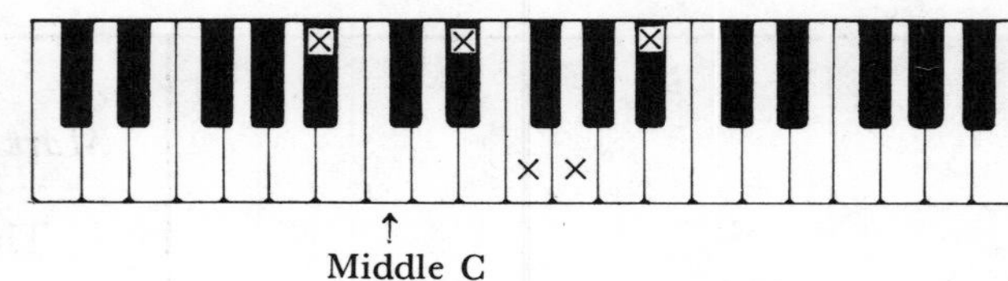

Middle C

8.

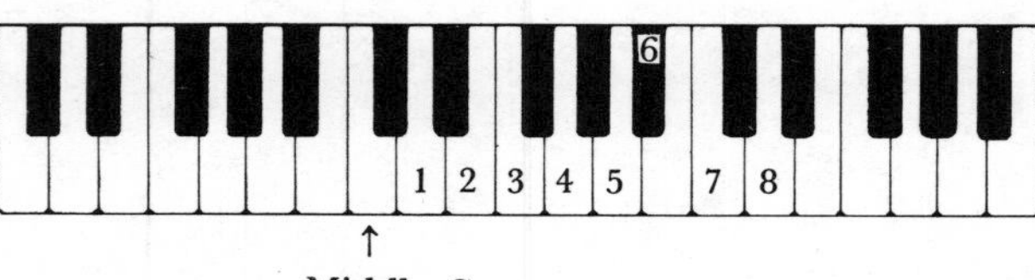

Middle C

9. C B B-flat A A-flat G G-flat F E E-flat D D-flat C

From your score determine if you can omit portions of the text.

CHAPTER 9 The Piano Keyboard

Understanding musical concepts requires continual association of cognitive concepts with the aural sounds. At every opportunity you should sing the music presented, find a piano or other instrument on which to play the music, use the records that are available with this book, and listen for these concepts in the music of everyday life.

Many fundamental concepts are reinforced by visual representation such as that provided by the piano keyboard. The keyboard is such an excellent device that there is a real danger of its becoming a crutch that the elementary teacher depends on. The teacher should be able to relate musical concepts not only to the keyboard but also to the musical staff and to aural sound itself.

Pianos are located in many classrooms; many college programs for elementary classroom teachers emphasize keyboard skills; paper keyboards are available for purchase or can be constructed; plastic keyboards with raised keys are standard equipment in many elementary schools; and with the advent of the electronic piano laboratory, one can assume that the piano will be increasingly available and used in teaching music in the classroom as well as in teacher training.

After doing the exercises in this chapter, the student should be able to (1) name all the keys of the keyboard by pitch name, (2) play accurately pitches from the treble and bass clefs, and (3) use the keyboard effectively for exercises in subsequent chapters.

The standard piano keyboard consists of 52 white and 36 black keys for a total of 88 notes: seven octaves plus two notes. Other keyboards, such as the electronic piano, plastic, and paper keyboards, will have a smaller range. All keyboard instruments are built on the half-step concept, the notes within one octave appearing thus:

Each octave is an exact repetition of the above scheme. In using the piano keyboard it is necessary to have a firm idea of the exact placement of keys and the names of the notes.

In one keyboard octave, there are ______ white and ______ black keys (if necessary, look at the drawing).

The names of the seven white notes beginning with C are ___ ___ ___ ___ ___ ___ ___.

The black keys are grouped, one group of ______ notes and another group of ______ notes.

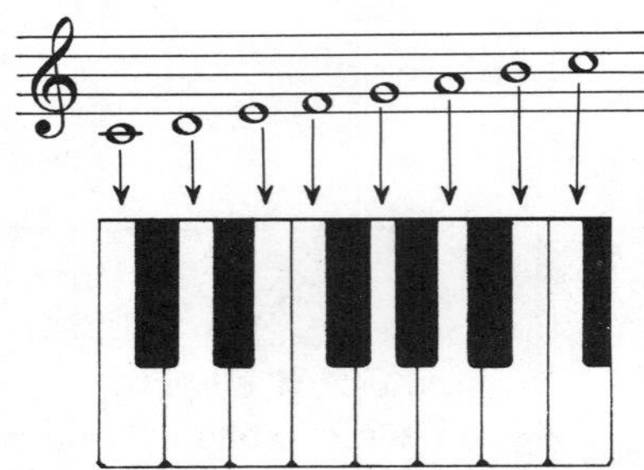

154

8, 5.

C D E F G A B.

2, 3.

154

In order to be able to give a starting tone or to determine if the class of singers has ended a song on the correct pitch, the teacher needs to be able to find the various pitches. The pitch C is always found immediately below (to the left of) the group of two black keys. The pitch F is found below (to the left of) the group of three black keys.

Label all the C keys and all the F keys.

155

155

The names of the notes on the keyboard should be associated with the staff.

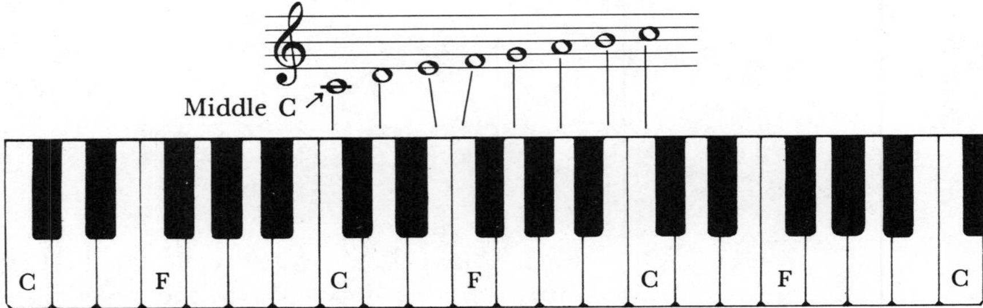

Other pitches can be found by counting up alphabetically from C or F, or by establishing other guideposts. For example, D is always between the two black keys; B is always just above (to the right of) the group of three black keys.

Label all D and all B keys on the keyboard.

156

156

Mark the letter names of the white keys. (C is given.) Skip around as you do it or the task will be too simple. For example, first mark in all the A's, then all the D's, the G's, and so forth.

157

157

Although the lines and spaces on the great staff appear to be equidistant, the pitch distances represented vary slightly. The pitches on the great staff are a whole step apart with two exceptions: between E and F is a half step and between B and C is a half step. Compare the staff with notes on the piano keyboard. The lines and spaces stand for the white keys; the white keys are separated by a black key in all instances except B–C and E–F.

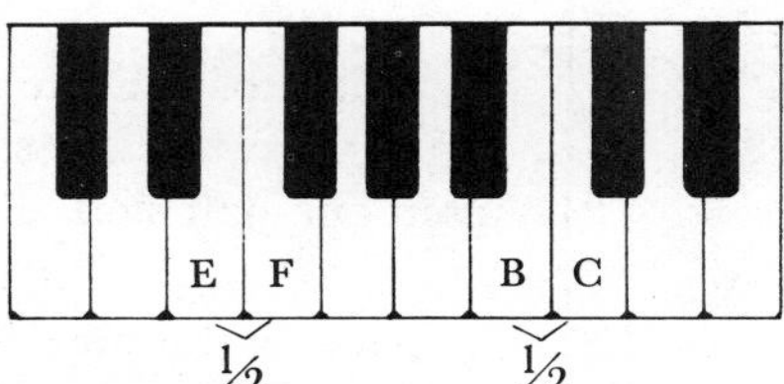

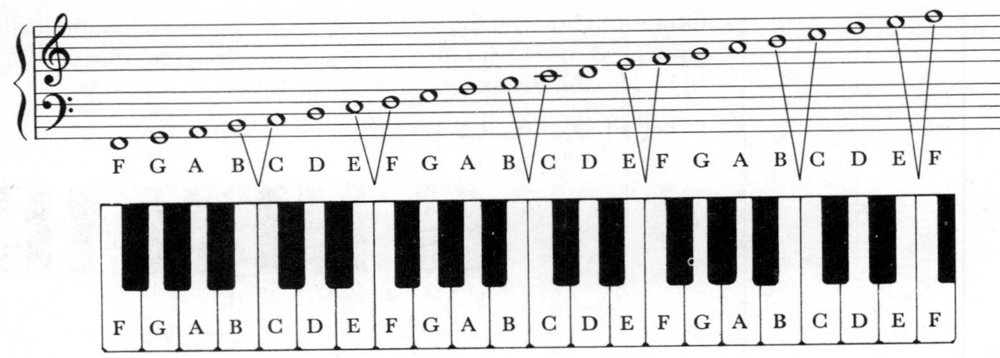

In the music of the Western world pitches are usually not closer together than a half step. When you play C on the piano keyboard and move to the black note just above it, you have moved up one half step, the shortest possible distance in piano music. The note just below C is a white note, B, and the distance between B and C is also one half step. Adjacent piano keys are one half step apart in pitch. One whole step, then, consists of two half steps. C to D is a whole step, one half step from C to the black key, one half step from the black key to D.

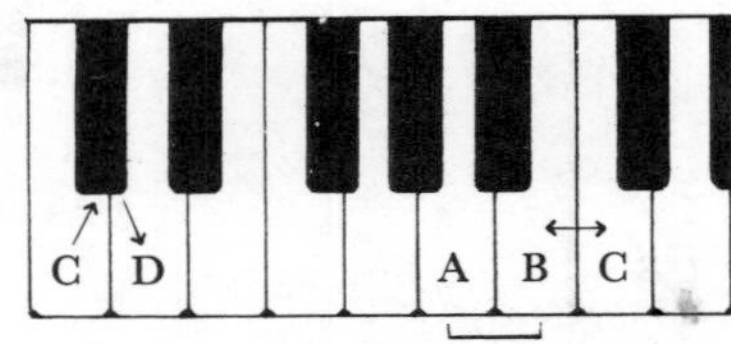

What is the distance between A and B? ________________.

Pitches closer together than half steps can be sung by the human voice and played on string instruments and trombones. Almost all other musical instruments are constructed with the half step being the smallest interval.

158

One whole step.

In order to indicate the "black-note pitches," accidentals may be used. The two common accidentals are the ♯ (sharp), which raises a pitch one half step, and the ♭ (flat), which lowers the pitch one half step. These accidentals are always written to the left of the note and on the same line or space as the note. For example, D-sharp: G-flat:

Write these quarter notes: C-sharp, E-sharp, D-flat, A-sharp, F-sharp, E-flat (use either clef).

159

Either octave:

159

Use either a piano or the large paper keyboard at the back of the book. Locate the accidentals named below. Remember, the sharp (♯) raises the pitch one half step and is sounded by the black key immediately right. The flat (♭) lowers the pitch one half step and is sounded by the black key immediately left.

Indicate the placement of these notes on a keyboard.

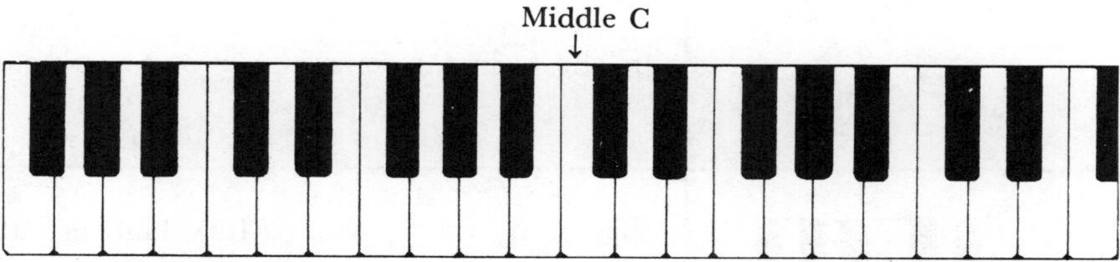

160

160

Write in the names of all the black and white keys on the keyboard below. Skip around to make it more interesting.

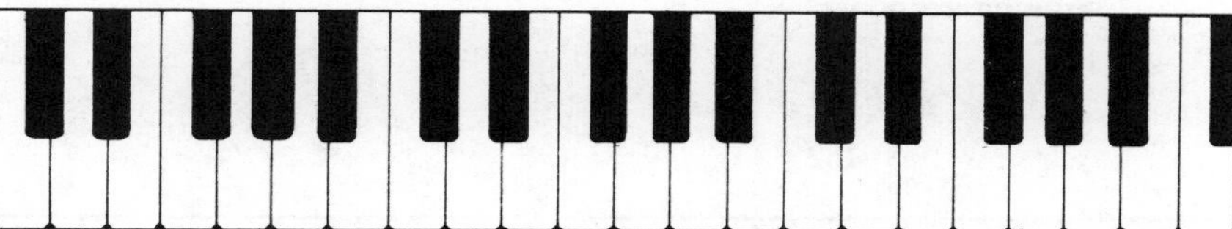

161

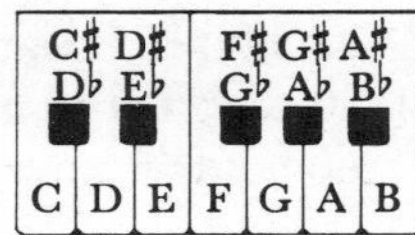

161

Tunes may be played on the keyboard simply by using the ear to help find the correct notes. Play "Mary Had a Little Lamb" on the piano, starting on E. If a piano is not available, play it on a paper keyboard and think what the sounds would be. Determine if the tune goes up or down, if it proceeds by step (scalewise) or skip, and where it repeats the same pitch. The tune uses only four pitches, E, D, C, and G. On the keyboard below, write these letter names on the keys used to play "Mary Had a Little Lamb." Sing the song with letter names.

Is the G in the song higher or lower than the other pitches? ______________

162

EDCDEEE, DDD, EGG,
EDCDEEEEDDEDC

Singing response.

Higher.

162

Beginning on A, play "Mary Had a Little Lamb" on the piano. Use A, G, F, and C. Thinking the tune as you play it is one important aspect of musical memory. Now play the same tune, beginning on B. What pitches are used? ___ ___ ___ and ___. Write them on the keyboard below.

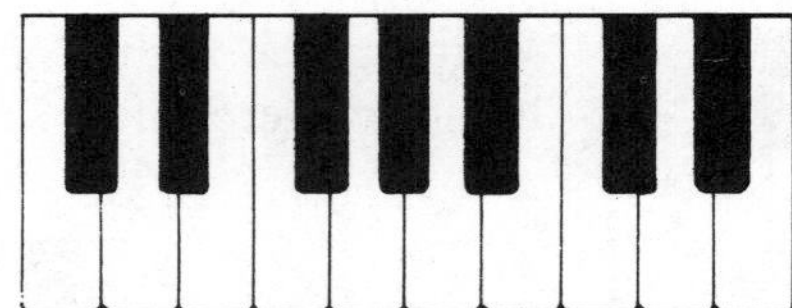

163

B, A, G, D.

163

Look at the notation for "Hot Cross Buns." Play it on the piano. Count the rhythm, using 1 & 2 &, etc. for the   's.

Play the tune starting on A; name the pitches used. ______________

Play it starting on G; name the pitches. ______________

Play it starting on C-sharp; name the pitches. ______________

164

Playing and counting response.

A, G, F.

G, F, E-flat.

C-sharp, B, A.

164

Mark the number on the keyboard that corresponds to the note.

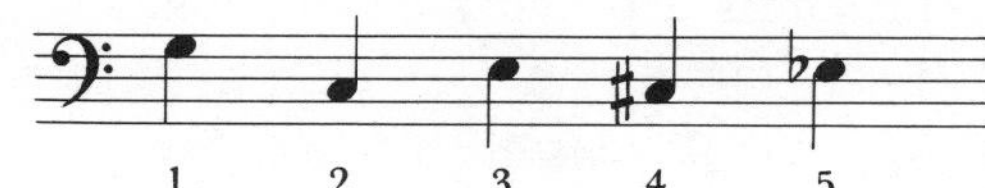

165

165

Mark the number on the keyboard that corresponds to the note.

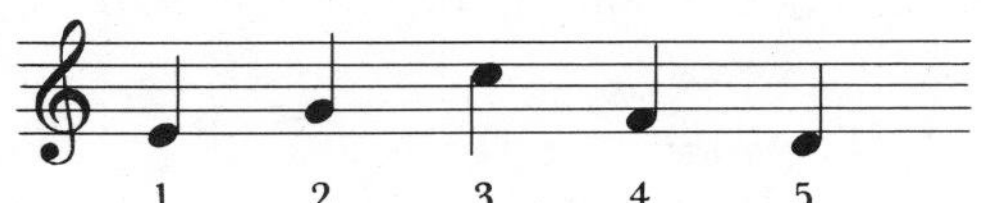

166

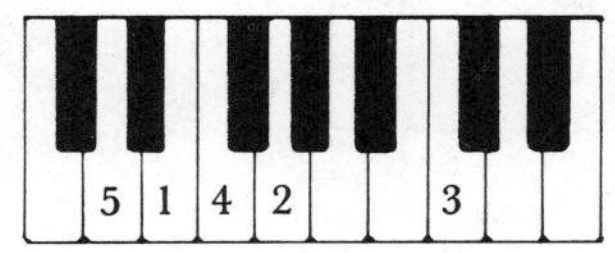

166

Mark the number on the keyboard that corresponds to the note.

Make up additional exercises in both clefs to develop your music reading skill. Mark them as rapidly as possible. If you have a piano, play and sing the exercises.

167

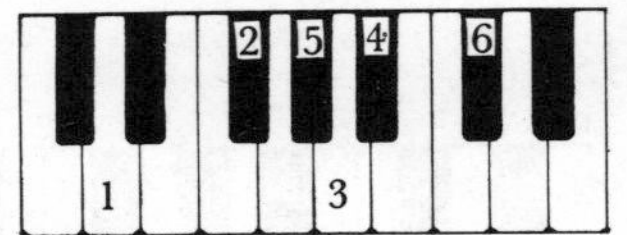

167

The half steps may be notated on the staff in one of two ways. The lower note may be sharped to raise it a half step or the higher note may be flatted to lower it a half step. For example, the half-step pitch between C and D can be C-sharp or D-flat; the sound is the same but it has two different names depending on the notation. This is called enharmonic notation.

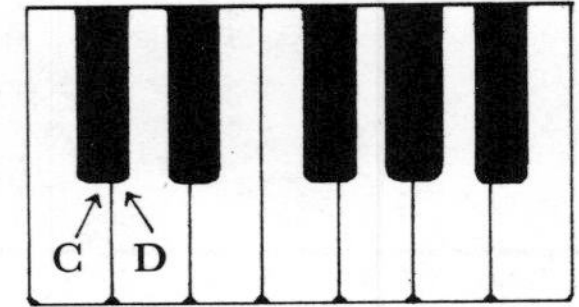

What other note is identical to A-sharp? ______ A-flat? ______ D-sharp? ______ F-sharp? ______

Give the enharmonic names for the half step between F and G: ______ ______ and between A and B: ______ ______.

Use the keyboard to assist you.

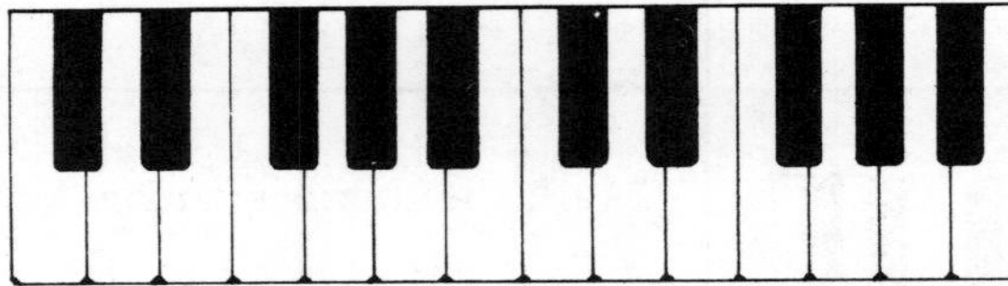

168

B-flat, G-sharp, E-flat, G-flat.

F-sharp, G-flat, A-sharp, B-flat.

168

Following each note write its enharmonic notation.

169

169

Using half notes, write *both* enharmonic notations for the half step between D and E; between F and G; between G and A; between A and B. Use treble clef.

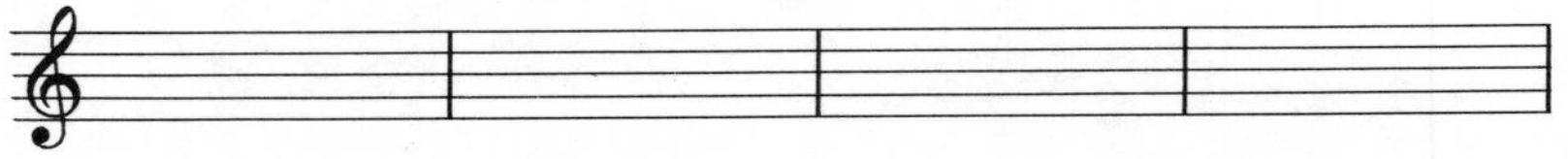

The function of a sharp sign in front of a note is to ______________ it ______________ step.

170

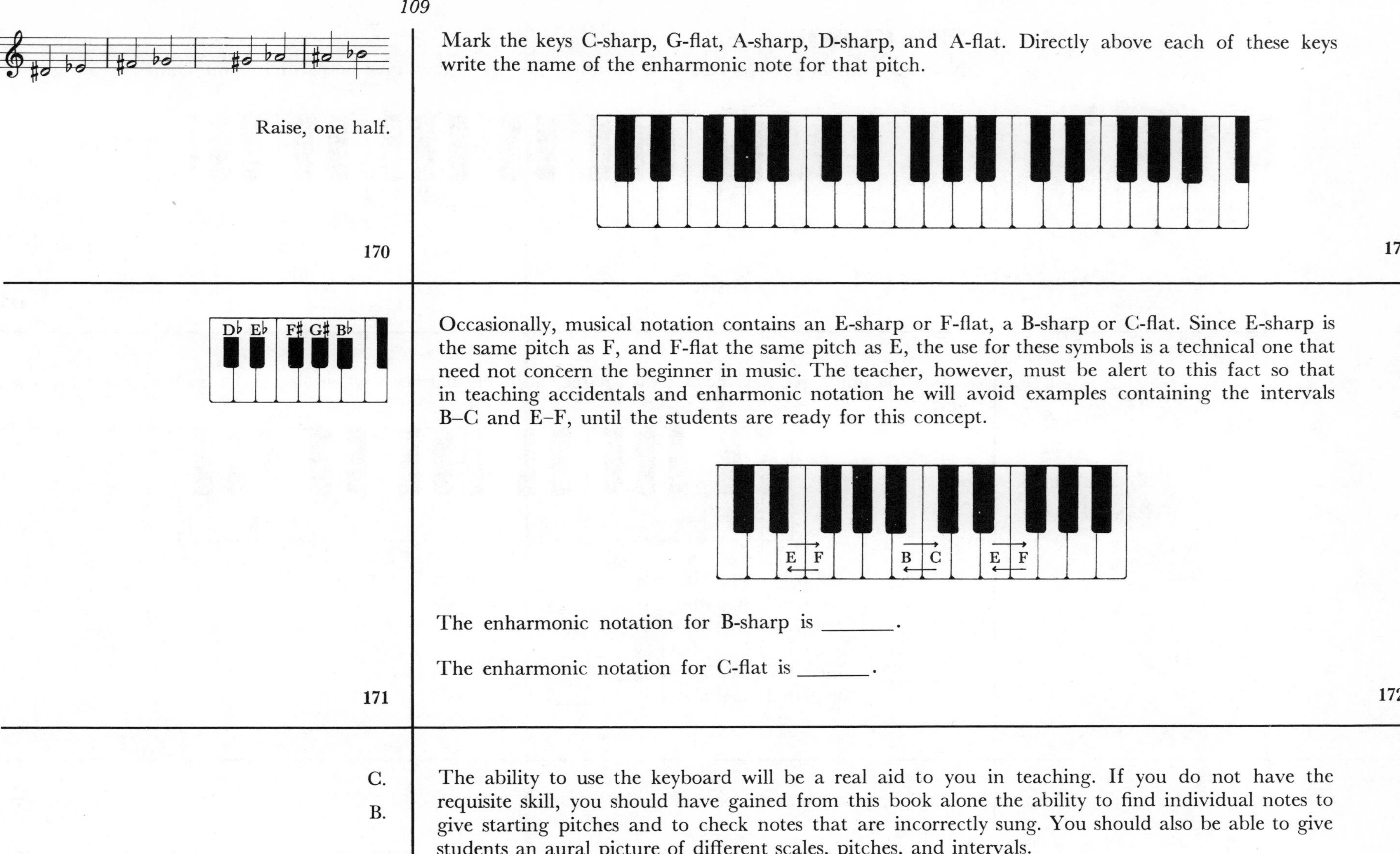

Raise, one half.

170

Mark the keys C-sharp, G-flat, A-sharp, D-sharp, and A-flat. Directly above each of these keys write the name of the enharmonic note for that pitch.

171

171

Occasionally, musical notation contains an E-sharp or F-flat, a B-sharp or C-flat. Since E-sharp is the same pitch as F, and F-flat the same pitch as E, the use for these symbols is a technical one that need not concern the beginner in music. The teacher, however, must be alert to this fact so that in teaching accidentals and enharmonic notation he will avoid examples containing the intervals B–C and E–F, until the students are ready for this concept.

The enharmonic notation for B-sharp is ______.

The enharmonic notation for C-flat is ______.

172

C.

B.

172

The ability to use the keyboard will be a real aid to you in teaching. If you do not have the requisite skill, you should have gained from this book alone the ability to find individual notes to give starting pitches and to check notes that are incorrectly sung. You should also be able to give students an aural picture of different scales, pitches, and intervals.

OPTIONAL KEYBOARD WORK

Name the numbered keys below. When there are black keys, give both enharmonic names.

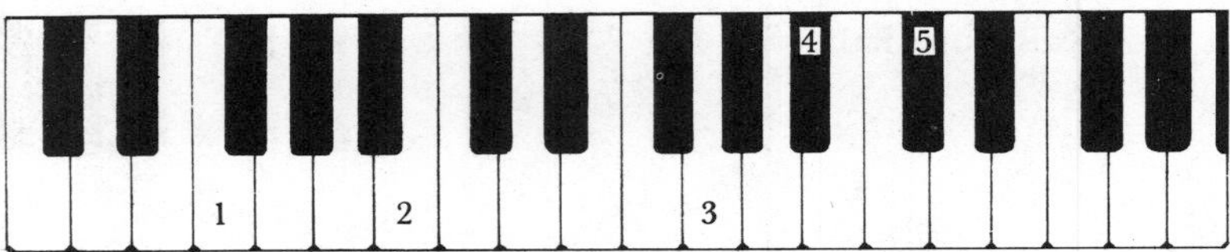

1. ______ 2. ______ 3. ______ 4. ______ and ______ 5. ______ and ______.

173

---

1. F.

2. B.

3. G.

4. B-flat, A-sharp.

5. C-sharp, D-flat.

173

Name the numbered keys below; then name the pitch that lies a whole step above each numbered key.

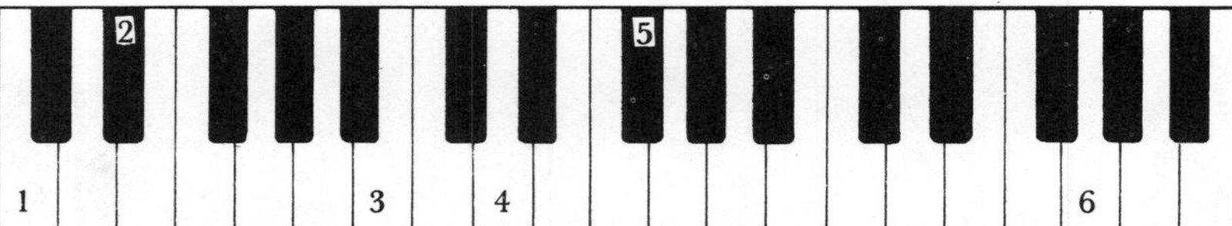

1. ______. One whole step above is ______.
2. ______. One whole step above is ______.
3. ______. One whole step above is ______.
4. ______. One whole step above is ______.
5. ______. One whole step above is ______.
6. ______. One whole step above is ______.

174

---

1. C, D.

2. E-flat or D-sharp, F.

3. B, C-sharp or D-flat.

4. D, E.

5. F-sharp or G-flat, A-flat or G-sharp.

6. G, A.

174

Using numbers, mark the pitches on the keyboard.

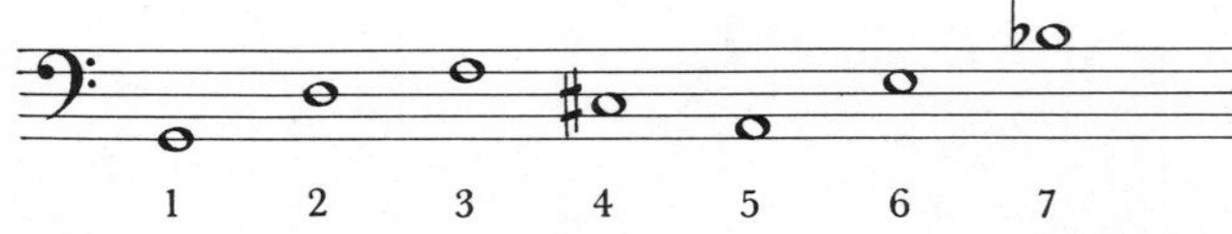

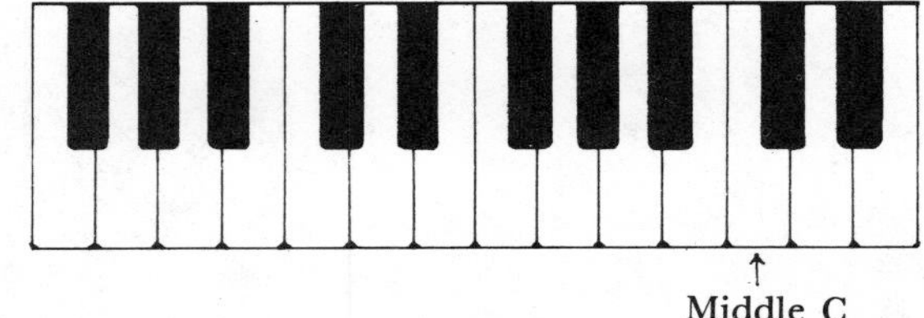

175

175

Some of the keys below are incorrectly named. Place an X through those that have the wrong letter names.

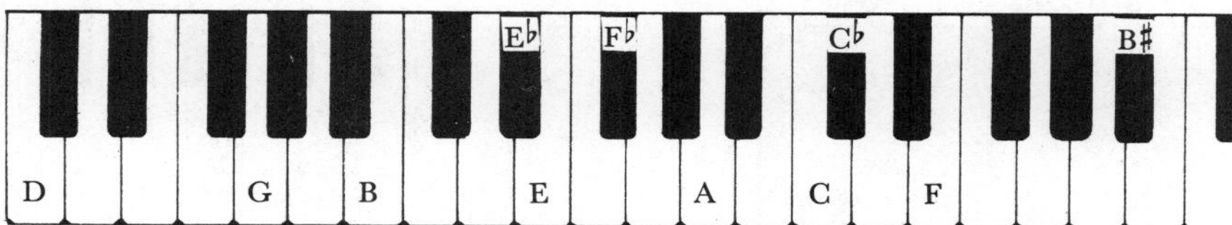

176

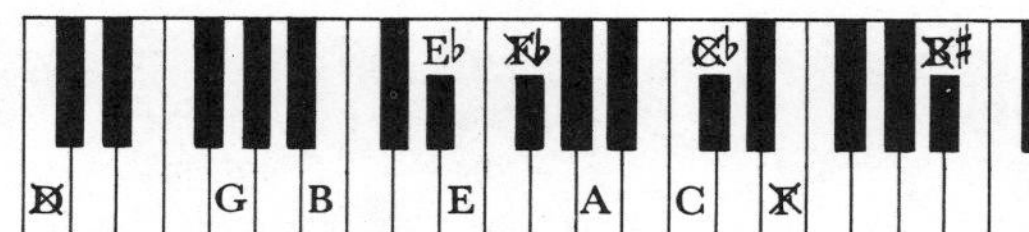

176

Name the keys.

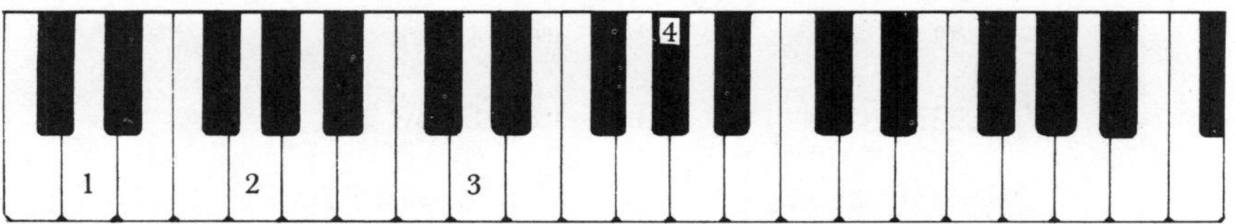

1. ______________ 2. ______________ 3. ______________ 4. ______________
5. ______________

177

1. D.

2. G.

3. D.

4. G-sharp or A-flat.

5. D-sharp or E-flat.

177

Place an X on each key that is incorrectly marked.

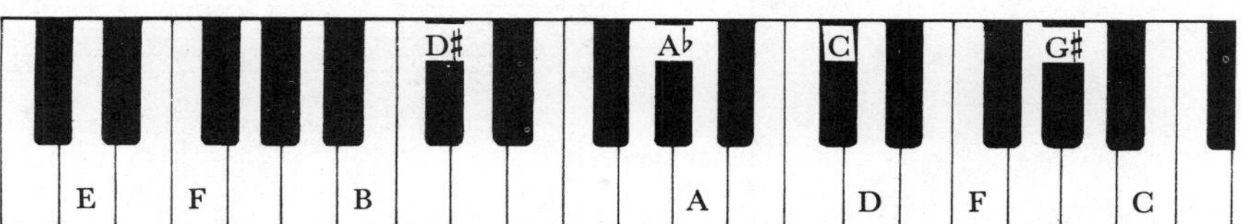

178

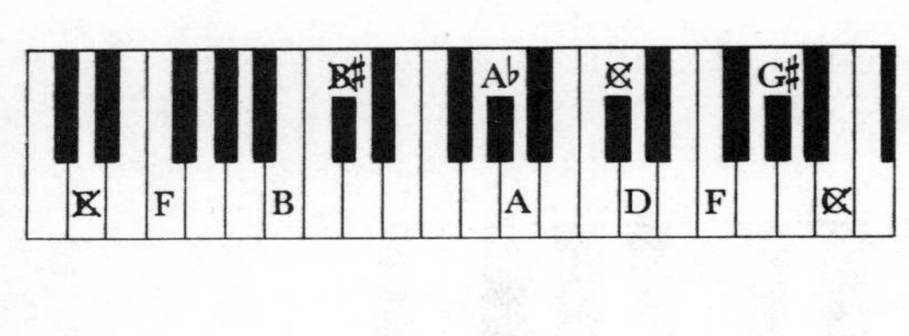

178

Identify the distance (interval) between each two notes that are marked.

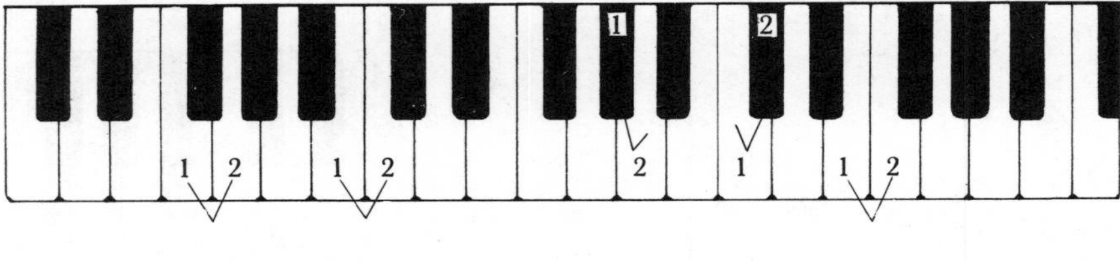

179

Whole step.

Half step.

Half step.

Half step.

Half step.

179

Write on the staff the pitch an interval of

1. half step above
2. half step below
3. whole step above
4. whole step below

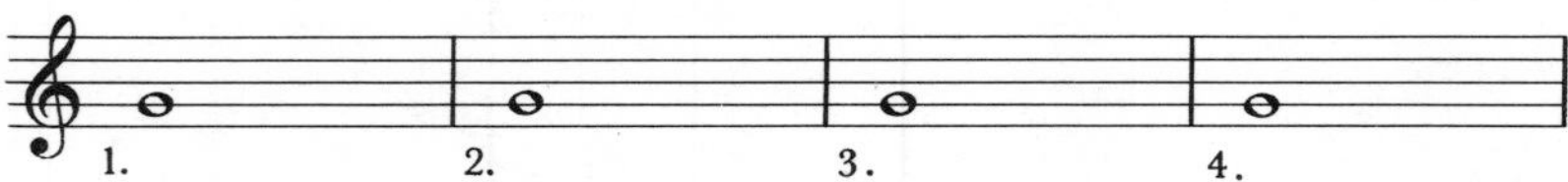

180

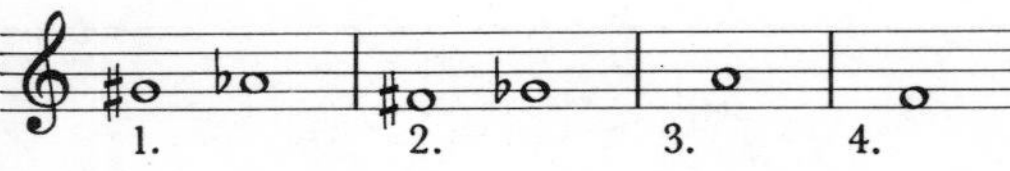

180

Using their numbers, mark these notes on the keyboard.

181

5 2 1 3 4 6

181

Examine the numbered keys and write on the staff the pitch each represents.

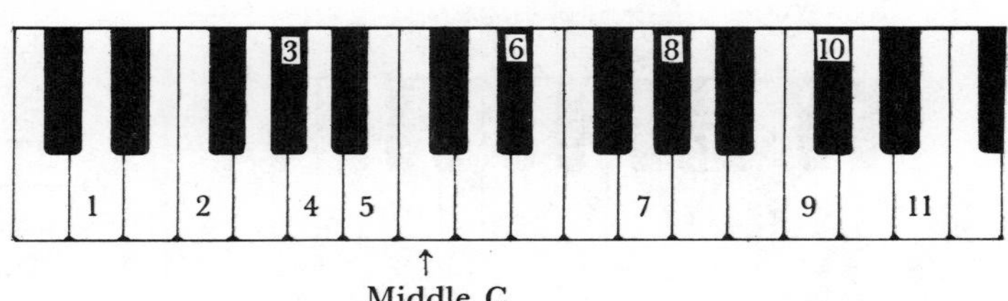

182

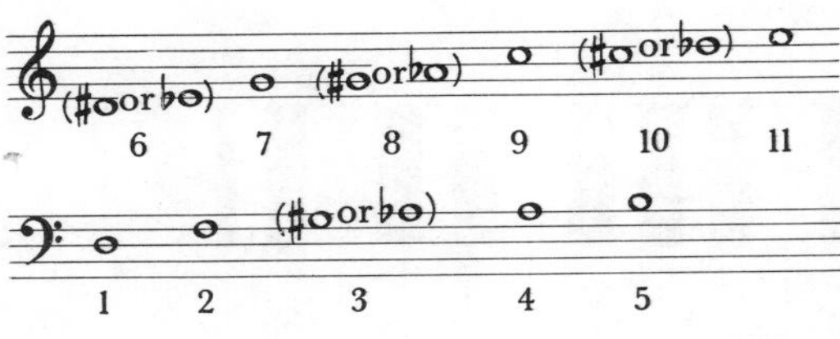

182

Write on the staff the interval one whole step above each pitch. Use the pitch that represents the next letter above each note. Give the name of each pitch. Use the piano to help you.

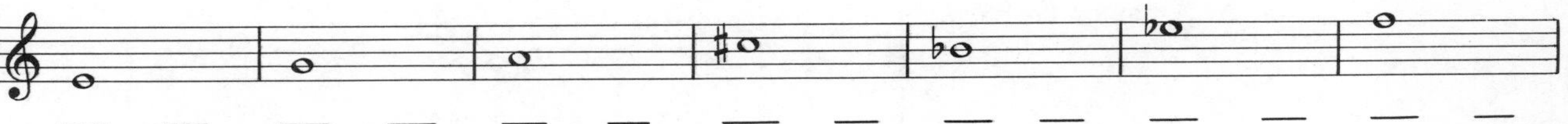

___ ___ ___ ___ ___ ___ ___ ___ ___ ___ ___ ___ ___ ___

183

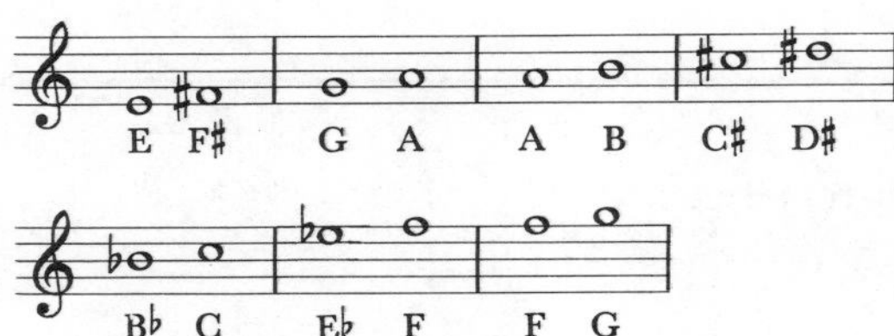

183

Name the numbered keys below. Give both enharmonic names for the black keys.

1. _______ 2. _______ and _______ 3. _______ and _______ 4. _______ 5. _______ 6. _______ and _______ 7. _______ 8. _______ and _______ 9. _______ 10. _______

184

1. C; 2. D-sharp or E-flat; 3. F-sharp or G-flat; 4. B; 5. D; 6. G-sharp or A-flat; 7. A; 8. C-sharp or D-flat; 9. E; 10. G.

184

Name the numbered keys below; then name the pitch that lies one-half step below each numbered key.

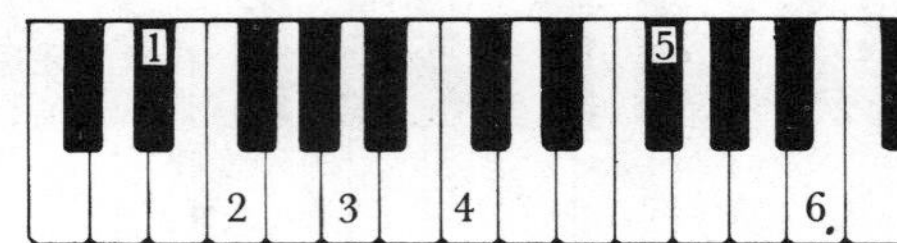

1. ______. One-half step below is ______.
2. ______. One-half step below is ______.
3. ______. One-half step below is ______.
4. ______. One-half step below is ______.
5. ______. One-half step below is ______.
6. ______. One-half step below is ______.

185

1. E-flat or D-sharp, D.
2. F, E.
3. A, A-flat or G-sharp.
4. C, B.
5. F-sharp or G flat, F.
6. B, B-flat or A-sharp.

185

Mark the pitches on the keyboard using numbers.

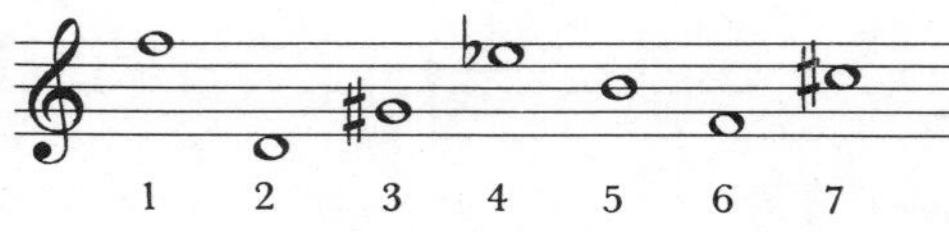

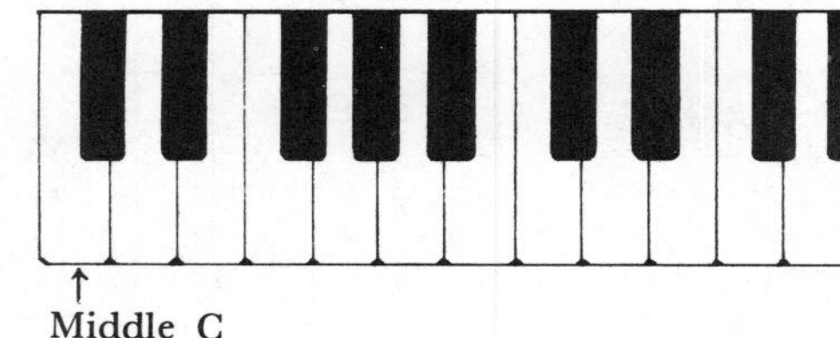

186

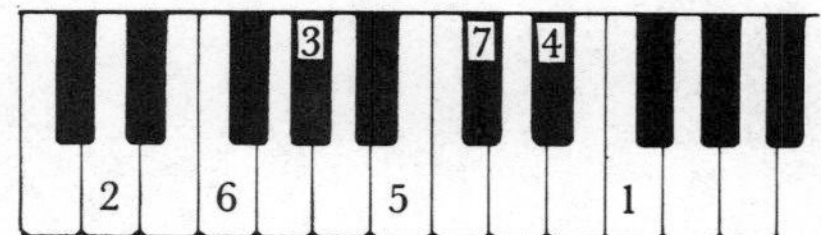

186

Examine the numbered keys and write on the staff the pitch each represents.

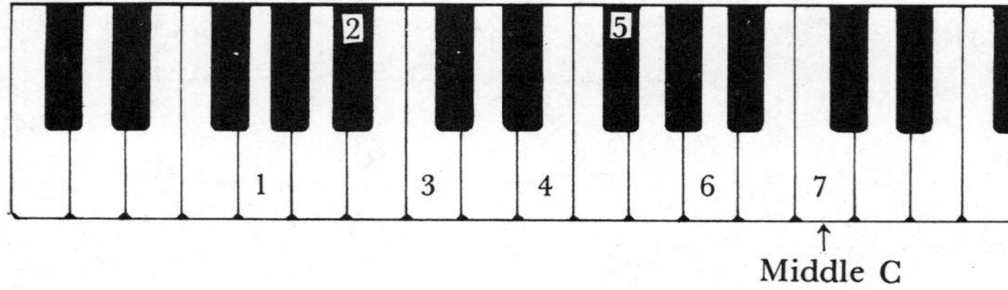

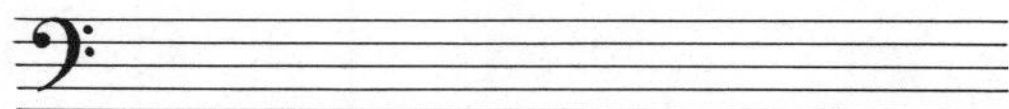

187

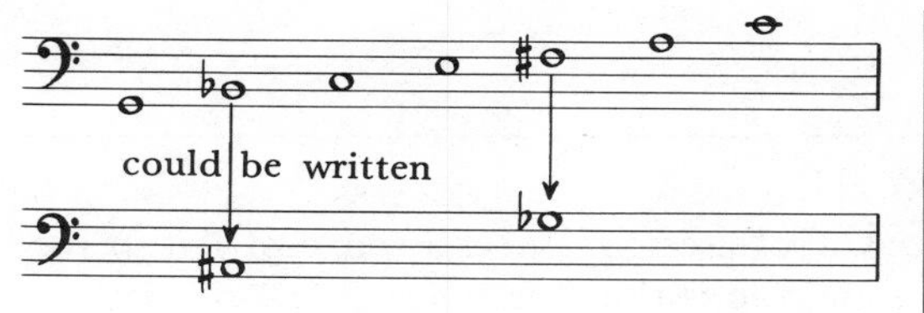

187

Examine the numbered keys and write on the staff the pitch each represents.

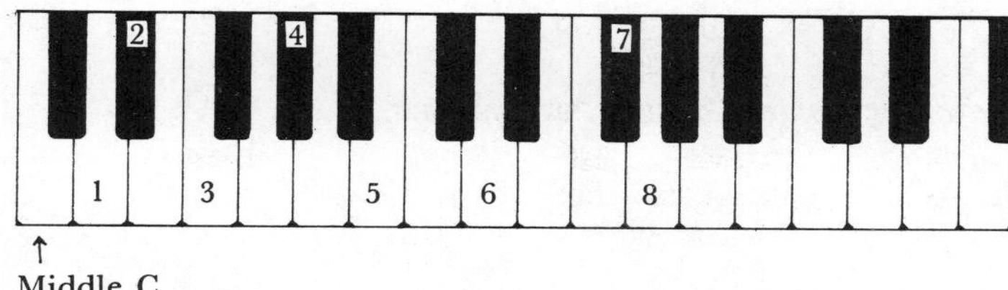

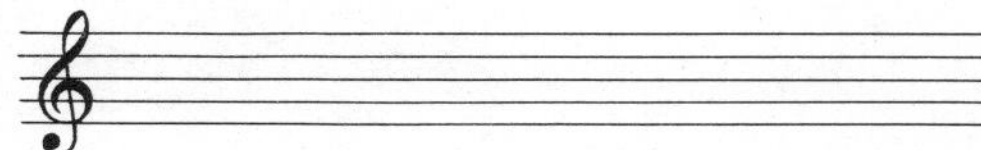

188

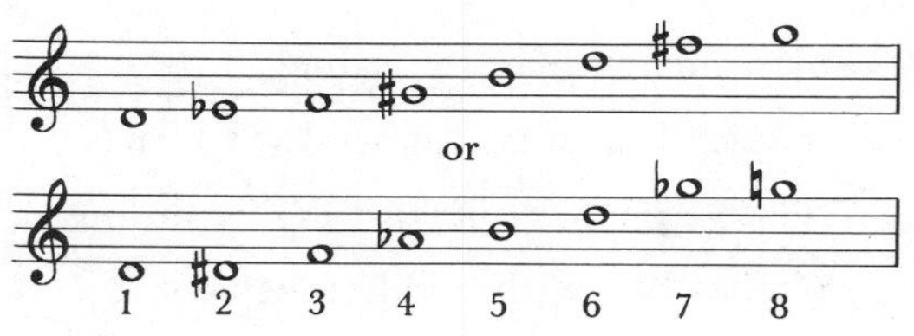

188

Find the errors in the names of the keys. Place an X through the incorrect letter name.

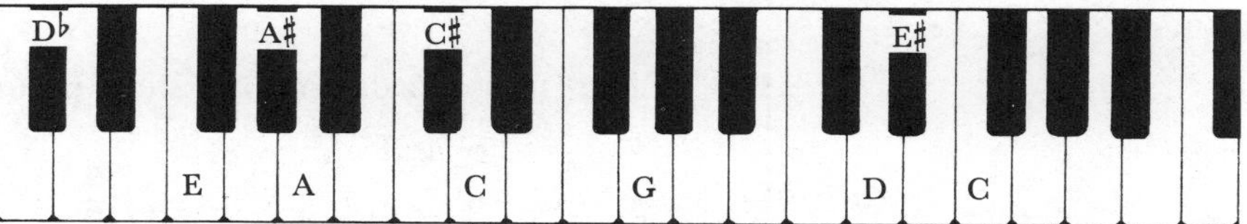

189

189

Name the interval indicated by the brackets by writing 1/2 (half step) or 1 (whole step).

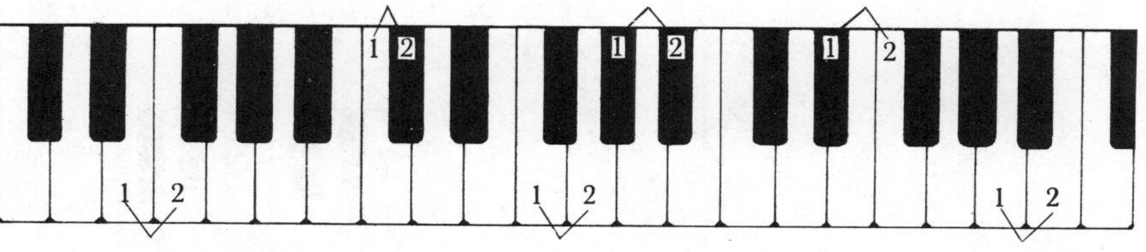

190

1/2; 1/2; 1; 1; 1; 1.

190

PRETEST for Chapter 10: Scale

Mark the correct answer or *answers.*

1. Which passage(s) move(s) scalewise?

2. In a major scale the half steps occur between:

—— a. 6 and 7

—— b. 2 and 3 and 5 and 6

—— c. 3 and 4 and 7 and 8

—— d. 1 and 2

3. Using the piano keyboard, indicate by [symbol] between the white notes where the whole steps occur.

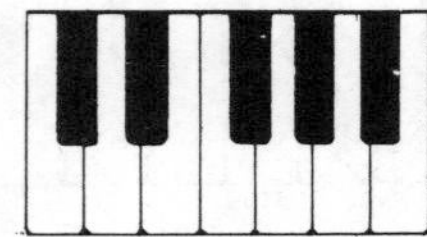

4. T F Whole steps can be identified visually, for they are written farther apart than are half steps.

5. On the piano the smallest interval that can be played is the:

—— a. step

—— b. quarter tone

—— c. half step

—— d. whole tone

6. The symbol used to cancel a sharp or flat in the key signature is the:

—— a. sharp sign

—— b. flat sign

—— c. natural sign

—— d. dal segno sign

7. Transposition means play the same:

—— a. pitches but start higher or lower

—— b. relative pitches but start higher or lower

—— c. pitches but with a different timbre

—— d. pitches but with a different nuance

8. Identify the notes that will sound the same by circling them and connecting them with a line:

9. In a diatonic scale:

—— a. the notes move by half steps

—— b. each letter of the scale is used only once

—— c. the intervals are half steps and whole steps

—— d. the scale moves by leaps

10. Construct a major scale beginning on E. indicate where the half steps occur. Use accidentals and no key signature.

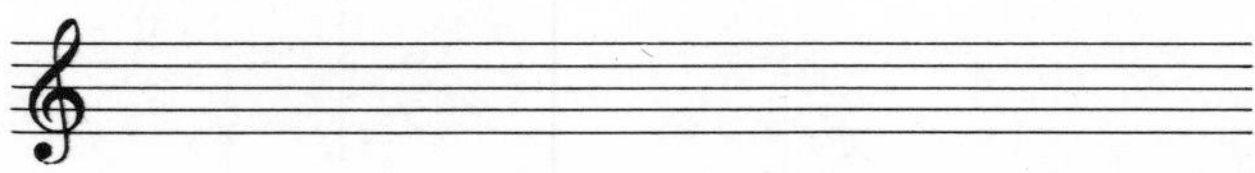

11. Below is "Go Tell Aunt Rhody" based on an F scale. Write it based on a D scale.

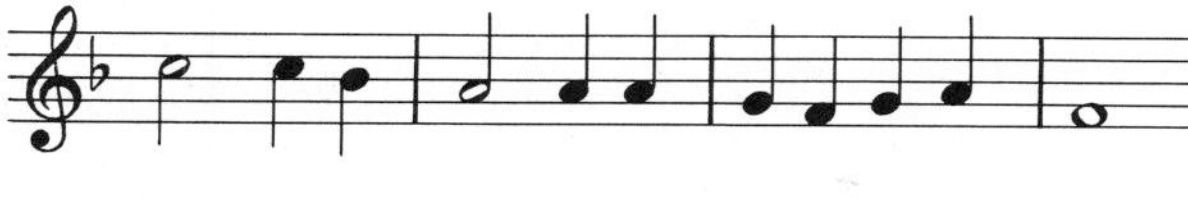

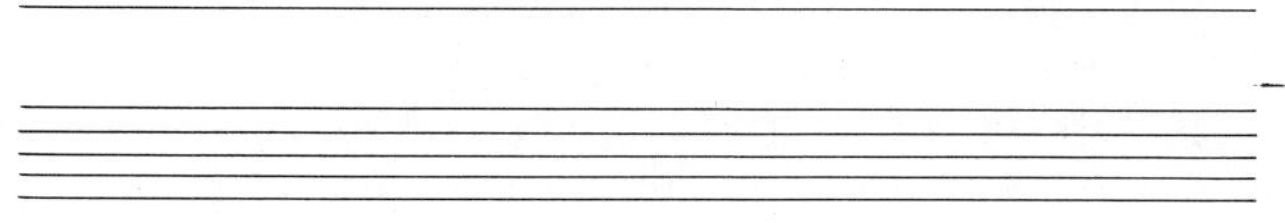

12. Examine the pitches. Add accidentals to construct a major scale.

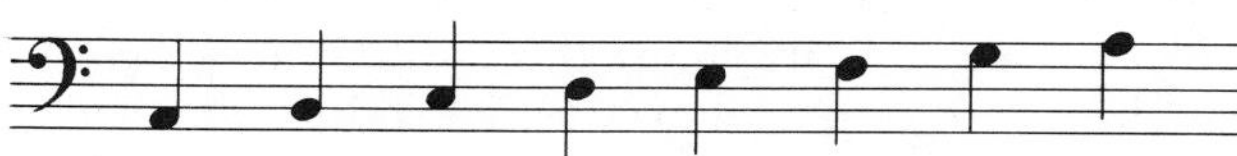

13. A scale composed entirely of half steps is a:

—— a. diatonic scale

—— b. chromatic scale

—— c. major scale

—— d. minor scale

Answers

1. 1, 3.
2. c.
3.

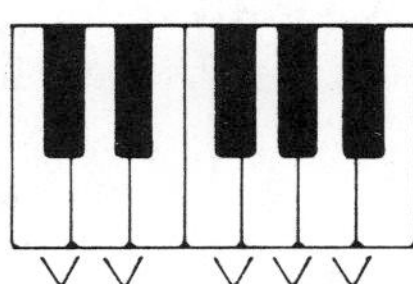

4. false.
5. c.
6. c.
7. b.
8.

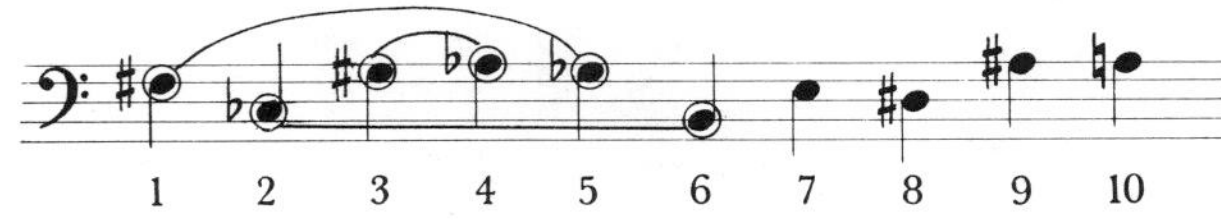

9. b, c.
10.

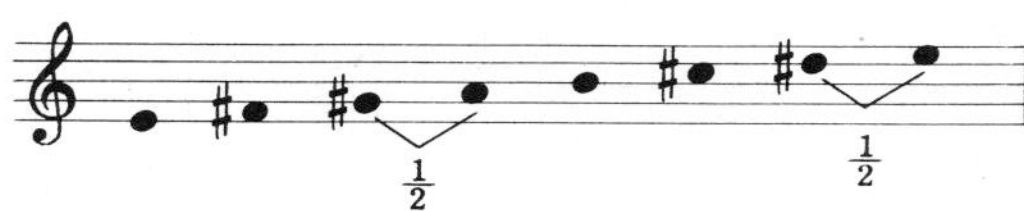

11.

12.

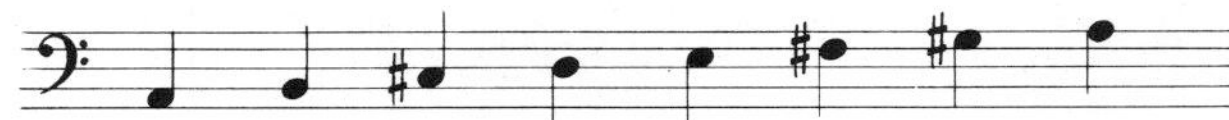

13. b.

From your score determine whether you can omit sections of the text.

CHAPTER 10 The Concept of Scale

Pitches are usually organized into scales. Since almost all of the music we hear and use is based on the scale, a thorough understanding of scales helps greatly in listening to music, learning it, and teaching it. Objectives for this chapter include: (1) knowledge of the structure of the major scale and the chromatic scale; (2) ability to write all major scales on the staff, using accidentals; (3) ability to play all major scales on the keyboard; and (4) understanding of transposition and ability to transpose simple melodies.

In music of the Western world a scale is defined as a group of consecutive pitches that center around one pitch as "home tone," or "key." They may ascend or descend, but they must be in order to be a scale. For instance, three different scales built on C are shown below. Each uses somewhat different pitches than the others, but all start on C and move consecutively to the C an octave distant.

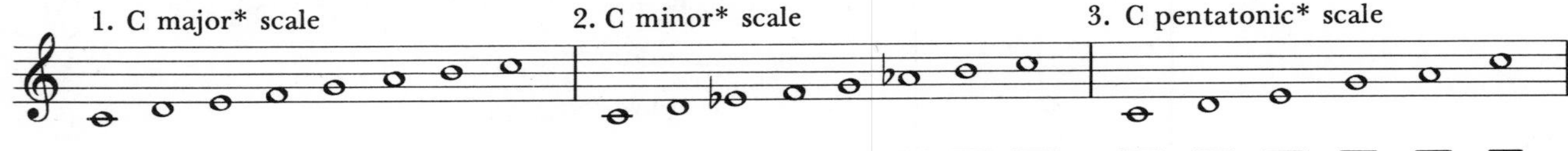

Write note names under each scale.

* These terms will be explained in succeeding frames.

191

1. C D E F G A B C.
2. C D E-flat F G A-flat B C.
3. C D E G A C.

191

Pitches do not form a scale when they are used at random. In the example below the beginning pitch is C, and all the other letter names are used, but this is not a scale. These sounds move nonscalewise; they leap or skip.

Write the letter names underneath the notes. Try to sing these pitches.

192

Singing response.

192

There are many different kinds of scales. The scale formed by placing a note on each line and space of the staff from C to C (see frame191) is called a C major scale. The major scale is widely used in music of the Western world. Other cultures make use of scales that sound different from the major scale. Some have many more pitches within the octave limit, and others have fewer pitches than the major scale. When the pitches are few in number, the distance between them is usually greater, as was illustrated by scale 3 in frame 191. When there are many notes in a scale, pitches are very close together, so close that they cannot always be indicated on the great staff.

The term "scalewise" means a group of ______________ pitches, either up or down.

193

Consecutive.

193

Many musical concepts are clearer to adults and children alike if reference is made to a musical instrument and the learning visualized at the piano keyboard or with an Autoharp. Sound should be produced in order to relate the cognitive concept to the aural aspect of music. For example, in learning about scales singing is valuable, but the singer may not produce the scale pitches as accurately as necessary. Playing the white notes of the piano consecutively from C to C produces a major scale. Use of the ukulele or guitar is also satisfactory, for each fret on a single string produces consecutive pitches.

The C major scale on the staff and on the keyboard looks like this:

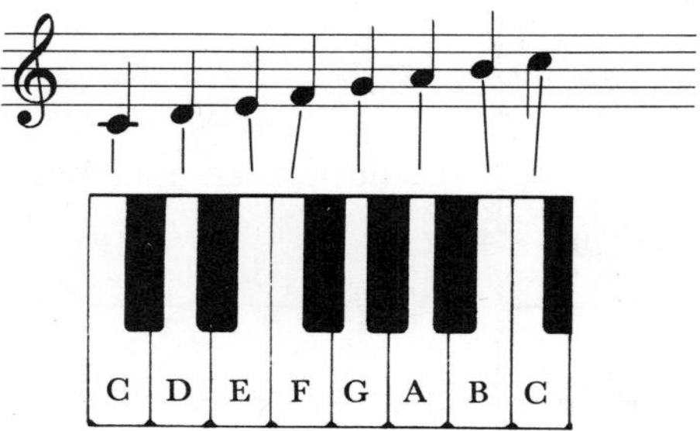

The piano keyboard will be used extensively in the remainder of this text; nevertheless, it does not substitute for listening. Although the application material at the end of the section is optional, listening is important to ensure clarity for these concepts. Example 1 below is *scalewise* or conjunct. Compare it with the other two examples which move by leaps or skips (disjunct motion). The second example obviously skips but the third example is often confused with scalewise motion by inexperienced people.

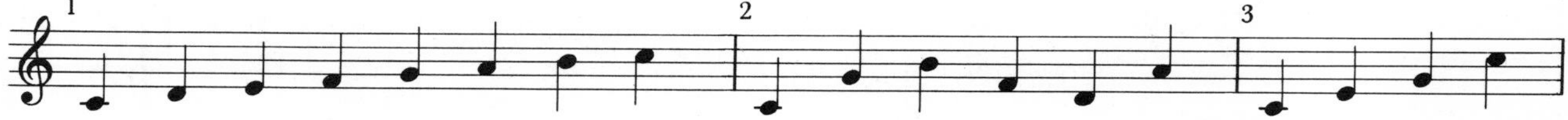

Play these examples on the keyboard.

194

Playing response.

The black and white notes on a piano keyboard help illustrate how a major scale is constructed. The white notes of the keyboard follow the letter names of the lines and spaces on the staff. The distance from a white note to the adjacent black note is called a half step; therefore it is two half steps, or one whole step, from F to G. Between B to C, however, there is no black note, so B and C are only a half step apart, as are E and F.

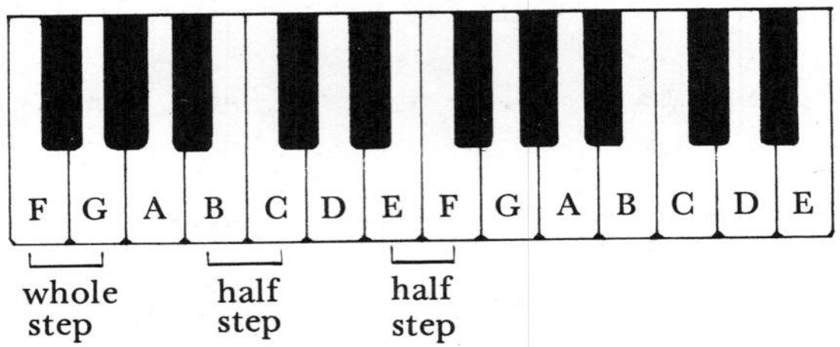

Any major scale has the following order of whole and half steps:

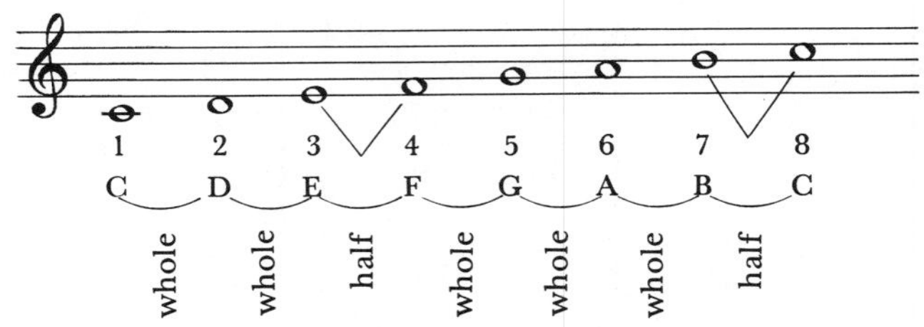

Using the letter names, sing the C scale. Using numbers, sing the scale.

194

195

Singing response.

The major scale pattern is one of all white notes on the piano when you begin on C, a scale of whole steps with half steps between 3–4 and 7–8. All major scales follow the same pattern: half steps between pitches 3 and 4 and pitches 7 and 8, whole steps between all other consecutive pitches.

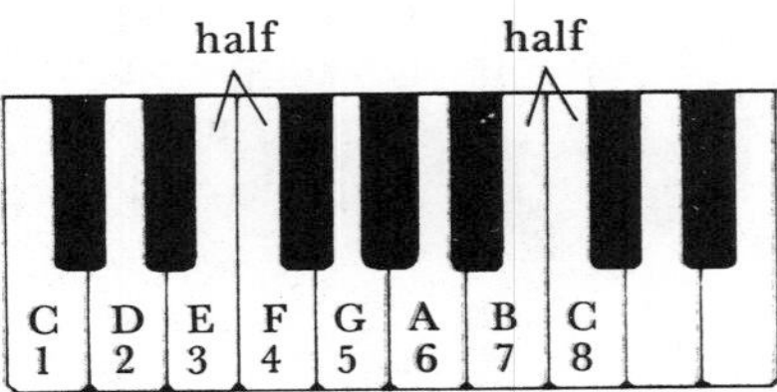

Play a C scale on the piano and sing it with letters and numbers.

195

196

Playing and singing response.

196

All major scales follow the pattern illustrated by the C scale: the pitches are a whole step apart except 3 to 4, and 7 to 8, which are half steps.

In a C major scale, the half steps occur between pitches ______ and ______ and between pitches ______ and ______ (use letter names).

Numerically, the notes that are a whole step apart in a major scale are ______ to ______, ______ to ______ , ______ to ______ , ______ to ______ , ______ to ______.

197

E, F, B, C.

1–2, 2–3, 4–5, 5–6, 6–7.

197

A scale of seven notes using each letter name only once is a diatonic scale.

The major scale is a diatonic scale because each consecutive pitch has a new letter name, with the final or eighth pitch repeating the beginning pitch name. The distance between the first pitch (in this example C) and the last pitch (also C) is called an octave. The scale below is a one-octave C major scale.

One scale, the *chromatic* scale, uses only half steps. Thus, it includes every pitch that can be played on the piano keyboard. Compare the number of notes in the chromatic scale with those in the *diatonic* scale.

The C major scale has ______________ pitches, and the chromatic scale has ______________.

What accidental sign is used in the scale above? ______________

198

7 (8).

12 (13).

Sharp.

198

Custom dictates that in writing the letter names of a chromatic scale that sharps are used ascending, flats descending.

Write the names of the notes for a one-octave chromatic scale, ascending and descending, beginning on A. Use letter names.

If you need assistance, use the keyboard.

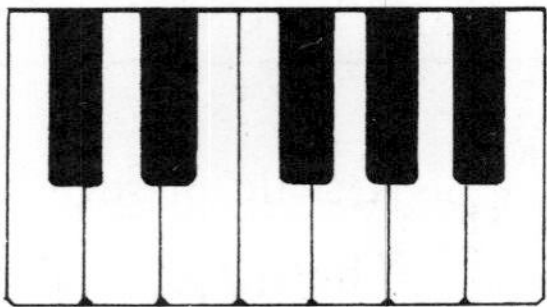

199

A A♯ B C C♯ D D♯ E F F♯
G G♯ A A♭ G G♭ F E E♭
D D♭ C B B♭ A.

199

On the keyboards below, label with the correct letter name each key used in the chromatic scale. Remember that the black keys are sharps when ascending, flats when descending.

ascending

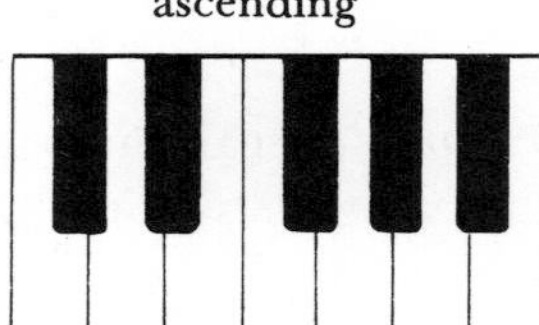

descending

200

---

ascending

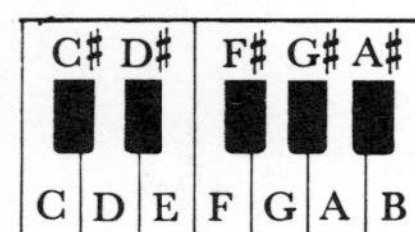

descending

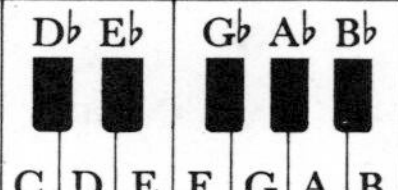

200

A major scale beginning on any pitch other than C must use accidentals to create the correct pattern of half and whole steps. For example, the scale beginning on D would use these notes on the staff: D E F G A B C D. Would the scale be diatonic? _______
1 2 3 4 5 6 7 8
Since the distance between E and F on the staff is a half step, F must be sharped (raised) to create a whole step between 2 and 3 of the scale. This nicely results in the half step between 3 and 4. Similarly, B and C are a half step apart, so C must be sharped (raised) to make a whole step between 6 and 7, which makes a half step between 7 and 8.

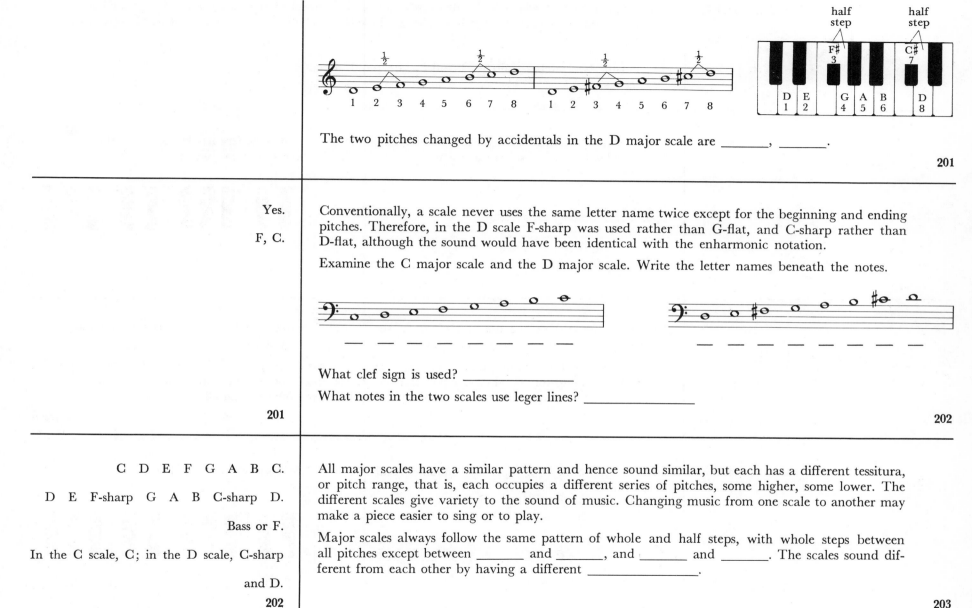

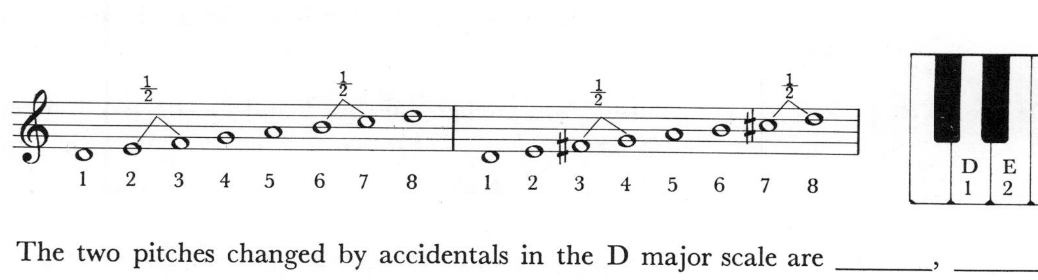

The two pitches changed by accidentals in the D major scale are ______, ______.

201

Yes.

F, C.

201

Conventionally, a scale never uses the same letter name twice except for the beginning and ending pitches. Therefore, in the D scale F-sharp was used rather than G-flat, and C-sharp rather than D-flat, although the sound would have been identical with the enharmonic notation.

Examine the C major scale and the D major scale. Write the letter names beneath the notes.

__ __ __ __ __ __ __ __   __ __ __ __ __ __ __ __

What clef sign is used? ______________

What notes in the two scales use leger lines? ______________

202

C D E F G A B C.

D E F-sharp G A B C-sharp D.

Bass or F.

In the C scale, C; in the D scale, C-sharp and D.

202

All major scales have a similar pattern and hence sound similar, but each has a different tessitura, or pitch range, that is, each occupies a different series of pitches, some higher, some lower. The different scales give variety to the sound of music. Changing music from one scale to another may make a piece easier to sing or to play.

Major scales always follow the same pattern of whole and half steps, with whole steps between all pitches except between ______ and ______, and ______ and ______. The scales sound different from each other by having a different ______________.

203

3 and 4, 7 and 8.

Tessitura, or pitch range.

203

This arrangement of whole and half steps is the basic concept of the major scale. Other kinds of scales have different patterns, but all scales are based on some systematic arrangement of consecutive pitches.

The outside two pitches—pitches 1 and 8—are the distance of an ______________.

204

Octave.

204

Examine the pattern of the G scale pitches. Place the accidental(s) where needed to make the G major scale. Do this by constructing the proper half and whole step arrangement.

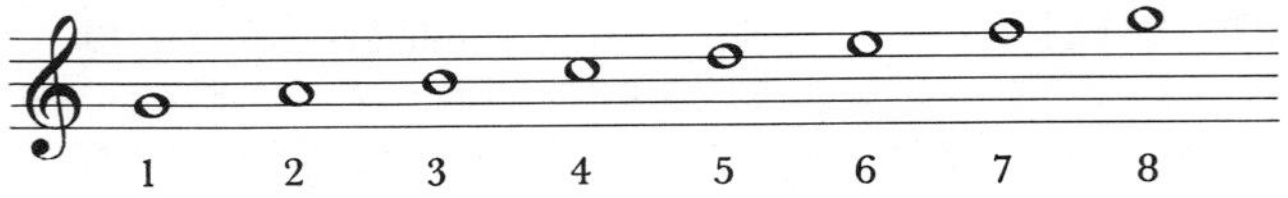

1 2 3 4 5 6 7 8

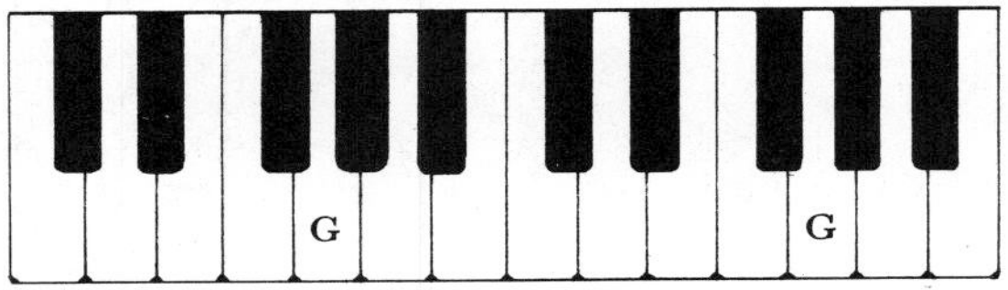

G G

205

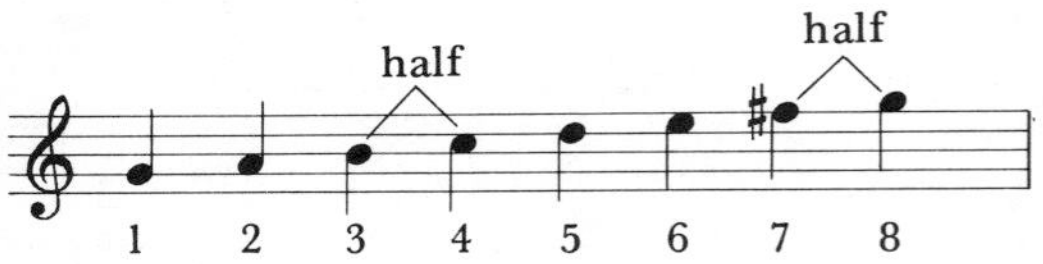

half half

1 2 3 4 5 6 7 8

205

In the previous frame the use of F-sharp in the G scale created a whole step between pitches number ______ and ______ and a half step between pitches number ______ and ______.

Pitch 7 is called the "leading tone" because it leads the ear to pitch 8, the home tone or resting place. The leading tone is always a half step below the final note of the scale (pitch 8). Play a scale on the piano and listen for this "leading" quality between pitches 7 and 8.

206

---

6 and 7, 7 and 8.

206

Examine the pattern of the E scale pitches. Place the accidental(s) where needed to make an E major scale.

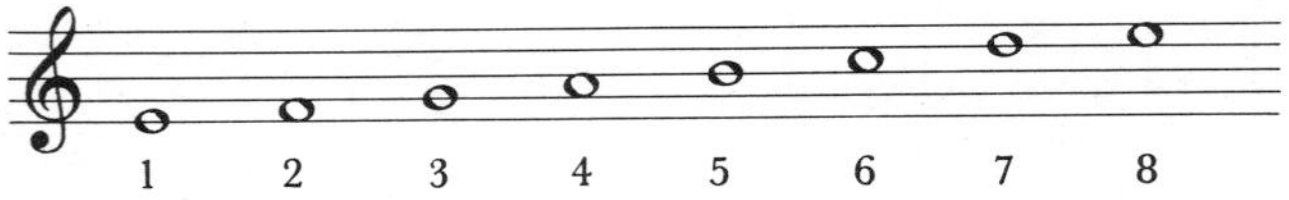

1 2 3 4 5 6 7 8

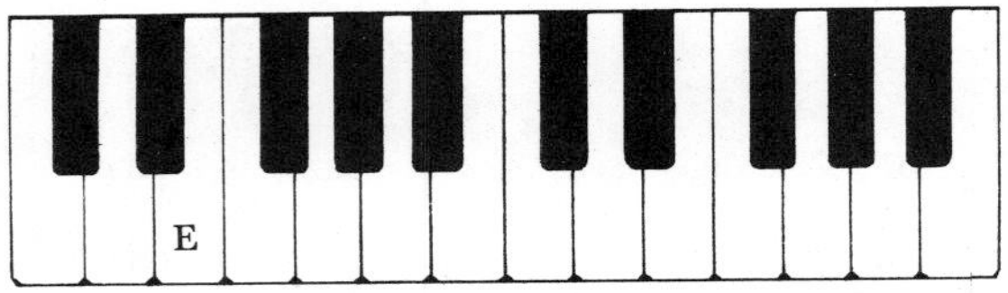

E

What is the name of the note that is called the leading tone? ______

207

half
half
1 2 3 4 5 6 7 8
HOT CROSS BUNS
Version 1
Hot cross buns, Hot cross buns, One a pen-ny two a pen-ny, Hot cross buns.
Version 2
Hot cross buns, Hot cross buns, One a pen-ny two a pen-ny, Hot cross buns.

D-sharp.

207

Below is the children's song, "Hot Cross Buns," written based on the C scale. (1) Notice that only three pitches are used for the song. "Hot Cross Buns" can be written based on any other scale. The second version below (2) is based on what scale? _______ What accidental is used? ____________

208

D, F-sharp.

208

Write "Hot Cross Buns" in the bass clef. Base it on the C scale.

209

209

Another children's song, "All My Little Ducklings," moves up the scale, then back down. Some notes are repeated. Version 1 is written using the F scale. Notice that B-flat makes the necessary half step between pitches 3 and 4. Version 2 gives the first two measures of the same song written using D scale. Write the last half, fitting it to D scale. Make the rhythm identical to version 1.

ALL MY LITTLE DUCKLINGS

Version 1

All my lit - tle duck-lings swim - ming in the sea, Heads are in the wa - ter, tails look up at me.

Version 2

All my lit - tle duck-lings swim - ming in the sea, Heads are in the wa - ter, tails look up at me.

What accidental did you use? _______

* The flat affects all repetitions of that pitch within the same measure: 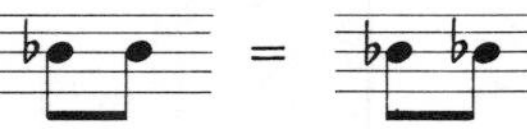

210

F-sharp.

210

The song "America" can be written based on the C scale or on any other note of the keyboard. In C the melody is rather low for children's voices; it is easier to sing when the range is somewhat higher. We can write "America" based on the D scale, which will make all of the pitches one step higher. To move a melody to a different scale is to *transpose* it. "America" (or any melody) can be transposed to any scale, as long as accidentals are used to create the proper scale pattern.

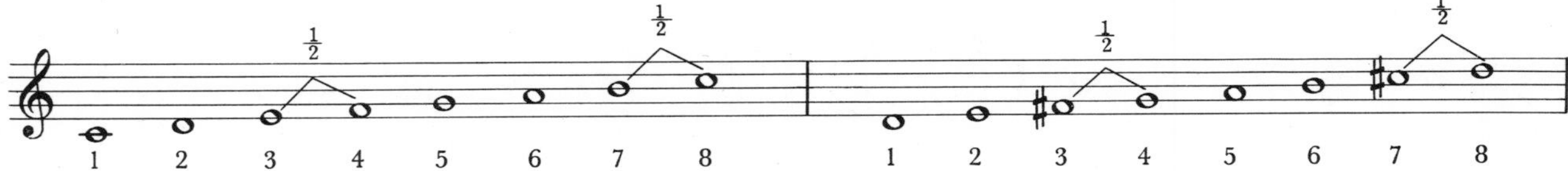
½ ½ ½ ½
1 2 3 4 5 6 7 8
1 2 3 4 5 6 7 8

AMERICA

C scale

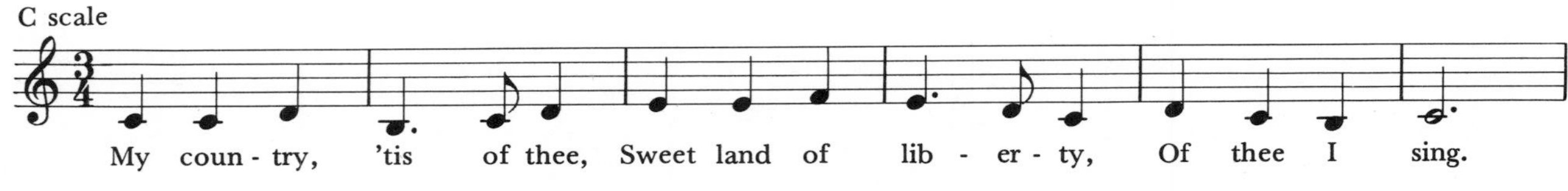
My coun - try, 'tis of thee, Sweet land of lib - er - ty, Of thee I sing.

D scale

My coun - try, 'tis of thee, Sweet land of lib - er - ty, Of thee I sing.

The C scale and the D scale are *diatonic* major scales. A scale made up solely of half steps is a _______________ scale.

Complete a one-octave rising chromatic scale. Put in the octave note. Use sharps for any accidentals.

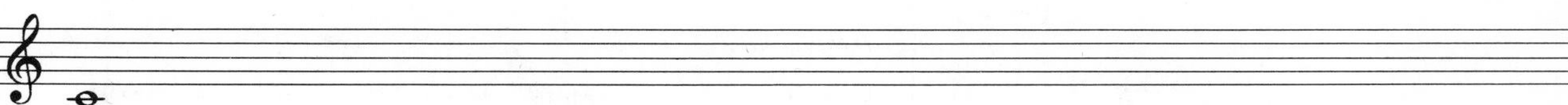

How many notes did you have to add? _______

211

Chromatic.

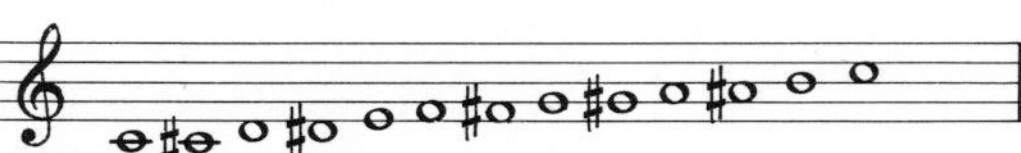

12 if you added the octave C.

211

"America" is usually sung based on the F scale or the G scale. Below are the pitches of the F scale. Inspection of these pitches indicates that the whole step and half step arrangement is correct except between pitches 3 and 4, and 4 and 5. If step 4 is flatted (B becomes B-flat), a half step is created between pitches 3 and 4, and a whole step is created between 4 and 5, making the scale correct. Make this correction.

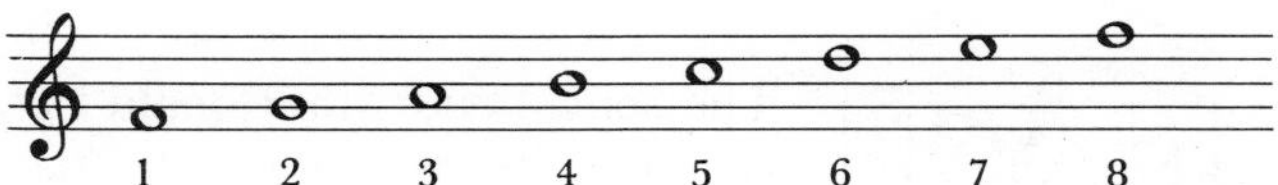

A sharp is used to raise the pitch of a note one half step and a flat is used to _______________ the pitch of a note one half step.

212

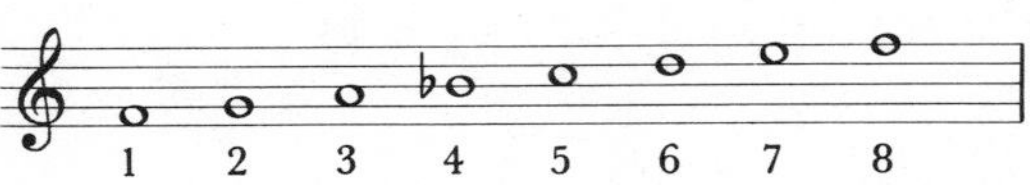
1 2 3 4 5 6 7 8

Lower.

212

Transpose the first six measures of "America" to the scale of F. The starting and ending pitches will be F (first space). Place a flat in front of the pitch B when it is used in the melody. Be sure the pitch and rhythm of the melody are exactly like that given in the version built on the C scale except that the notes must all relate to F.

AMERICA

C scale

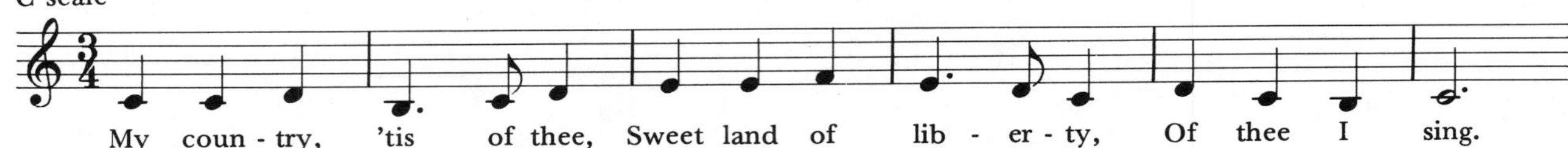
My coun - try, 'tis of thee, Sweet land of lib - er - ty, Of thee I sing.

F scale

Write the names of the notes under the F version.

213

F F G E F G A A B♭
A G F G F E F

213

The song "Old MacDonald" uses only five notes on the keyboard. Mark the five notes on the keyboard below, using letter names. Learn to play the song.

OLD MACDONALD

Old Mac - Don - ald had a farm, ee - ii - ee - ii - o, And
on this farm he had a pig, ee - ii - ee - ii - o.

Middle C

If you were to play "Old MacDonald" alla breve, the meter would be _______________.

214

$\frac{2}{2}$ or ¢

214

The keyboard is useful to practice the scales. Mark in order (using numbers) the keys used in playing the D major scale, the A major scale, and E major scale.

D Major

A Major

E Major

Double check your answer by seeing if the half steps fall between 3 and 4 and between 7 and 8.

Using letters and numbers, sing the scale.

215

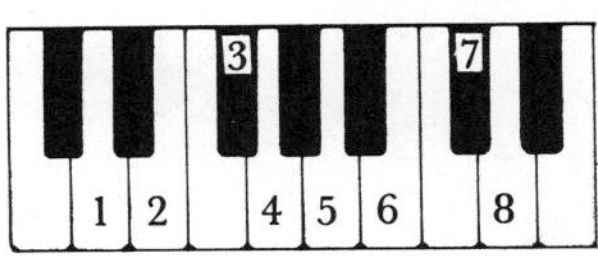

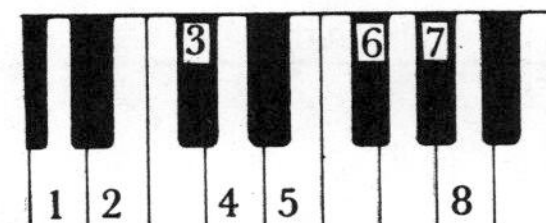

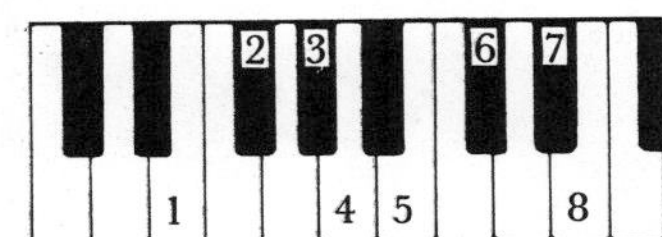

Singing response.

215

The same method of measuring whole steps and half steps is used to play a scale beginning on a black note. Mark in order (using numbers) the keys used in playing the B-flat major scale. Sing the scale using letters and numbers. Why is the pitch E flatted? ____________________

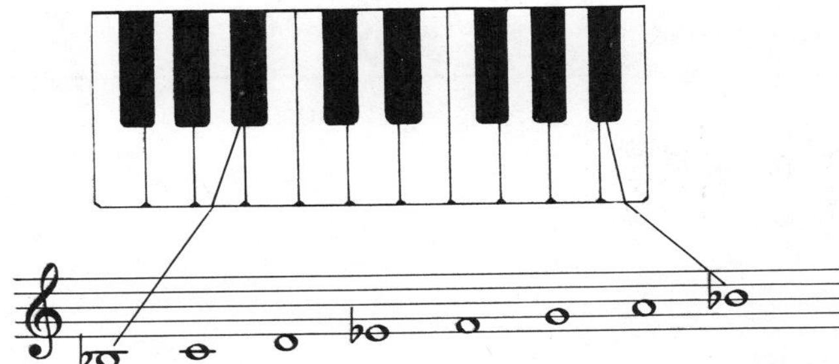

216

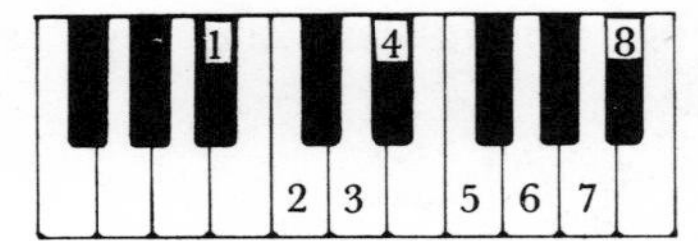

Singing response.

To create a half step between 3 and 4.

216

The Afro-American game song below uses five notes on the keyboard. Mark the five notes on the keyboard, using letter names. Learn to play the song. Learn to sing the song. What scale is this song based on? _______

OH MARY MACK

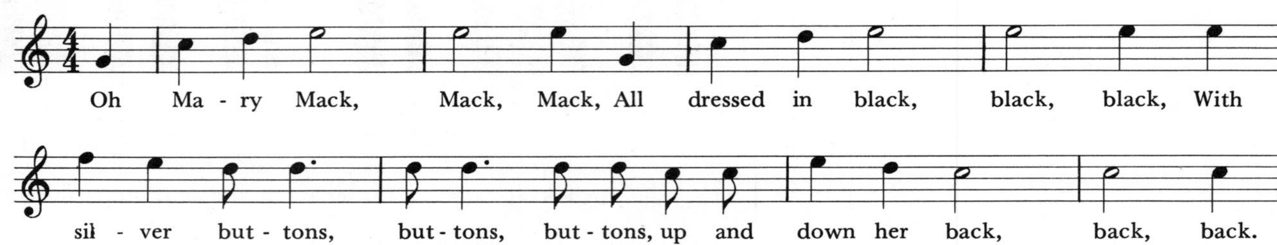

Oh Ma - ry Mack, Mack, Mack, All dressed in black, black, black, With
sil - ver but - tons, but - tons, but - tons, up and down her back, back, back.

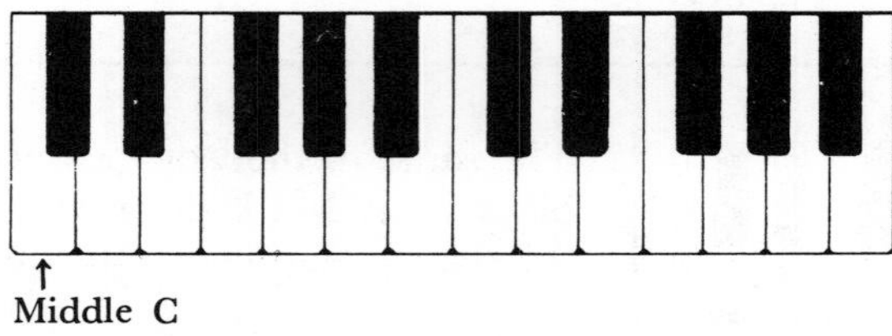

Middle C

217

G
C D E F

Playing and singing response.

C.

217

PRETEST for Chapter 11: Key Signature

Mark the correct answer or *answers.*

1. Name the following major keys:

   a. 1 sharp ______

   b. ______

   c. F♯ C♯ G♯ ______

   d. 5 flats ______

2. The following major scale is in the key of ______ .

3. Sharps and flats in the key signature should be placed:

   —— a. right of the clef sign

   —— b. right of the time signature

   —— c. right of the key signature

   —— d. right of the tempo sign

4. A natural sign:

   —— a. cancels all accidentals for one measure

   —— b. cancels a sharpening or flattening of the note beside which it is placed for one phrase

   —— c. cancels a sharpening or flattening of the note beside which it is placed for one measure

   —— d. cancels accidentals for one phrase

5. In the key of B, which pitches are sharped? ______

   Which pitches are flatted? ______

6. List the sharps in order for the major key signature of F-sharp major.

   ______

7. If D-flat were flatted by a key signature, you could be sure there would be at least how many flats in the key signature?

   —— a. 2

   —— b. 3

   —— c. 4

   —— d. 5

8. Identify the following major keys.

   a.____ b.____ c.____ d.____ e.____ f.____

9. Which key signatures are written incorrectly?

   ______

   a. b. c. d. e. f.

10. Write the seven flats in order on the staff.

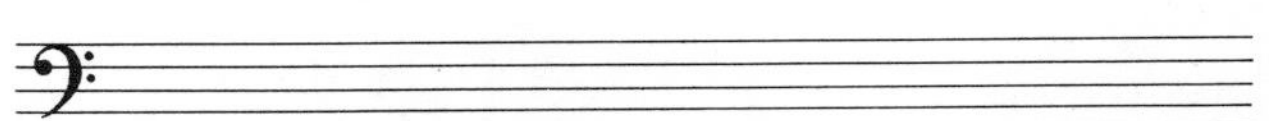

11. The possible number of different major key signatures is:

    —— a. 15

    —— b. 14

    —— c. 7

    —— d. 8

12. Complete the missing keys in the circle of fifths.

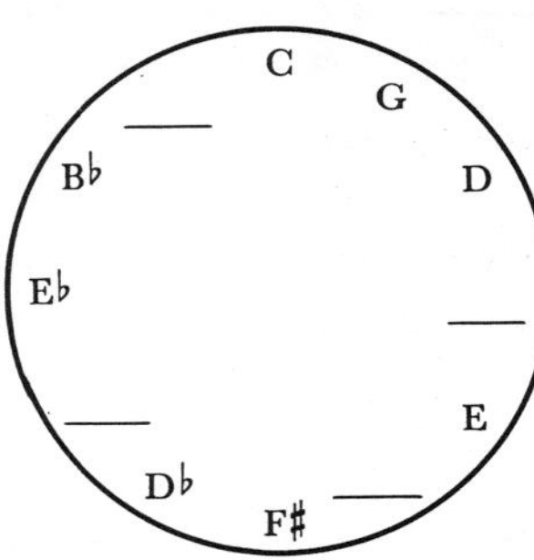

Answers

1. a. G; b. E-flat; c. A; d. D-flat.
2. F.
3. a.
4. c.
5. F, C, G, D, A, none
6. F-sharp C-sharp G-sharp D-sharp A-sharp E-sharp.
7. c. (BEAD)
8. a. A; b. G; c. F; d. F; e. E; f. A-flat.
9. a, b, c.
10. 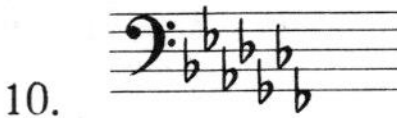
11. a.
12. 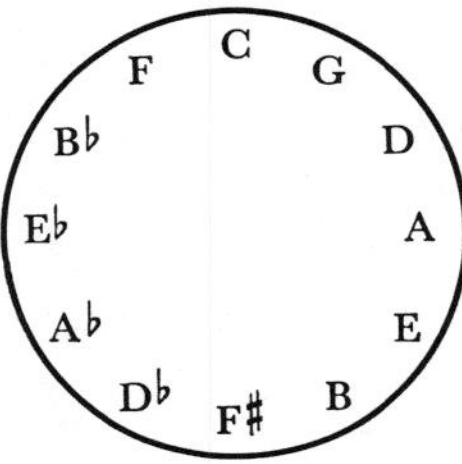

From your score determine if you can omit sections of the text.

CHAPTER 11 The Concept of Key Signature

In writing a piece of music with numerous sharps or flats, placing the accidental before each note that requires it would be time consuming; therefore a short cut is used. This short cut is the key signature. A key signature is composed of the flats or sharps needed for any particular scale. These sharps or flats affect that note throughout the entire piece of music. They are placed immediately to the right of the clef sign.

The objectives of this chapter are (1) knowledge of the sharps or flats that comprise each major key signature; (2) ability to name the major key represented by any key signature; (3) knowledge of the correct construction of major signatures.

BLOW THE MAN DOWN

Come, all ye young fel - lows who fol - low the sea,
Yeo ho! Blow the man down! And please pay at - ten - tion and
lis - ten to me, Give us some time to blow the man down!

The sharp signs on the F line and the C space are indicators that every F and every C are to be raised one half step to F-sharp and C-sharp. Notice that when the music is more than one line in length, the key signature is repeated on each line, but the meter signature is not.

The song in this frame is based on the D scale. It is in the key of D major.

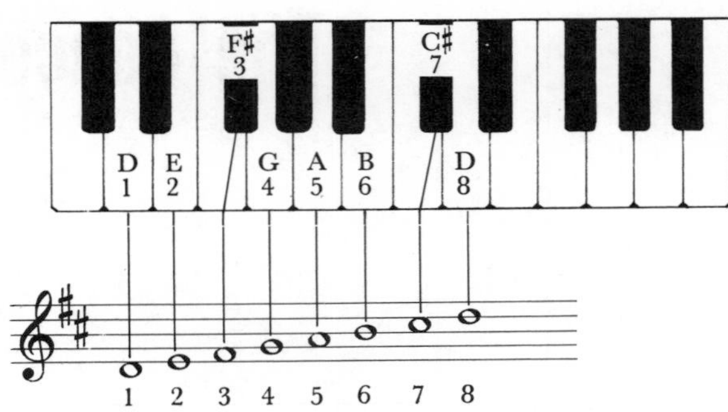

There are half steps between 3 and 4 (F-sharp and G) and between 7 and 8 (C-sharp and D), but there are whole steps everywhere else.

Music based on the F scale (even though the music is not all scales) is said to be in the key of _______________.

218

F major.

218

If a sharp or flat is to be cancelled, a natural sign ♮ is used to the left of the note. The sign must be centered on the same line or space as the note. In order to practice making this sign correctly, place natural signs in front of the following notes.

The ♮ is considered an accidental, as are the ♯ and ♭. The sign is centered on the line or space.

219

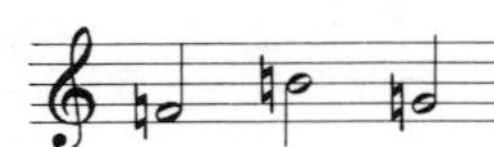

219

Because of the key signature, B and E are flatted throughout the following song:

BARNACLE BILL, THE SAILOR

1.
2.
3.
4.
Who's that knock - ing at my door? Who's that knock - ing at my door?

Identify the measure in which an accidental raises the pitch a half step. _______

Identify the measure in which an accidental cancels one of the flats of the key signature. _______

220

1 (also measure 3).

3.

220

When a natural sign is used to cancel a sharp or flat, it is effective only for the line or space it is placed upon and only for the measure in which it occurs.

In example 1 the ♮ does not apply to the fifth line F that follows it in the same measure nor to the first space F in measure 2. In example 2 fifth line F remains sharped the entire first measure.

When a sharp or flat is used as an accidental, it is also effective only for the line or space it is placed upon, and only for the measure in which it occurs. In the example below, circle all the notes flatted by the ♭. Place an X through the B pitches *not* affected by the ♭.

221

221

The name of a musical key is identical to the name of the scale having the same number of flats or sharps. The diatonic scale that uses only white keys begins on C and is called a C major scale. Another way of saying this would be that it is a diatonic scale in the key of C major.

Key of C major

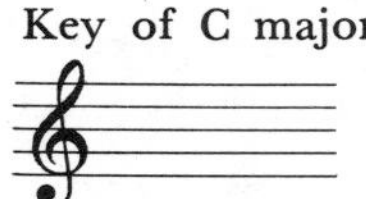

Key of F major

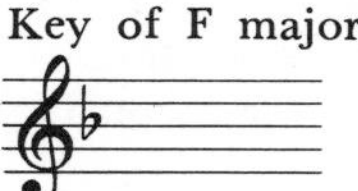

Key of G major

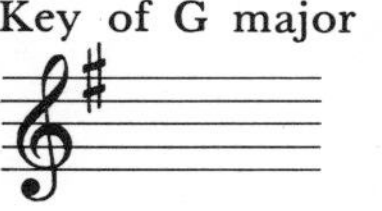

No sharps or flats in the key signature is the key of C major; one sharp is the key of G major; one flat is the key of F major.

Music based on the G major scale, having one sharp, F-sharp, in the key signature is said to be in the _______ of G.

Musicians memorize the signatures for the sharp and flat keys. An understanding of the system of sharps and flats will help you in memorizing the signatures.

222

Key.

222

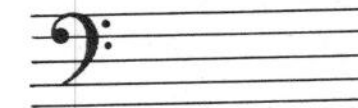

This key signature indicates the key of ______.

This scale is in the key of ______.

If your memory failed you for the scale with one flat, it might be helpful to inspect the scale. If there are half steps between 3 and 4 and 7 and 8 with whole steps elsewhere, it is a major scale with the key signature having the same name as the first note. Inspecting every scale, however, to determine where the half and whole steps lie is a very cumbersome method for determining the key. Musicians are concerned with the key signature not only to know what notes are to be sharped or flatted but also to know which pitch is "1" or the fundamental note (key note) of the scale upon which the music is constructed. The name of the key signature is the same as "1" or the fundamental. 223

C major.

F major.

223

The keys are determined by inspecting the arrangement of whole or half steps or by a variety of other means. Learning the seven keys that contain sharps and the seven keys that contain flats can be done in several different ways.

The first sharp key has one sharp, the second two sharps, the third three sharps, and so on. There is a total of seven sharp keys. The seven flat keys are those having one flat, two flats, three flats, and so on.
How many different pitches may be sharped or flatted? ______ 224

7.

224

In order to avoid figuring out the whole and half steps for every key and every piece of music, we learn the order of the sharps and flats as they are placed in the key signature. The first sharp is always F, the second is always C, and so forth. Each additional sharp is placed to the right of the last one, on the proper line or space of the staff. The order of the sharps is F–C–G–D–A–E–B. Can you construct a mnemonic device to use in remembering the sharps in order?

Mnemonic devices such as Fat Chicken, Good Dinner, All Eat Bird; Frank Can Go Down An Elevator Backward; etc., the first letter of each word, abound. Whether or not to teach these devices is frequently argued among music teachers.

Alternative

Another way to remember the order of the sharps is to count up five pitch names from the previous sharp, calling the previous sharp "1":

F g a b C d e f G a b c D e f g A b c d E f g a B
1 2 3 4 5 2 3 4 5 2 3 4 5 2 3 4 5 2 3 4 5 2 3 4 5
(1) (1) (1) (1) (1)

Key of G | Key of D | Key of A | Key of E | Key of B | Key of F♯ | Key of C♯

The seven sharp key signatures are given above, in order. Practice writing these if you need to develop more skill in drawing sharps on a line or space.

In the bass clef the sharp on the second space is ________________. It is always the ________________ sharp.

The sharp on the third line, bass clef, is ________________. It is always the ________________ sharp.

225

C-sharp, second.

D-sharp, fourth.

225

These sharps or flats are placed ________________ the meter signature.
(before or after)

226

Before.

226

Although writing key signatures is frequently necessary for the teacher, more often he needs to identify the key from key signatures printed in the music. The sharps will already be in the correct order on the musical page. For sharp signatures in major keys, the key is always the note above the last sharp. For example, when there is one sharp in the signature 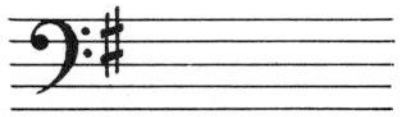 , this sharp is F-sharp. F-sharp, being the only one, is also the last sharp in that signature; count up one half step to the next letter in the alphabet—F-sharp–G. The major key for one sharp is thus G.

With two sharps 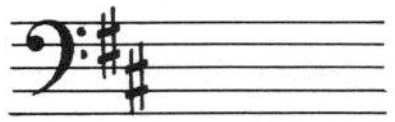 (F-sharp and C-sharp) the last sharp (the farthest one to the right in the key signature) is C-sharp. Count up one half step from C-sharp to D. The major key for two sharps is D. For some, visualizing the one half step up is easier with the piano keyboard.

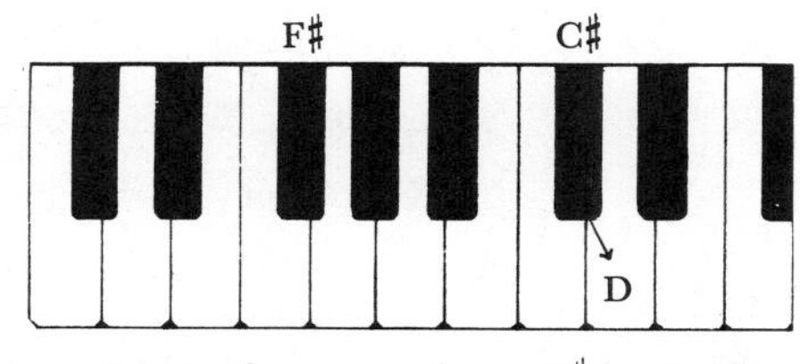

One-half step up from C♯ is D.

Circle all the key tones in this song.

Bracket the places where half steps occur in the melody 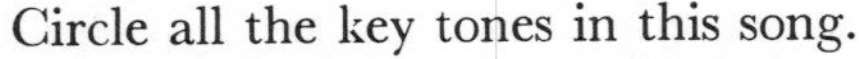

THE CLAPPING LAND

As I was trav - ling o'er the sea, I met a man who said to me.

The key for this song is ______ major.

227

E.

227

Circle all the key tones in this song.

Bracket the places where half steps occur in the melody.

THE GALLANT SHIP

Three times a-round went the gal - lant ship, And three times a- round went she.

The key for this song is ______ major.

228

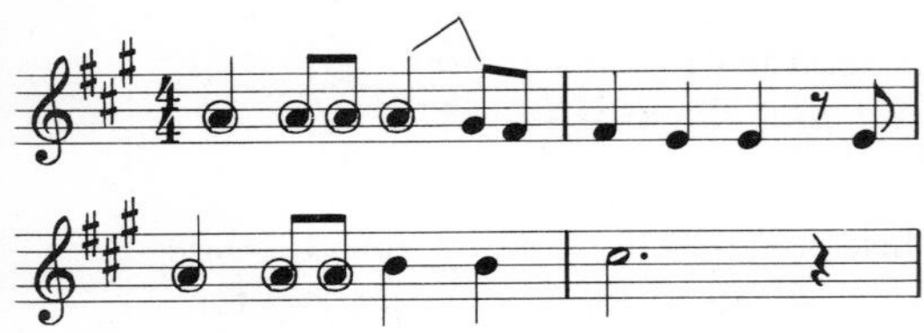

A.

228

Elementary teachers often give students the same rules in a different form: to determine the major key, call the last sharp 7 and count up to 8; or, if they use syllables, the last sharp to the right is called "ti" and the student counts up to "do."

Many teachers have students count down 7 (to the octave) rather than up 1 to find "do" or the key tone. Although this involves more counting, it is done to put "do" in the singing range of the child and a ready association with "do" as written in the music.

What is the key of the song below? _______

What two pitches are sharped in this key? _______

Only one of the sharped pitches appears in the melody given below. Which pitch is it? ______

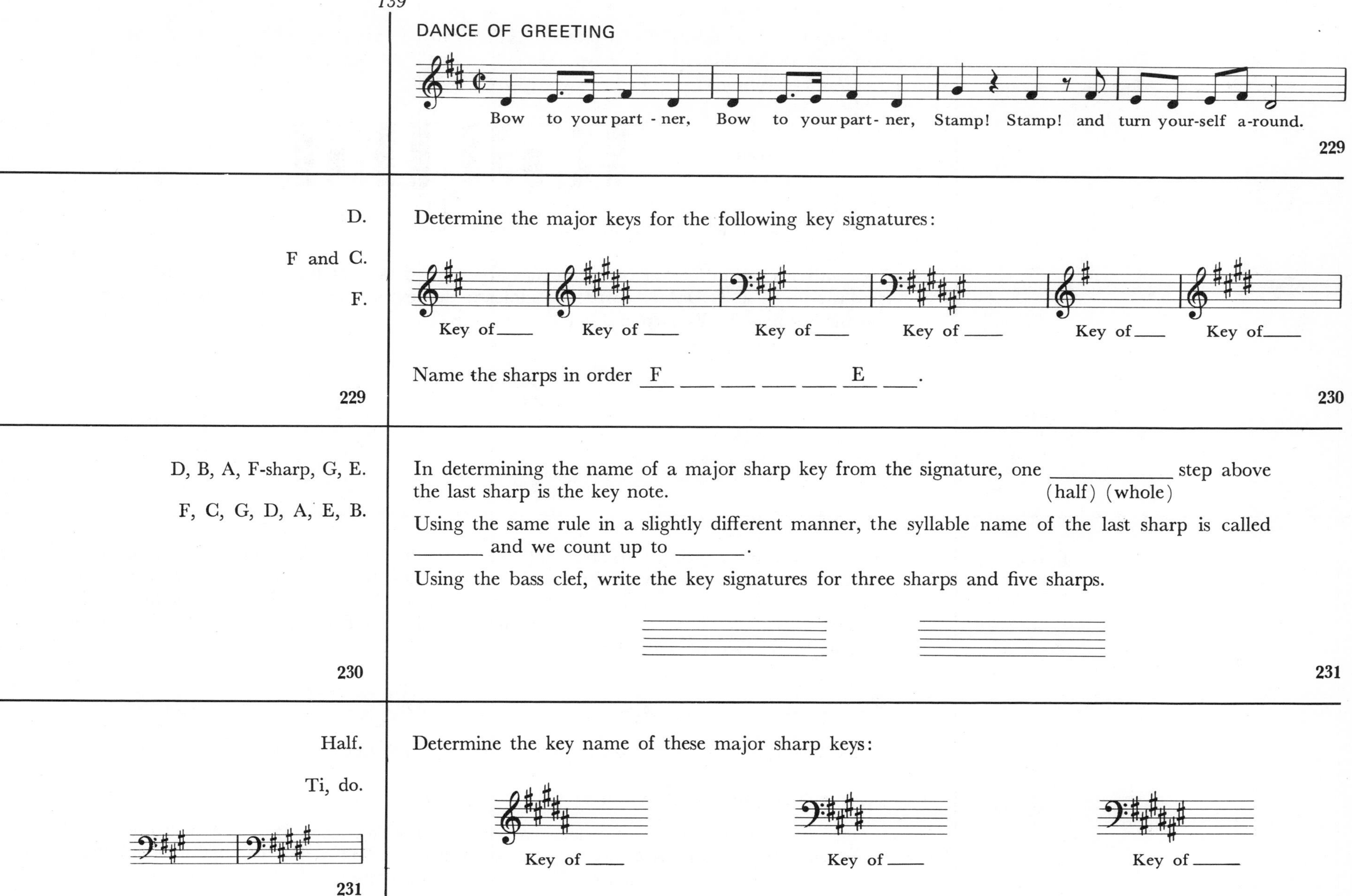

DANCE OF GREETING

Bow to your part - ner, Bow to your part- ner, Stamp! Stamp! and turn your-self a-round.

229

D.

F and C.

F.

229

Determine the major keys for the following key signatures:

Key of ___ Key of ___ Key of ___ Key of ___ Key of ___ Key of ___

Name the sharps in order F ___ ___ ___ ___ ___ E ___.

230

D, B, A, F-sharp, G, E.

F, C, G, D, A, E, B.

230

In determining the name of a major sharp key from the signature, one ___________ step above the last sharp is the key note. (half) (whole)

Using the same rule in a slightly different manner, the syllable name of the last sharp is called _______ and we count up to _______.

Using the bass clef, write the key signatures for three sharps and five sharps.

231

Half.

Ti, do.

231

Determine the key name of these major sharp keys:

Key of ___ Key of ___ Key of ___

The last answer is the key of F-sharp, not F. This can be checked in either of two ways: (1) One half step above E-sharp is F-sharp (remember that in enharmonic notation E-sharp is the same note as F-natural).

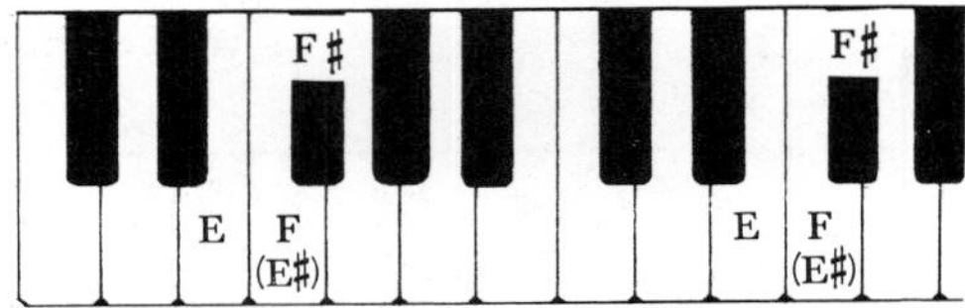

(2) A second check is to look at the notes that are sharped as a result of the key signature. With six sharps they are F C G D A E. Inspection indicates that every F in the selection is to be sharped and thus the key must be F-sharp and not F.

What major key is shown? ______

232

B, E, F-sharp.

C-sharp.

232

The teacher needs the same two abilities with flats as with sharps: the ability to write them in the correct order to designate keys and the ability to determine the key from a properly written key signature of flats. Placing flats in the key signature also proceeds from left to right. The first flat is always B-flat, the second E-flat, and so on. The first four flats are BEAD; the word "bead" is often used as a mnemonic aid in remembering them.

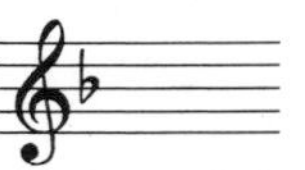

Key of F major

Key of B♭ major

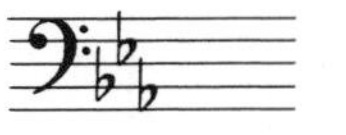

Key of E♭ major

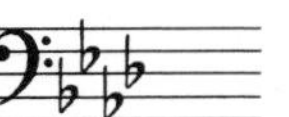

Key of A♭ major

The seven flats in order are BEADGCF.

Again, make up a mnemonic device to assist you in remembering them. If you learned the seven sharps well enough to recite them forward and backward, you will notice that the order for flats is exactly the reverse of that for sharps, BEADGCF for flats and FCGDAEB for sharps.
The seven flats, in order, are ______________.

233

B♭ E♭ A♭ D♭ G♭ C♭ F♭.

233

The seven flat keys are written as follows:

PUT YOUR LITTLE FOOT

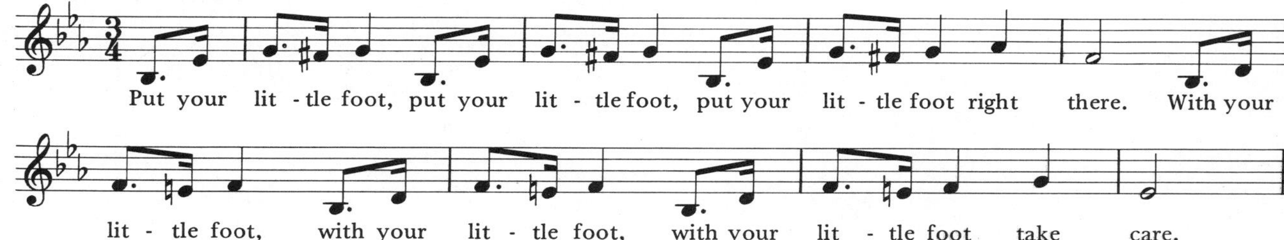

Name the major key of the song. ________________

What is the term applied to the first two notes? ________________

In measures 1, 2, and 3, F is sharped to make a half step interval for the word "little foot" ; in measures 5, 6, and 7 why is a natural sign used instead of a sharp for "little foot"? ________________________

How many dotted rhythm patterns are there? _______

234

E-flat.

Pick-ups.

A half step is created by the ♮, because E is flatted in the key of E-flat.

12.

234

OLD TEXAS

Name the major key of the song. _______

How many notes are in the pick-up? _______

How many counts does the word "leave" receive? _______

How many tied notes are present in the music? _______

235

F.

3.

2 1/2.

4.

In determining flat key signatures in major, the easiest rule to remember is "the next to the last flat is the key." For example, with two flats, B-flat and E-flat, the next to the last flat is B-flat, which is also the name of the major key. If you have three flats, B-flat, E-flat, and A-flat, the key is _______.

Which major key has four flats? _______

This system works for every key except that of one flat in which there is no next to the last flat. Here, one must memorize that the key of one flat is F major or else use one of the other rules.

235 | 236

E-flat.

A-flat.

Another rule is that the last flat is always the fourth degree of the major scale. Count down to 1 to determine the key note or "do." In the case of one flat, call B-flat 4 and count down to (1) (F); thus the major key is F.

Syllables may be used: the last flat is "fa" and you count down "fa-mi-re-do."

Some students prefer to visualize the keyboard to count down.

Using the keyboard, which key has three flats (B-flat, E-flat, and A-flat)? _______

Which key has five flats (B-flat, E-flat, A-flat, D-flat and G-flat)? _______

236 | 237

E-flat.

D-flat.

You have probably noticed that with the exception of one flat, the key of F major, flat keys always have the word "flat" in them. This is comparable to the designation of the last two sharp key signatures, six sharps (F-sharp major) and seven sharps (C-sharp major): the note has already been altered.

When there are three flats, B-flat, E-flat and A-flat, the key is E-flat major rather than E. Because of the key signature, all the E's in the music are to be flatted, and E natural is not present in the scale.

237

A third but slightly more cumbersome method of determining the names of the flats and the keys is by counting up four. Starting with B-flat, the next flat is four after it:

1 234 1 234 1 234
B♭ cd*E*♭ fg*A*♭ bc*D*♭ ef*G*♭ ab*C*♭ de*F*♭

(The starting pitch is called "one.") The keys follow an identical order only beginning with

1 234 1 234
*F*ga*B*♭ cd*E*♭ fg*A*♭ bc*D*♭ ef*G*♭ ab*C*♭

Using any rule, determine the keys in the following:

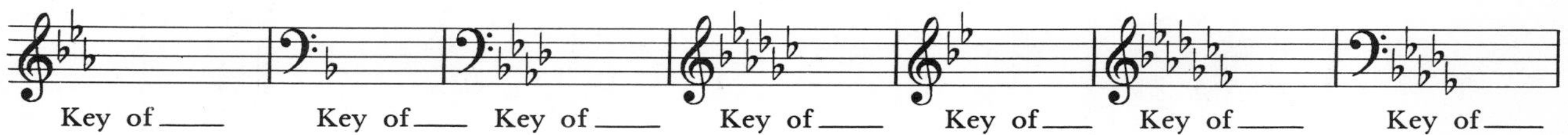

238

E-flat, F, A-flat, G-flat, B-flat, C-flat D-flat.

238

In determining the name of a major flat key from the signature, one rule is to call the last flat ________________ and count down to ________________.

239

---

4 or "fa."

1 or "do."

239

Another rule for finding the name of a major flat key signature when you have two or more flats is to look at the ________________ to the last flat, and it will be the key name.

240

Next.

240

To make key signatures as readable as possible, the sharp or flat on a line is always placed with the line running exactly through the center: ♯ and ♭. The sharp or flat for a space is centered on the space: ♯ and ♭. Some pitches occur twice on the staff (E and F in the treble staff, A and G in the bass staff). In a key signature, the sharp or flat is placed only once for each pitch, but applies to all pitches of that letter name. The usual placement for sharps is:

for flats is:

Write the key signature for five sharps in both the bass and treble staves.

241

241

Write the key signature for five flats in bass and treble staves.

242

242

Unscramble the signatures and write the sharps or flats in the correct arrangement.

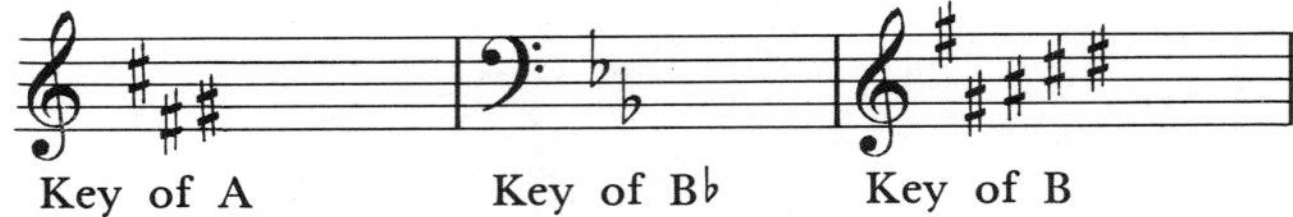

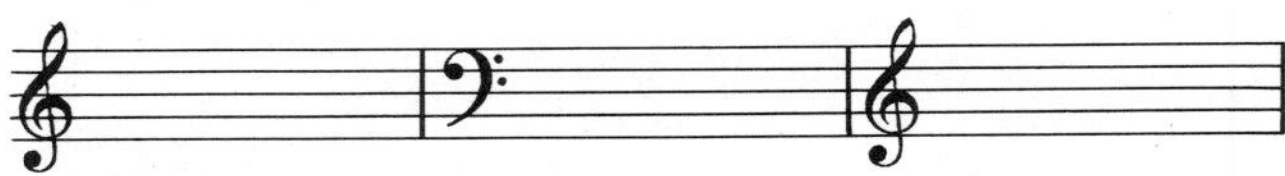

243

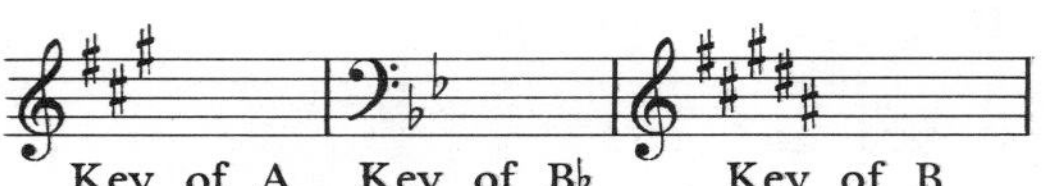

243

When given a key, the beginner is often at a loss as to whether it has sharps or flats, and without that knowledge selection of the correct rule to use is impossible.

All flat keys with the exception of one flat, the key of F, have the word flat in them: F, B-flat, E-flat, A-flat, D-flat, G-flat, C-flat. With the further exception of the key of C, which has no sharps or flats, all plain keys will be sharp keys:

G, D, A, E, B, (F-sharp, and G-sharp).
↑ ↑ ↑
1 2 3 etc. sharps

Write the signatures for the major keys given. Be sure observe the clef sign.

244

244

By counting to determine the order of the sharps and flats we have discovered that there is a relationship among the sharps and flats.

This relationship is shown by diagram A below and is known as the "circle of fifths."

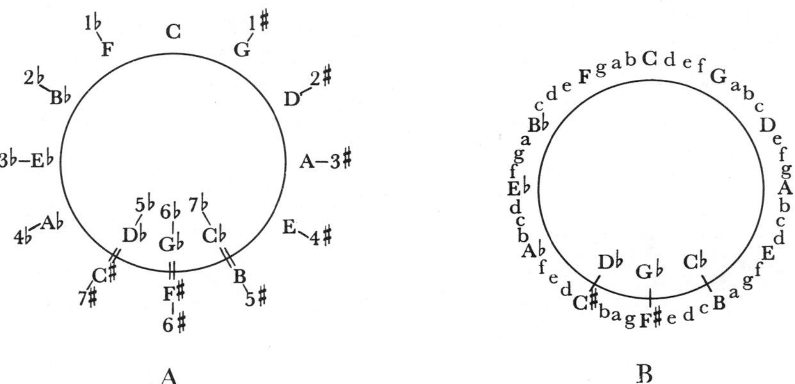

If you begin with C at the top of diagram B and count in the circular alphabet by fives, you will see that all the major key signatures appear in order, ending again with C. Can you also see the sharps in order going clockwise and the flats in order going counterclockwise?

The major key signatures above have the correct *number* of sharps or flats for the key given, but they contain one or more errors. Correct the signatures, using the staff below.

245

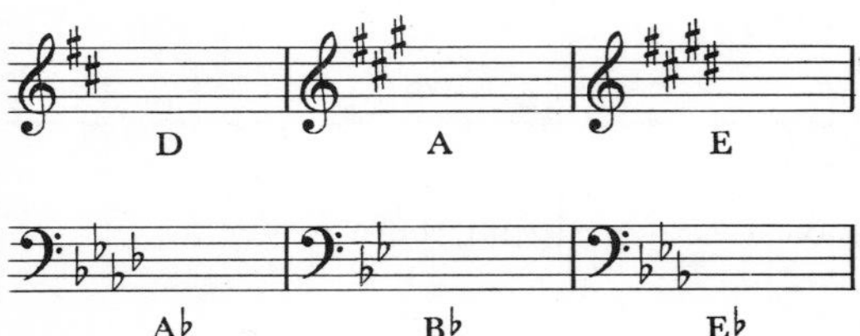

245

Write on the lower staff "do," or the key note, for each of the following key signatures. Make your answer similar to the first example.

246

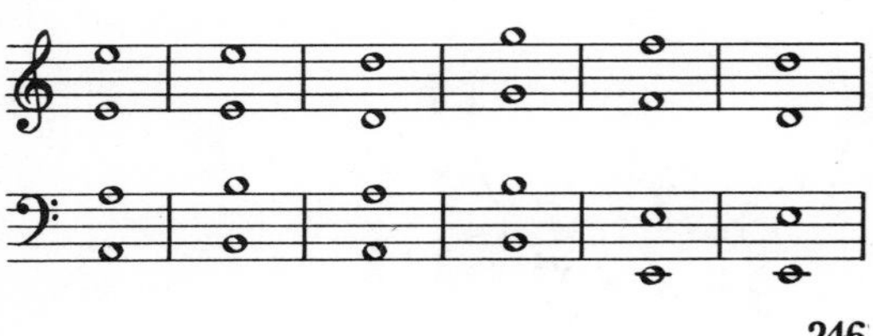

246

PRETEST for Chapter 12: Tonal Center

Mark the answer or *answers that are correct.*

1. Tonal center is the:

—— a. fundamental note of the scale

—— b. in tuneness of a note

—— c. middle section of a piece

—— d. note on the bottom line of the staff

2. If you sing "America" in the major key of F, the tonality is:

—— a. F

—— b. one sharp

—— c. C

—— d. written in the bass clef

3. A feeling for tonal center aids in:

—— a. establishing perfect pitch

—— b. playing or singing in tune

—— c. placing the clef sign

—— d. recognizing the rhythm

4. The tonal center sounds like:

—— a. an anacrusis

—— b. a resting place

—— c. it should lead to "do"

—— d. a tuning note

5. Which of the following songs begins on the tonal center?

—— a. "Jingle Bells'"

—— b. "America"

—— c. "The First Noel"

—— d. "Three Blind Mice"

Answers

1. a.
2. a.
3. b.
4. b, d.
5. b.

From your score determine if you can omit sections of the text.

CHAPTER 12 The Concept of Tonal Center

In determining the major key in music we have been dealing with something that can be seen on the musical page, indicated by the key signature. But in music we are always dealing with something that can be heard. Music built upon the major scale revolves around the keynote—the note for which the scale is named. The "pull" created by the keynote establishes what is known as the tonality, or key of a song. Much tonal music ends on the keynote and much also begins on the keynote. This basic pitch (note) is also called the tonic, the tonal center, "1," or "do."

This chapter has two objectives: (1) an understanding of tonality or tonal center and (2), more important, the aural ability to recognize the tonal center of songs in major keys. Since aural recognition requires practice in listening, use the records, sing, and use the keyboard.

Sing "America." The first note of the melody is the keynote or tonal center. The final note of the melody is also the tonal center. Hum this pitch. It should have a feeling of rest, or finality.

AMERICA

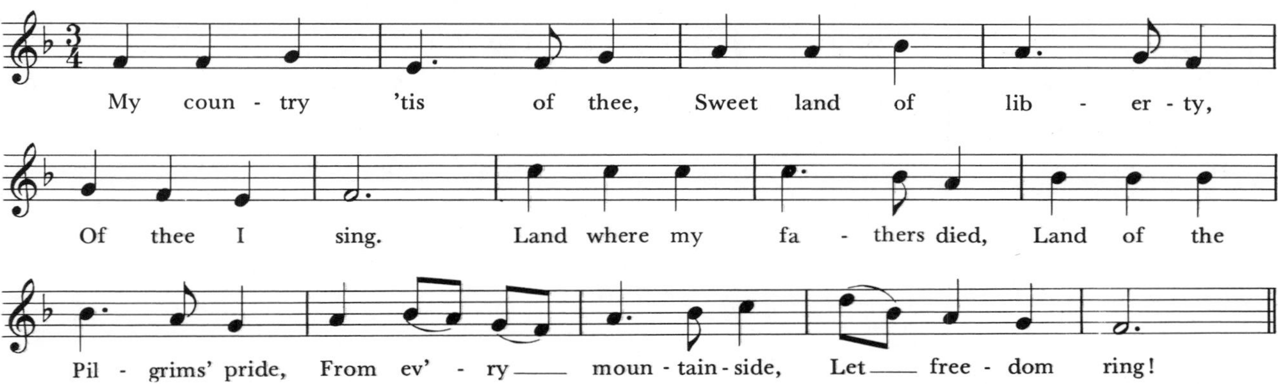

My coun - try 'tis of thee, Sweet land of lib - er - ty,
Of thee I sing. Land where my fa - thers died, Land of the
Pil - grims' pride, From ev' - ry moun - tain - side, Let free - dom ring!

Singing response.

247

In what major key is "America"? ______

What is the letter name of the first note? ______ Last note? ______

The key or tonality of "America" is F and the entire song is often thought of in relation to this key tone.

Use the application section to hear this tonal center for "America."

248

F.

F, F.

248

In most traditional music the key tone provides a central focus or a place of rest. Recognizing the key tone helps one follow the music with understanding. Beyond the ability to identify key signatures, ability to hear the tonal center is important, because key signatures can have more than one meaning, as later chapters will show.

The tonal center is the same as "do," or ______________

249

"1," keynote, tonality, tonic.

249

A feeling for tonal center is important and is the basis for many musical experiences.

Students learn to sing in tune not by developing a sense of perfect pitch but rather by relating one pitch to another. For example, if you are to sing

it would be very difficult unless someone were to give you the pitch of the first note, G. Once you can securely sing the G, it is relatively easy to sing the next pitch, which is ______. This pitch is ______________ step above G.

250

A.

One (whole).

250

Because so much music of our culture is tonal, learning to sing or to play an instrument in tune is based on the ability to consciously or unconsciously relate to the tonal center of the piece.

You may have heard a chorus find their pitches after someone has played a note on a piano or a pitch pipe, or have heard an orchestra tune up from the oboist sounding a single pitch. They are relating to a single pitch.

The ability to sing or play in tune is related to one's ability to hear the ______________ ______________ of the music.

251

Tonal center.

251

WHEN THE SAINTS GO MARCHING IN

What is the key of "When the Saints Go Marching In"? _______

Does the song begin on the keynote (tonic)? _______

Does the song end on the tonic? _______

Does the final pitch sound like a resting place? _______ Notice how the frequent use of E-flat emphasizes the tonal center. Sing the song.

252

E-flat major.

Yes.

Yes.

Yes.

Singing response.

252

Sing the song, "Aunt Rhody." Hum the key center. What is the key of the song? _______ Is the final note of the song the keynote? _______ Is the first note of the song the keynote? _______ Hum the key center or play it on the piano. Does this match the pitch of the final note? _______

AUNT RHODY

253

Singing response.

F major.

Yes.

No.

Yes.

253

In this frame "Aunt Rhody" appears in a different key. Moving music from one key to another key is called ______________. The letter name of the keynote in this version is ______________. What is the meter? ______________.

Sing "Aunt Rhody" in the new key by playing D on the piano or on a pitch pipe. Can you find the starting pitch? Singing in a new key does not require thinking about the sharps and flats; the tune will remain the same. The primary difference is that the song will have a different range (highest and lowest notes) and revolve around a different tonal center.

AUNT RHODY

Go tell Aunt Rho - dy, Go tell Aunt Rho - dy,

Go tell Aunt Rho - dy the old grey goose is dead.

254

Transposing.

D.

$\frac{2}{4}$

254

Think of several short songs you know well, for example, "Row, Row, Row Your Boat," "Mary Had a Little Lamb," "Three Blind Mice," and so forth. Sing each of them aloud and try to determine which pitch is the tonal center, or "do," and if the song begins on the tonal center.

Of the three songs named above, which ones end on "do"? ______________

Which ones begin on "do"? ______________

255

Singing response.

All three.

"Row, Row, Row Your Boat."

255

PRETEST for Chapter 13: Minor Mode

Mark the correct answer or *answers.*

1. Mode is equivalent to:

—— a. scale

—— b. interval

—— c. style

—— d. key tone

2. A chromatic scale consists of:

—— a. a specified mixture of half steps and whole steps

—— b. consecutive half-step intervals

—— c. color tones used in a regular major or minor scale

—— d. a minor scale with a raised seventh

3. Natural minor scales have half steps between:

—— a. e–f and b–c

—— b. 3–4 and 7–8

—— c. b–c and e–f

—— d. 2–3 and 5–6

4. Mark the whole steps in the following minor scale by bracketing them.

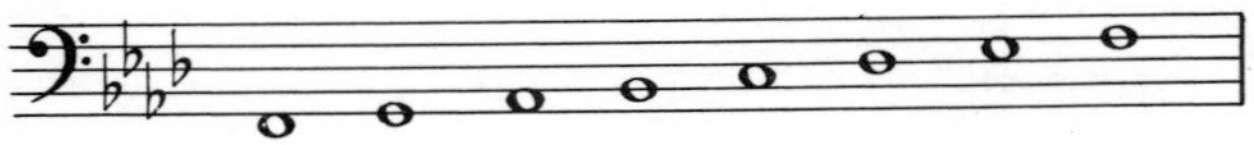

5. Which key signature is indicated?

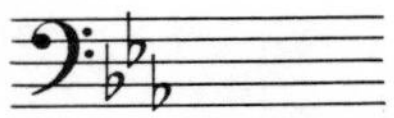

______ major and ______ minor

6. Which two keys may be indicated by a signature of four sharps?

______ major

______ minor

7. The major key related to d minor is ______.

8. The minor key related to B major is ______.

9. When a major and minor key are related, they have the same:

—— a. tonality

—— b. beginning note

—— c. key signature

—— d. ending note

10. Minor scales sound different from major scales because they:

—— a. are written lower

—— b. are written higher

—— c. have different combinations of sharps and flats

—— d. have a different arrangement of whole and half steps

11. If you know the key signature of a major key, you can:

    —— a. count 1 1/2 steps up to find the starting note of the relative minor

    —— b. count 1 1/2 steps down to find the starting note of the relative minor

    —— c. count 1 1/2 steps up to find the key signature of the related minor

    —— d. count 1 1/2 steps down to find the key signature of the related minor

12. The rule(s) to determine the major key signature(s) is (are):

    —— a. the note above the last flat is the key

    —— b. the note above the last sharp is the key

    —— c. the next to the last flat is the key

    —— d. the next to the last sharp is the key

13. What is the key signature for (give number and name of sharps or flats, for example, 2 sharps, F and C)?

    —— a. a minor

    —— b. e-flat minor

    —— c. g minor

    —— d. f-sharp minor

14. Look at this melody. What is the key?

15. In the harmonic minor scale:

    —— a. the sixth and seventh are raised

    —— b. the fifth is lowered

    —— c. the seventh is raised

    —— d. notes ascend only by half and whole steps

16. List the sharps in order. ______________

Answers

1. a.
2. b.
3. d.
4. 
5. E-flat, c.
6. E, c-sharp.
7. F.
8. g-sharp.
9. c.
10. d.
11. b.
12. b, c.
13. a. no sharps and flats.
    b. 6 flats, B-flat, E-flat, A-flat, D-flat, G-flat, C-flat.
    c. 2 flats, B-flat, E-flat.
    d. 3 sharps, F-sharp, C-sharp, G-sharp.
14. a minor (harmonic).
15. c.
16. F, C, G, D, A, E, B.

From your score determine if you can omit sections of the text.

CHAPTER 13 The Concept of Minor Mode

When the basis of a musical composition is the major scale, we say the piece is in the major mode. The major mode has been the most widely used basis for writing music in the Western tradition. It is by no means the only one. In the continual search for new and expressive sounds, composers utilize various other modes as the basis for composition. The chromatic scale with its series of half steps has been mentioned; much contemporary music makes use of the chromatic scale because of its freedom. Two other important modes are the minor mode and the pentatonic mode. Although there are additional modes, they are beyond the scope of this text.

When you complete this chapter, you will be able to (1) identify the minor key that is related to each major key; (2) distinguish the difference between natural and harmonic minor; (3) find the basic tonality of any song in a major or a minor key; (4) if you complete the optional section, you will be able to write a natural and a harmonic minor scale in any key.

The distinguishing characteristic of a mode, or scale—that which makes it sound different—is its pattern of whole steps and half steps, and in some cases the use of even wider distances than whole steps between two consecutive pitches.

The minor scale, like the major scale, consists of seven different pitch names plus a repetition of the first pitch name, the octave, at the end of the scale pattern.

When the distance between pitches 3 and 4 and between 7 and 8 is one-half step and all other intervals in the scale are a step apart, the scale is a ______________ scale.

256

Major.

256

The natural minor scale, like the major scale, is constructed of a combination of whole and half steps but here the half steps occur between pitches 2 and 3 and between pitches 5 and 6. All other pitches are a whole step apart. In the example a natural minor scale has been constructed beginning on the pitch A. The half steps are between B and C (pitches 2 and 3), and between E and F (pitches 5 and 6).

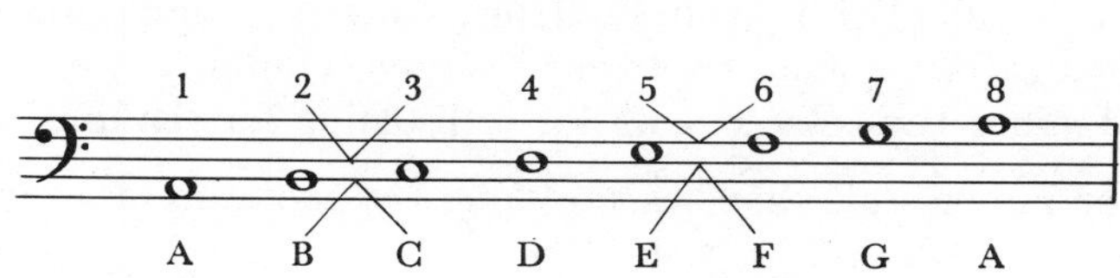

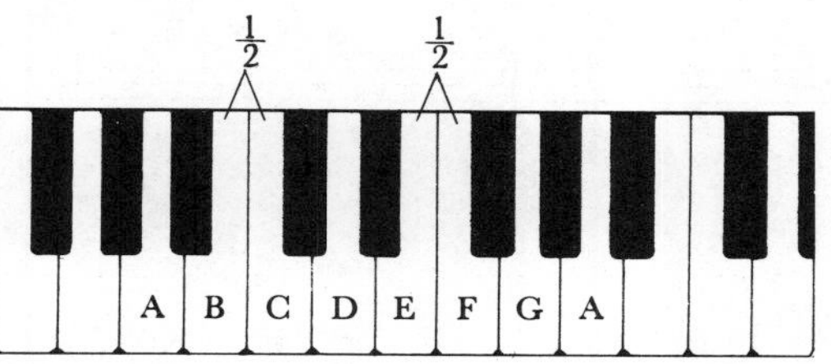

The half steps in a natural minor scale occur between pitches _______ and _______; _______ and _______. (use numbers)

The distance between all other consecutive pitches in a natural minor scale is a ___________ step.

257

2, 3; 5, 6.

Whole.

The natural minor scale beginning on A can be played on the keyboard using only the white notes. Thus, a* minor uses the same notes as C major, but the difference is in the beginning and ending notes.

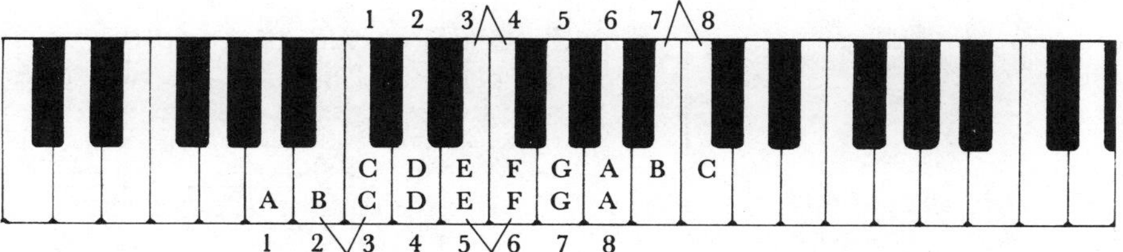

Because the starting and ending notes are different, the half steps E–F and B–C occur at different places in the scale, and the tonal center is different—C for the major scale and a for the minor.

Because no accidentals are needed for the a natural minor scale, its key signature is identical to the key signature for C major, i.e., there are no sharps or flats. Since these two scales share the same key signature, we think of them as being related: a minor is the *relative* minor of C major, and C major is the *relative* major of a minor.

Using quarter notes, write a one-octave a natural minor scale. Use treble clef, half note as the unit beat, and quadruple meter.

* Minor keys and scales are referred to by lowercase letters and major keys and scales are referred to by uppercase letters, for example, a minor and A major.

257

258

258

Since there are only seven notes, A,B,C,D,E,F, and G in music, there can be only seven sharps or flats, A,B,C,D,E,F, and G. Thus, when key signatures are used, there will be minor keys having identical key signatures to major keys. The only way a major key can be distinguished from a natural minor key is by looking for or listening for the tonal center.

The minor scale that has the same key signature as a major scale is called the ______________ minor of that major scale.

259

Relative.

259

The a natural minor scale and the C major scale use exactly the same notes on the staff. Music written in a minor, however, centers around A as the tonic pitch. The music often begins on A and usually ends on A. The different tonic or tonal center, with the resulting different arrangement of half and whole steps, causes the two scales to sound quite different.

If music written in C major is based on the C major scale, music written in the key of a minor might be based on the ______ natural minor scale.

260

---

a.

260

Sing the C major scale; then find the pitch A and sing several times the a natural minor scale. Play it on the piano and listen to the two scales on the record in the application section.

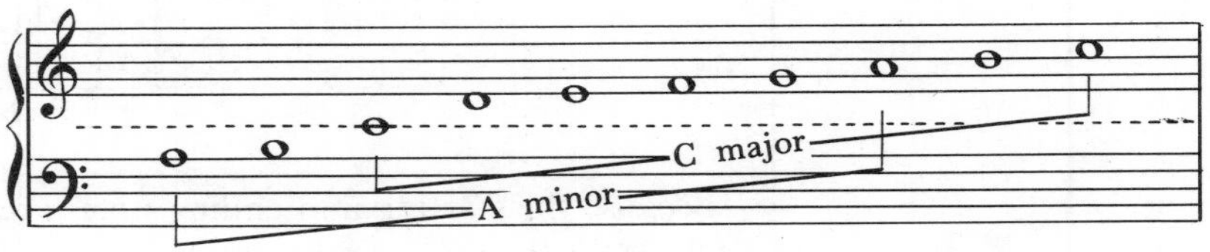

261

Singing response.

261

In constructing minor scales, the same procedure is followed as for major scales. A natural minor scale can be written using any note as tonic. To obtain the correct arrangement of half steps (between 2 and 3 and 5 and 6) one can either (1) use accidentals or (2) use the correct key signature.

If you know the major keys well, relating the minor to the major is the most practical approach. The minor with the same key signature as the major is always located 1 1/2 steps *below* the major. For example, we have been using C major and a minor, both having a key signature of no sharps and flats.

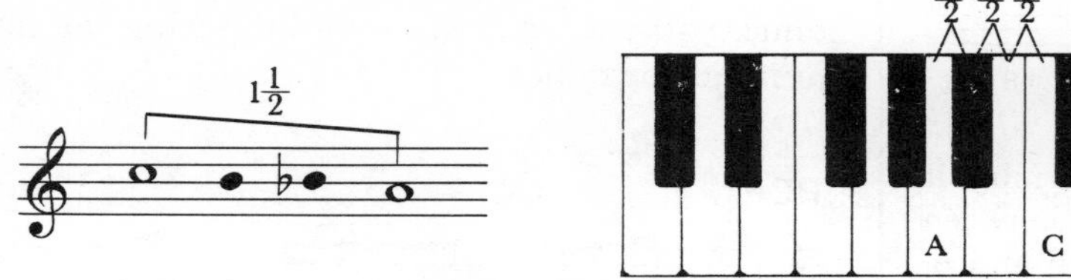

Inspection of the keyboard confirms that a is 1 1/2 steps (three half steps) below C.

A good knowledge of the major keys is important to the understanding of material about relative minor keys.

Write the key signatures for the following major keys. Use treble clef,

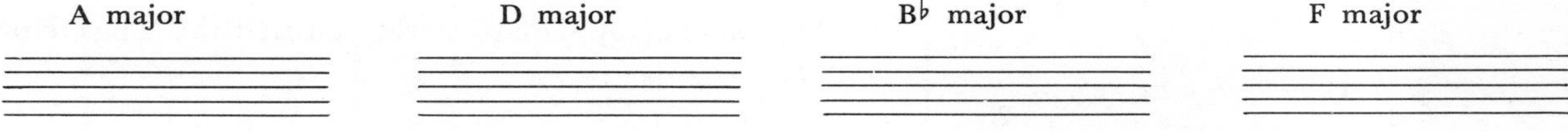

262

262

If you need to construct a minor scale related to a major scale, determine the number of flats or sharps in the major key; then count down 1 1/2 steps from the tonality of the major to determine the tonality of the minor. Place the key signature on the staff and write the scale.

Write the natural minor scale that is related to G major.

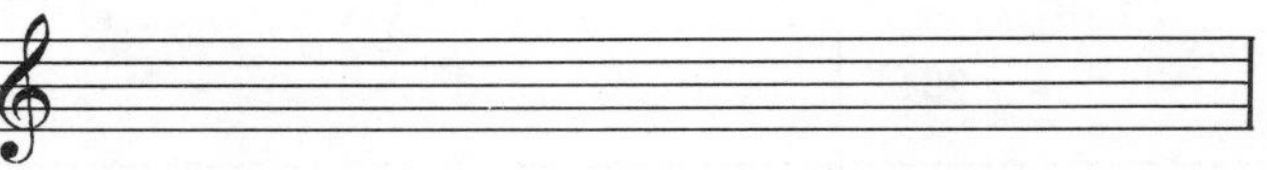

263

If you wish to check yourself determine if the half steps occur between 2 and 3 and between 5 and 6.

263

The reason for the importance of this knowledge is that the classroom teacher must be able to determine, without hearing a song but seeing the music, the tonal center of music and know if the song is in major or minor.

Looking at the key signature tells you that the song "Hora" is either in ______ major or ______ minor.

264

F, d.

264

The tonal center of "Hora" is D, so the key is d minor.

Write the natural minor scale that is related to E-flat major. Check the intervals to be sure that you are correct.

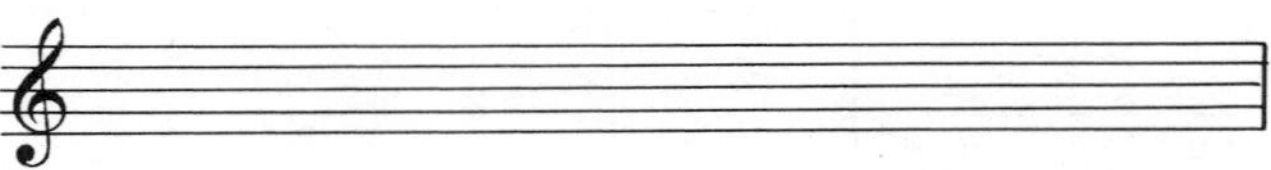

265

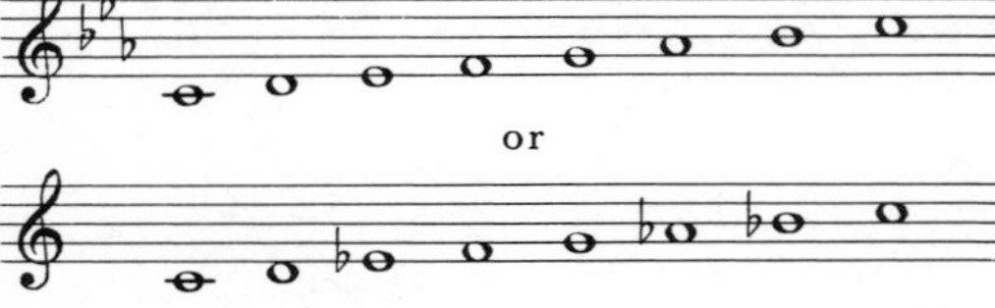

265

Determine that the key signature for E-flat major is three flats. (The next to the last flat is the key—the flats in order are B, E, A, D, G, C, F.)

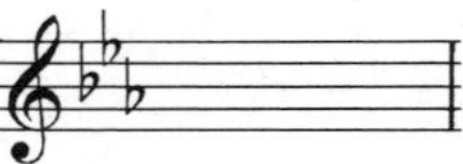

Count down three half steps (1 1/2 steps) from E-flat to determine the keynote of the relative minor. This note is C.

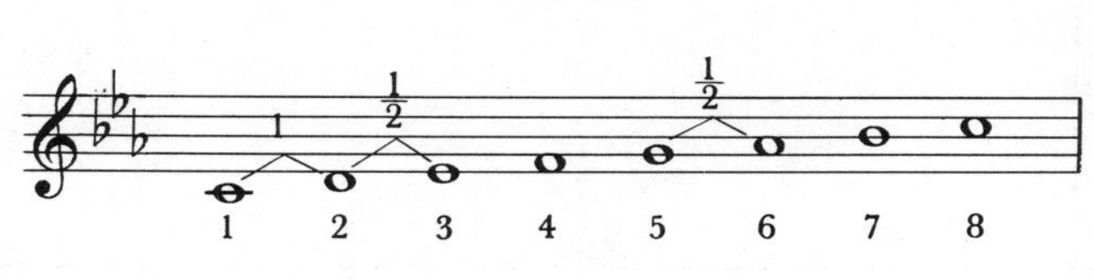

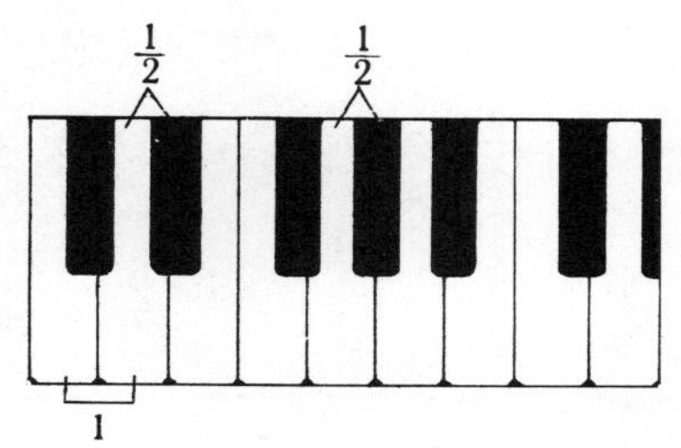

Another method to determine the relative minor key is to find the sixth note in the scale of the major key. For example, the sixth note in C major is A. The relative minor of C major is the key of a minor. In this method the relative minor to E-flat major is ________________.

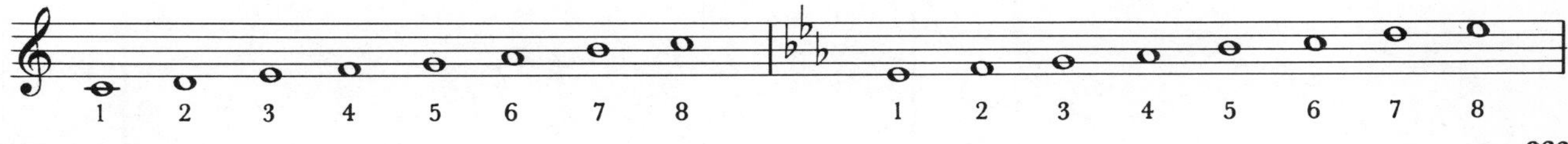

266

---

c minor.

266

The relative minor to A major is ________________.

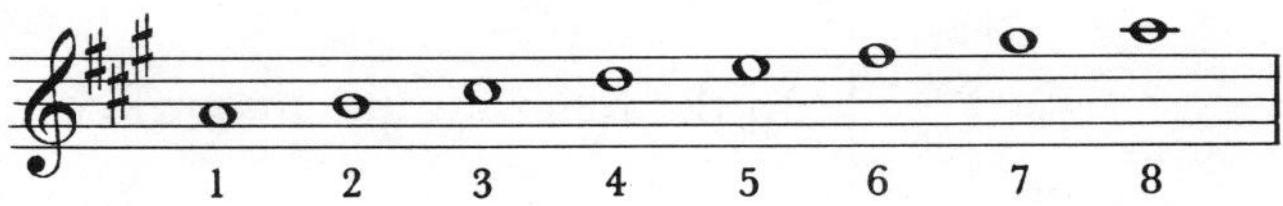

Remember that F is sharped in the key of A major. ________________

As you have realized by now, the pitch 1 1/2 steps down from the keynote and the sixth pitch of the scale are the same.

267

---

f-sharp minor.

267

This is the key signature for the minor key of ________________.

268

c-sharp minor. 268	This is the key signature for the major key of _______ and the minor key of _______. 269
D. b. 269	The method of determining minor signatures for the flat keys is identical to that for the sharp keys. The relative minor is 1 1/2 steps below the major (or the sixth degree of the major scale). For example, B-flat major has a relative minor of g which also has two flats, B-flat and E-flat. $\frac{1}{2}$ $\frac{1}{2}$ $\frac{1}{2}$ G G In the following the major key is ________________ and its relative minor is ________________. 270
F major. d minor. 270	When the major key is E-flat, the relative minor key would be ________________. 271
c minor. 271	What is the major key? ________________. What is the minor key? ________________. 272

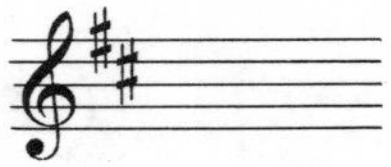

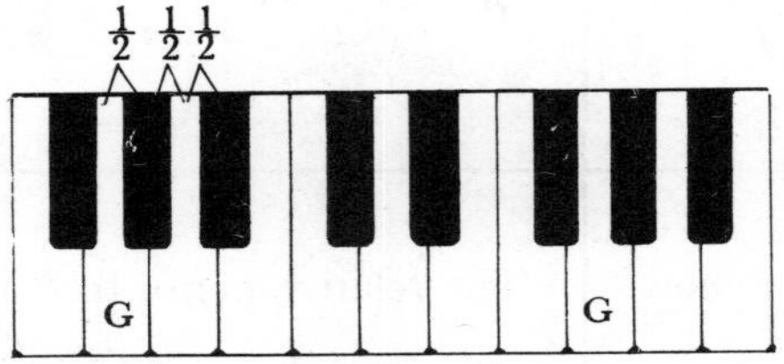

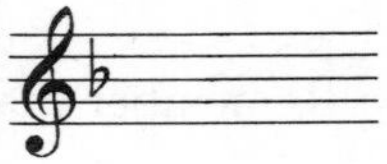

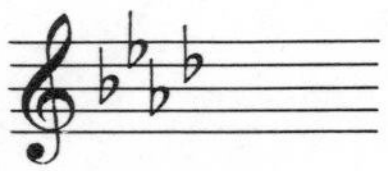

A-flat major.

f minor.

272

Remember, if the tonal center for a minor scale is sharped or flatted, that sharp or flat is part of the *key name,* just as in major. For example, this signature stands for E major and c-sharp minor.

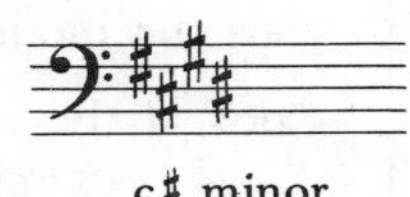

c♯ minor

Calling it c minor is incorrect, because c minor's signature has three flats: c minor

Counting up or down the 1 1/2 steps would not be possible if the key name were not accurately given.

Write the name of the major key and minor key for each of the following signatures:

Major: ______ ______ ______ ______ ______ ______ ______ ______ ______ ______

Minor: ______ ______ ______ ______ ______ ______ ______ ______ ______ ______

273

Major: E-flat, D, B, F, A, B-flat, A-flat, C, E, G.

Minor: c, b, g-sharp, d, f-sharp, g, f, a, c-sharp, e.

273

Draw the key signatures for

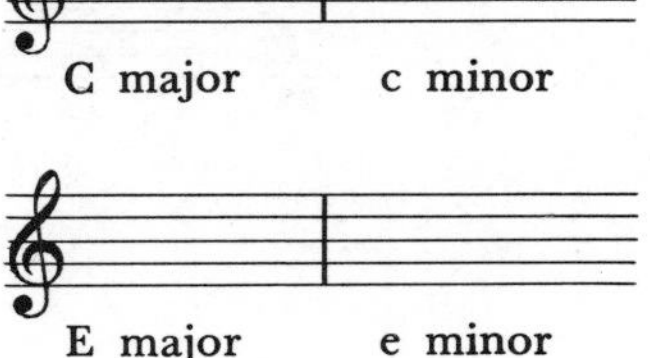

C major c minor

E major e minor

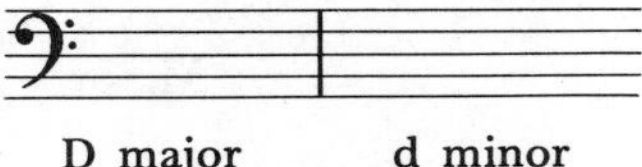

D major d minor

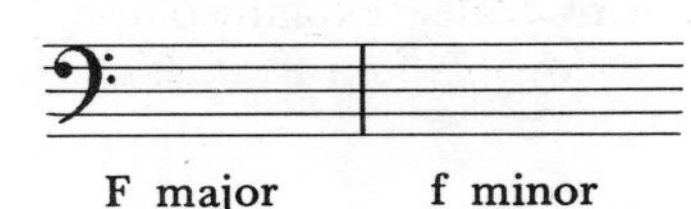

F major f minor

274

274

Since a key signature is shared by more than one mode, the only way to determine if a piece is in major or minor is to listen or to look at the music itself. The ending pitch, the beginning pitch, and the pitch around which the music seems to revolve help us to determine the key center and thus the mode.

Look at the song below. The flat in the key signature is ______. This indicates the major key of ______ or minor key of ______. "Joshua" is in the ______________ mode because
(major or minor)

______________________.

JOSHUA

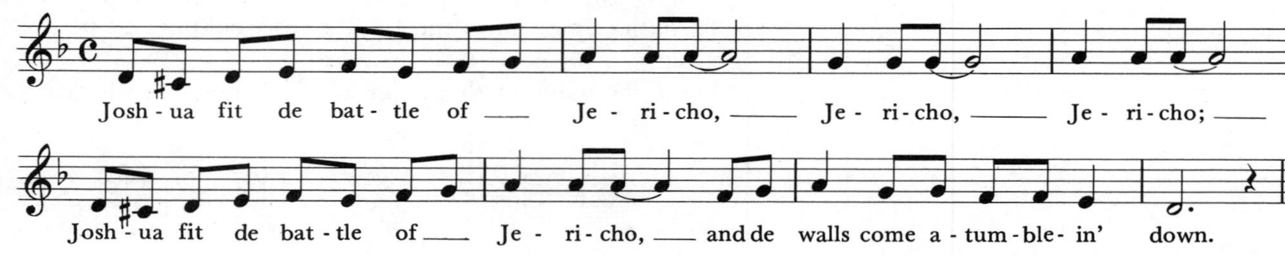
Josh - ua fit de bat - tle of ___ Je - ri - cho, ___ Je - ri - cho, ___ Je - ri - cho; ___
Josh - ua fit de bat - tle of ___ Je - ri - cho, ___ and de walls come a - tum - ble - in' down.

275

B-flat.

F.

d.

Minor

Tonal center of "d"; first and last note is "d"; raised seventh degree of scale (explained in the following four frames).

275

There is a slight variation of the natural minor scale called harmonic minor, which is more typical of what we recognize as a minor scale. Listen to a harmonic minor scale in the application section. In harmonic minor the seventh degree (pitch or note) of the scale is raised one half step above that in the natural minor.

1 2 3 4 5 6 7 8

______ natural minor

276

d.

276

If you raise the seventh note C to C-sharp you will construct a d harmonic minor scale. This seventh note of the scale is also called the leading tone. It is the tone just before "do" in an ascending scale and seems to "lead" to it. Raising this gives a strong feeling in minor of leading to the octave.

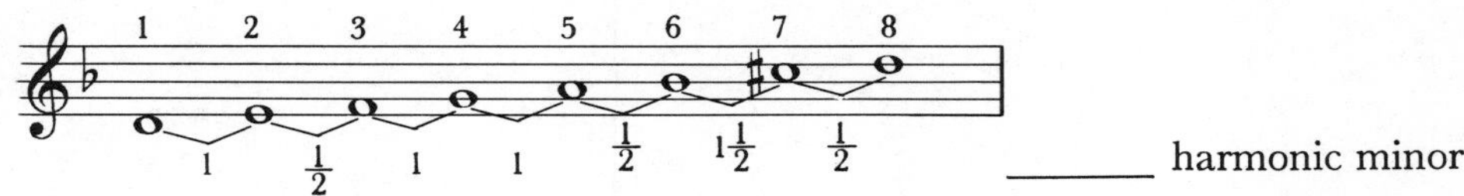

______ harmonic minor

Play the scale in frame 276 and the scale in this frame to hear the difference.

277

---

d.

Playing response.

277

Although the intervals are as indicated above, again it is not necessary to rely on the interval scheme to construct the scale. The simplest method for constructing harmonic minor scales is to rely on your knowledge of the key signature and raise the seventh pitch one half step.

Accidentals are used to raise the seventh degree of the scale. The natural minor key signature continues to be used.

JOSHUA

Notice in the song "Joshua" that each time C is written it is raised by a sharp. In a d minor scale, C is the seventh degree of the scale; thus "Joshua" is written in d harmonic minor mode. The song is not in F major; one clue is that it begins and ends on d. A raised seventh is also confirmation of minor tonality. If you listen to it, the minor modality can be plainly heard.

Review the relationship between major and minor keys. Relative minor shares a common key signature with its relative major, but lies 1 1/2 steps *below* the major. E major is related to _______ minor.

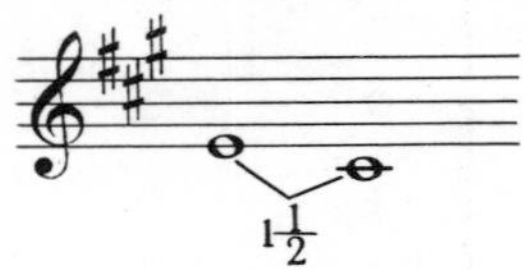

B-flat major is related to _______ minor.

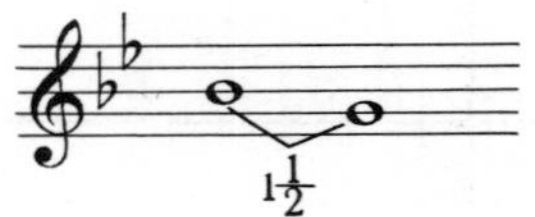

278

---

c-sharp.

g.

Conversely, the relative major lies 1 1/2 steps *above* the minor: c-sharp minor is related to _______ major.

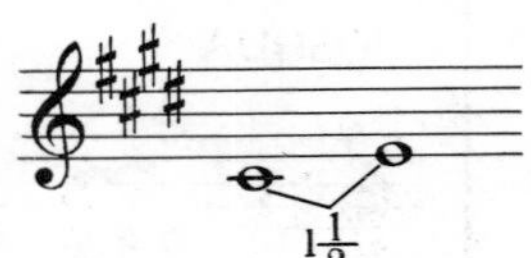

g minor is related to _______ major.

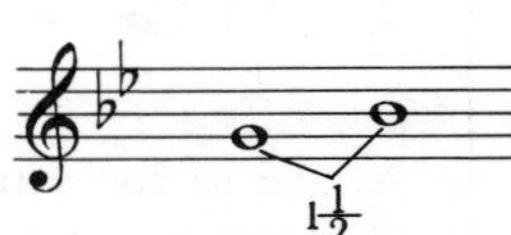

278

279

E.

B-flat.

279

Minor may be natural minor (using the key signature with no changes) or harmonic minor (using the key signature and raising the seventh step), but it is still relative to the major key 1 1/2 steps above it.

Give the kind of minor scale, its key, and the relative major.

_____ ______________________ minor

__________ relative major

_____ ______________________ minor

__________ relative major

280

---

b harmonic.

D.

g natural.

B-flat.

280

As previously stated, a practice usually followed is to indicate major keys with capital letters and minor keys wih small letters: B major = key of B, B minor = key of b. This practice omits the necessity of writing out major and minor for each reference to a key. Abbreviations are also used: "maj." for major, "min." for minor, as well as "M" for major and "m" for minor.

Remember, the minor related to a major key has the same key signature and its scale begins 1 1/2 steps below the major.

The relative minor keys of these major keys are:

G: ______, D: ______, E: ______, A: ______, B-flat: ______.

281

---

e, b, c-sharp, f-sharp, g.

281

This song is in minor. What is the key? ______________

Is it an example of harmonic or natural minor? ______________ Reason ______________

WAYFARING STRANGER

I am a poor way-far-ing stran-ger, just travel-ing thru this world be-

low. There is no sick-ness, toil nor dan-ger in that bright world to which I go.

282

d minor.

harmonic.

raised seventh note, which is C.

One other type of minor scale is the melodic minor scale. It has a similar relationship to a major key. Its characteristic is that the sixth and seventh degrees of the scale are raised when ascending scales are used but the regular natural minor is used for descending scales.

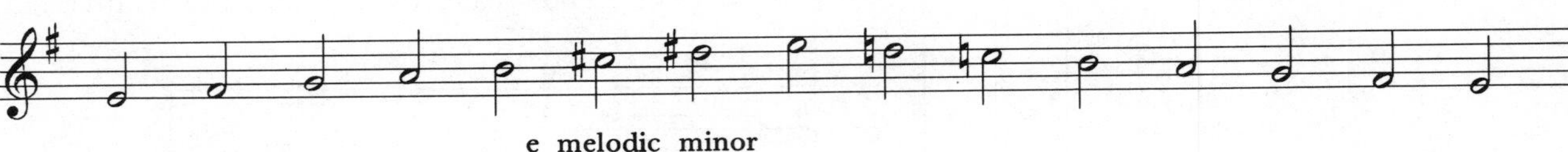

e melodic minor

Because it is not widely used in elementary songs, no exercises have been provided for this scale.

282

OPTIONAL SECTION: Minor Mode

Often you will have the beginning note of the minor scale and will need to determine its key signature in order to ensure the proper arrangement of the half and whole steps in the scale. The process is exactly reversed from that followed in the preceding frames: count up 1 1/2 steps to determine the related major key and its key signature. For example, if the task is to write a natural minor scale on F-sharp, you would count up 1 1/2 steps from F-sharp:

The key signature of f-sharp minor is identical to that of A major: three sharps, F-sharp, C-sharp and G-sharp.

If you have forgotten how to determine the number of sharps in the key of A major, recall the rule that the note above the last sharp is the key. Reversing this, the last sharp will be the note below the key.

Given the key of A, we count down one half step to G-sharp, the last sharp. Knowing our *f*at *c*hicken *g*ood *d*inner, *a*ll *e*at *b*ird, we can count until we get to G, the last sharp: fat chicken *g*ood.

Draw a treble or bass clef, put in three sharps, and write a scale beginning on F-sharp. You will have correctly written the f-sharp natural minor scale. Use quarter notes.

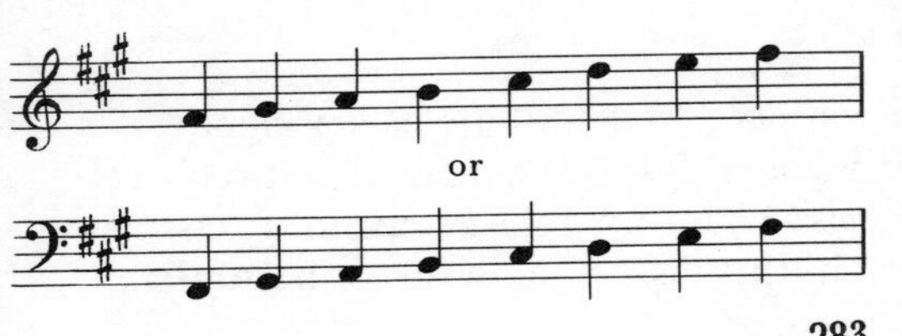

283

The key signature of G major is one sharp. Write the relative minor scale (natural minor).

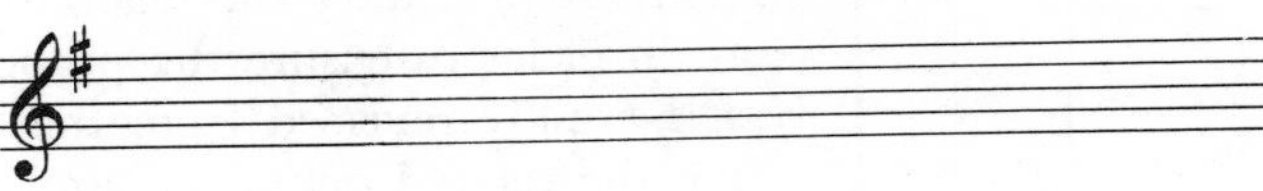

284

284

1 1/2 steps below G is E.

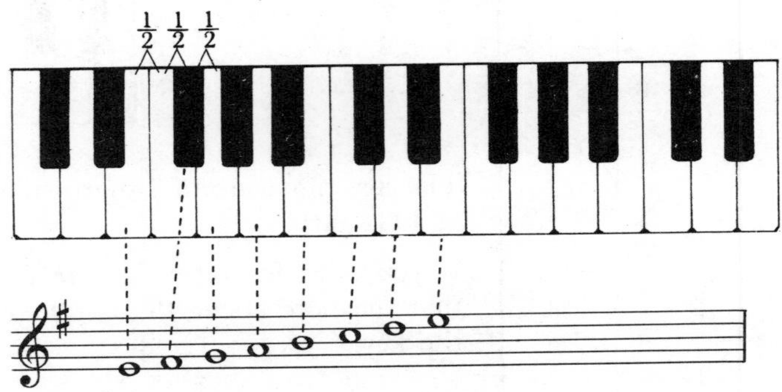

Construct a minor scale on C and make all the checks to ensure accuracy.

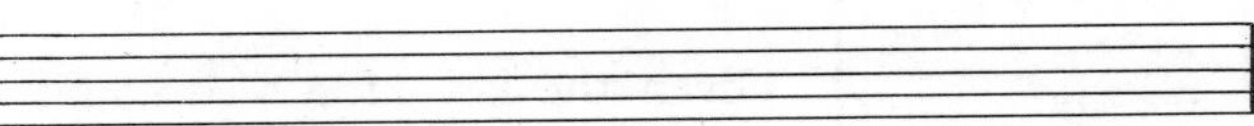

Since this integrates so much past knowledge, you may wish to give yourself more exercises. Check them by the half–whole step relationship.

Play as many of these scales as possible on the piano. Sing them.

285

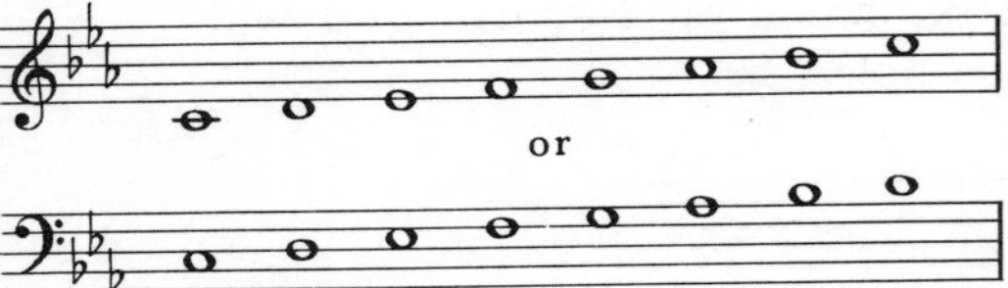

Playing or singing response.

285

Construct a natural minor scale beginning on G-sharp.

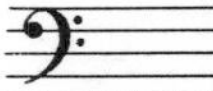

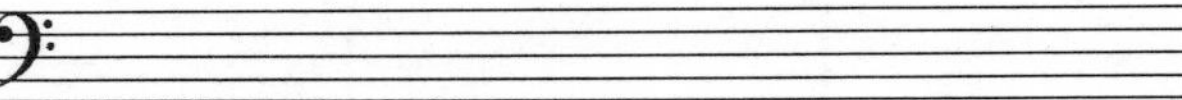

And one more just for practice. Construct a natural minor scale on E.

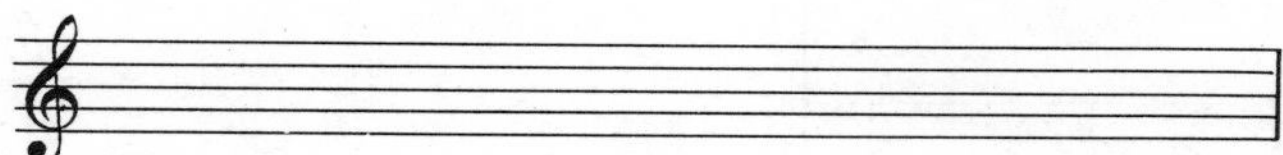

286

286

Writing natural minor scales in flat keys is identical to writing them in sharp keys. We have to be able, however, to recall the major flat keys and their rules.

To construct a natural minor scale on F, count up 1 1/2 steps:

F–F-sharp: 1/2 step
F-sharp–G: 1/2 step
G–G-sharp: 1/2 step

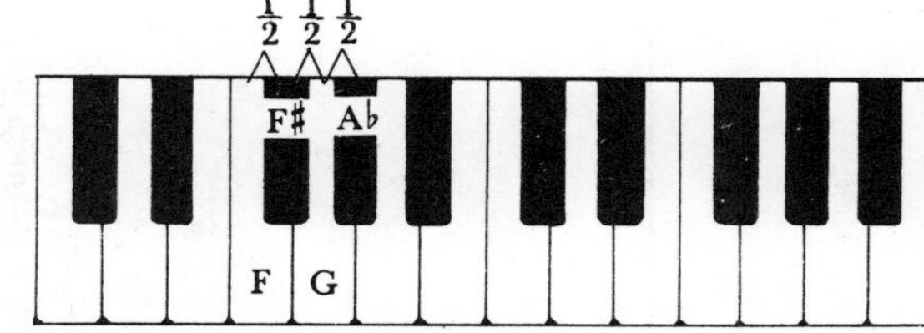

Can we build an f-minor scale using the signature for G-sharp major? No, because there is no key of G-sharp major. Since the enharmonic notation for G-sharp is A-flat, counting up 1 1/2 steps from F also brings us to A-flat.

To determine how many flats there are in the key of A-flat major, use the following rule: the next to the last flat is the key. To reverse this rule, if A-flat is the key, we merely have to name the flats out to A-flat plus one more.

Four flats is the signature for A-flat major. B E A plus one—D. (Recall that the flats in order were B E A D G C F and you were to have made up some mnemonic device to help you remember.)

Draw the clef sign, put in the four flats, and construct the natural minor scale beginning on F.

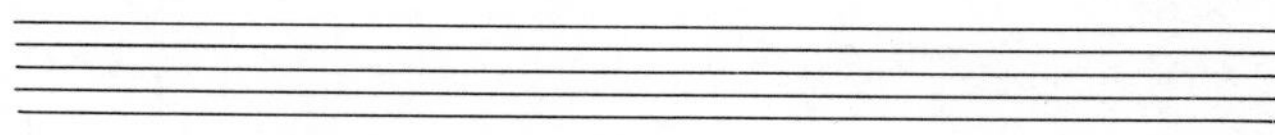

Check to see if the half and whole steps are in their proper places, half steps occurring between 2 and 3 and 5 and 6, with whole steps elsewhere.

287

287

Write a *harmonic* minor scale built on E.

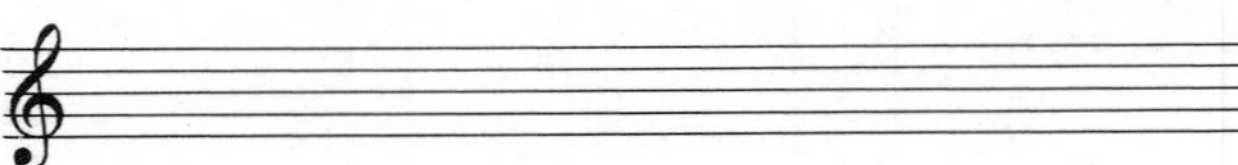

288

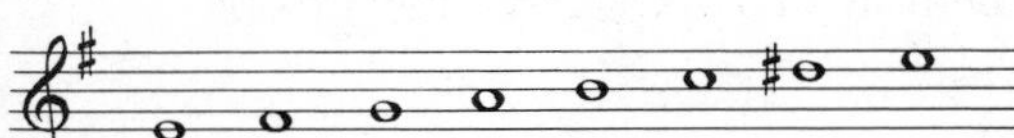

288

In raising the seventh degree of the scale for harmonic minor, care must be taken to determine the present pitch rather than automatically adding a sharp sign. For example, the note may be flatted by the key signature. In this case, the natural (♮) sign would be used to cancel the flat and raise the seventh degree a half step. For example:

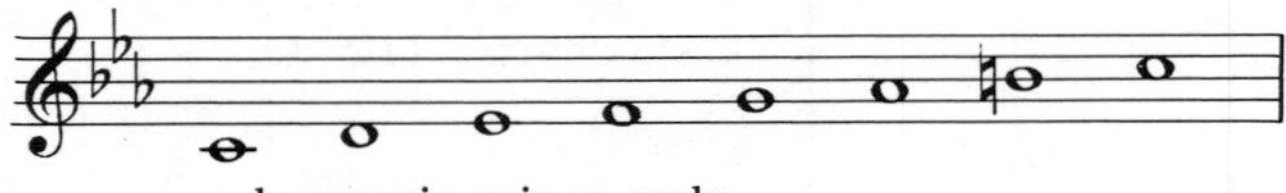

APPLICATION: Tonal Center and Minor Mode

Exercise 33: "America" is shown here as it was in frame 247. The key tone (tonal center) will be sounded and then "America" played. Keep the key tone in mind as you listen. Notice how the music seems to center around F.

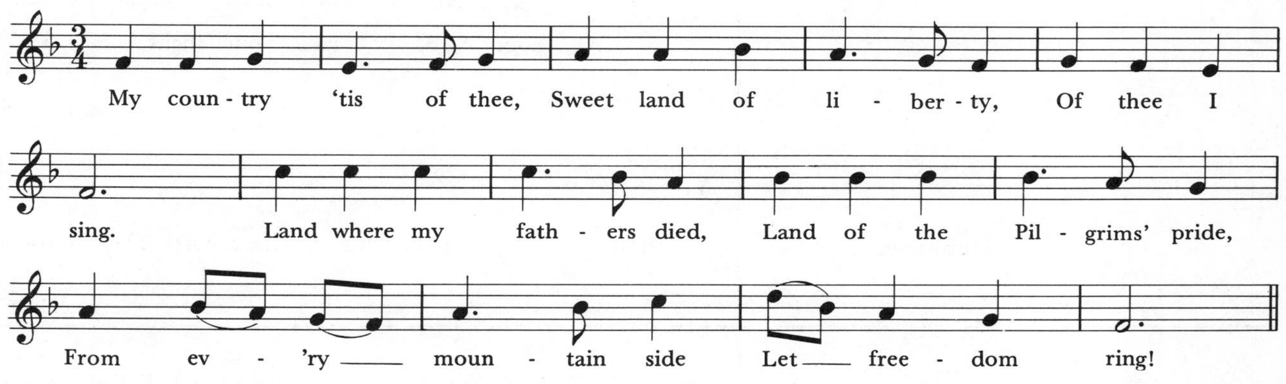

Listening response.

Exercise 34: Listen to "Grandma Grunts." Immediately after listening to the song, try to sing or hum the tonal center. It will then be given on the recording so that you can check your answer.

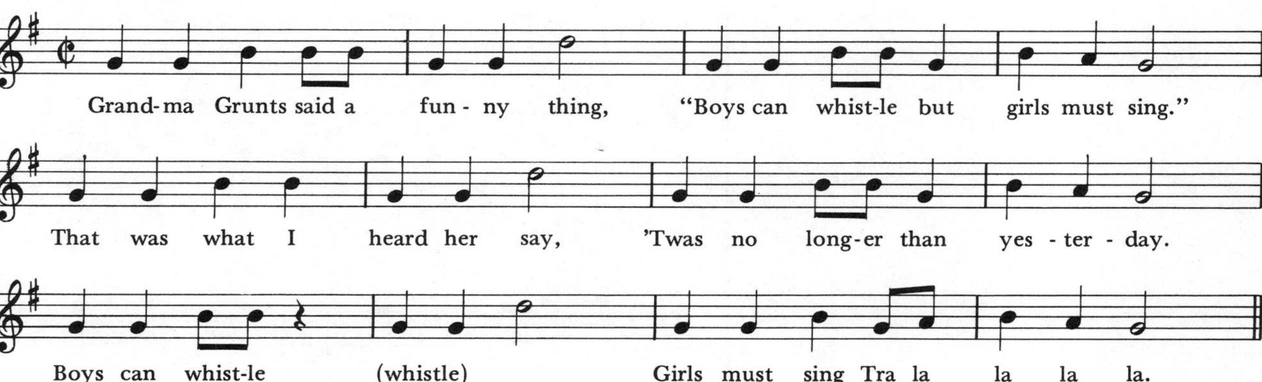

33

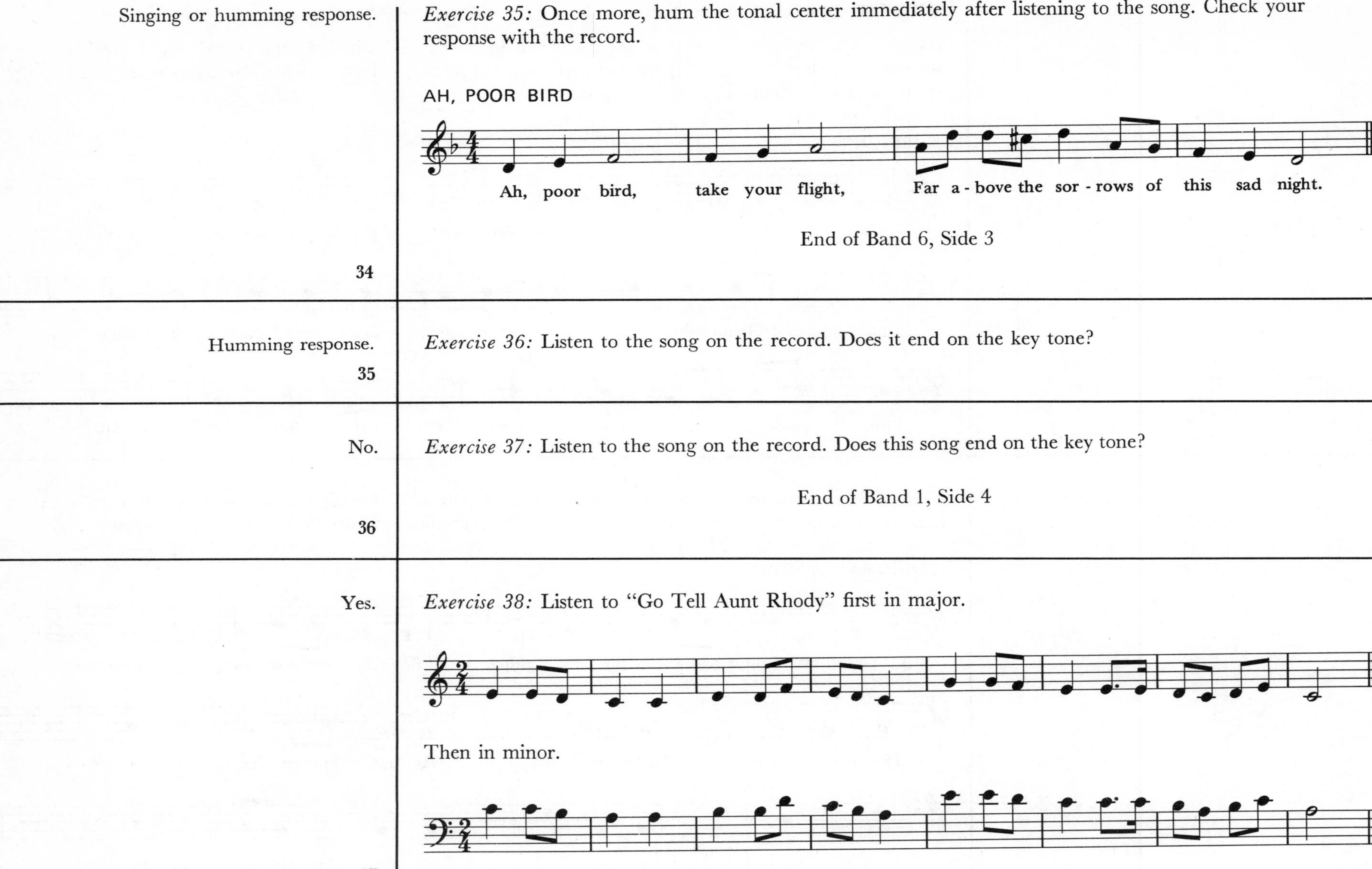

Singing or humming response.

34

Exercise 35: Once more, hum the tonal center immediately after listening to the song. Check your response with the record.

AH, POOR BIRD

Ah, poor bird, take your flight, Far a - bove the sor - rows of this sad night.

End of Band 6, Side 3

Humming response.

35

Exercise 36: Listen to the song on the record. Does it end on the key tone?

No.

36

Exercise 37: Listen to the song on the record. Does this song end on the key tone?

End of Band 1, Side 4

Yes.

37

Exercise 38: Listen to "Go Tell Aunt Rhody" first in major.

Then in minor.

Listening response.

38

Exercise 39: Listen to the major scale and its relative natural minor to hear the difference.

C major

a minor

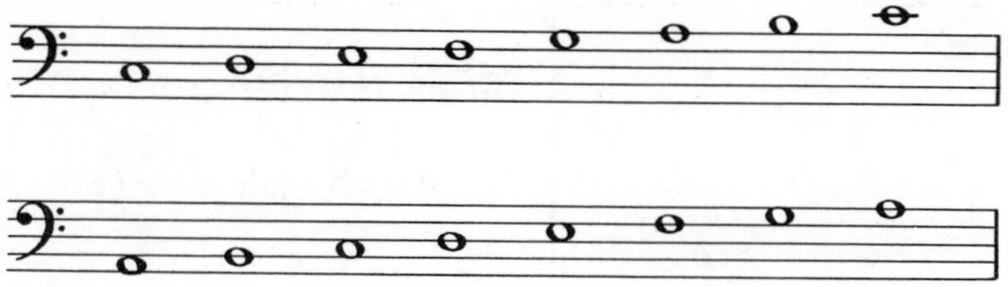

Listening response.

39

Exercise 40: Listen to a harmonic minor scale and then to "Joshua Fit de Battle," which is based on a harmonic minor scale.

JOSHUA

Josh-ua fit de bat-tle of___ Jer - i - cho,___ Jer - i - cho,___ Jer - i - cho,___

Josh-ua fit de bat-tle of___ Jer - i - cho,___ and de walls come a - tum-ble - in' down.

End of Band 2, Side 4 (A STOP BAND)
End of Application Section 3

Listening response.

40

PRETEST for Chapters 14–15: Pentatonic and Interval

Mark the correct answer or *answers.*

1. Which scale(s) is(are) tonal pentatonic? ______

a.
b.

c.
d.

2. Use of only the black keys on the piano forms a:

—— a. major scale

—— b. minor scale

—— c. whole-tone scale

—— d. pentatonic scale

3. A pentatonic scale has:

—— a. 5 different notes

—— b. 6 different notes

—— c. 7 different notes

—— d. 4 different notes

4. The interval from

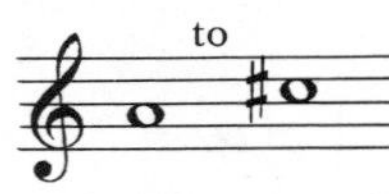
to

would be:

—— a. major third

—— b. minor third

—— c. major second

—— d. minor second

5. The following song is in the:

—— a. major mode

—— b. minor mode

—— c. pentatonic mode

SEE MY PONY

See my po - ny, See my po - ny,

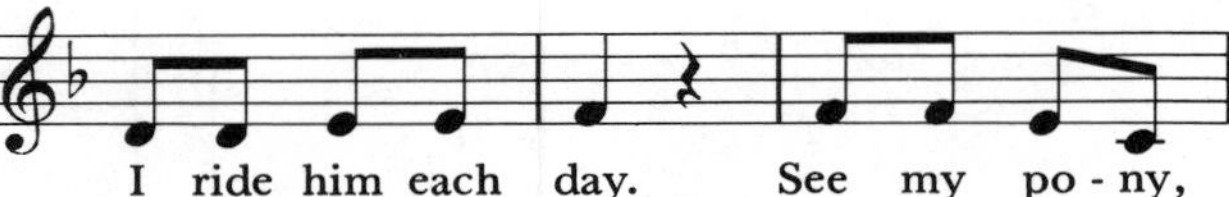
I ride him each day. See my po - ny,

See my po - ny, I ride him each day.

Answers

1. a, c, d.
2. d.
3. a.
4. a.
5. a.

From your score determine if you can omit portions of the text.

175

CHAPTER 14 The Concept of Pentatonic Mode

In addition to the major scale, the minor scales, and the chromatic scale, the pentatonic scale is also important. The goals of this chapter are (1) that you be able to recognize songs written in a pentatonic mode and (2) that you understand the construction of the commonly used pentatonic scales. "Penta" means "five"; the pentatonic scale contains only five pitches before it repeats the first pitch (the octave). The pattern of the pentatonic scale usually looks like this:

This is also pentatonic:

The tonal pentatonic scale is widely used today in elementary music. It is easy for young children to sing because it does not have any intervals as small as the half step. Although the two forms of the scale given in the preceding frame are the most common, the tonal pentatonic scale can be defined as any scale of five pitches with no interval smaller than a whole step. There are still other pentatonic scales: a Javanese scale in which the five pitches are equidistant and a semitonal scale of five pitches which omits either the second and fifth or second and sixth degrees of the regular scale. Only the tonal pentatonic will be discussed here.

The pentatonic scale is composed of ______ pitches plus a repetition of the first pitch.

Five.

289

Play the black keys on the piano. Start on F-sharp and stop on the F-sharp an octave above. You have played a pentatonic scale.

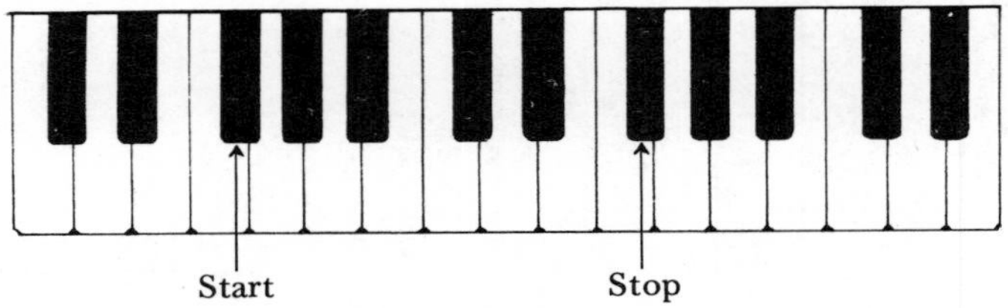

Start Stop

290

Playing response.

290

Compare this tonal pentatonic scale with the major scale. They are identical except that the pentatonic scale does not have the fourth and seventh degrees of the major scale.

1 2 3 4 5 6 7 8

Sing the major scale with numbers. Sing it again, omitting pitch 4 and pitch 7. Sing it several times to gain familiarity with the pattern. Then look at the pentatonic scale and try to sing it with numbers, duplicating the pitches you have been singing. Use the piano to help you in singing.

291

Singing response.

291

Another common form of tonal pentatonic is given below. It is identical to the major scale with the third and seventh omitted.

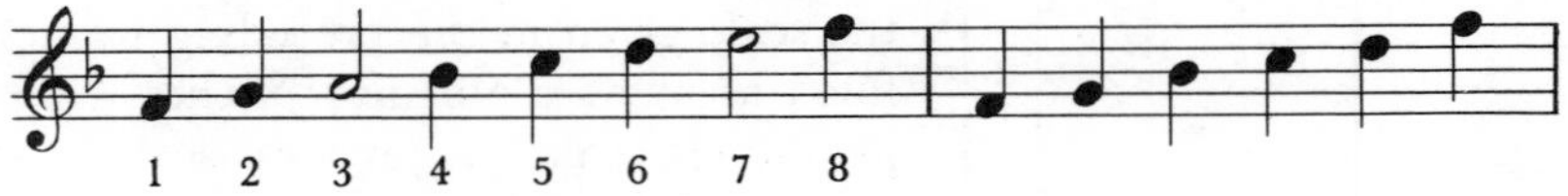

1 2 3 4 5 6 7 8

Again, sing the major scale with numbers, then sing it again omitting pitches 3 and 7. Use the piano to aid your singing. If you play the black keys of the piano from C-sharp to C-sharp an octave higher, you will have this version of the pentatonic scale.

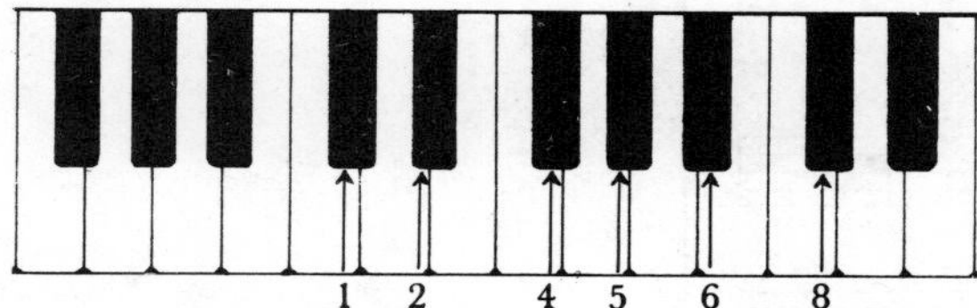

292

Singing response.

292

Pentatonic scales may be constructed on any degree of the chromatic scale. The key signature for the major scale is used—the differences being (1) the absence of half steps and (2) only five notes (plus the octave).

Which of the following is not a tonal pentatonic scale? ______

1.

2.

3.

293

2.

293

Using key signatures, write a tonal pentatonic scale beginning on A and one on C.

A:

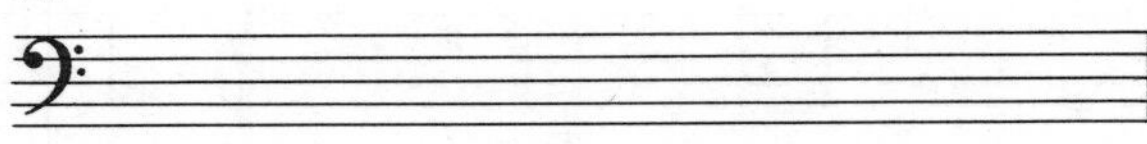

C:

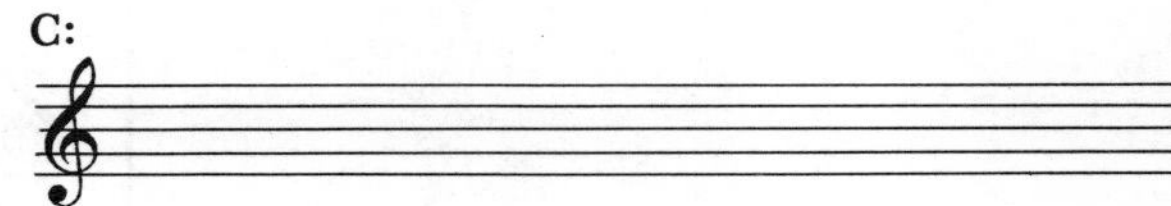

294

294

Technically, the pentatonic scale does not have a fundamental or tonic pitch. Pentatonic melodies can begin and end on any step of the scale.

Using the black notes on the piano, make up a tune starting on any black key and ending on any black key. As long as you avoid the white keys, you will be creating a tonal pentatonic melody.

295

Playing response.

295

The children's song below comes from Singapore. The key signature is for C. When compared to C major scale, what pitches (letter names) are omitted in this song? _______________ Is it in pentatonic mode? ______

THE NEW DRESS

With new cloth my ma - ma sews A new
dress for me with bows. Ma - ma's face will
be so proud and gay When I wear my new dress to - day.

From the UNICEF Book of Children's Songs, *ed. William Kaufman. Used by permission of Stackpole Books.*

296

F and B (4 and 7).

Yes.

296

Examine the following scales. Scale number _______ is not a tonal pentatonic scale.

1.
2.
3.

297

1.

297

Many teachers believe that children's early experiences with singing should be through the use of pentatonic melodies. The wider skips of the pentatonic scale are easier to sing than the half steps present in major and minor, and the patterns seem to be closer to the natural chants that children make up in their play.

Two important recent movements in elementary music—those of Carl Orff and Zoltan Kodály—make great use of pentatonic melody. The Orff system begins with the exclusive use of pentatonic, then later introduces major, and much later minor.

Orff often uses songs that have less than the five notes of the pentatonic scale. The songs below are used in the Orff system. Learn the songs and sing them.

BOBBY SHAFTO

Bob - by Shaf - to's gone to sea, Sil - ver buck - les at his knee;
He'll come back and mar - ry me, Bon - ny Bob - by Shaf - to.

"Bobby Shafto's Gone to Sea" from Book I, Pentatonic of the Orff Schulwerk Music for Children. Copyright © 1956 by B. Schott's Söhne.

How many different pitches in this song? _______

298

Singing response.

3.

298

Sing this song.

THE BELLS IN THE STEEPLE

"The Bells in the Steeple" from Book I, Pentatonic of the Orff Schulwerk Music for Children. Copyright © 1956 by B. Schott's Söhne.

How many different pitches in this song (not counting the octave)? ______ 299

Singing response.

5.

299

Sing this song.

DING DONG

Ding, dong, di - gi - di - gi dong, di - gi - di - gi dong, the cat is gone.

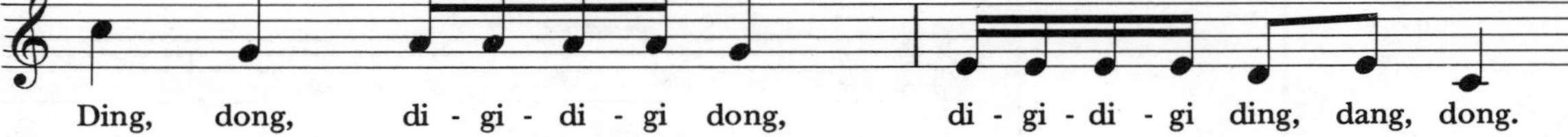

Ding, dong, di - gi - di - gi dong, di - gi - di - gi ding, dang, dong.

"Ding Dong" from Book I, Pentatonic of the Orff Schulwerk Music for Children. Copyright © 1956 by B. Schott's Söhne.

Note the following pattern in the pentatonic melody above: 

It is the typical childhood call used spontaneously in play. 

Find this pattern in the songs in frames 298 and 299.

The number of different notes in "Ding Dong" is ______. 300

Singing response.

5.

300

Inspect and sing the song in this frame and the two following frames. Determine if each is in major mode, minor mode, or pentatonic mode.

MINKA

From the Vol - ga I was rid - ing On my great horse nob - ly strid - ing,
When I saw in sha - dows hid - ing, Min - ka, charm - ing Min - ka.

Is this song in major, minor, or pentatonic mode? ______________

301

Singing response.

Minor.

301

HOW OLD ARE YOU?

How old are you my pret- ty lit -tle miss? How old are you my ho - ney? She
an - swered me with a tee - hee - hee, "I'll be six - teen this Sun - day."

"How Old Are You?" from Book I, Pentatonic of the Orff Schulwerk Music for Children. Copyright © 1956 by B. Schott's Söhne.

Is this song in major, minor, or pentatonic mode? ______________

302

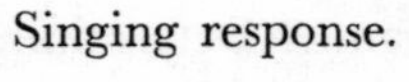

Singing response.

Pentatonic.

302

EARLY ONE MORNING

Ear - ly one morn - ing be - fore the sun had ri - sen, I heard a
blue - bird in the fields — gai - ly sing, "South winds are blow - ing,
Green grass is grow - ing, We — come to her - ald the mer - ry — spring."

Is this song in major, minor, or pentatonic mode? ______________

303

Singing response.

Major.

303

CHAPTER 15 Optional Section: The Concept of Interval

To understand the meaning of interval is simple: an interval is the distance between two pitches. In discussing scales we considered intervals of half step and whole step. The half step is the smallest interval used in the music of the Western world; the whole step is simply two half steps. In finding the relative minor from the major key, we used an interval of 1 1/2 steps.

To measure intervals and learn to recognize them when listening to or performing music is *not* so simple, but a knowledge of intervals and their sounds is very helpful in singing new music at sight and in helping children learn music.

The aims of this chapter are to help you (1) learn to identify intervals by number (seconds, thirds, fourths, etc.); (2) understand major, minor, and perfect intervals; and (3) begin to use intervals in listening and singing.

Intervals are measured from the bottom pitch. By using the major scale one can easily understand how intervals are measured and labeled. In the C scale, for example, the distance from C to D, which we have called a whole step, is labeled a second. From C to E a third, from C to F a fourth, and so on. Examine the diagram below.

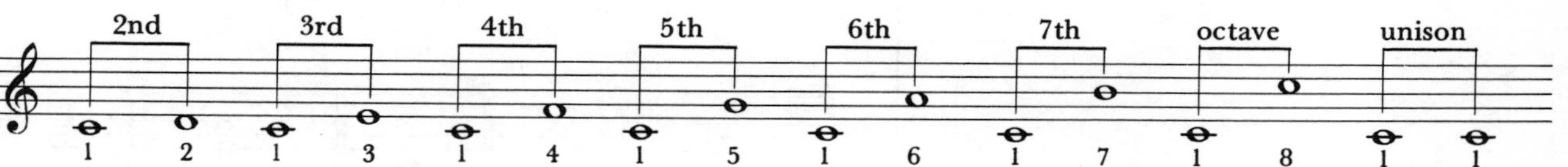

In measuring intervals, call the ______________ pitch "one." Count both the starting and ending pitch to determine the name of the interval. For example C to D is a second; *C* D *E*, a third;
1 2 3

C D E F G A *B*, a seventh; and so on.
1 2 3 4 5 6 7

Lower or bottom.

304

Write the name of each of these intervals:

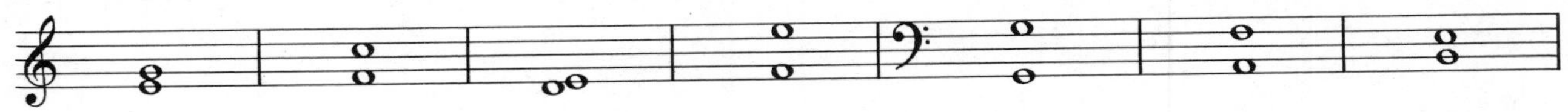

In frame 300 this interval was given as the typical childhood call. What interval is it? _______

305

3rd, 5th, 2nd, 7th, octave, 6th, 4th.

3rd.

305

Besides having the numerical designation of 2nd, 3rd, 4th, and so on, intervals are also labeled major, minor, perfect, augmented, and diminished. We need only consider major, minor, and perfect.

An interval from C–E is considered a major 3rd because E is a note in the C-major scale.

C to A is a major 6th.

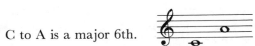

When the top note of an interval fits into the major scale of the bottom note, the interval is major (4ths and 5ths are called perfect rather than major.)

Label each interval below, using both the numerical designation, 2nd, 3rd, 4th, etc., and P (perfect) or M (major). Remember, 2nds, 3rds, 6ths, and 7ths are major; 4ths and 5ths are perfect.

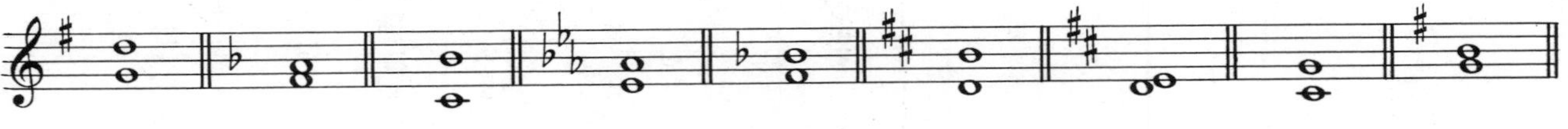

Play the intervals on the piano.

306

P 5th, M 3rd, M 7th, P 4th, P 4th, M 6th, M 2nd, P 5th, M 3rd.

Playing response.

306

When major intervals are made a half step smaller, they become minor intervals. Examine the intervals below:

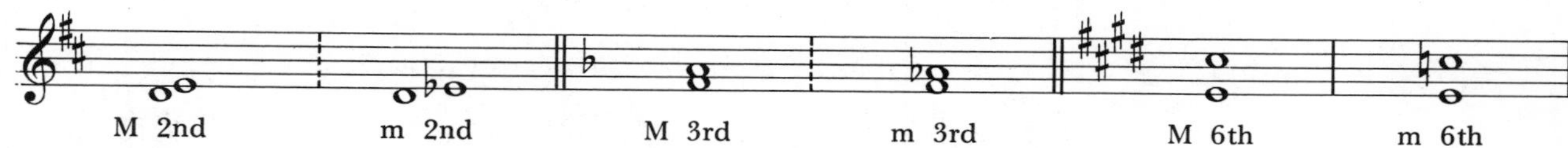

The perfect intervals, 4ths and 5ths, may also be made smaller, but their alteration is not important in classroom music and therefore is omitted here.

Label the following intervals. Use numerical labels plus M, m, or P.

Play the intervals on the piano. Sing them.

307

P 5th, M 3rd, P 4th, m 3rd, M 6th, P 4th, Octave, P 5th, m 7th.

Playing and singing response.

307

PRETEST for Chapter 16: Harmony

Mark the correct answer or *answers.*

1. Harmony can be created by:
   —— a. adding a descant
   —— b. singing a round
   —— c. more than one voice singing a single part
   —— d. singing a cadenza

2. A triad consists of:
   —— a. the root, fundamental, and octave
   —— b. the fundamental, third, and fifth
   —— c. the root, second, and third
   —— d. the root, third, and fifth

3. One can visually recognize a triad because the notes are:
   —— a. written on consecutive lines
   —— b. written on consecutive spaces
   —— c. written on consecutive pitches
   —— d. written for consecutive strings on the guitar

4. Write major triads above these notes.

5. A triad is also:
   —— a. an arpeggio
   —— b. a descant
   —— c. an appoggiatura
   —— d. a chord

6. Write a IV chord in D major, bass clef.

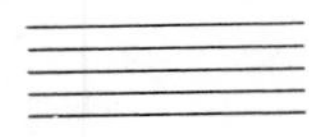

7. Write the I, IV, V^7 chords in the key of B♭ major.

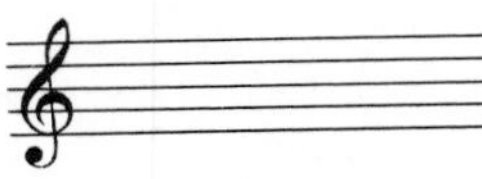

8. Write the I, IV, V^7 chords in b minor (watch the V^7 in minor).

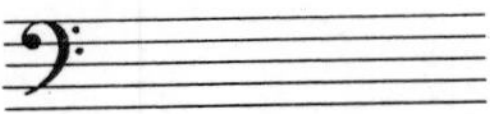

9. Identify the following chords. Use letters.

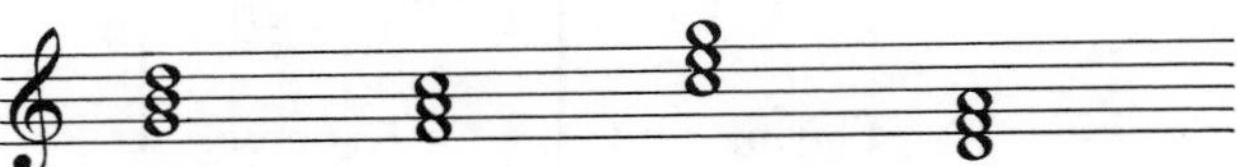

10. Identify the pitches of triads in the following keys. Use letters.

Key of B-flat

I ____________

IV ____________

V^7 ____________

Key of E

I ____________

IV ____________

V^7 ____________

11. Construct a chord on the fifth degree of the scale in the key of A-flat.

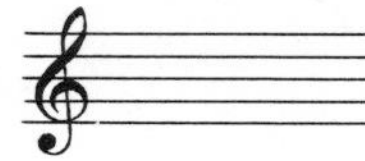

12. Which of these chords are minor chords in a major key?

—— a. I (i)

—— b. II (ii)

—— c. III (iii)

—— d. IV (iv)

13. Change the following major chords to minor chords:

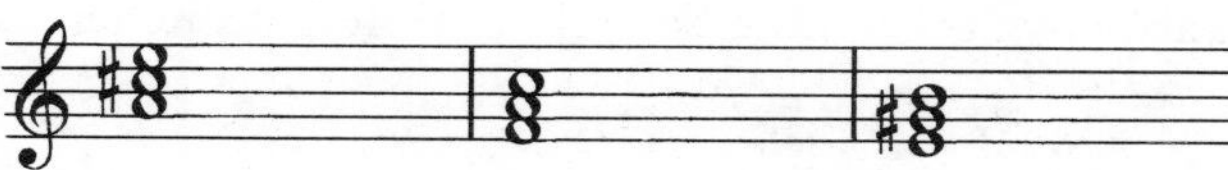

14. Construct a V^7 chord in g minor.

15. Which chords are written incorrectly?

Answers

1. a, b.
2. b, d.
3. a, b.
4.

5. d.
6.

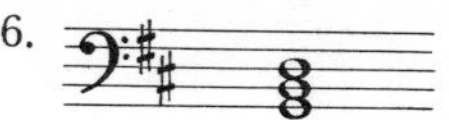

7.

I IV V^7

8.

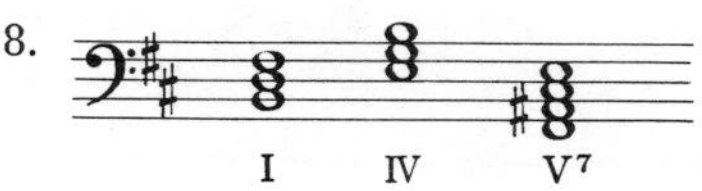

9. G, F, C, d.
10. Key of B-flat.
    I = B-flat, D, F.
    IV = E-flat, G, B-flat.
    V^7 = F, A, C E-flat
    Key of E:
    I = E, G-sharp, B.
    IV = A, C-sharp, E.
    V^7 = B, D-sharp, F-sharp, A.
11.

12. b, c.
13.

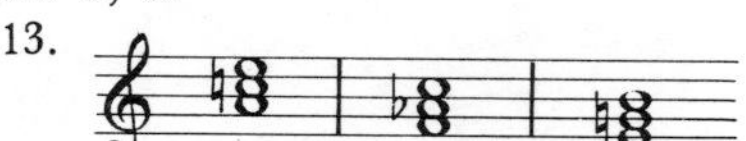

14.

15. a, b.

From your score determine if you can omit portions of the text.

CHAPTER 16 The Concept of Harmony

The four basic ingredients (concepts) of music are duration, pitch, amplitude, and timbre. Timbre, you recall, is the quality of an instrument, that which distinguishes a clarinet from a cornet while each plays the same pitch. Duration, pitch, and amplitude have been previously discussed. Each of these concepts can be discussed simply, but each also offers more complex insights as one's knowledge of music increases. Harmony is one aspect of the concept of pitch; rather than a single pitch being sounded, two or more pitches are sounded together to create harmony.

When harmony occurs, at least _______ different pitches that seem to fit together are being sounded.

308

Two.

Much singing in the elementary grades is unison singing—everyone singing the same pitch. Upper elementary students who have an adequate background in music, however, should be able to sing in parts, another way of saying two or more pitches sounded at the same time. Part singing is often called harmonizing.

The round is a unique form of harmony. Everyone sings the same melody (or "part"), but groups of singers enter at different points in the melody, thus combining two, three, or more pitches to make harmony. A round is easy to learn, for all the students sing the identical melody. Inexperienced singers, however, gain little concept of harmony from singing rounds because they tend to pay attention only to their own part.

TEETH AND GUMS

*
Thir - ty white hor-ses up-on a red hill, Now they champ, now they tramp, now they stand still. ___

From "Homer's Woe." Copyright 1967, 1968 by Boosey & Hawkes, Inc.

Learn the two-part round above. If possible, find another person to sing it as a round with you. The second person begins when the first sings the first "now."

308

309

Singing response.

309

As the student's musical knowledge increases, he can learn to sing music written in five, six, or more parts or by playing an instrument he can participate in band or orchestra in which as many as twenty different parts are involved, all fitted together by the composer to produce the desired sound.

When the student begins to participate in making harmony—even simple two-part harmony— his musical independence becomes crucial. With unison singing, he can lean upon others; when a second part is added, he must know which sounds are his and perform them accurately. Although many classroom activities are group activities, musical independence remains the primary objective.

The combining of two or more musical parts may be a complicated experience for the student. The teacher helps prepare him for this experience by adding harmony to the unison singing in the early grades. The teacher's ability to add a harmony part is therefore important. There are many ways in which the teacher can create harmony with the unison singing of the class: he may sing a second part or play it on a songflute or recorder; he may play chords on the piano that fit the melody being sung; a chordal accompaniment may be played on the Autoharp, guitar, or ukulele; a simple two- or three-note part may be played by an advanced pupil with the teacher's help. One objective of this chapter is to provide an understanding of the function of harmony so that the acquisition of harmonic skills may be at least begun. Another objective is the ability to write the principal chords—I, IV, and V—in any key. The third objective is the recognition of harmonic symbols in order to use them with Autoharp, ukulele, piano, or some other chording instrument.

A simple way to introduce two-part singing is through the use of descants. A *descant* is often a florid melody sung by a few select voices added to the regular melody. In elementary music the term is used to indicate a simple second part using two or three harmonizing pitches. It may be either a higher or lower part. After the entire class has learned the melody of the song, part of the class (or all of it) may learn the descant; then the two parts can be sung together.

When you have one-half of your class sing "Row, row, row your boat gently down the stream" and the other half of the class begins the song when the first half has finished the word "stream," elementary harmony is produced and the class is singing a ______________.

310

Round.

310

A simple descant may be added to the well-known singing game "Paw-Paw Patch." First, learn the song.

Melody

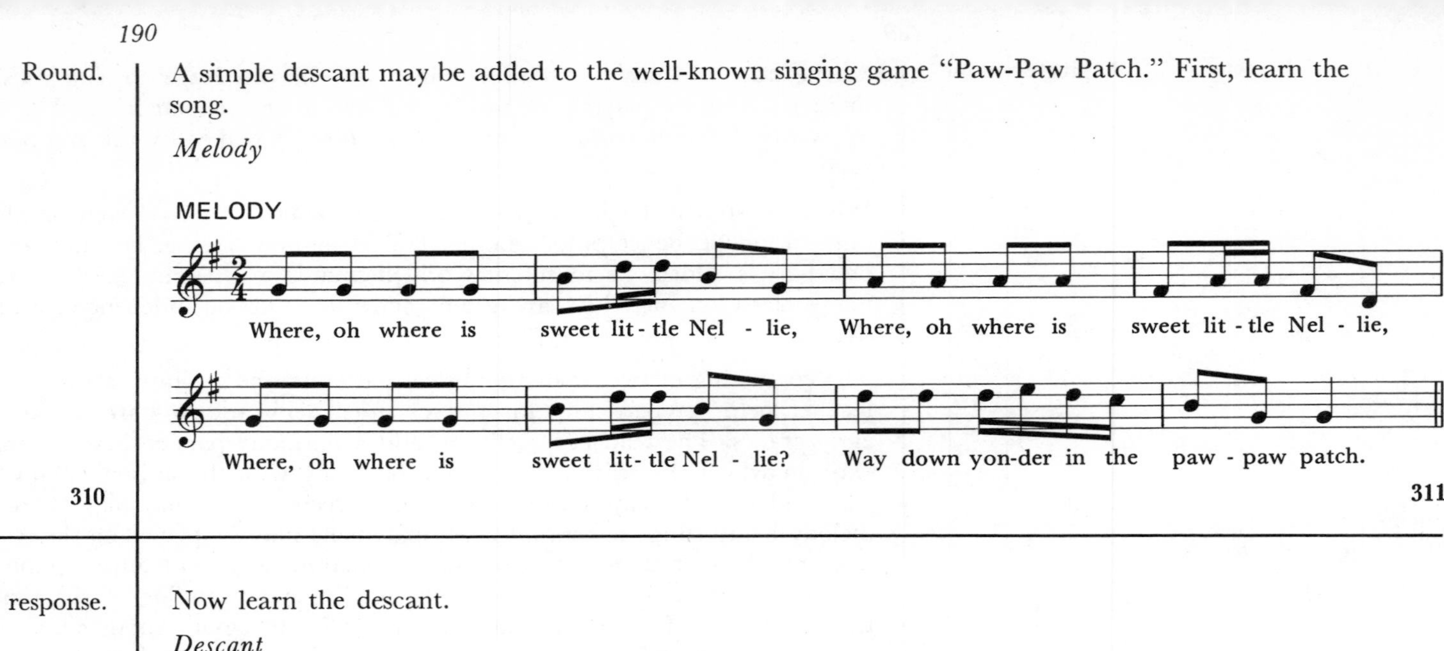

311

Singing response.

311

Now learn the descant.

Descant

Combine the melody and the descant.

312

Singing response.

A descant may be either written out or improvised by using tones from the chords that fit the melody. Thus, understanding chord structure is important, for almost all harmony parts are built out of chords. A chord is three or more pitches sounding together. There are many different kinds of chords, but the most common is the triad. A triad is a three-tone chord made up of the root, or fundamental (the bottom note), plus the pitches a third and a fifth above. The pitches "third" and "fifth" are so named because they are the third and fifth notes of the scale built on the fundamental.

5 fifth
3 third
1 root

Play these triads on the piano.

312 | 313

Playing response.

Identify those chords which are triads. _______

1 2 3 4

313 | 314

1, 4.

When a triad is written in the normal position, if the root is written on the second space, on which line or space will the third of the chord be written? ________________

314 | 315

Third space.

If the root of a chord is C, what note is the fifth? _______

315 | 316

G.

If the third of a chord is A, what note is the root? _______

316 | 317

F. The eighth note or octave above the root (fundamental) is often added to the triad. The addition of this note does not change the chord structure because the octave is a repetition of the fundamental pitch (root). Triads in regular position are easy to recognize visually because all three pitches fall on either adjacent lines or adjacent spaces. For example, in the treble clef, middle C is on a line, and so the triad C–E–G will fall on three adjacent lines. In the bass clef, C is on a space; the triad C–E–G falls on three adjacent spaces—the C space and the two spaces immediately above.

With octave:

Write triads above these notes. The given note is the fundamental or root.

The name of a triad is the name of the note that is the fundamental or root. For example,

is called an F chord or F triad because F is the root.

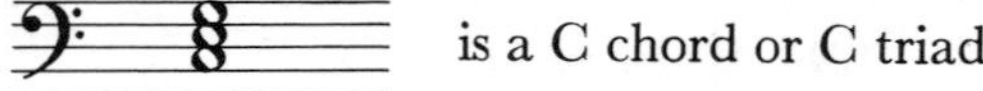 is a C chord or C triad.

317

318

318

Identify these chords (triads) by their letter names.

319

C, E-flat, A.

A, D, C.

319

Chords, like scales, can be major or minor. To determine the major or minor quality of a chord depends on knowledge of the key signature. Knowing the key signature is important for many aspects of music.

The key of D major has ______ sharp(s). They are ______________

The key of F major has ______ flat(s). They are ______________

The key of E-flat major has ______ flat(s). They are ______________

320

2, F-sharp C-sharp.

1, B-flat.

3, B-flat E-flat A-flat.

320

A triad in which all three pitches fit into the key of the root is a major triad. That is, if the third and the fifth above the root are the third and fifth notes of that major scale, the triad is a major triad.

For example, is a major triad.

The key of F major has one flat, B-flat; thus the scale is

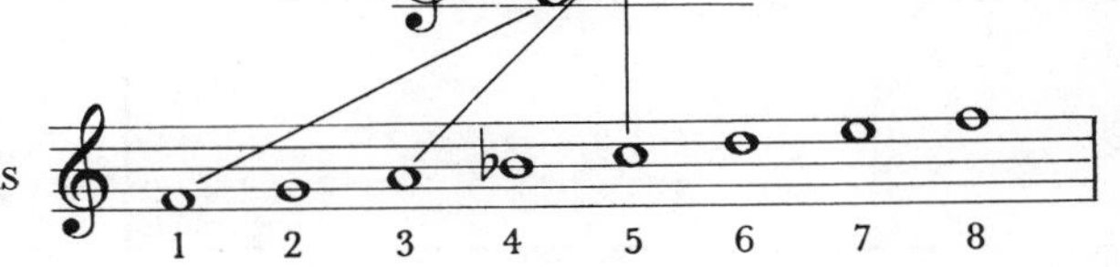

The root, F, the third, A, and the fifth, C, are identical in the scale and in the chord.

Draw an X through the triads that are major triads.

321

321

Draw an X through the chords that are major triads.

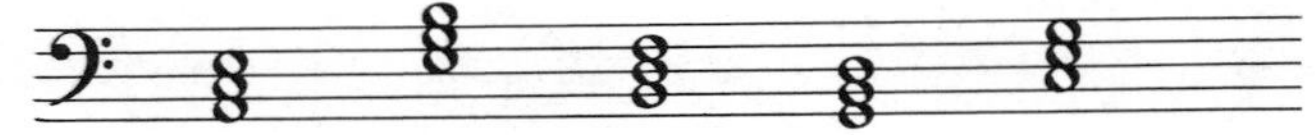

322

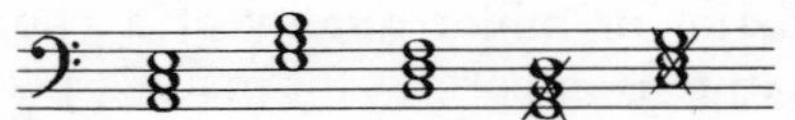

322

Often the terms "chord" and "triad" are used interchangeably. When no other label is given to the chord than its letter name (C chord, G chord, etc.), a major triad is indicated.

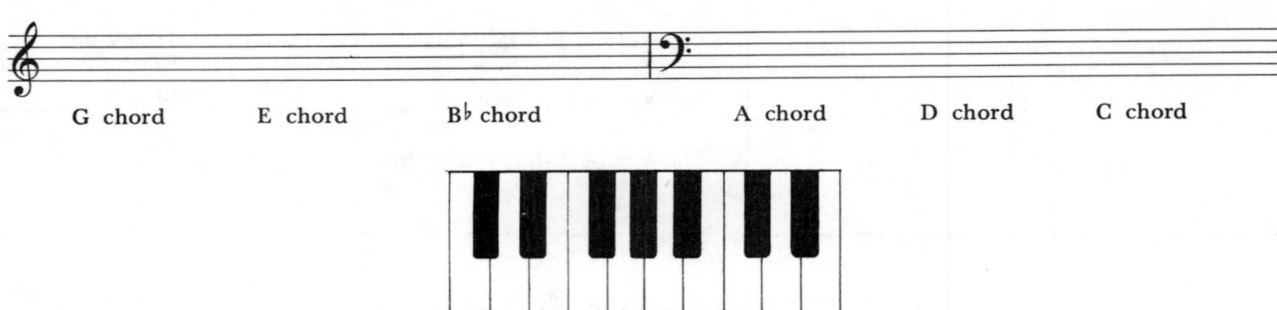

Write the chords (major triads) indicated on the staff, using accidentals where necessary. Use your knowledge of key signatures. One can count up two whole steps from the root to correctly identify the third and 1 1/2 steps from the third to find the fifth, but this is cumbersome and does not make use of the important concept of key signatures and tonality. If possible, play the chords on the piano.

323

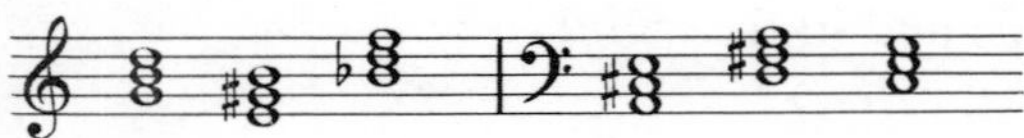

Playing response.

323

Make the triads below major triads by writing in the key signature. The name of the key is identical with the name of the root. Name the chord.

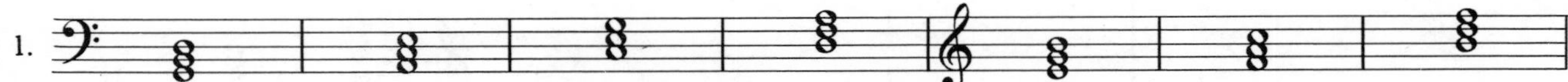

Make the triads below major triads by using an accidental in front of the note(s) that need(s) it. If the root is sharped or flatted, this still indicates the name of the key signature and knowledge of the key signature is needed to determine which accidentals are required.

324

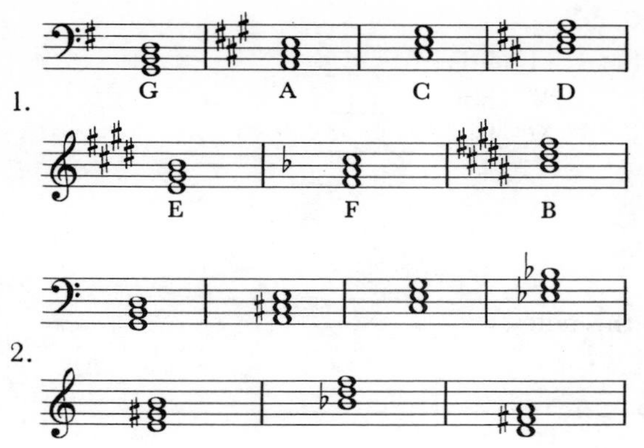

In any major key, triads whose fundamentals are either the first, fourth, or fifth note of the scale (counting up from one as the tonal center) are always major chords. Many songs can be harmonized using these three major chords. Since these are major chords in any key, it is more meaningful to identify them by function rather than by the name of the fundamental or root note. The name given is their function in the scale, I, IV, or V; chords are designated by roman numerals and pitches by arabic numbers. They are called "one chord," "four chord," and "five chord."

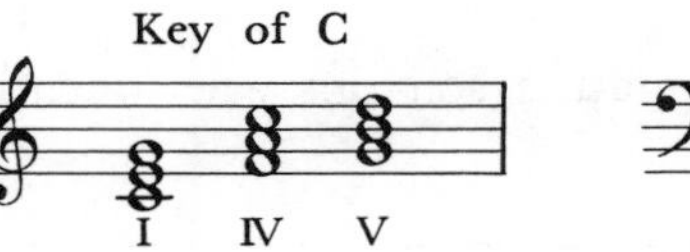

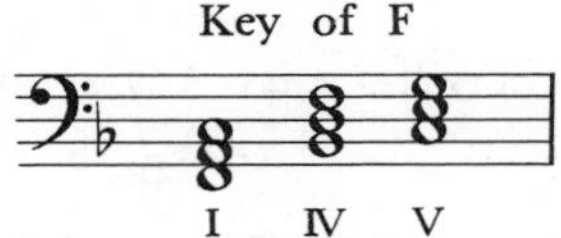

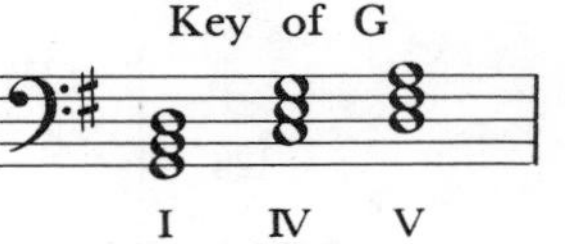

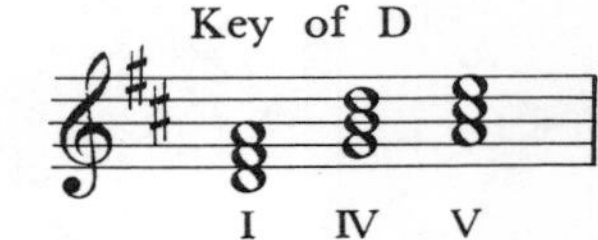

If you compare the chord tones above with the scales as shown below, you will notice that the I, IV, and V are always major chords.

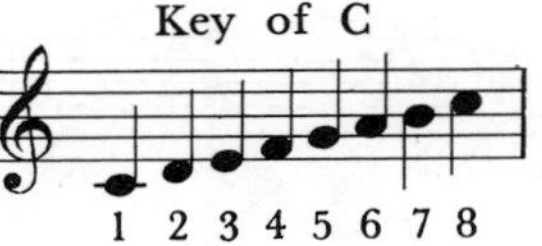

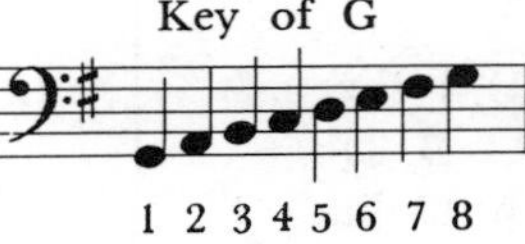

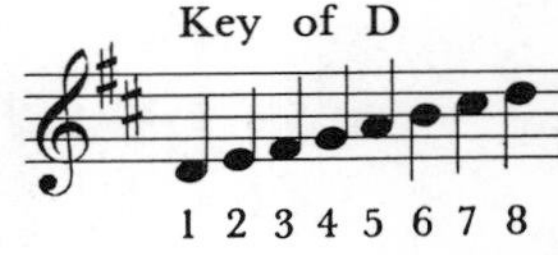

Play these chords on the piano, Autoharp, or other instrument. Try to play them without looking at the notation.

Playing response.

Chords are named by the root (fundamental)—C chord, F chord, B-flat chord, etc.—as well as by number—I, IV, V—either designation indicating a major triad. In order to harmonize a melody, we must be able to find the I, IV, and V in the key of the melody. When these three important chords are located, we can call them by letter name or number name. For example,

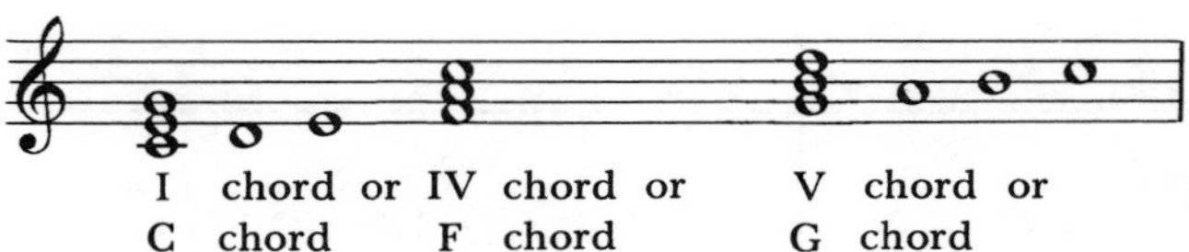

Give the letter name (root) for these chords:

Key of G major: I chord _______
IV chord _______
V chord _______

Key of F major: I chord _______
IV chord _______
V chord _______

G major: G
C
D

F major: F
B-flat
C

326

For practice, write the letter names of the chord *notes* for

Key of G: I chord ______
IV chord ______
V chord ______

Key of D: I chord ______
IV chord ______
V chord ______

Key of B-flat: I chord ______
IV chord ______
V chord ______

(Remember what each key signature contains when identifying the notes.)

327

G: G, B, D.
C, E, G.
D, F-sharp, A.

D: D, F-sharp, A.
G, B, D.
A, C-sharp, E.

B-flat: B-flat, D, F.
E-flat, G, B-flat.
F, A, C.

327

The song below uses only the I and V chords for harmony. Write these two chords on the staff below. Play the two chords on the piano.

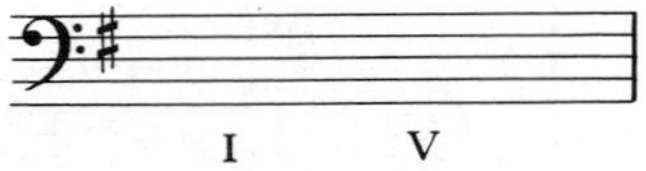

I V

Learn the song. Play the chords while you sing the song.

CLEMENTINE

I I I V
Oh my dar - ling, Oh my dar - ling, Oh my dar - ling Cle - men - tine, You are

V I V I
lost and gone for - ev - er, dread - ful sor - ry Cle - men - tine.

328

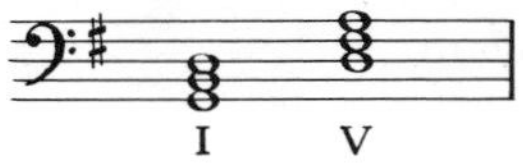

I V

Playing and singing response.

328

When a chord accompaniment is used with a song, the chords are played on the strong beat(s) of the measure—count ONE in duple or triple meter, counts ONE and THREE in quadruple meter (unless the tempo is so fast that only one chord is needed for the measure). When no chords are indicated for a melody and you wish to create an accompaniment "by ear," the chord is usually chosen that matches the melody note on the strong beat(s). For example, the melody below has F on the strong beat of measure 1 and G on the strong beat of measure 2. The I chord (F chord —FAC) goes with F in the first measure; the V chord (C chord—CEG) goes with G in the second measure.

However, the ear must be a guide since there may be more than one chord that matches the melody note. Students should begin at an early age to listen carefully to music and decide on the appropriateness of chords through their own judgments. Experimenting with an Autoharp, piano, or other instrument is an important step in understanding this concept.

The Autoharp is commonly used to accompany songs in the classroom. It is an excellent instrument to use when learning to harmonize melodies. It is played by depressing bars on which chord names are written and strumming to produce the sound.

The song below can be harmonized with the Autoharp or with the piano by playing the designated chords on the *downbeat* of each measure. Play these on an Autoharp.

SANDY LAND

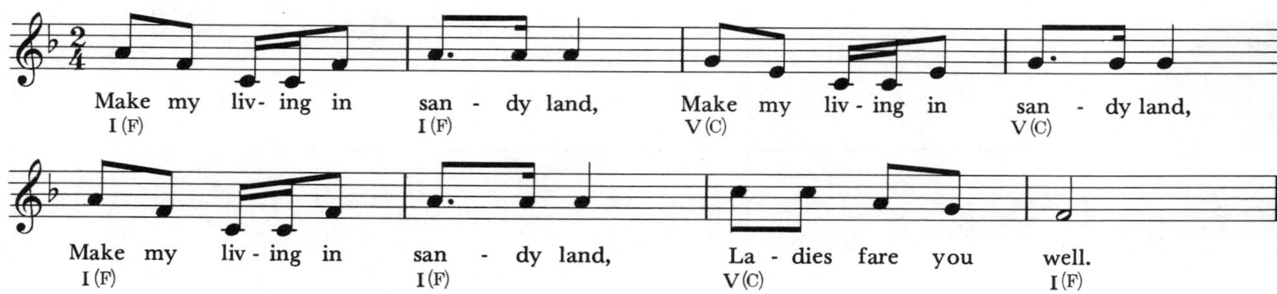

In addition to triads, chords of four or more notes are often used. A four-note chord is called a seventh chord because the fourth pitch is seven notes above the root.

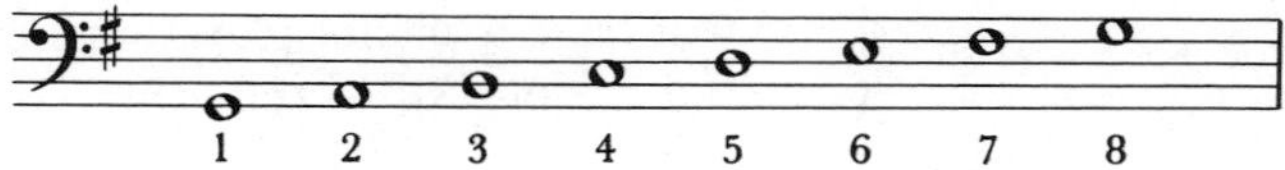

A seventh chord with a root of G would be G, B, D, F-sharp and designated I^7 in the key of G.

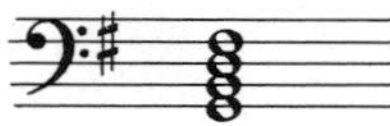

The most common seventh chord (four-note chord) in elementary music is the V^7. Construct a V^7 based on the G scale.

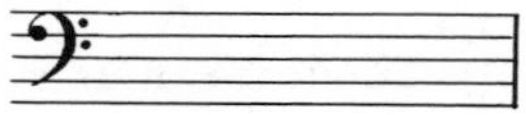

Playing response.

329

If you used the regular V chord  and added the note on the next higher line (the seventh note above D, you probably understand how to construct seventh chords.

Write the I, IV, V, and V^7 chords in the key of B-flat. Put in the key signature.

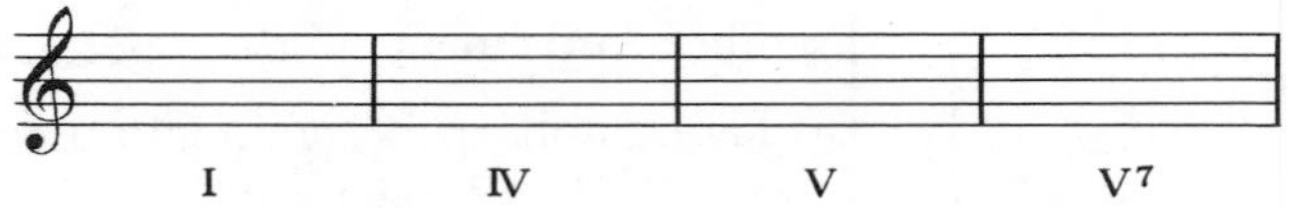

I IV V V^7

330

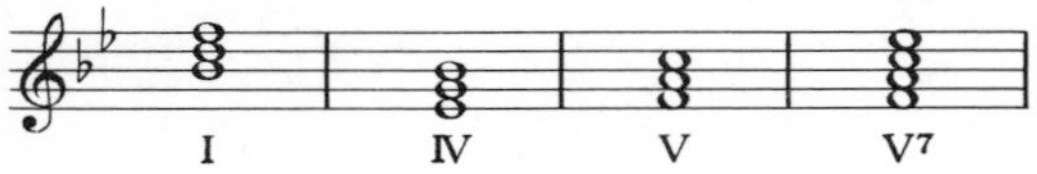

I IV V V^7

330

Identify the incorrect chords by drawing an X through them.

I IV V^7 I V I

331

I IV V^7 I V I

331

Although chords built on the 1, 4, and 5 pitches of the scale are the most common, chords can be built on any step of the scale.

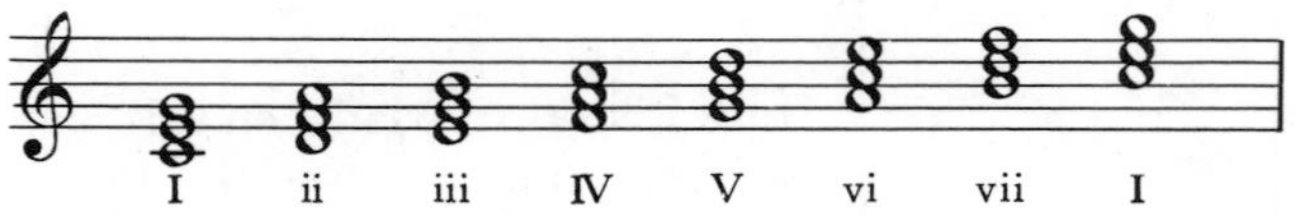

I ii iii IV V vi vii I

If you have a piano, play the above chords. Notice that only the C, F, and G (I, IV, and V) triads sound major. All of the other chords except B are minor triads.

332

Playing response.

332

If you are familiar with major key signatures, the reason why certain chords are major and certain are minor may be apparent to you. The minor chords each have one note, the third, which is not in the key of the root of that chord. For example, the ii chord in C major is D–F–A. F is not in the key of D, but F-sharp is. (The key of D has two sharps, F-sharp and C-sharp.) Check each of the other minor chords in the same manner. B is not minor because it has two notes that are not in the key of the root; it is called a diminished triad.

Since the minor triad has only one pitch different from the major triad, it is easy to change a chord from major to minor: merely lower the middle note (3rd of the chord) by one half step.

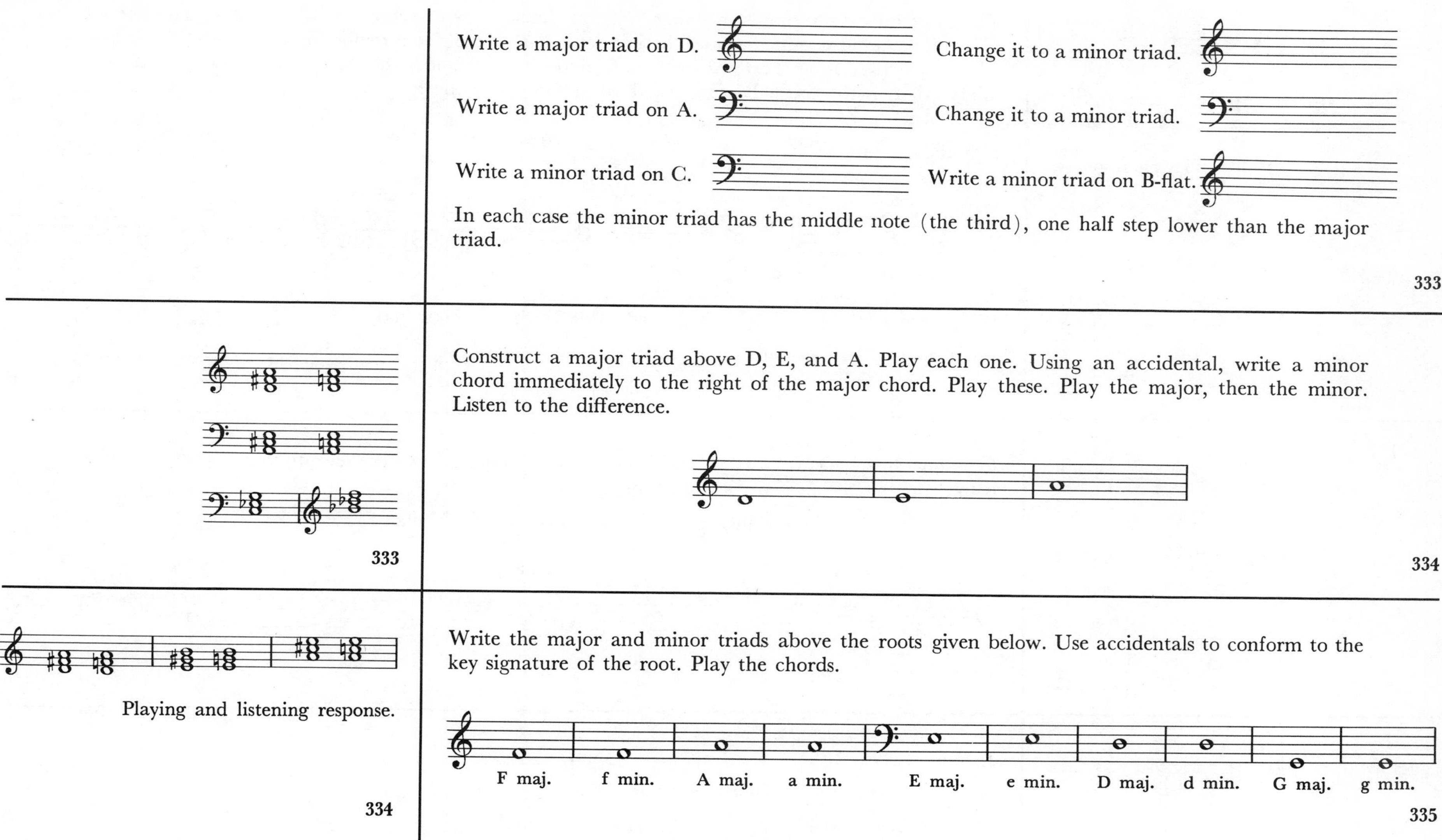
Write a major triad on D.
Change it to a minor triad.
Write a major triad on A.
Change it to a minor triad.
Write a minor triad on C.
Write a minor triad on B-flat.
In each case the minor triad has the middle note (the third), one half step lower than the major triad.
333
333
Construct a major triad above D, E, and A. Play each one. Using an accidental, write a minor chord immediately to the right of the major chord. Play these. Play the major, then the minor. Listen to the difference.
334
Playing and listening response.
334
Write the major and minor triads above the roots given below. Use accidentals to conform to the key signature of the root. Play the chords.
F maj.
f min.
A maj.
a min.
E maj.
e min.
D maj.
d min.
G maj.
g min.
335

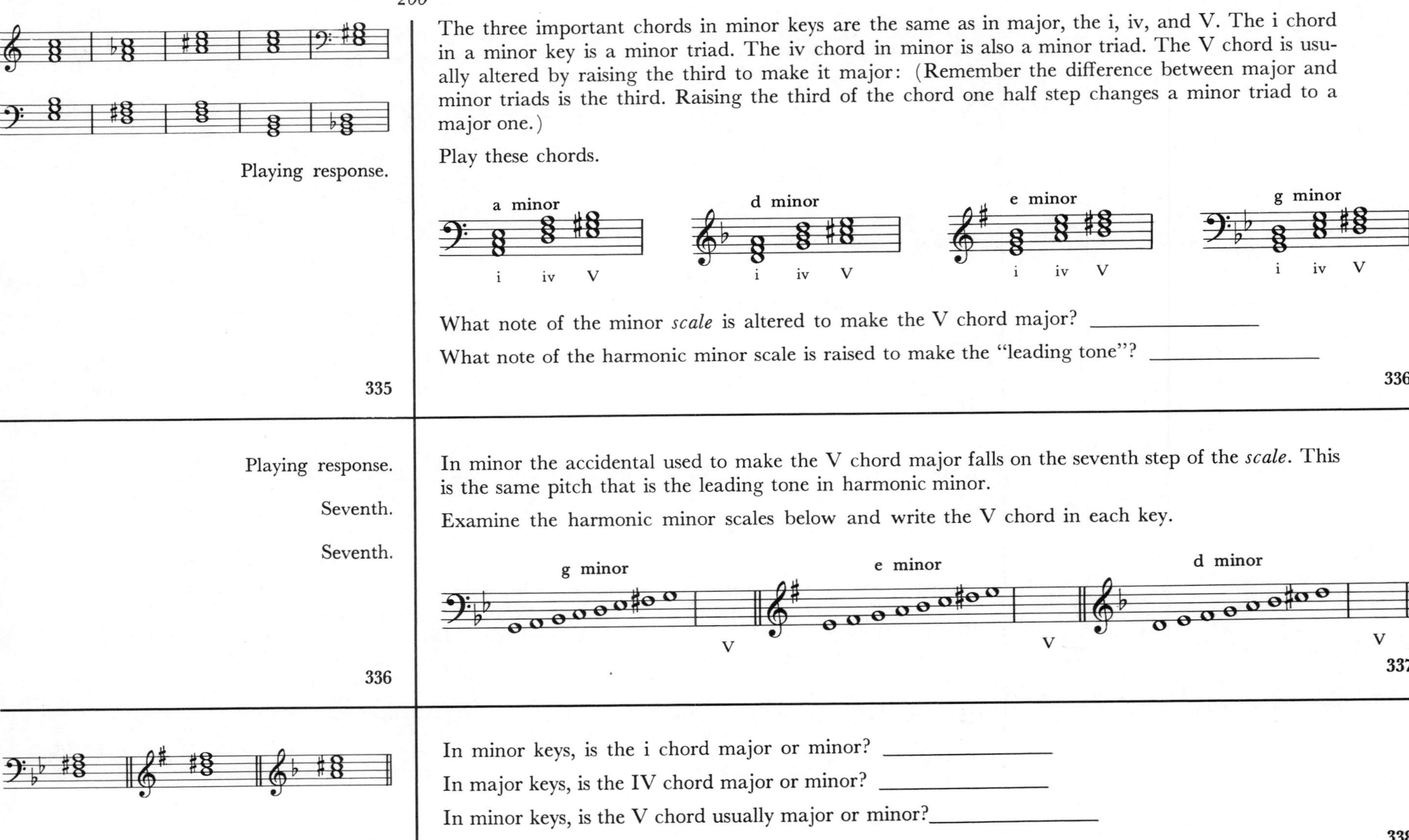

Playing response.

335

The three important chords in minor keys are the same as in major, the i, iv, and V. The i chord in a minor key is a minor triad. The iv chord in minor is also a minor triad. The V chord is usually altered by raising the third to make it major: (Remember the difference between major and minor triads is the third. Raising the third of the chord one half step changes a minor triad to a major one.)

Play these chords.

What note of the minor *scale* is altered to make the V chord major? ______________

What note of the harmonic minor scale is raised to make the "leading tone"? ______________

336

Playing response.

Seventh.

Seventh.

336

In minor the accidental used to make the V chord major falls on the seventh step of the *scale*. This is the same pitch that is the leading tone in harmonic minor.

Examine the harmonic minor scales below and write the V chord in each key.

337

337

In minor keys, is the i chord major or minor? ______________

In major keys, is the IV chord major or minor? ______________

In minor keys, is the V chord usually major or minor? ______________

338

Minor.

Major.

Usually major because it is usually altered.

338

The song below is in the key of c minor. Write the chords that could be used to add harmony. Learn the song; then play the chords while you sing the melody.

SONG OF HOPE

Hope and faith are still with - in the He-brew heart, Peo - ple of Zi - on do not drift a -part.

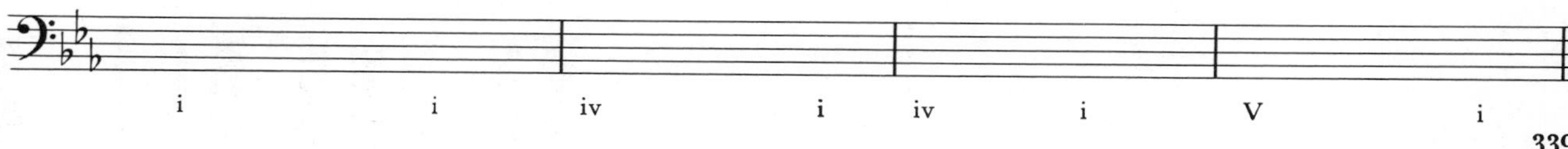
i i iv i iv i V i

339

I IV I IV I V I

Playing and singing response.

339

Write the i, iv, V triads in the following minor keys:

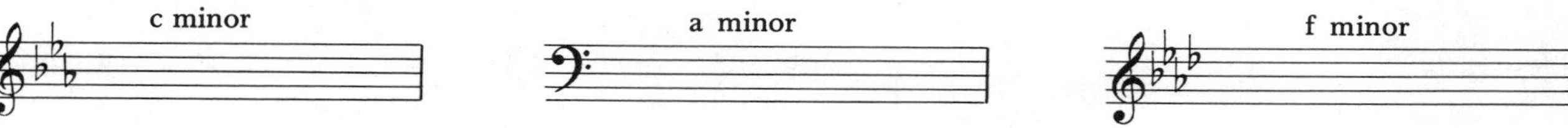
c minor
a minor
f minor

When key signatures are used, the only accidental needed is the one that raises the third of the V chord (seventh of the scale).

Be careful to place the notes on the proper line or space to create the chords correctly.

340

340

In minor keys as well as major keys, the V chord is frequently played with the fourth pitch added—the seventh above the root. It is designated by a small 7 to the right of the chord letter name or numeral (see frames 329–330 for review).

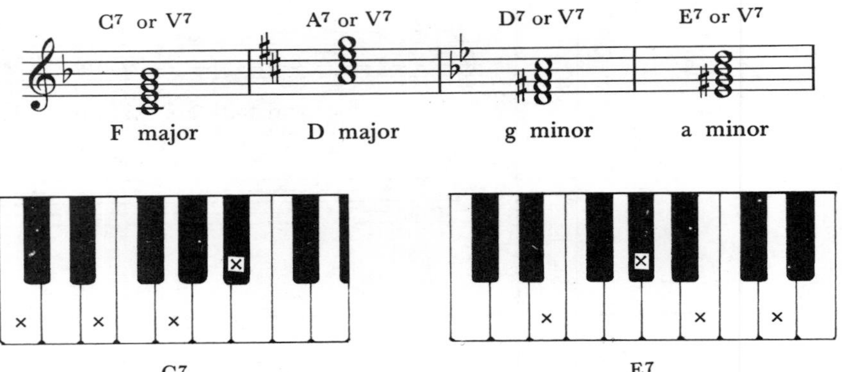

The V^7 chord is always a major triad with a minor seventh added.

Write the V^7 chords in the keys below. Use the usual form of the V chord in minor, that is, raise the third of the chord by means of an accidental.

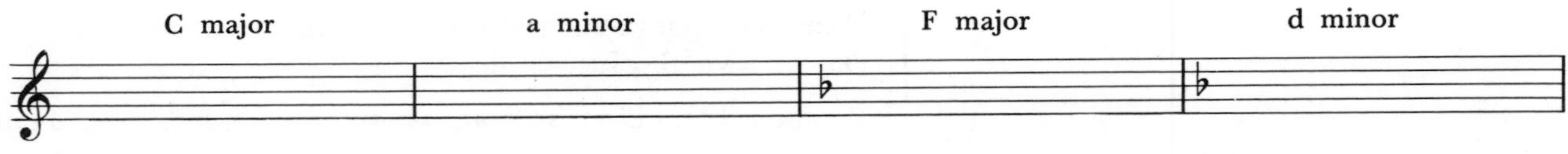

Is any accidental needed for the seventh of the V^7 chord? ______________
(yes or no)

341

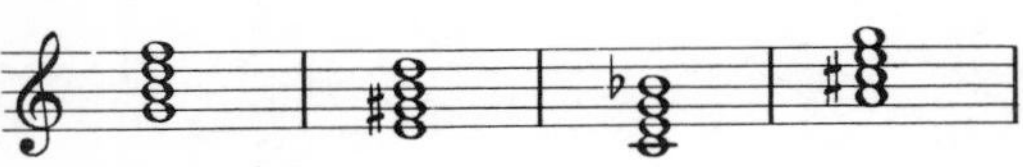

No, not if a key signature is used.

341

Write the designated chord above each fundamental; use accidentals whenever necessary. Play the chords. Make the 7th chords V^7 chords by writing in the appropriate major key signature.

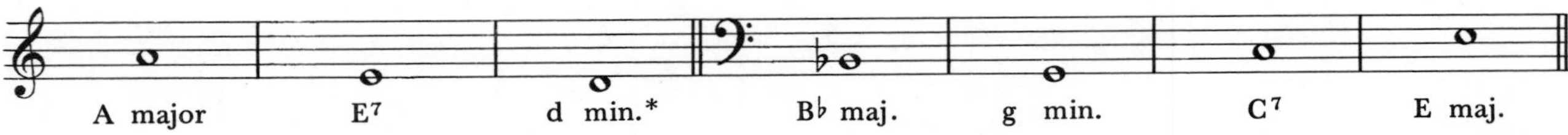

* Min. is an abbreviation for minor.

342

Playing response.

342

What is the key of this song? ______________ What is the letter name for the I chord? _______, the IV chord? _______, the V^7 chord? _______ Learn the chords and play them with the song.

THE CRAWDAD HOLE

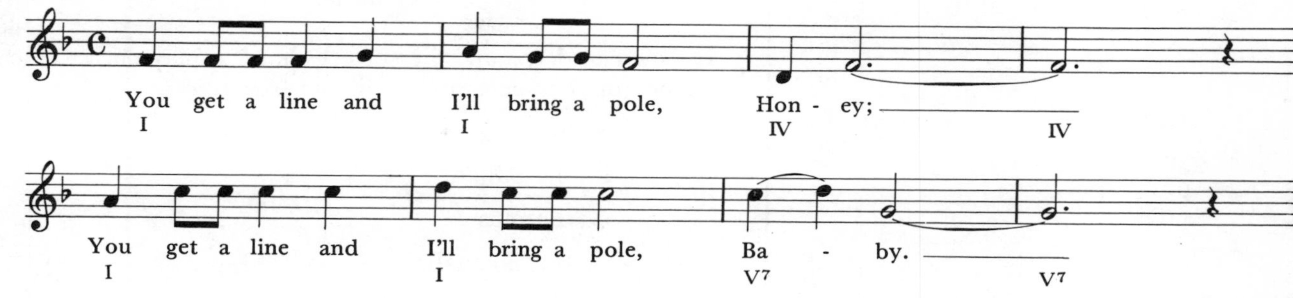
You get a line and I'll bring a pole, Hon - ey;
I I IV IV
You get a line and I'll bring a pole, Ba - by.
I I V^7 V^7

343

F major.

F.

B-flat.

C^7.

The chords you played were:

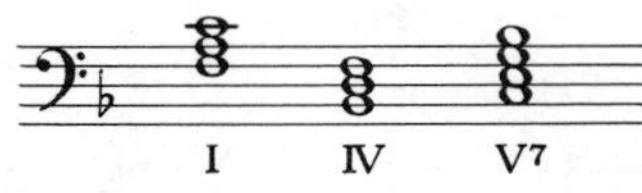
I IV V^7

343

PRETEST for Chapters 17–18: Playing Accompaniments

Mark the correct answer or *answers.*

1. One can determine the correct chord to play on the guitar to accompany singing from:
   —— a. listening
   —— b. the tablature
   —— c. the music
   —— d. the incanabula

2. An x over a string in guitar music means to:
   —— a. depress the string
   —— b. leave the string open
   —— c. do not strike the string
   —— d. accent the string

3. In order to raise the pitch of a string one must:
   —— a. depress the string on a fret
   —— b. depress the string between the frets
   —— c. depress the string on the nut
   —— d. depress the string between the nuts

4. The ukulele has:
   —— a. 4 strings compared to 6 on the guitar
   —— b. 6 strings compared to 4 on the guitar
   —— c. strings tuned to A, D, F-sharp, B
   —— d. strings tuned to E, A, D, G, B, F

5. Mark the correct playing position to produce the following chords on two hypothetical instruments.

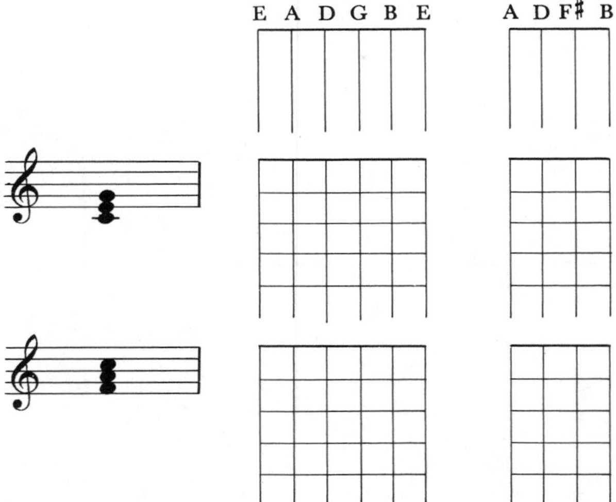

6. Identify the following chords by roman numerals and by letter names.

7. With a 12-bar Autoharp, one can:
   —— a. play a tonic chord in each of the twelve keys
   —— b. play major, minor, and seventh chords
   —— c. play the I, IV, V^7 in three major keys
   —— d. play chords only in major keys.

8. Why would you want an Autoharp that could play both a C chord and a C^7 chord?

   ____

9. The 15-bar Autoharp allows one to:
   —— a. play 3 chords in three additional keys
   —— b. play the I, IV, V^7 in additional keys
   —— c. add minor chords to major keys available on the 12-bar model
   —— d. play the I, IV, V^7 chords in five major keys.

10. Which buttons on the Autoharp should be depressed to play the chords in the following song?

DID YOU EVER SEE A LASSIE?

Answers

1. a, b, c.
2. c.
3. b.
4. a, c.
5.

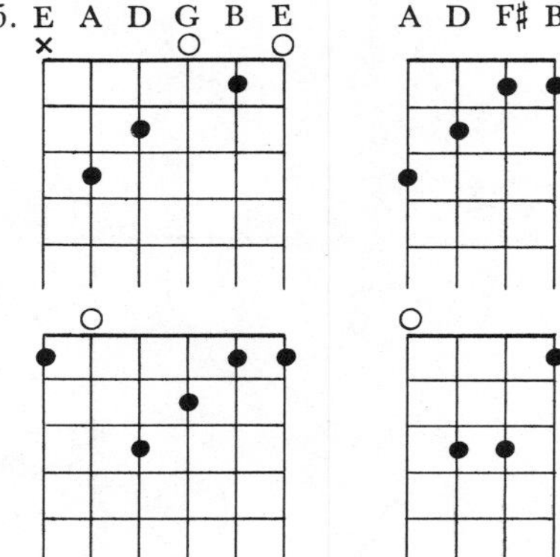

6. IV, V^7, V^7, vi, D, $B\flat^7$, $E\flat^7$, b.
7. b.
8. The C chord serves as the I chord in C, the C^7 as the V^7 in the key of F.
9. b.
10. G, G, D^7, G, G, G, D^7, G.

From your score determine if you can omit sections of the text.

CHAPTER 17 Playing Accompaniments

Many people teach themselves to play accompaniments on the piano, Autoharp, guitar, or ukulele without knowing how to read music. They simply play by ear, listening carefully for the sounds they want to create. All major triads sound somewhat alike; all minor triads sound somewhat alike; the pattern I–IV–V^7 sounds similar in any major key and also in any minor key. To play by ear means to recognize these sounds and search for them on the instrument.

For most people, however, an understanding of how to read the symbols for ukulele, guitar or Autoharp is very helpful in learning to play accompaniments. The purposes of this chapter are (1) to help you understand how chords are played on the Autoharp, ukulele, and guitar and (2) to acquaint you with the symbols used in reading music for the ukulele and the guitar. The exercises in the chapter are not designed to develop skill on these instruments, but to offer a description of them.

THE AUTOHARP

The Autoharp is the simplest of all accompanying instruments. On it chords are formed by depressing a bar with one hand while strumming with the other hand. The player needs only to know what chord he wants and find the bar so named. No special symbols or notation are needed; the player reads the chord names printed on the instrument.

Children in the classroom can accompany with the Autoharp, experimenting with rhythm patterns which enhance the song. The disadvantage of the Autoharp is that it has limited chord possibilities. There are two sizes, the 12-bar Autoharp and the 15-bar Autoharp.

12-bar Autoharp. Oscar Schmidt International, Inc.

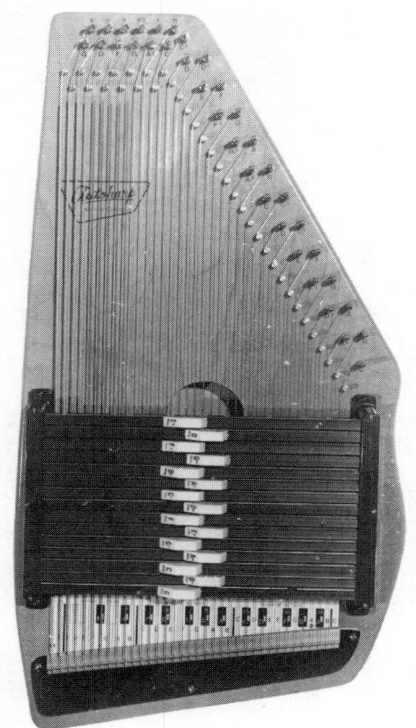

15-bar Autoharp. Oscar Schmidt International, Inc.

The chord bars of the 12-chord Autoharp are arranged like this:

Gm		A^7		Dm		E^7		Am		D^7	
	B♭		C^7		F		G^7		C		G

Autograph Bridge—12-bar model.

Are all the chords major? ______

344

No.

Look at the bar designations.

How many major triads can be played on the 12-bar Autoharp? ______

For what keys is the I chord possible? ______________

How many minor triads can be played on the 12-bar Autoharp? ______

What seventh chords can be played on the 12-bar Autoharp? ______________

These would be V^7 chords for which keys? ______________

344 345

4.

B-flat, F, C, G.

3.

A^7, C^7, E^7, G^7, D^7.

D, F, A, C, G.

For most songs the I, IV and V or V^7 chords will be needed to play accompaniments in frame 346. With the 12-bar Autoharp, these three chords are available in the following keys: F major, C major, and G major; d minor and a minor.

In F major the IV chord is a __________ (letter name) chord; the V^7 chord is a __________ (letter name) chord.

In C major the IV chord is a ______ chord; the V^7 is a ______ chord.

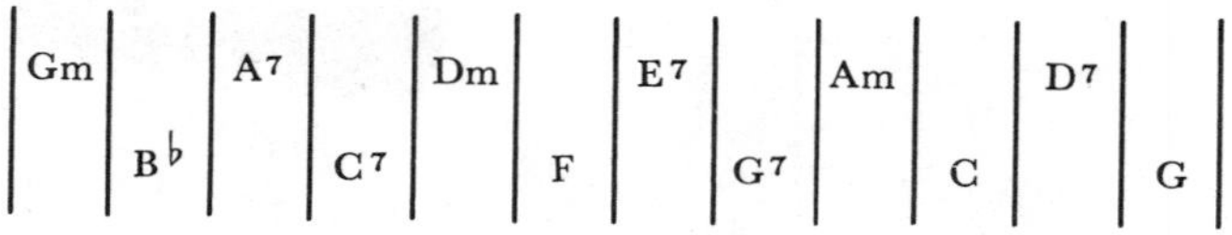

Gm | B♭ | A^7 | C^7 | Dm | F | E^7 | G^7 | Am | C | D^7 | G

345 346

B-flat.

C^7.

F.

G^7.

In the key of F major name the I chord. ______

name the IV chord. ______

name the V^7 chord. ______

Mark the bars for the I, IV, and V^7 chords in F major on the Autoharp diagram.

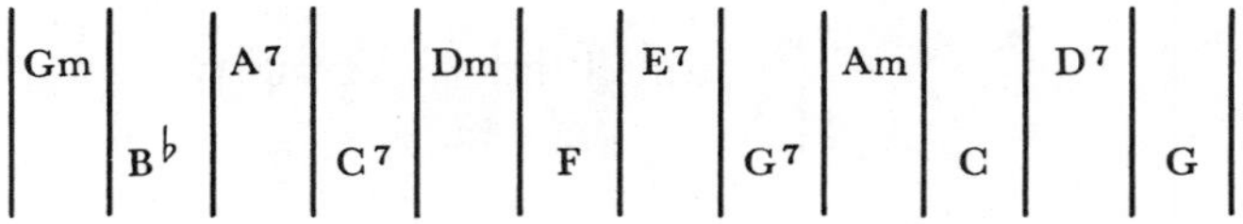

Gm | B♭ | A^7 | C^7 | Dm | F | E^7 | G^7 | Am | C | D^7 | G

346 347

F.

B-flat.

C^7.

Gm	~~B♭~~	A⁷	~~C7~~	Dm	~~F~~	E⁷	G⁷	Am	C	D⁷	G

347

In the key of C major identify the I chord. ______letter name)
In the key of C major identify the IV chord. ______ (letter name)
In the key of C major identify the V^7 chord. ______ (letter name)

Mark these three bars on the Autoharp diagram:

Gm	B♭	A⁷	C7	Dm	F	E⁷	G7	Am	C	D⁷	G

The Autoharp has both a C and a C^7 to allow a I chord in C and a V^7 chord in F; a G and G^7 to allow a ______ chord in G and a ______ chord in C.

348

C.

F.

G^7.

Gm	B♭	A⁷	C7	Dm	~~F~~	E⁷	~~G7~~	Am	~~C~~	D⁷	G

I (G).

V^7 (C^7).

348

In the key of G major another name for the I chord is a ______ major chord.

In the key of G major another name for the IV chord is a ______ major chord.

In the key of G major another name for the V^7 chord is a ______ major chord.

Mark the three bars on the Autoharp diagram.

Gm	B♭	A⁷	C7	Dm	F	E⁷	G7	Am	C	D⁷	G

349

G.

C.

D7.

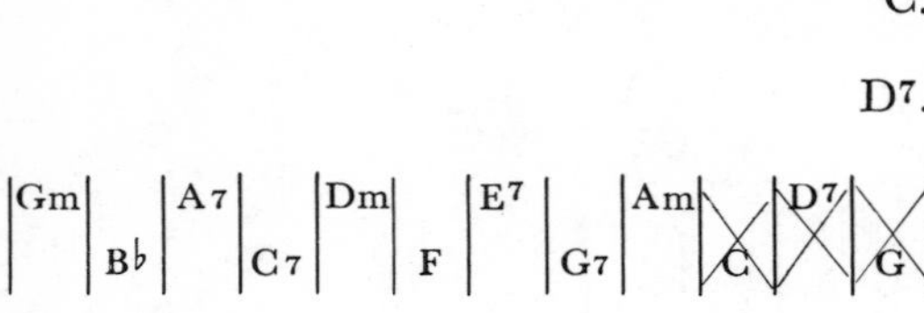

349

Determine the key for the song below. ______ Find the chords used in the song. Accompany the song on the Autoharp by strumming on every beat.

GOOD DAY, GOOD DAY TO YOU

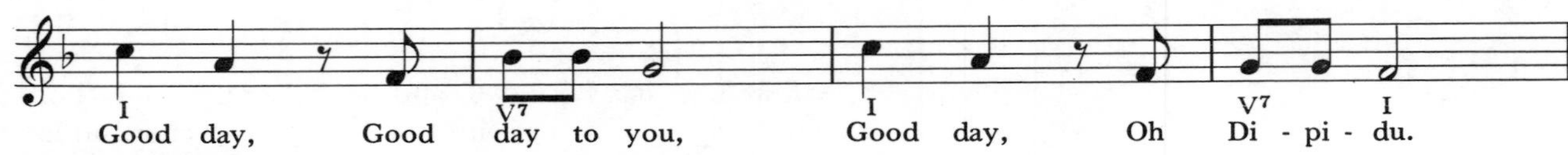

From the UNICEF Book of Children's Songs, *ed. William Kaufman. Used by permission of Stackpole Books.*

What is the tempo of the song? ______________

350

F major.

Strumming response.

Moderato (moderate).

350

Which buttons on the Autoharp should be depressed to play the chords in the following song?

LITTLE DAVID

351

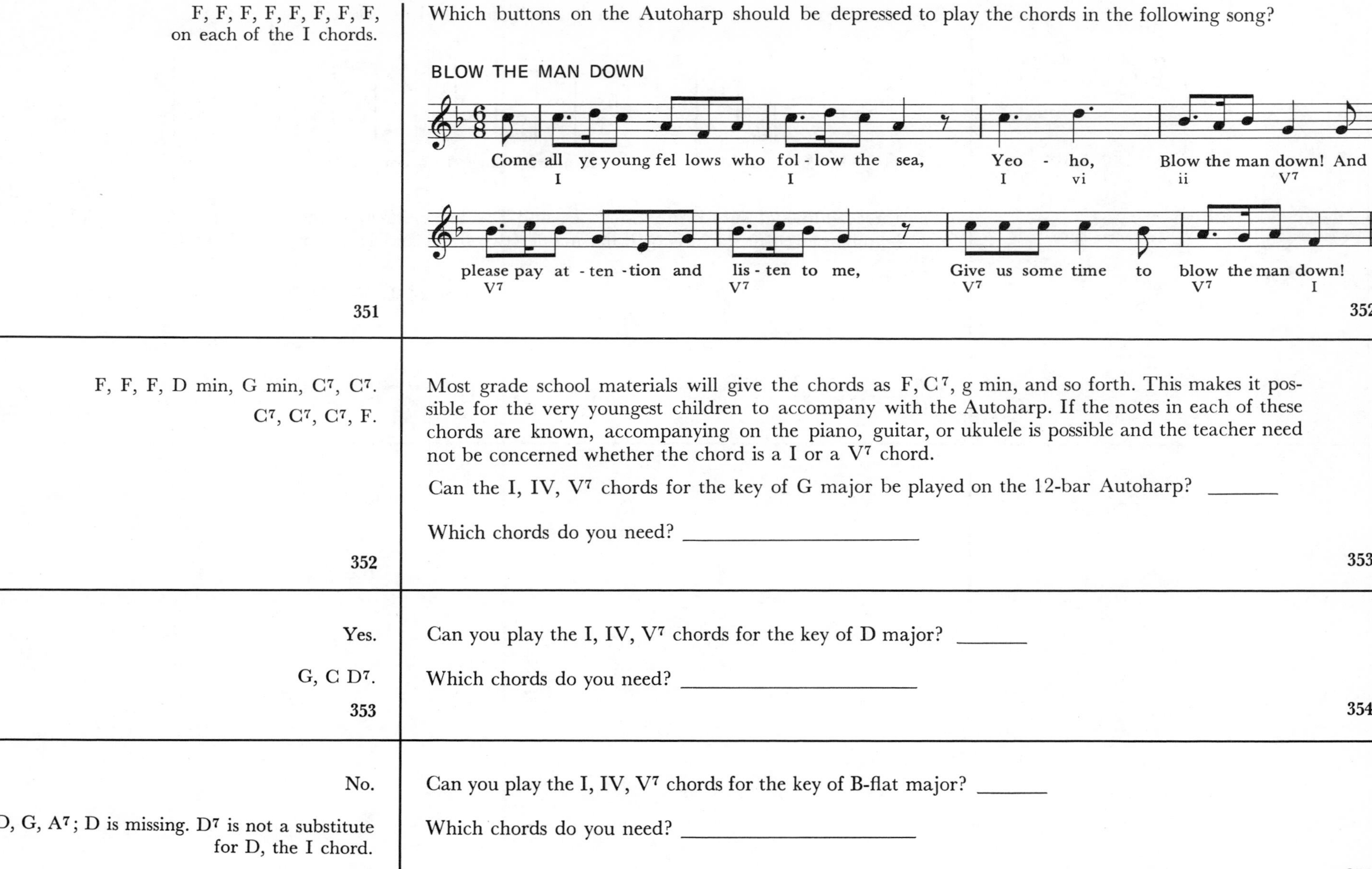

F, F, F, F, F, F, F, F, on each of the I chords.

351

Which buttons on the Autoharp should be depressed to play the chords in the following song?

BLOW THE MAN DOWN

352

F, F, F, D min, G min, C^7, C^7. C^7, C^7, C^7, F.

352

Most grade school materials will give the chords as F, C^7, g min, and so forth. This makes it possible for the very youngest children to accompany with the Autoharp. If the notes in each of these chords are known, accompanying on the piano, guitar, or ukulele is possible and the teacher need not be concerned whether the chord is a I or a V^7 chord.

Can the I, IV, V^7 chords for the key of G major be played on the 12-bar Autoharp? ______

Which chords do you need? ____________________

353

Yes.

G, C D^7.

353

Can you play the I, IV, V^7 chords for the key of D major? ______

Which chords do you need? ____________________

354

No.

D, G, A^7; D is missing. D^7 is not a substitute for D, the I chord.

354

Can you play the I, IV, V^7 chords for the key of B-flat major? ______

Which chords do you need? ____________________

355

No.

B-flat, E-flat, F^7; F^7 could be substituted for F, but E-flat is still needed.

The chord bars for the 15-chord Autoharp are arranged as below:

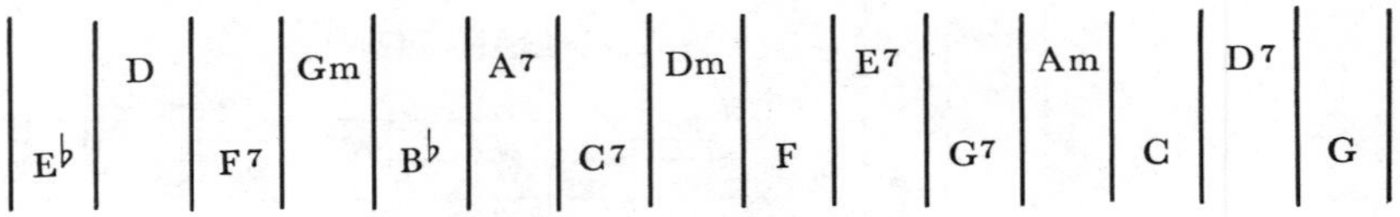

E♭	D	F7	Gm	B♭	A7	C7	Dm	F	E7	G7	Am	C	D7	G

Autoharp Bridge—15-bar model

The three additional chords are E-flat, D, and F^7. These three chords allow the I, IV, and V^7 chords to be played in the keys of B-flat major (two flats) and D major (two sharps).

Key of B-flat: I = B-flat

IV = ____

V^7 = F^7

Key of D: I = D

IV = ____

V^7 = ____

355

356

E-flat.

G.

A^7.

356

CHAPTER 18 Optional Section: The Guitar

In order to read guitar music one should understand the simple diagram called the tablature. The tablature shows the six strings of the guitar, and has dots to indicate where the fingers should be placed.

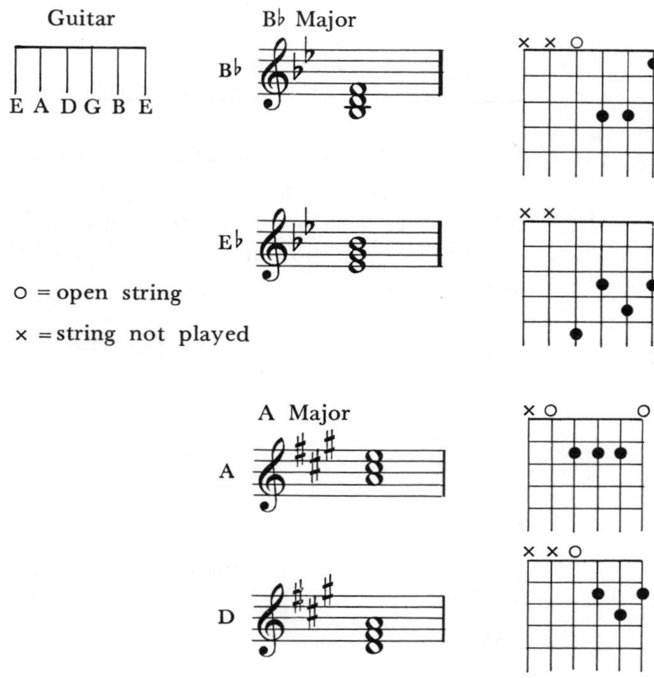

The six vertical lines in the diagram represent the six strings of the guitar. They are tuned (from left to right) to pitches E, A, D, G, B, E. The crosswise lines represent frets, narrow metal strips placed on the fingerboard of the guitar underneath the strings. The player's fingers are placed between these frets.

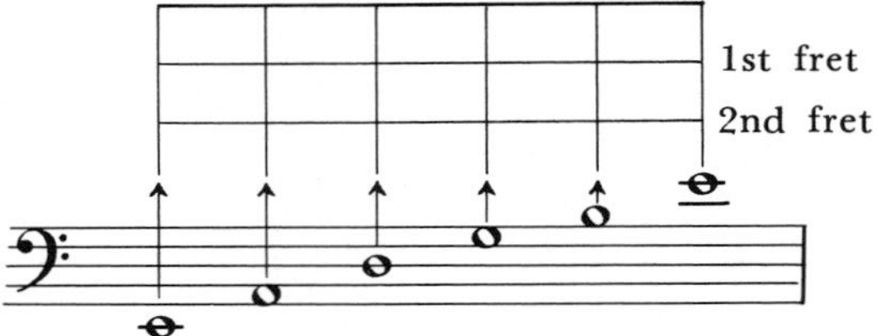

The pitches of the guitar strings, from lowest to highest (left to right in the tablature) are: ______________

The fret is represented in the tablature by a ________________ line.
(horizontal or vertical)

357

E, A, D, G, B, E.

Horizontal.

357

The guitar is held so that the fingertips of the left hand may change the pitches by depressing the strings, while the right hand strums to create the sound. As the player holds the instrument in playing position, the lowest pitched string is at the top of the fingerboard, the highest pitched string on the bottom. The top line of the diagram (tablature) represents the nut adjacent to the tuning pegs.

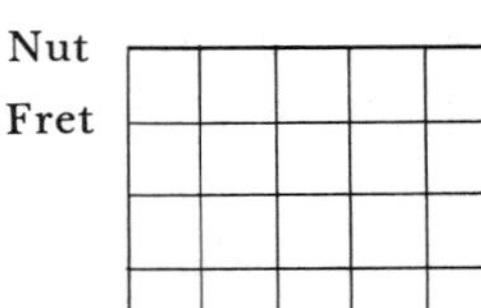

The guitar is held so that the low ____________ string is at the top of the fingerboard.
(name of pitch)

358

E.

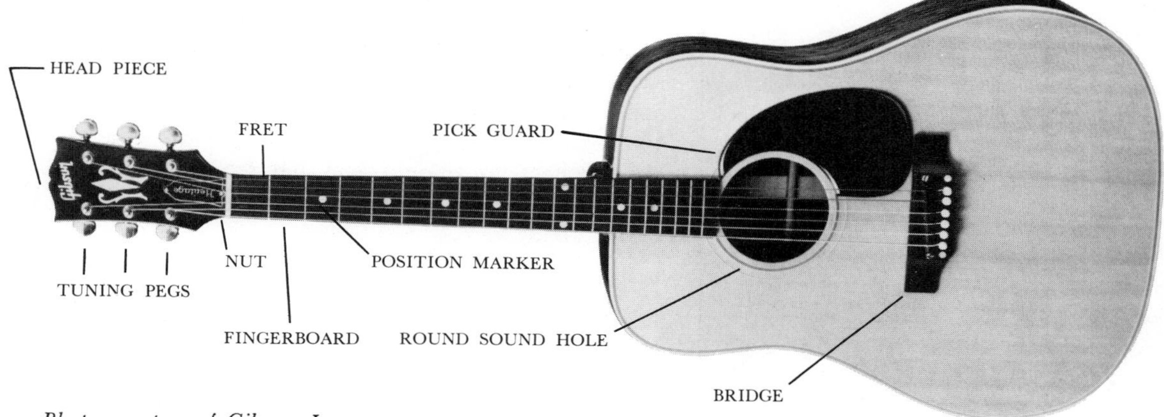

Photo courtesy of Gibson, Inc.

	6	5	4	3	2	1
	Low →					High
Strings	E	A	D	G	B	E
Frets 1						
2						
3						
4						
etc.						

The names of the strings, from left to right in the tablature, are E, A, D, G, B, E; if a finger is placed on any string *between* the nut and the first fret, the pitch of the string will be raised one half step. The frets are spaced so that placing the finger on the string between each succeeding fret raises the pitch of that string one half step higher than at the preceding fret.

	E	A	D	G	B	E	
1st fret							- - raises pitch 1/2 step
2nd fret							- - raises pitch another 1/2 step
3rd fret							- - raises pitch another 1/2 step - - (1 1/2 steps above pitch of open string.)

The frets are indicators of where to place the fingers to produce higher pitches on the strings, but the finger is not placed directly on a fret. The pitch distance between any two adjacent frets is ______________ step(s).

If you remember the names of the strings plus the above information, with adequate time you could determine the notes from any tablature or play any chord on the guitar.

One half.

359

The tablature below indicates the C major chord. The first and second fingers depress the E and A strings (the lowest pitched strings) between the second and third frets, raising the pitch 1 1/2 steps to sound G and C. The third string, D, is depressed, which raises it one step to E. The next string, G, is left open. The B string is depressed to produce the pitch C, and the E string is left open. The sounds thus produced are G, C, E, G, C, E—the pitches of the C-major chord. Knowing chord note names plus how the guitar operates will allow a teacher to quickly chord to elementary songs. There are many songs that require only one or two chords for accompaniment. In determining which fret produces which note, remember that there is only a half step between E and F and B and C.

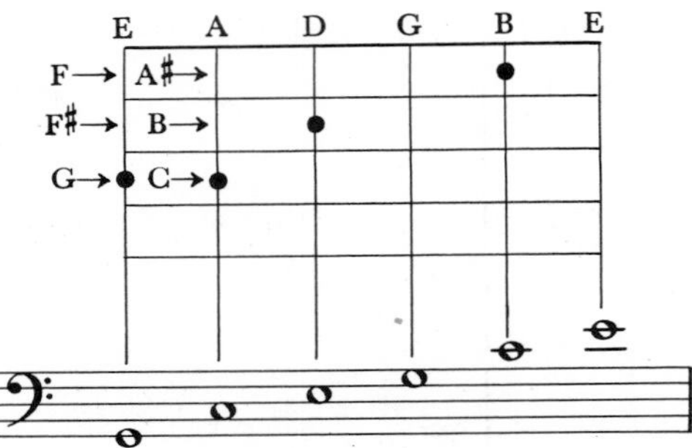

Each chord on the guitar can be "figured out" by ear. If we know the names of the pitches in a desired chord, then we position our fingers on each string near the fret that will produce the pitch desired in the chord.

Which notes are indicated by the tablature? ________________

Which chord does this combination of pitches produce? ________________

E A D G B E

* optional

360

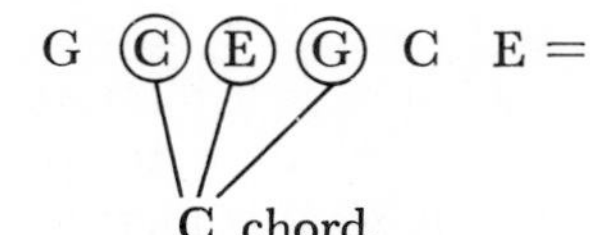

Other pitches are duplicates of these.

360

The order of the pitches in a chord is not critical. The notes may be mixed up, but C–E–G, G–E–C, E–G–C, etc. are all considered the same chord, the C chord. Pitches may be doubled and put in any order to facilitate playing.

Examine the first example below and then determine what chord is present in the other examples.

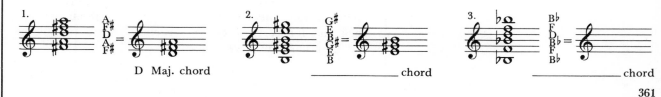

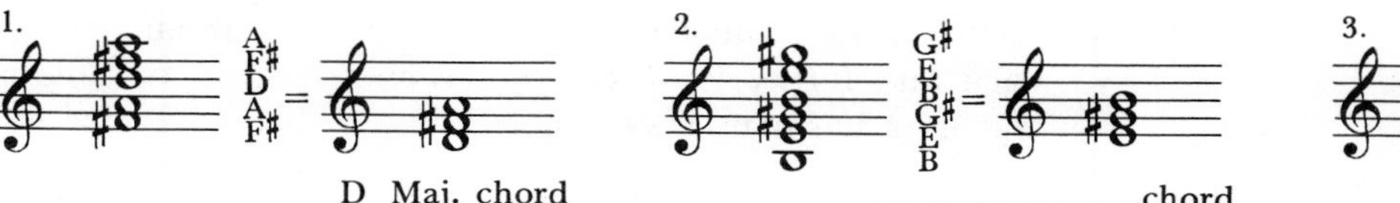

361

2. E major chord.

3. B-flat major chord.

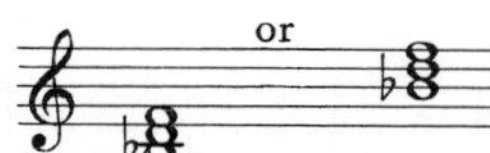

361

In guitar tablature an X is placed above strings that are not to be played. An O is placed above strings that are to be played open (no fingers down). The C chord may be played as a four-string chord, following the tablature below. In such case, the player must take care to strum only the four higher pitched strings.

Name in order (lowest to highest) the four pitches that would sound if the chord were played.

____

362

E, G, C, E.

362

Complete the following tablature to indicate an F chord. Mark any open and unused strings.

363

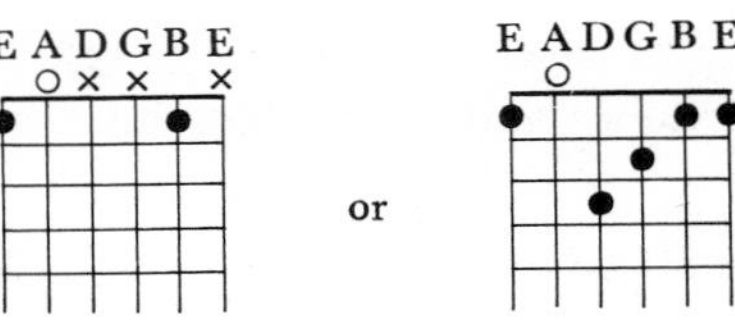

A knowledge of chord structure is not necessary to play the guitar by ear, but it is necessary in order to teach playing by ear. Attentive practice in reading the tablature will increase one's skill so that the guitar can readily be used for accompanying simple tunes. In reading, the player simply places his fingers where the diagram indicates; he does not need to know anything about chords, although he must be able to hear whether the sound is correct or incorrect for the melody he is accompanying. For songs requiring only one chord for accompaniment, the fingers are positioned for that chord and retain that position throughout the song. For two chords, only one change—back and forth—is necessary. Teachers should be able to assist students in their early efforts in playing a harmony instrument.

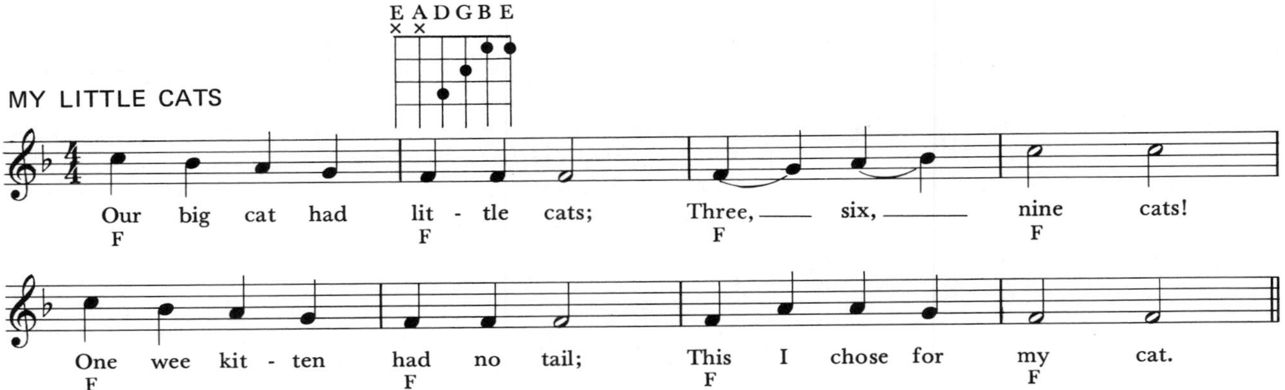

E A D G B E
MY LITTLE CATS
Our big cat had lit - tle cats; Three, six, nine cats!
F F F F
One wee kit - ten had no tail; This I chose for my cat.
F F F F

Name the pitches in the F chord as given in the tablature above. ________________

The song above may be accompanied using only the F chord. Learn to play the chord while you sing the song.

F, A, C, F.
Playing and singing response.

364

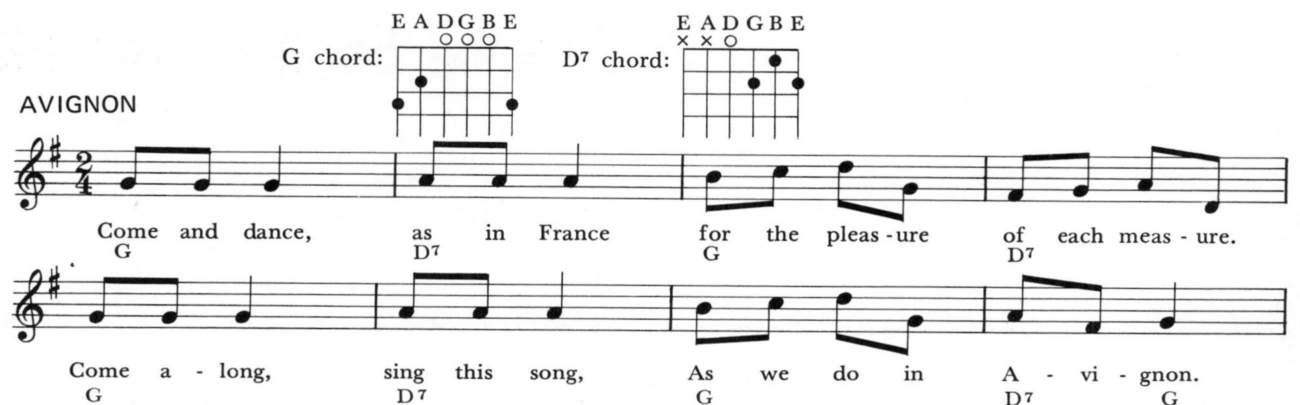
E A D G B E
G chord:
E A D G B E
D7 chord:
AVIGNON
Come and dance, as in France for the pleas - ure of each meas - ure.
G D7 G D7
Come a - long, sing this song, As we do in A - vi - gnon.
G D7 G D7 G

The pitches in the G chord indicated in the above tablature are ________________.

Name the pitches in the D⁷ chord, as given in the tablature. ________________

Learn to play the chords while you sing the song.

Many students only look at the tablature without identifying the names of the notes. That is why with little knowledge but finger positions for three chords, C(I), F(IV), and G(V), they can accompany many songs—as long as the songs are sung in the key they know—in our example, the key of C. Beginners on the guitar learn the chords in two or three of the keys most frequently used and play all their accompaniments in those keys.

365

G, B, D, G, B, G.

D, A, C, F-sharp.
Playing and singing response.

365

CHAPTER 19 Optional Section: The Ukulele

The ukulele is a more economical instrument to purchase than the guitar. It has only four strings which are usually tuned to the pitches A, D, F-sharp, and B (left to right in the tablature). (The standard tuning was once G, C, E, A, but the higher tuning is now preferred.)

The ukulele is a ______ stringed instrument with pitches of ______________ from left to right
(number)
in the tablature. Notice that the pitches do not consistently move from low to high.

366

4.

A, D, F-sharp, B.

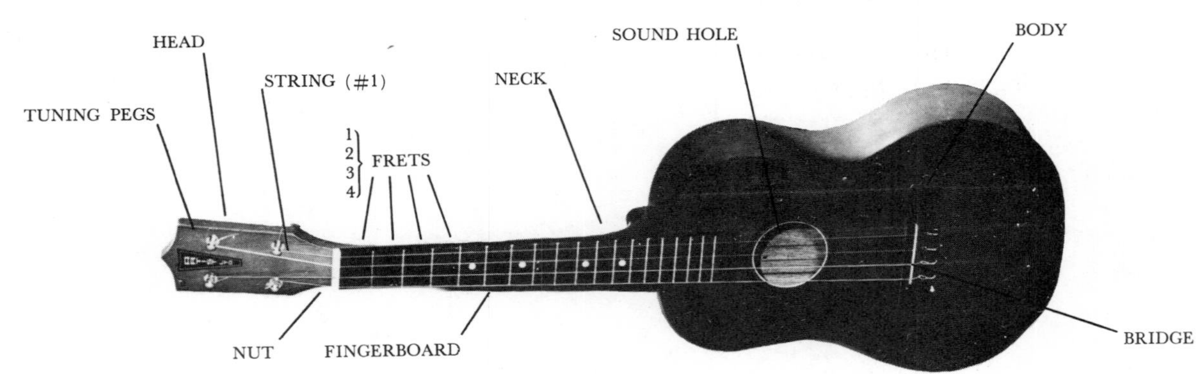

Rhythm Band, Inc.—manufacturer and distributor of elementary musical instruments.

366

Ukulele tablature is identical to guitar tablature except that the diagram uses only four lines to represent the four strings. The D-major chord can be formed by depressing the B string to sound the pitch D. As on the guitar, depressing a string one fret raises the pitch of the string by one half step. The other three strings fit into the D-major chord.

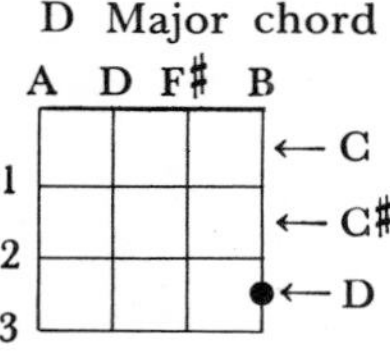

The pitch D is _______ steps above the pitch B.

367

---

1 1/2.

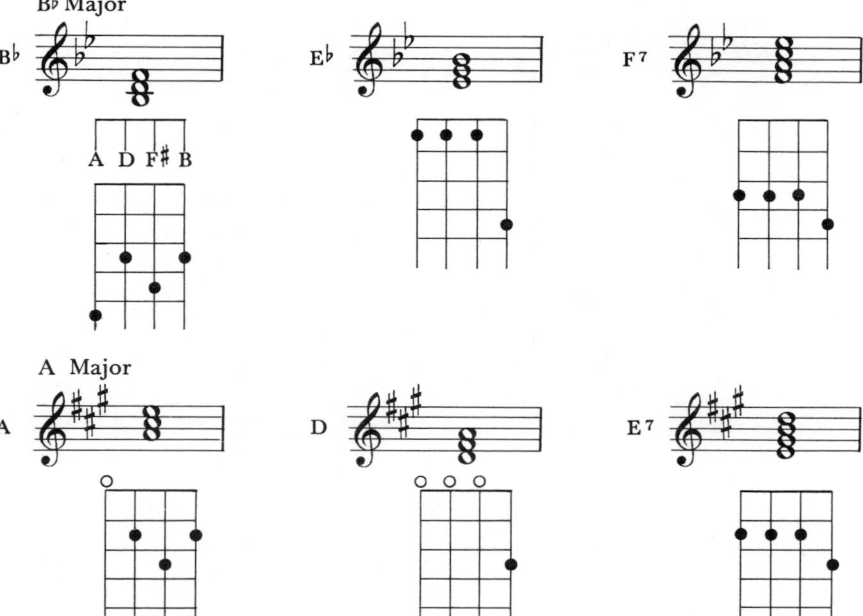

Look at the diagrams to ensure that you understand the tablatures and that the fingering indicated will produce only the notes in the chord.

367

Identify errors in the following tablatures by placing an X on the incorrect finger placement:

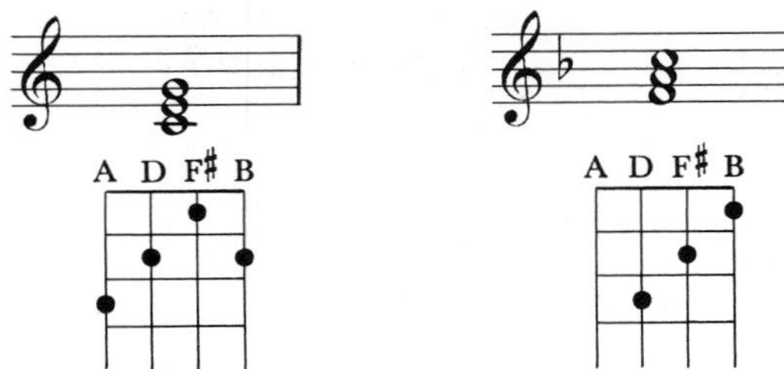

368

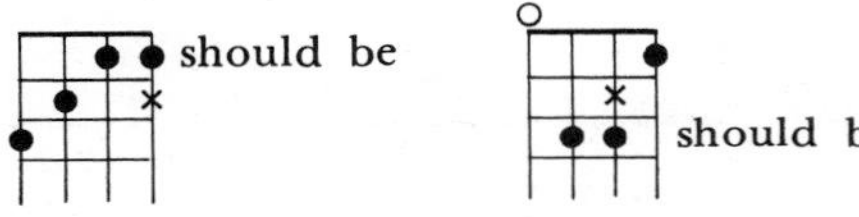

368

In the tablatures below are the I and V⁷ chords in the key of D. Name the notes for these chords beginning with the root: I chord ________________; V⁷ ________________.

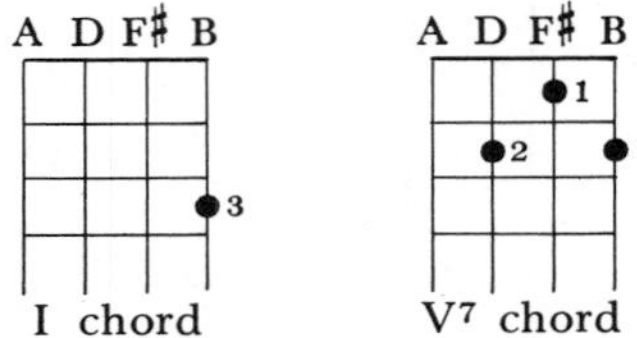

From left to right name the pitch sounded by each string in the tablature for the I chord ________________; for the V⁷ chord ________________. Practice playing these chords on the ukulele.

369

D, F-sharp A.

A, C-sharp, E, G.

A, D, F-sharp, D.

A, E, G, C-sharp.

Playing response.

369

Play the accompaniment for the song below on an instrument. What is the key of the song? ______________

BOBBY SHAFTO

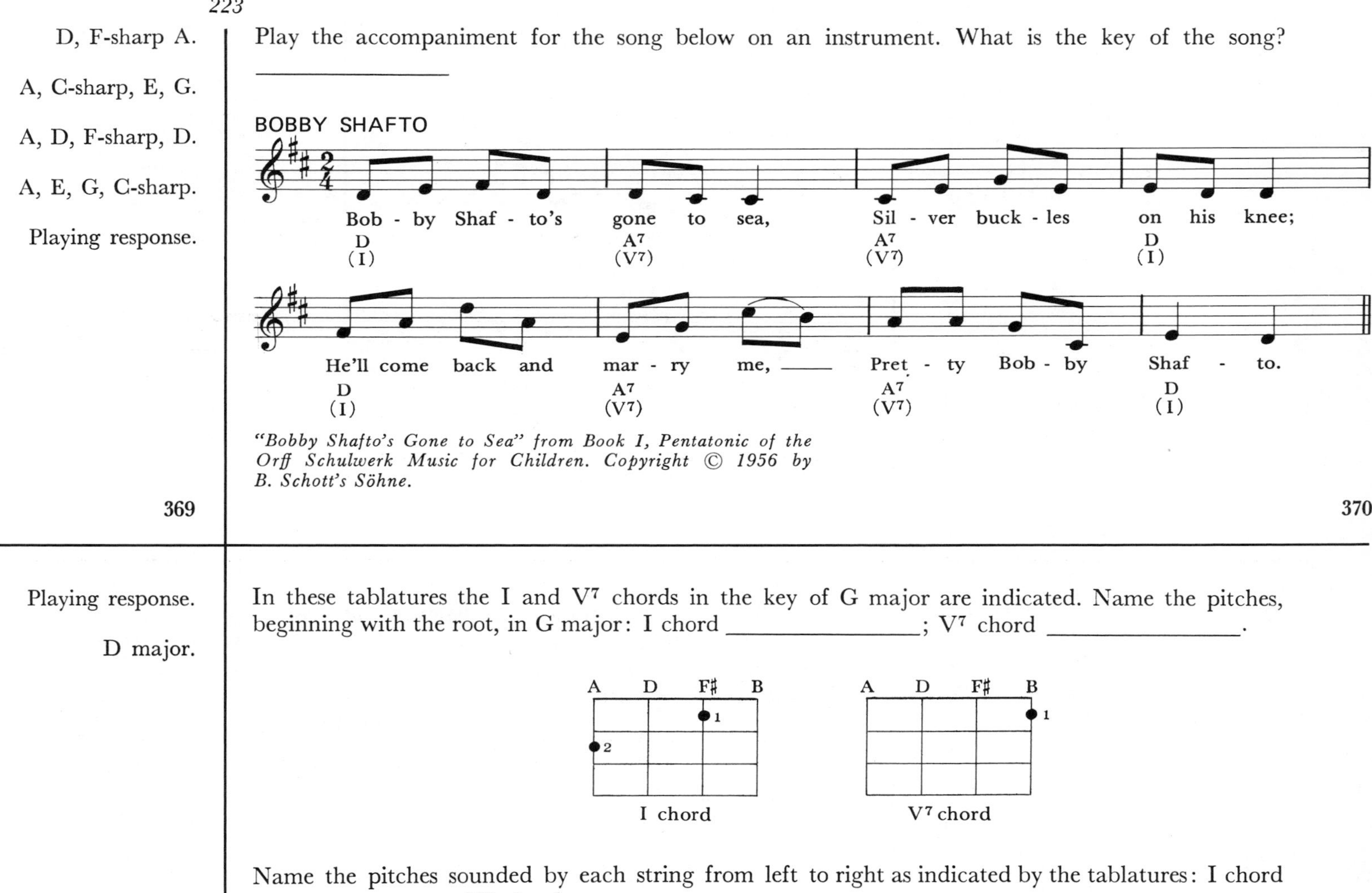
Bob - by Shaf - to's gone to sea, Sil - ver buck - les on his knee;
D (I) A7 (V7) A7 (V7) D (I)
He'll come back and mar - ry me, —— Pret - ty Bob - by Shaf - to.
D (I) A7 (V7) A7 (V7) D (I)
A D F♯ B
1 2
I chord
A D F♯ B
1
V7 chord

"Bobby Shafto's Gone to Sea" from Book I, Pentatonic of the Orff Schulwerk Music for Children. Copyright © 1956 by B. Schott's Söhne.

370

Playing response.

D major.

370

In these tablatures the I and V^7 chords in the key of G major are indicated. Name the pitches, beginning with the root, in G major: I chord ______________; V^7 chord ______________.

Name the pitches sounded by each string from left to right as indicated by the tablatures: I chord ______________; V^7 chord ______________.

371

G, B, D.

D, F-sharp, A, C.

B, D, G, B.

A, D, F-sharp, C.

371

Play the accompaniment for the song below. Name the key of the song. ______________ It is in the major mode.

MY DONKEY

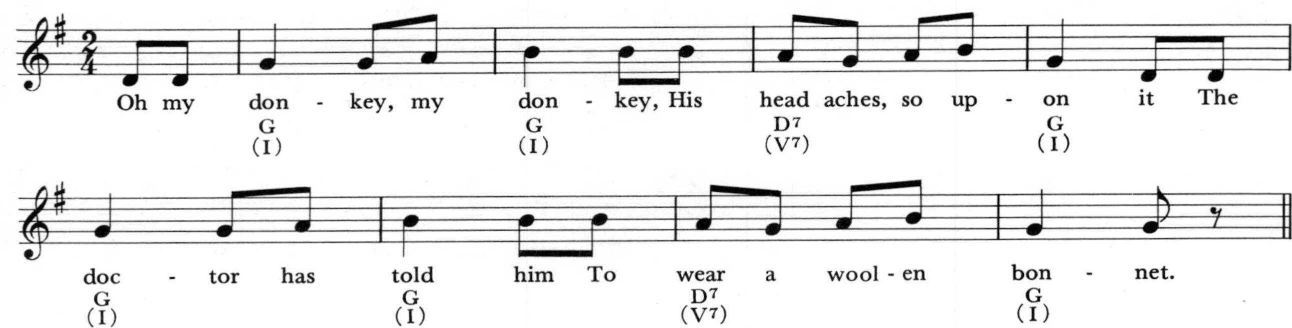

372

G major.

372

Almost all grade school music texts designate the chordal accompaniment for the songs. Some use the letter name designation and others use the roman numeral designation. The teacher should become proficient at using chords by both letter name and roman numeral so that he may be able to provide accompaniments.

Practice the accompanying chords for the song in the next frame. Use either piano, guitar, ukulele, or Autoharp. Sing the song and play the accompaniment. What is the key of the song? ______________

373

Singing and playing response.

G major.

373

SHOO FLY

Flies in the but-ter-milk, shoo fly shoo, Flies in the but-ter-milk, shoo fly shoo,
I I V7 V7
Flies in the but-ter-milk, shoo fly shoo, Skip to my loo my dar - ling.
I I V7 I

Practice the chords for the minor song. Use either piano, guitar, ukulele, or Autoharp. Sing the song and play the accompaniment. In what key is the song? ________________

GO DOWN, MOSES

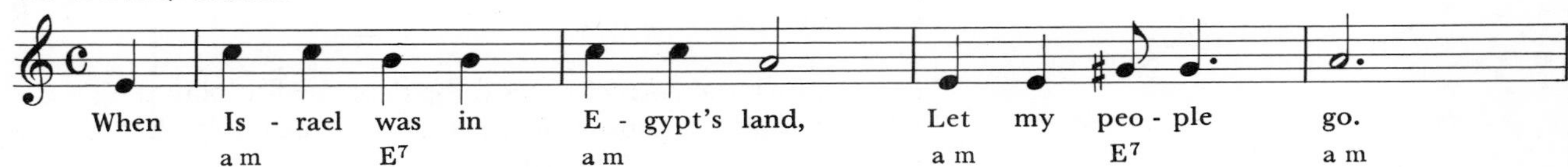
When Is - rael was in E - gypt's land, Let my peo - ple go.
am E7 am am E7 am

What does the **C** meter signature indicate? ________________ 374

Singing and playing response.

a minor.

$\frac{4}{4}$ time (common time).

374

PRETEST for Chapter 20: Piano Technique

Mark the correct answer or *answers.*

1. You need to play a chord using the left hand on C, E, and G. Which fingers would be used?

 ____

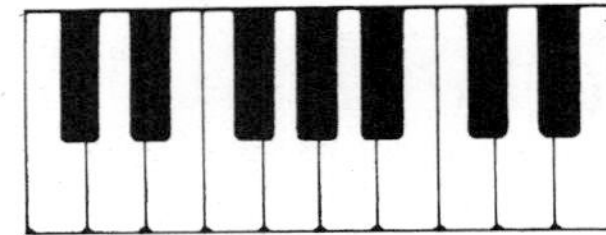

2. Using only black keys, name the notes used in a five-finger pattern. ____________________

3. Mark the correct notes to be depressed to play the I and V^7 chords in the following example. Use an x for the I chord, o for the V^7.

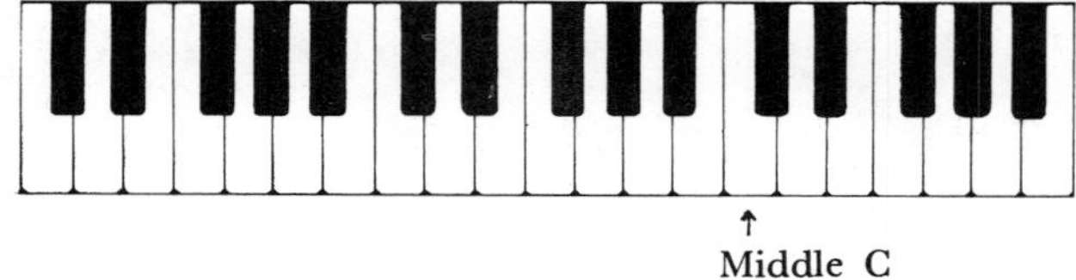

4. The note most commonly omitted from the V^7 chord is:

 —— a. the root

 —— b. the third

 —— c. the fifth

 —— d. the seventh

5. What are the letter names of:

 first inversion of an F chord ______________

 Second inversion of a C chord ______________

 root position of a G chord ______________

 first inversion of a D chord ______________

6. In the key of A major the letter name of the V^7 chord is______. In the key of A major, the letter name of the iii chord is ______.

7. Rearrange the following triads into root position:

 E–G–C _____
 E–A–C _____
 F–B–D _____
 A–F–C _____

8. The V^7 chord is different from a V chord because it:

 —— a. has seven notes rather than five

 —— b. is an inverted chord

 —— c. contains the seventh degree of the scale

 —— d. is a four-note chord

Answers

1. 5 3 1.
2. C-sharp, D-sharp, F-sharp, G-sharp, A-sharp or D-flat, E-flat, G-flat, A-flat, B-flat (any order).
3. 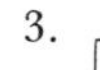

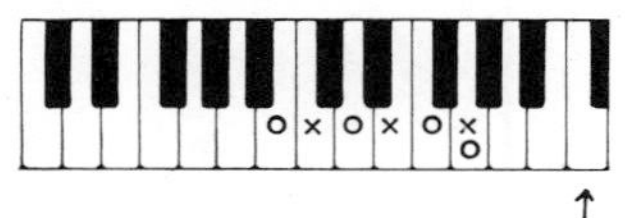

4. c.
5. A–C–F.
   G–C–E.
   G–B–D.
   F-sharp–A–D.
6. E^7, C-sharp.
7. C–E–G.
   A–C–E.
   B–D–F.
   F–A–C.
8. d.

From your score determine whether you can omit sections of the text.

CHAPTER 20 Optional Section: Piano Technique

The piano keyboard has been introduced as a useful tool for learning scales and chords. Even a paper keyboard can help children see relationships in scales and chords. Proficiency in playing the piano is an aid the teacher should avail himself of because use of the piano can enhance nearly every aspect of musical learning: rhythm, harmony, melodic movement, dynamics, and so forth. Listening can also be aided by introduction of motifs and themes on the piano.

When you have completed this chapter, you should (1) be able to recognize and write inversions of triads and seventh chords in all major keys and (2) know how to use the I, IV, V^7 chords in playing accompaniments. Since this knowledge will be of little value to you unless you apply it, the necessity for using the piano to practice all possible exercises is great.

Knowledge of correct finger position makes mastering the keyboard easier. Fingering for piano is numbered from the thumb outward.

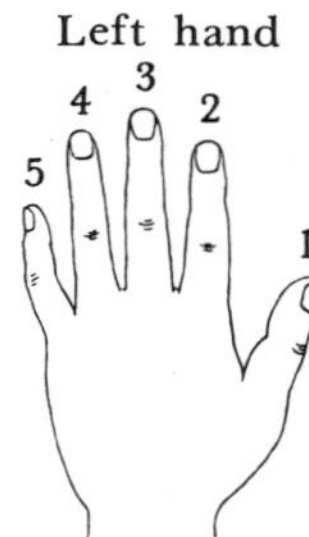

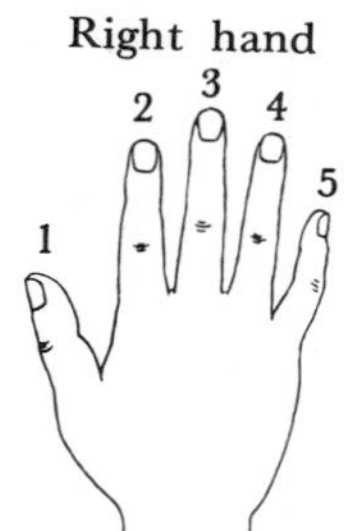

Five-note patterns or melodies are played by placing the five fingers over the keys to be used and striking the keys with the same fingers each time. Notice in the song below that G is always played with the fifth finger, C with the thumb, and so forth. Much initial work on the piano can be done with five-finger patterns.

375

Playing response.

375

Triads in root position are played on the piano using fingers 1–3–5 in the right hand and 5–3–1 in the left hand. The diagram below gives the fingering for triads.

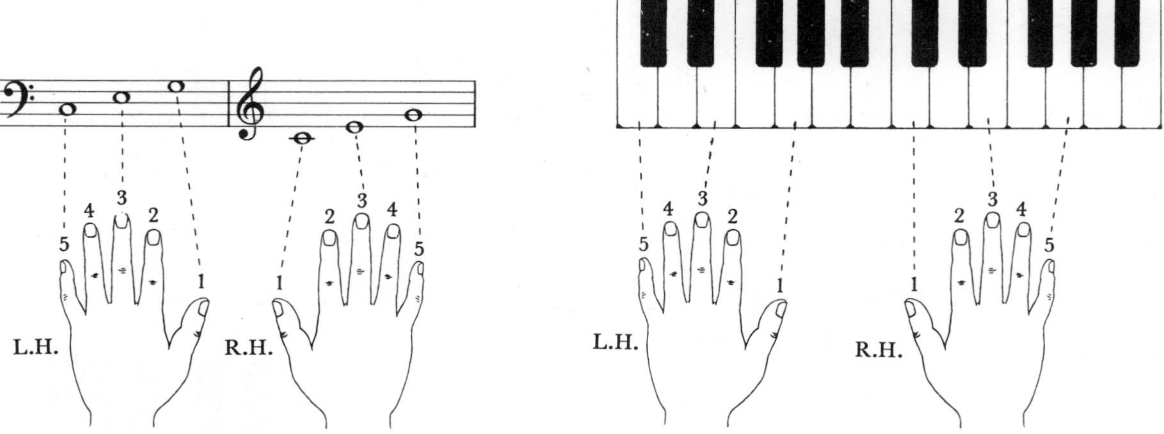

Play the I, IV, V chords in the keys of C, G, and F; use the paper keyboard in the back of the book or preferably a real piano keyboard.

376

Playing response.

376

Mark the I chord in the key of C with x's. Mark the IV chord with y's and the V chord with z's.

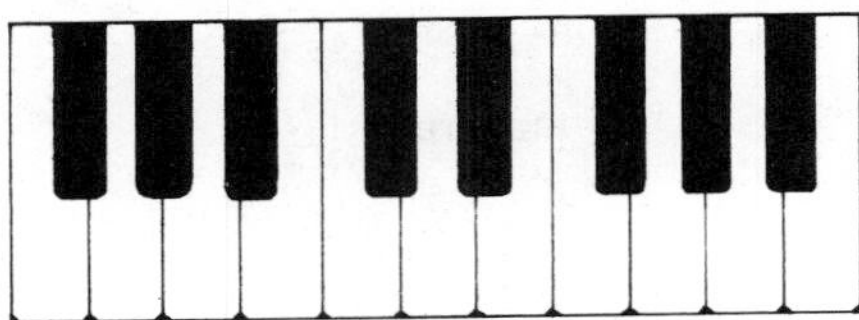

377

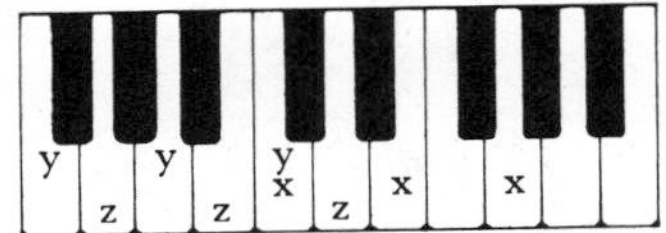

377

Play the song with the right hand. If possible, play the accompanying chords with the left hand and sing the melody. If you know some piano, play with both hands together.

OLD WOMAN

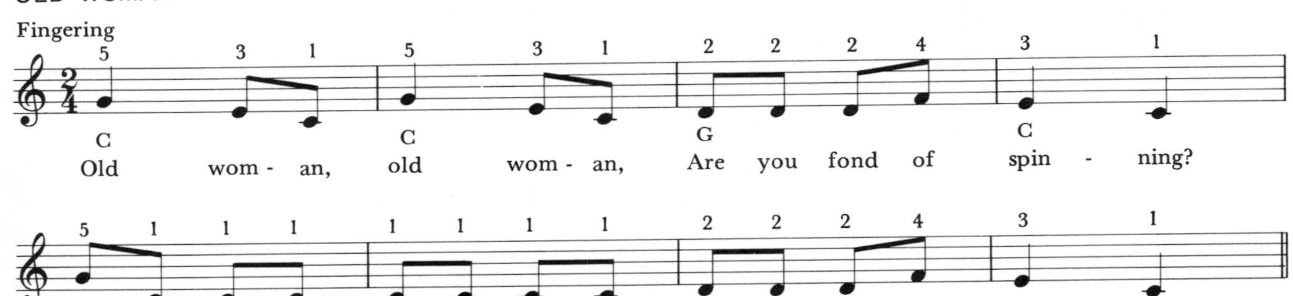

378

Playing and singing response.

378

Mark the I chord in the key of E with a's, the IV chord with b's, and the V chord with c's.

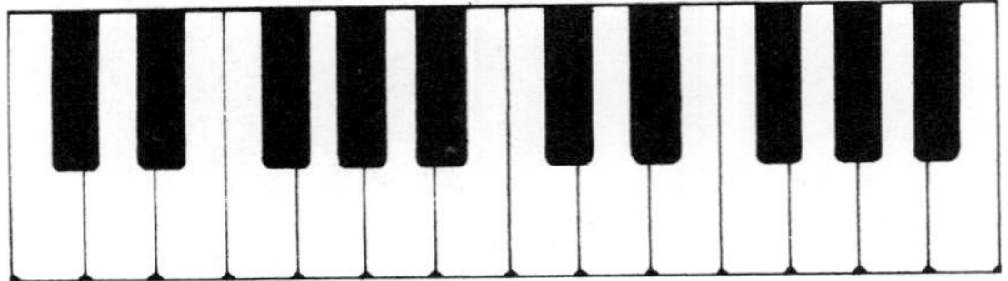

379

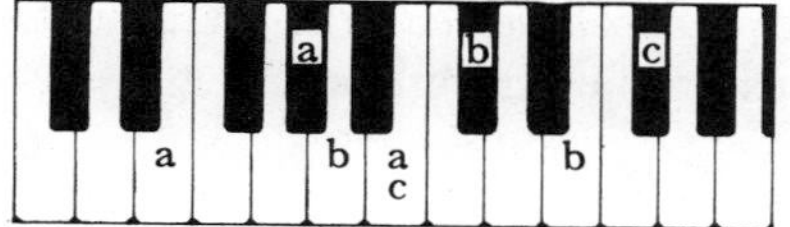

379

Chords in root position (which means that the root is the bottom note, root–3rd–5th) have been introduced. Moving from the I to the IV and then to the V in root position on the piano is awkward and requires considerable movement. Even the use of only two chords in root position, such as you played in frame 378, is awkward. To reduce this movement, the same chord notes are played but in a different order. For example, in root position the I chord in C major is C–E–G with C the lowest note.

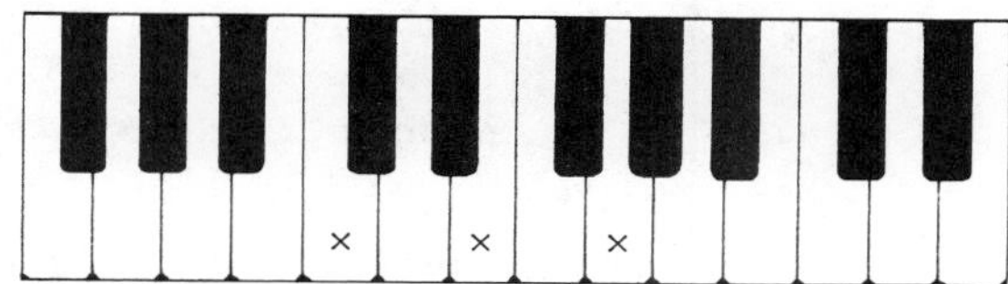

It is still a I chord with a slightly different sound if E is the lowest note and the order of the notes is E, G, C.

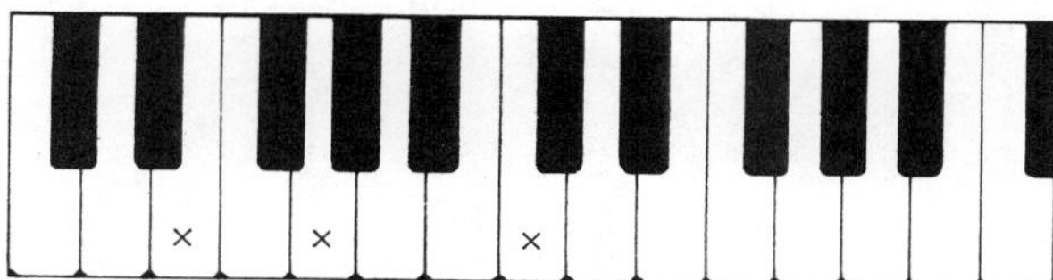

What other combination of notes is possible for a I chord in C major? ______________

380

G, C, E, with G on the bottom.

380

When the order of the chord notes is altered, the chord is said to be *inverted*. All triads can be played in three positions: root position, first inversion (the third as the bottom note), and second inversion (the fifth as the lowest note).

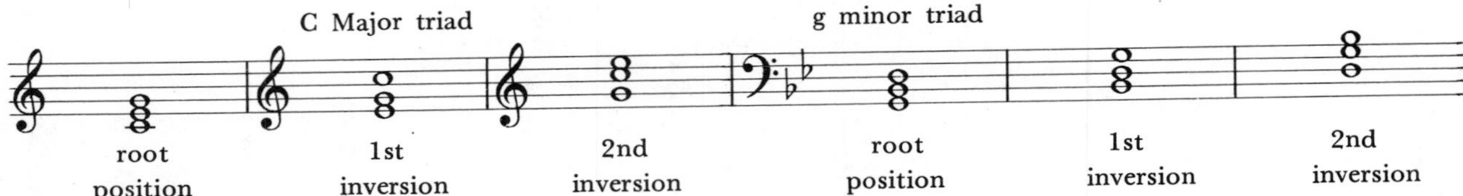

As the previous frame illustrated, the first inversion is made by placing the root tone, or fundamental, on the top of the chord rather than on the bottom. The second inversion is made by "turning the chord over" again so that the fundamental or root is in the middle of the chord and the fifth becomes the lowest tone.

Identify the position of these chords by writing root, 1st inversion, or 2nd inversion beneath each chord.

Play them on the piano.

381

Root, 1st inversion, 2nd inversion.
1st inversion, 2nd inversion, root.
2nd inversion, root, 1st inversion.
2nd inversion, 1st inversion root.

Playing response.

381

Below are triads in root position. Write these chords in first and second inversions.

382

382

Four-tone chords such as the V⁷ chord are inverted in the same manner as triads. If the chord tones are G–B–D–F in root position, in first inversion they will be B–D–F–G, second inversion D–F–G–B, and third inversion F–G–B–D, the first letter indicating the lowest tone. Thus, the four-tone chord has three inversions:

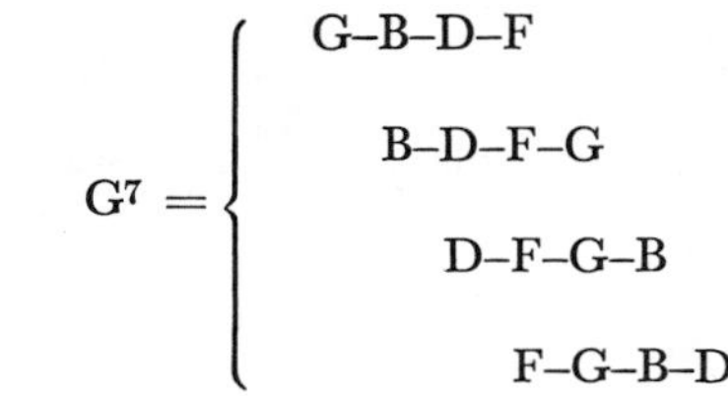

Notice in the accompaniment to "Bingo" the position of the chords, root or inversion. Draw an X through the chords that are inverted.

383

383

Write the V⁷ chord in root position for the keys of D and F. Write the three inversions for each of the two V⁷ chords.

384

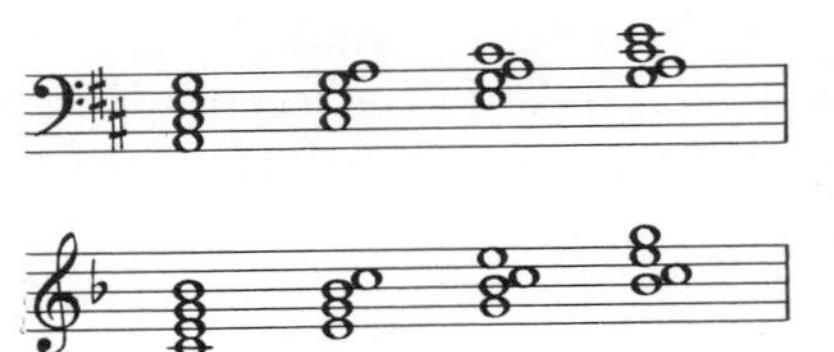

384

Chord inversions are used to make the playing of chord accompaniments easier. In moving from the I to the V^7 and back to the I, the hand is kept at approximately the same spot on the keyboard and the fingers are shifted to reach the notes of the next chord in an inverted position. The pattern below is commonly used. Which chord in the pattern is inverted? _______

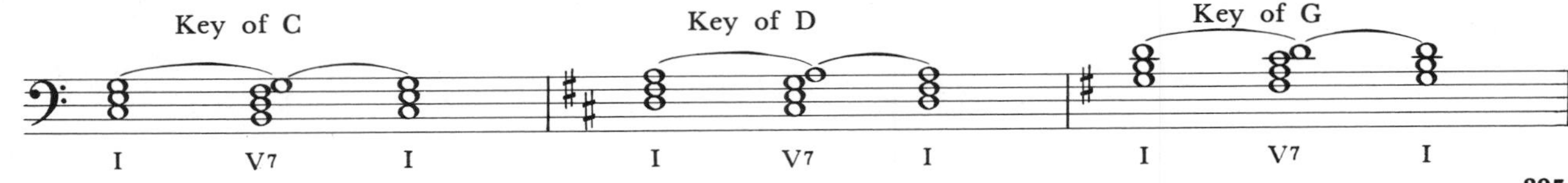

385

V^7.

385

For example, in the key of C no finger has to move more than one note up or down in order to strike the notes of the V^7 chord.

○ - indicates I
× - indicates V^7

Mark the root position of the I chord in C and the *root* position of the V^7 chord in C. Use o for I and x for V^7.

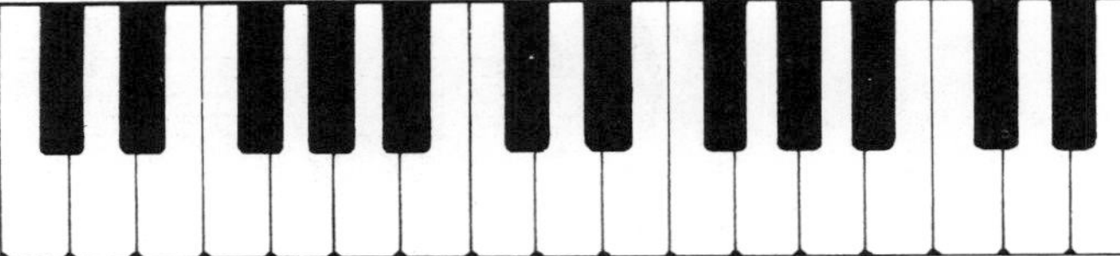

386

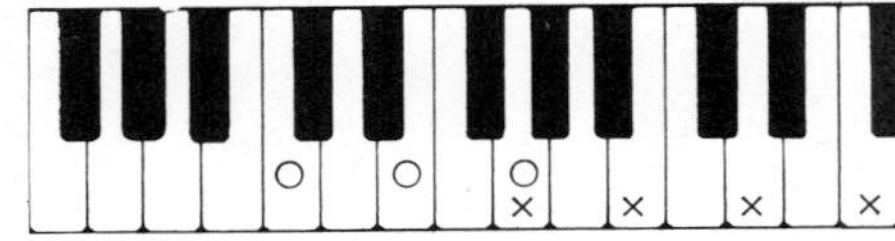

386

Mark the I chord, root position, and the V^7 chord, first inversion, key of D, on the keyboard below. Use o for I and x for V^7.

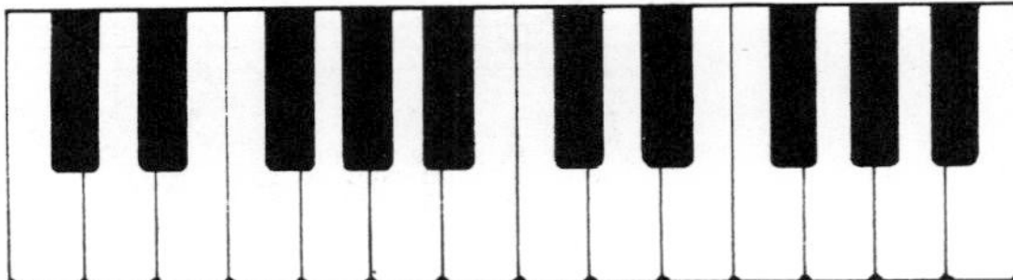

387

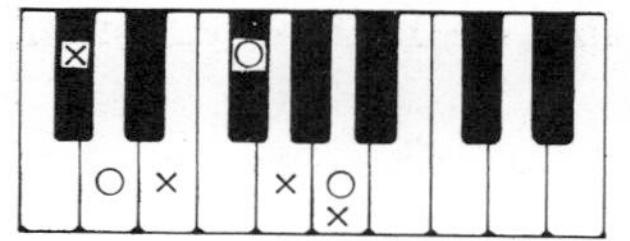

387

Inspection of the accompaniments of many elementary songs indicates that the V⁷ is most often written in first inversion, a practice that locates the notes close to those of the I chord in root position. Write the V⁷ chord, first inversion, for the keys of B-flat and D.

Play the chords.

388

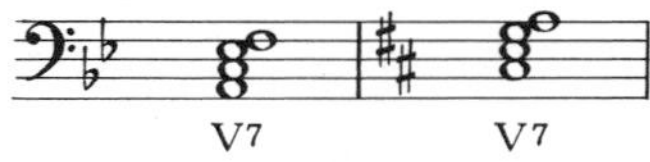

Playing response.

388

A second practice is the omission of certain chord notes. The fifth is often omitted from the V⁷ first inversion to facilitate performance without radically altering the sound.

What is the letter name of the omitted pitch in the V⁷ chord below? _______

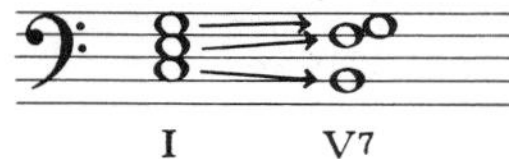

389

D.

389

Try playing this V⁷ chord on the piano to discover the difference made by omitting the fifth. (The o's are the I chord, the x's the V⁷ chord.)

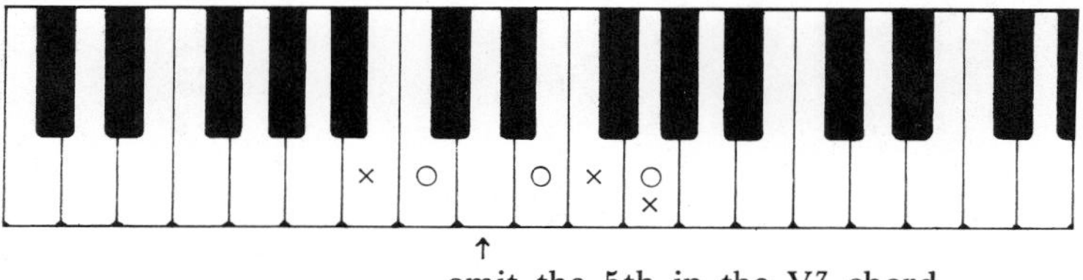

390

Playing response.

390

Note the practice in the following song. What is the letter name of the omitted pitch in the V^7 chord? _______

TROT, TROT MY LITTLE PONY

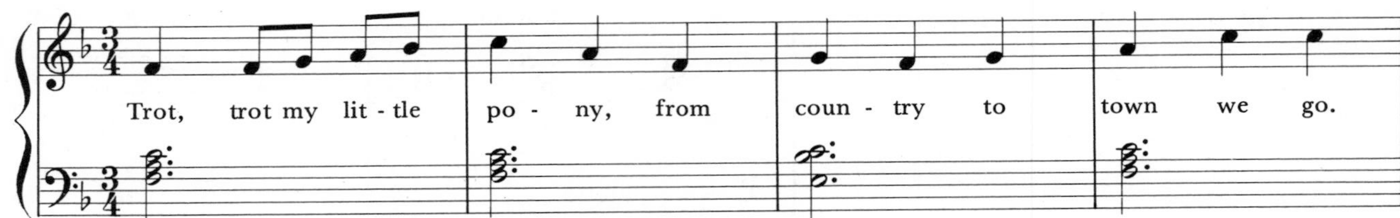
Trot, trot my lit - tle po - ny, from coun - try to town we go.

Trot, trot my lit - tle po - ny we trav - el se - cure - ly.

Often, other notes are omitted to make the accompaniments simple; many songs use only two notes of the chord. The teacher who knows the notes in the full chord can easily identify these two-note chords and thus assist the students in correct chording with an Autoharp, stringed instrument, or other chordal instrument.

391

G.

391

Write I, V^7 (first inversion), I in the keys designated. Omit the fifth in the V^7.

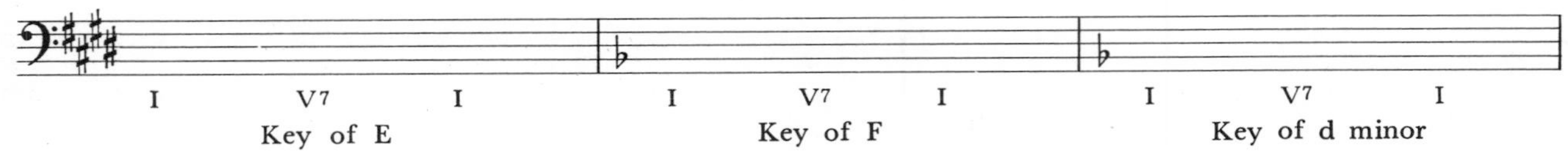
I V7 I
Key of E
I V7 I
Key of F
I V7 I
Key of d minor

Play the chords on the keyboard.

392

Playing response.

392

Write out the I, V^7 (first inversion), I for the key of G. Use the pattern you have written to accompany the song below.

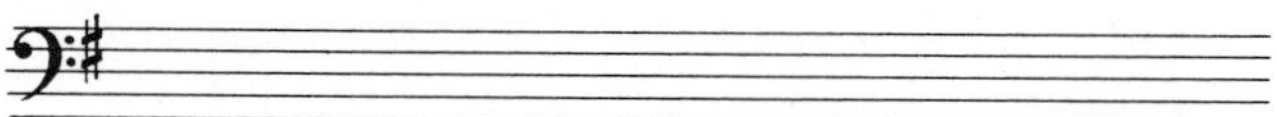

THE BRIDGE OF AVIGNON

On the bridge, round and round, Ev - ery - one is gai - ly danc - ing,
I V7 I V7
On the bridge, round and round, On the bridge of A - vi - gnon.
I V7 I V7 I

393

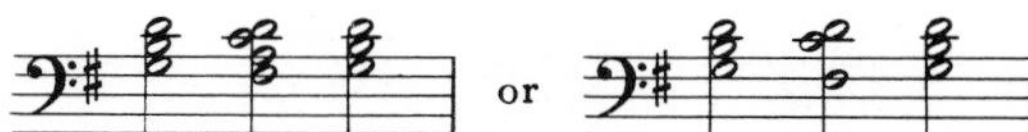
or

393

When the IV chord is used with the I and V^7 for accompanying, the simplest method is to play chord tones as close as possible to the preceding chord. The pattern below is widely used.

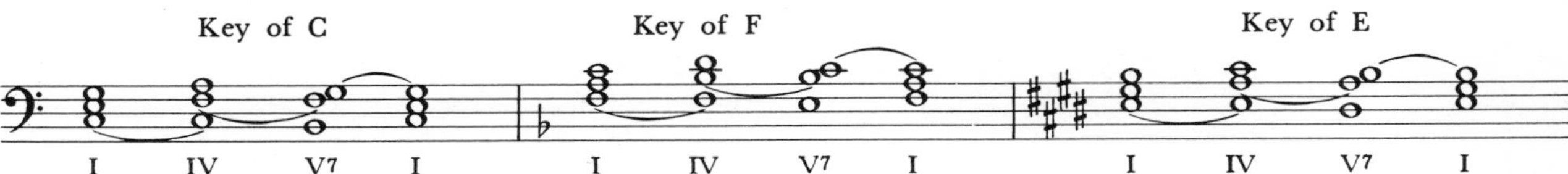
Key of C
Key of F
Key of E
I IV V7 I
I IV V7 I
I IV V7 I

Mark an X through the chords in root position.

Which inversion of the IV chord is used in each example? _______________

Which note is omitted from the V^7 chord? _______________

394

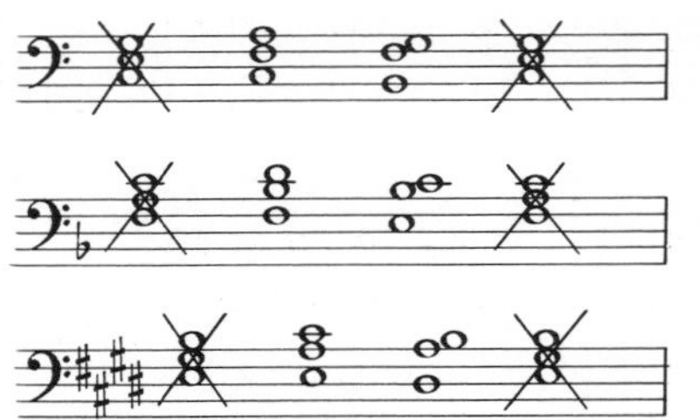

The second.

The fifth.

394

The pattern presented in the previous frame enables the player to move smoothly from one chord to the next. The I chord is played in root position. The root of the I is kept as the bottom note of the IV chord, the other two pitches moving up one scale step. From the IV to the V^7, the middle pitch of the IV (root) is kept, and the outer two pitches move down one scale step. Returning to I is done by keeping the top note (root) of the V^7 and moving the lower two notes to the pitches of the I chord.

On the keyboard mark the I chord notes with x, the IV chord notes with o, and the V^7 chord notes with √, in the key of C major. Use the pattern given in this frame.

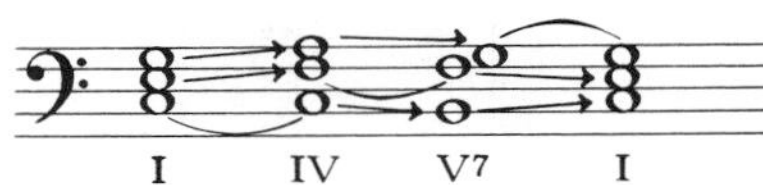

395

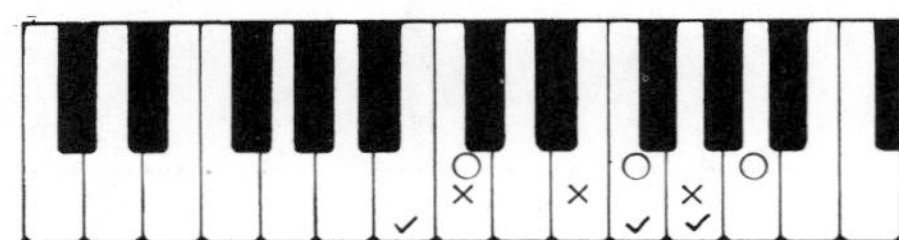

395

Write out the I, IV, V^7, I pattern in the keys indicated. Use identical movement to that in the preceding frame. Play the patterns.

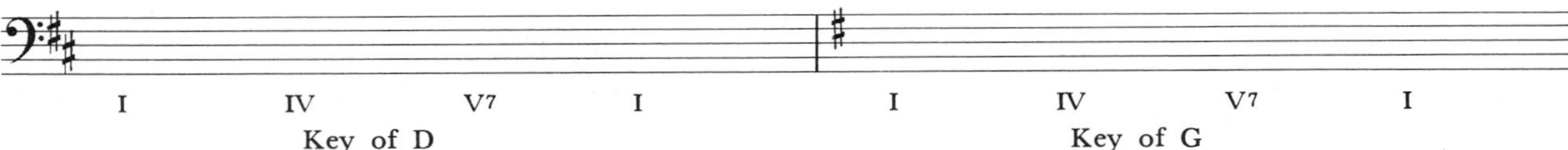

396

Playing response.

396

Practice the chordal accompaniment for the song below using inversions to make a smooth pattern. Write out the chords if necessary. Play the melody and accompaniment together. Give the roman numerals for the chords.

AIKEN DRUM

From The Fireside Book of Children's Songs. *Copyright © 1966 by Marie Winn and Allan Miller. Reprinted by permission of Simon and Schuster.*

397

I, IV, I, V^7, I, IV, I, V^7, I.

397

Inversions are used with the stringed instruments—guitar and ukulele—as they are with the piano, and for the same reason. Minimizing movement from one chord to another is important because it makes the accompaniment easier to play. We naturally invert chords on the stringed instruments, for we think of the name of the string and find the note of the chord closest to the pitch of the string.

Make up an exercise using the I, IV, V^7, I in an easy key for ukulele or guitar.

398

Composing response.

In the key of C, for example, the chords are usually played on the ukulele as shown below. The I chord is in root position; the IV chord and V^7 chord are inverted.

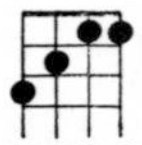

C (I) CEGC 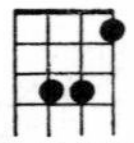 F(IV) AFAC 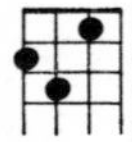 G (V7) BFGB

What is the inversion of the F chord? ________________

What is the inversion of the G^7 chord? ________________

What pitch is omitted from the G^7 chord? ________________

398

399

First.

First.

D.

399

CHAPTER 21 Chord Singing

Singing chords in the classroom is fun and it helps teach the sounds of major and minor chords. An easy way to introduce chording is to have one part of the class sing the root, a second part of the class add the third of the chord, and the rest of the class sing the fifth, all holding their pitches until the chord is complete. The objectives of this chapter are to help you (1) recognize chord patterns when they occur in melodies and (2) be able to sing various forms of chord patterns.

Using the piano, play "1" and "3" of a major triad; then sing "5." Change around: sing the root, hold it while you play the third and fifth; play "1," sing "3," and play "5." Do this in several keys. After you sing a pitch, check it with the piano to be sure you have sung it accurately.

400

Playing and singing response.

400

The notes of the chord presented one at a time, in order, are called an arpeggio. In singing an arpeggio we may sing "1–3–5," or the letter names of the chord, or the syllables do–mi–so.

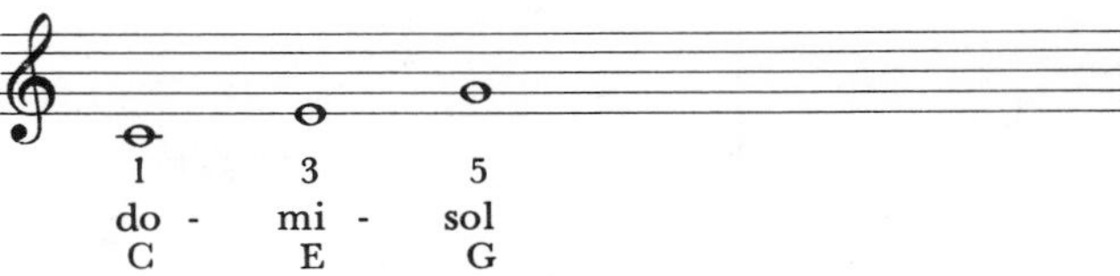

The pitches of a chord sounded one at a time, in order, create an ________________.

401

Arpeggio.

401

Singing the arpeggio for the tonic chord helps establish the tonal center or key feeling. Students may also practice singing the IV chord arpeggio and the V^7 chord arpeggio.

Play D on the piano. Sing the D arpeggio. Sing the d (minor) arpeggio. Check your singing with the piano.

Play B-flat on the piano. Sing the B-flat arpeggio. Sing the b-flat arpeggio. Check your singing with the piano.

Play E on the piano. Sing the E arpeggio and the e arpeggio. Check your singing with the piano.

402

Playing and singing response.

402

Label the chords given below in arpeggio form. Play F on the piano; then try to sing all three arpeggios without further help from the piano. Use letter names. Check your singing by playing the notes.

403

F, B-flat, C.

Singing response.

403

Remember that pitches may be omitted from the chord and the chord inverted, but it is still labeled by considering the lowest pitch, as if it were built in thirds (adjacent lines or spaces). Play the D chord; then sing the various inversions of the D chord. Check your singing by playing the inversions on the piano.

Name the chords below.

404

Playing and singing response.

C^7, D, D^7.

To identify an arpeggio in a pattern, inspect the pattern and name the notes. Rearrange the notes to fit a triadic pattern. For example, the notes A, C, F can be arranged:

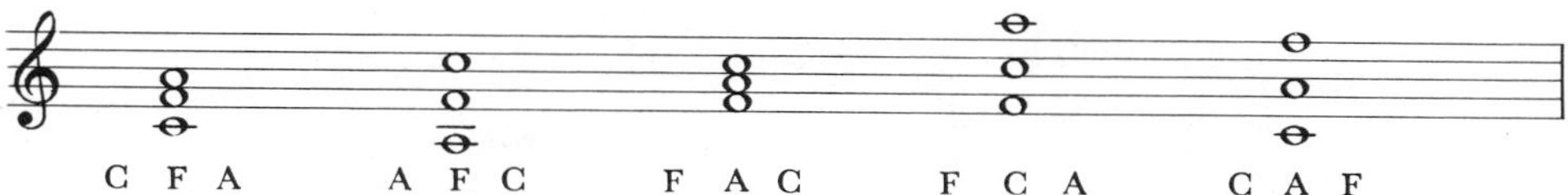
C F A
A F C
F A C
F C A
C A F

Only F–A–C is a triadic (line by line or space by space) pattern. Next, determine the key. F–A–C is a I chord in the key of F, a IV chord in the key of C, and a V chord in the key of B-flat.

With seventh chords there may be four notes to arrange. Also with a seventh chord one note may be omitted without destroying the arpeggio.

For example, F–G–B

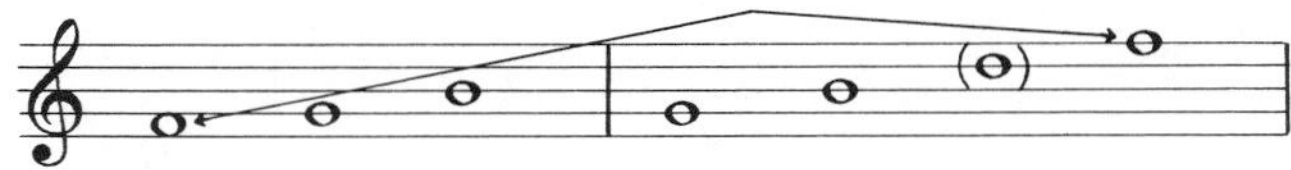

is an arpeggio of G–B(D)–F, a V^7 chord in the key of C.

In this song the melody in measures 1, 2, 5–6, and 7 forms arpeggios of chords in the key. What arpeggio is in measure 1? ________________; in measure 2 (one note of the chord is omitted)? ________________; in measures 5–6? ________________; in measure 7 (partial chord)? ________________

SWEET BETSY FROM PIKE

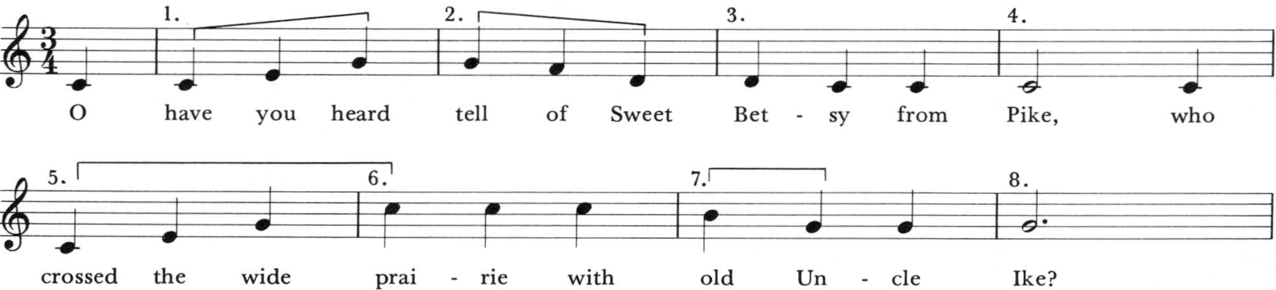
1.
2.
3.
4.
O have you heard tell of Sweet Bet - sy from Pike, who
5.
6.
7.
8.
crossed the wide prai - rie with old Un - cle Ike?

Play the C chord; then sing the bracketed arpeggios. Check with the piano.

C major.

G_7.

C major.

G(V).

Playing and singing response.

405

Triads and seventh chords are by no means the only chords used in music. A common practice in popular music and jazz is to use chords containing (or implying) five, six, or more pitches. A three-note chord is called a triad; 1–3–5. A four-note chord is called a seventh chord: 1–3–5–7. A five-note chord is called a ninth chord: 1–3–5–7–9. A six-note chord is called an eleventh chord: 1–3–5–7–9–11, and so forth. Play these chords.

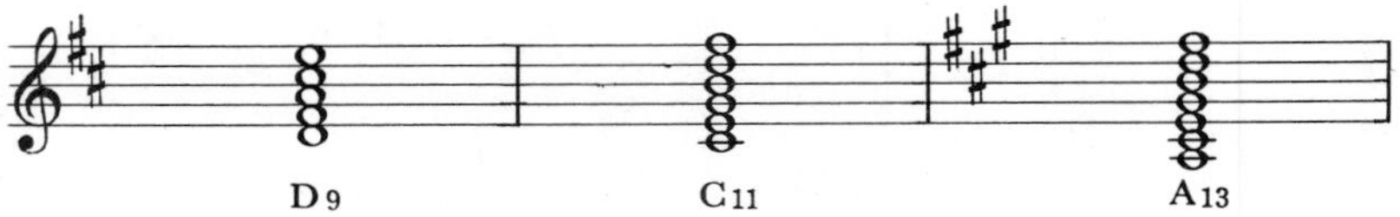

D9 C11 A13

406

Playing response.

406

Contemporary composers have made use of chords built upon intervals other than the third. Chords may be built in fourths, fifths, seconds, and sevenths (the interval between pitches is a fourth, fifth, etc.).

Play these chords on the piano. Listen to their sounds. Try to sing the pitches of each chord.

Chords built in fifths

Chords built in seconds

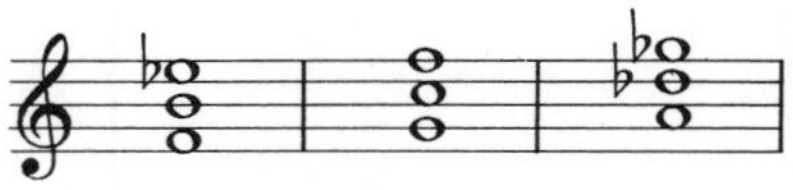

Chords built in fourths

407

Playing and singing response.

407

Examine the chords below. Determine the interval used to build each chord.

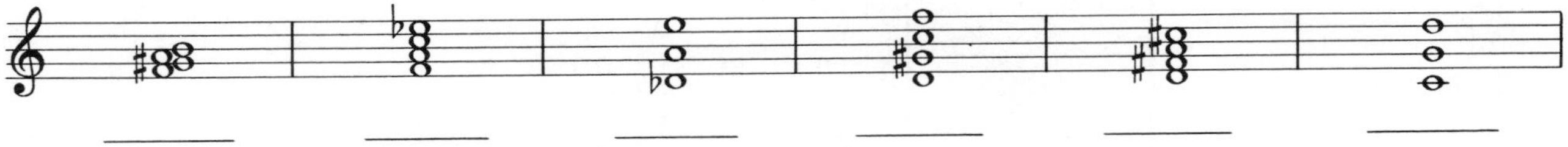

________ ________ ________ ________ ________ ________

Play the chords. Try to sing the pitches.

408

Seconds.

Thirds.

Fifths.

Fourths.

Thirds.

Fifths.

408

PRETEST for Chapter 22: Sight Singing

Mark the correct answer or *answers.*

1. The syllables in this musical passage are:

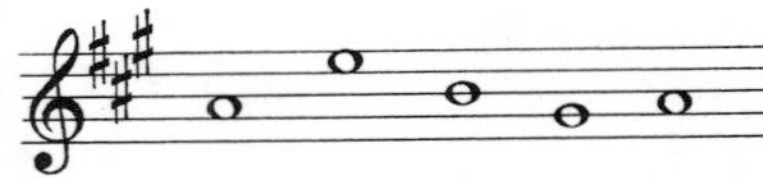

2. Which of the following is an arpeggio?

1. 2. 3. 4.

3. The minor scale always begins on:

—— a. do

—— b. me

—— c. so

—— d. la

4. An E-major scale would always begin on:

—— a. do

—— b. so

—— c. mi

—— d. la

5. In a major scale, fa is:

—— a. 1

—— b. 4

—— c. 6

—— d. 8

6. In an a minor scale, the note c is:

—— a. 3

—— b. 1

—— c. 5

—— d. 8

7. In an e minor scale, the note g is:

—— a. do

—— b. me

—— c. so

—— d. la

8. A clenched fist hand signal indicates:

—— a. me

—— b. fa

—— c. so

—— d. do

Answers

1. do, so, re, ti, do.
2. 1.
3. d.
4. a.
5. b.
6. a.
7. a.
8. d.

From your score determine whether you can omit sections of the text.

CHAPTER 22 Sight Singing

One of the most useful skills a teacher can help students achieve in music is the ability to sing new music at sight without depending on piano, record, or teacher. Much of what has already been presented in this book helps in sight reading: knowing durational values and meter signatures, understanding scalewise and skipwise intervals, knowing key signatures and their meanings, and recognizing tempo and volume terms. The exercises in this chapter are designed to give you (1) knowledge of syllables in major and minor, (2) knowledge of numbers in major and minor, (3) acquaintance with hand signals used with syllables, and (4) practice in applying these aids, as well as letter names, to sight singing.

Several methods exist for helping the singer to sight sing accurately. The following pages discuss three such methods: use of syllables, use of numbers, and use of letter names. It is also possible to sight sing depending only on a recognition of the distance (interval) between written pitches. For example, if you remember accurately the sound of the whole step, and if you recognize the written pitches as a whole step, you can sing the pattern on "la" or "loo" or whatever.

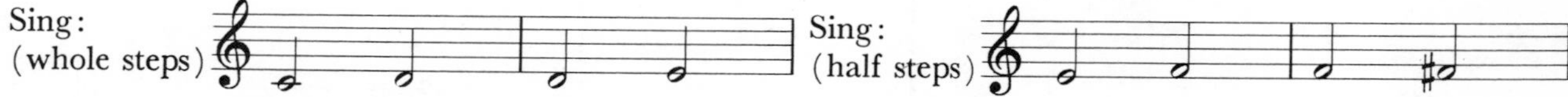

Check your answer with an instrument such as the piano.

409

Singing response.

409

When the intervals become larger than the half steps and whole steps of the scale, sight singing increases in its difficulty. The sound of larger intervals, however, can also be memorized: Sing

410

Singing response.

410

When you can retain the sound of the major third 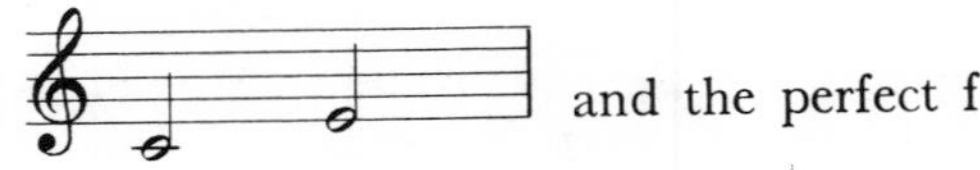 and the perfect fourth , you can accurately sing any two pitches that form these intervals.

These major thirds all sound alike  except that they lie on slightly different pitch levels. The same is true for these perfect fourths

 .

Sight singing simply on "loo" or "la" without depending on a method requires a keen memory for the sound of the intervals and an ability to recognize the intervals in the notation.
Sing these intervals, using the piano to assist you.

411

Singing response.

411

Unless we can sing notated pitches accurately, we are unable to sight sing. To aid himself in reading the pitches correctly, the singer can use several helps. The syllable system is often used to help in pitch recognition. The pitches of the major scale are each called by a syllable: do, re, mi, fa, so, la, ti, and do, from the lowest pitch to the highest. These syllables always have the same relationship to each other, regardless of what major key they are applied to. For example, in the key of C, do, re, mi applies to C, D, E; and in the key of D it applies to D, E, F-sharp.

The complete scale of syllables is:

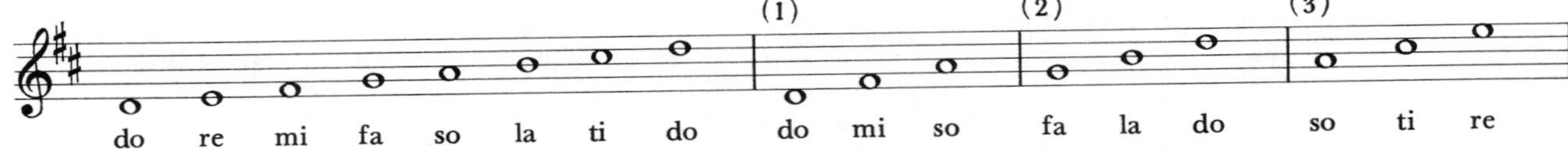

Sing the scale and chords above; use the syllable names. What chord is indicated by arpeggio (1)? ______________ (2)? ______________ (3)? ______________ Play the piano to check your accuracy of pitch.

412

Singing response.

I (D).

IV (G).

V (A).

Playing response.

412

The use of syllables is determined by the key signature. The keynote indicated by the major signature is always "do," with the other syllables always maintaining the same pattern in relation to "do." This is true for both major and minor keys.

The syllables for the C major scale are:

The syllables for a minor (relative to C) are:

C is "do" in both cases. The minor scale runs from "la" to "la," the major scale from "do" to "do."

The syllables for the c minor scale are:

What major key is indicated by the three-flat signature? ______________

413

E-flat major.

413

Knowledge of the major key allows one to know syllables in both major and minor.

Name the syllables.

Sing the syllables; check your accuracy with the piano.

414

Do, so. Singing response. 414	The syllable names for these notes are: ___ ___ ___ Sing and check. 415
Re, do, re. Singing response. 415	The syllables are: ___ ___ ___ Sing them. Check with the piano. 416
So, fa, la. Singing response. 416	The syllable names for these notes are: ___ ___ ___ ___ Sing with syllables. Check with the piano. 417
So, mi, do, la. Singing response. 417	Write the syllables under each note of the following scale: ___ ___ ___ ___ ___ ___ ___ ___ What is the key? _______ What kind of scale is it? ________________ Sing the scale. 418

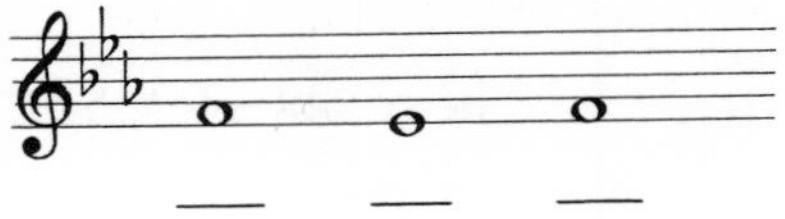

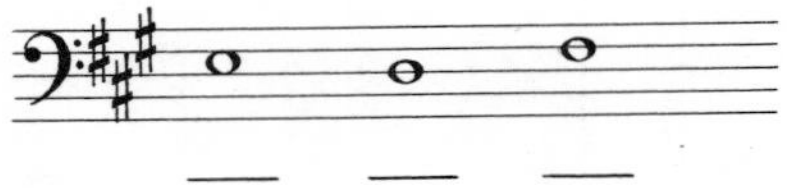

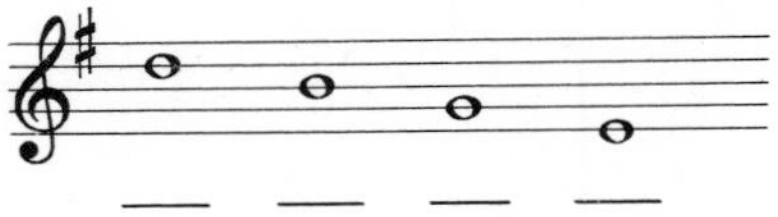

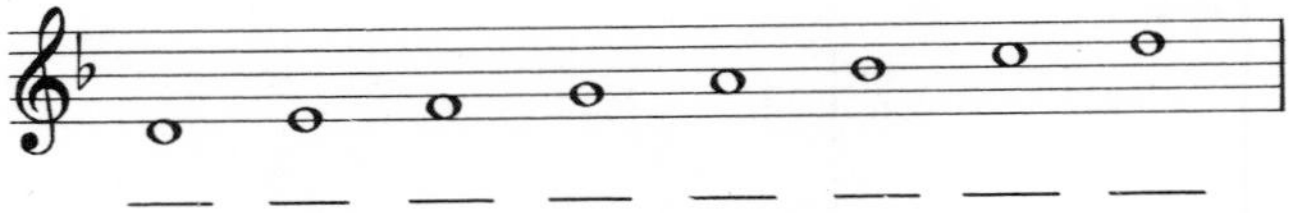

la, ti, do, re, mi, fa, so, la.

d.

Natural minor.

Singing response.

418

Once the key center, or "do," has been established, syllables can be applied to all the pitches of the melody to help in singing the song correctly.

The short phrase above appears in two different major keys. Determine the key center or "do." Write the syllables underneath the notes, and sing it in each key, first finding "do" on the piano. The melody should be identical in both keys. Check your accuracy with the piano.

419

Singing response.

419

With syllables, separate sounds are available for accidentals. For example, there is a sharp and a flat for "so": "so-sharp" is "si"; "so-flat" is "se." A complete list of these is found in the Glossary.

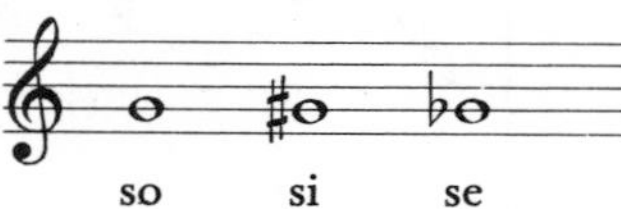

If we sing in the minor mode with syllables, the key tone is called "la." "Do" is the key tone of the major scale, and to find the relative minor we count down "do, ti, la" just as we do to find the minor key from the signature. The minor scale runs from "la" to "la." The pitch relationships always remain the same; the key center moves.

Using the syllables, sing the natural minor scales above. Check with the piano.

420

Singing response.

420

Write the syllables for the minor phrase. Sing the melody with syllables, first finding "la" on the piano. Use the piano to check your pitches.

WAYFARING STRANGER

421

---

la do re mi mi re mi do la la re re

re la do re mi

Singing response.

421

Do the same for "O Hanukkah."

O HANUKKAH

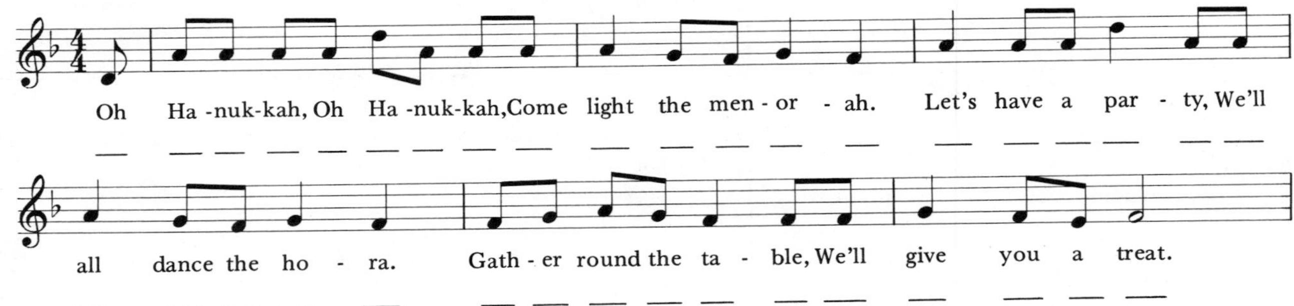
Oh Ha-nuk-kah, Oh Ha-nuk-kah, Come light the men-or-ah. Let's have a par-ty, We'll
all dance the ho-ra. Gath-er round the ta-ble, We'll give you a treat.

422

la mi mi mi mi la mi mi mi mi re do re do
mi mi mi la mi mi mi re do re do
do re mi re do do do re do ti do

Singing response.

422

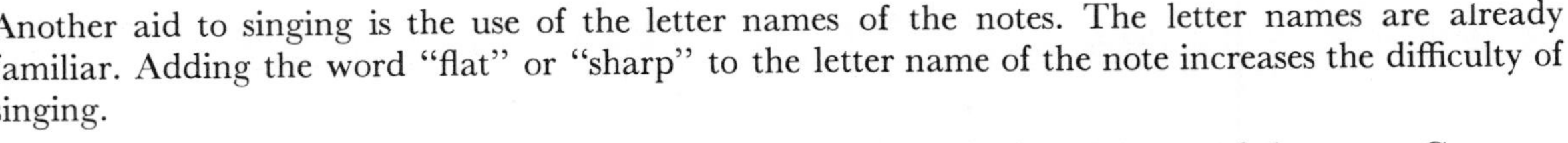

Another aid to singing is the use of the letter names of the notes. The letter names are already familiar. Adding the word "flat" or "sharp" to the letter name of the note increases the difficulty of singing.

Sing a tonic arpeggio in the key of D (D–F-sharp–A). Use the letter names of the notes. Compare this with singing these three pitches using do-mi-so.

423

Singing response.

423

Sing this scale and chords. Use the letter names and then use syllables. Check your accuracy with the piano.

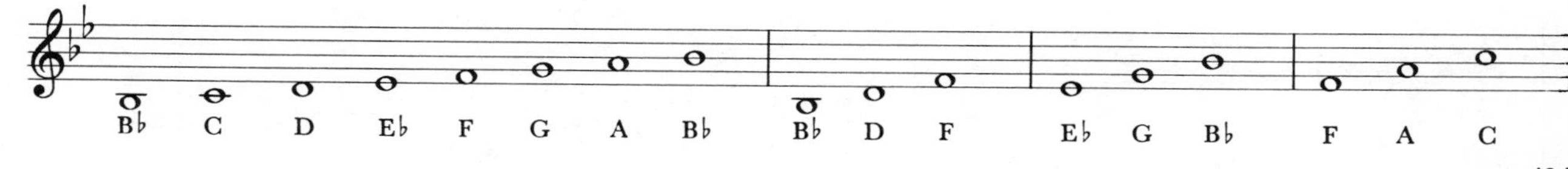

424

Singing response.

424

Write the syllables underneath the notes in the following song:

THE FARMER IN THE DELL
The farm - er in the dell, The farm - er in the dell,
Heigh - o the mer - ry - o, The farm - er in the dell.

Sing with the syllables. Sing with the letter names.

425

Singing response.

425

This is the same phrase in the same two keys that appeared in frame 419. Write the letter names underneath the notes. Sing the two phrases with letter names. Before you sing each phrase first play the key center on the piano. (Changing the key will not change the pitch relationship between the notes, and both phrases will sound alike.) With syllables, both phrases were sung alike; with letter names, "do" is F in the first phrase, C in the second.

426

Singing response.

426

A third system to aid in sight singing is the use of numbers. Numbers, like syllables, have the same relationship to each other regardless of the key. The pitches in the major scale are numbered 1, 2, 3, 4, 5, 6, 7, and 8, from the lowest pitch to the highest. The advantage of numbers over syllables is that the numbers are already familiar and syllables have to be learned. The disadvantage of numbers is that they are unmusical—they do not offer the open, vocal sounds of the syllables.

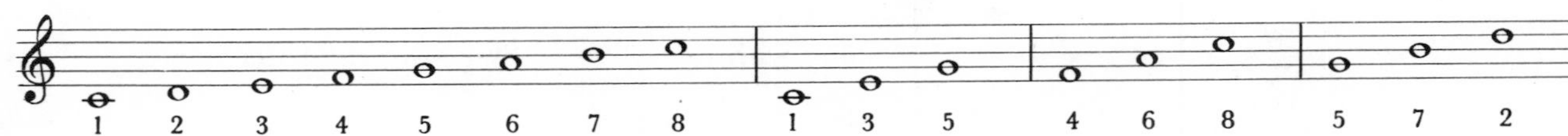

Sing this scale and chords. First use numbers; then use syllables and letter names.

427

Singing response.

427

Again the same phrase is presented in the same two keys. Write the number names beneath the notes. Sing the phrase with numbers after you have found "1" on the piano.

Considerable time has been spent on introducing various techniques that might aid music reading. The teacher will want to take advantage of all of them in order to help students gain musical independence and learn to sight sing.

428

Singing response.

428

Advocates of the syllable system and the number system believe these make sight singing easier because pitch relationships within each system remain stable. "Do" to "so" always sounds the same; 1 to 5 always sounds the same (they are the same interval); the singer simply applies his vocal tape measure to the key in which the piece is written. The system that determines "do" by the key signature is called the *movable "do"* system; "do" moves from key to key. The *fixed "do"* system is widely used in Europe; in this system "do" is always C, and use of syllables is identical in all respects to the use of letter names. The movable "do" system is used in American schools, but the fixed "do" system is seldom used.

In the fixed "do" system, what syllable is the pitch E? ______

429

Mi.

Syllables and letter names do not change according to mode, major or minor. If you sing in the minor mode with numbers, "1" is the key center. "One" is also the key center for the major scale; thus, when the minor scale is sung with numbers, 3, 6, and 7 will be lowered in pitch from their sounds in the major scale. The singer learns two sets of half and whole step relationships for numbers—the major scale relationships and the minor scale relationships.

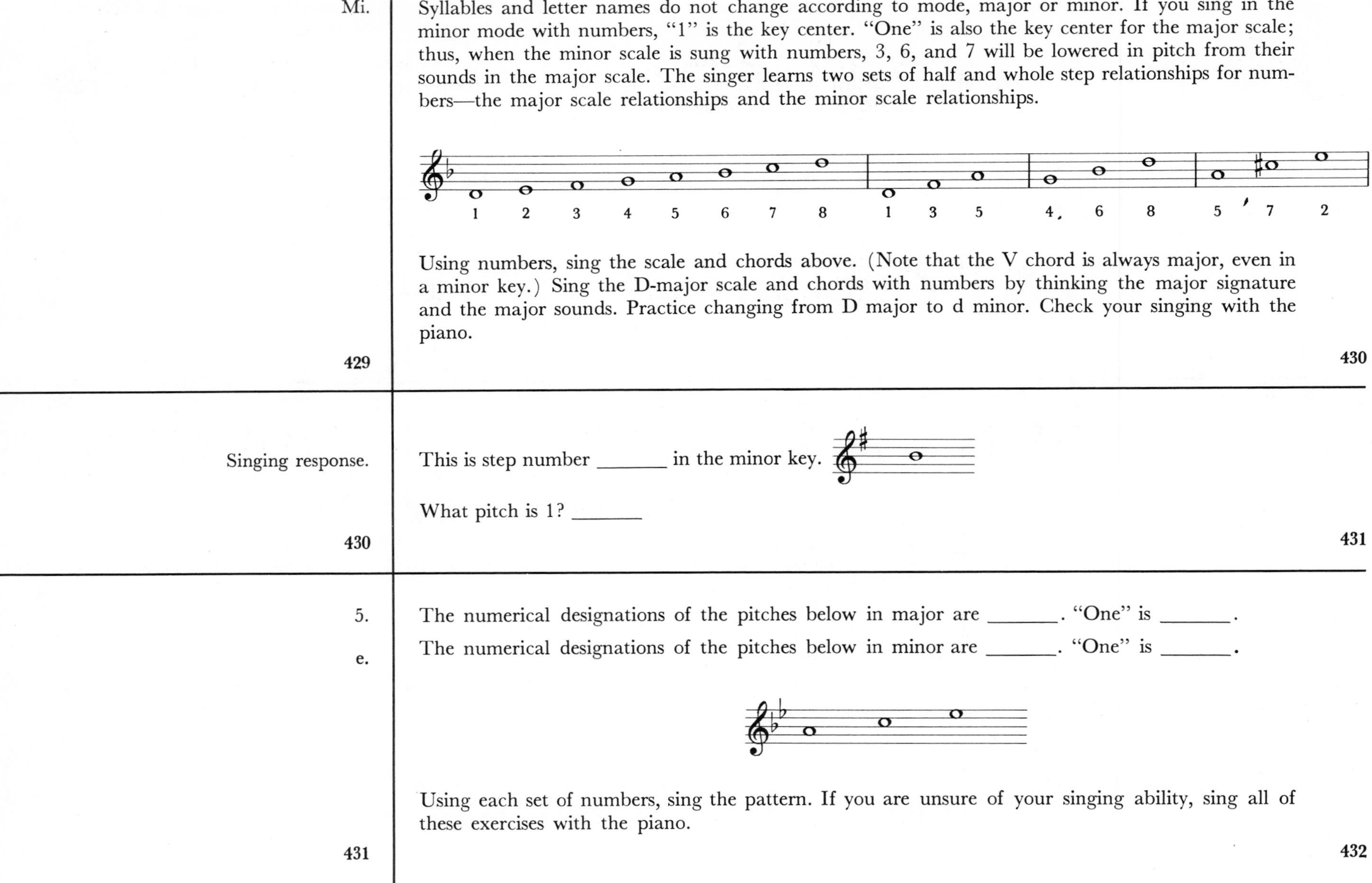

Using numbers, sing the scale and chords above. (Note that the V chord is always major, even in a minor key.) Sing the D-major scale and chords with numbers by thinking the major signature and the major sounds. Practice changing from D major to d minor. Check your singing with the piano.

429 430

Singing response.

This is step number ______ in the minor key.

What pitch is 1? ______

430 431

5.

e.

The numerical designations of the pitches below in major are ______. "One" is ______.

The numerical designations of the pitches below in minor are ______. "One" is ______.

Using each set of numbers, sing the pattern. If you are unsure of your singing ability, sing all of these exercises with the piano.

431 432

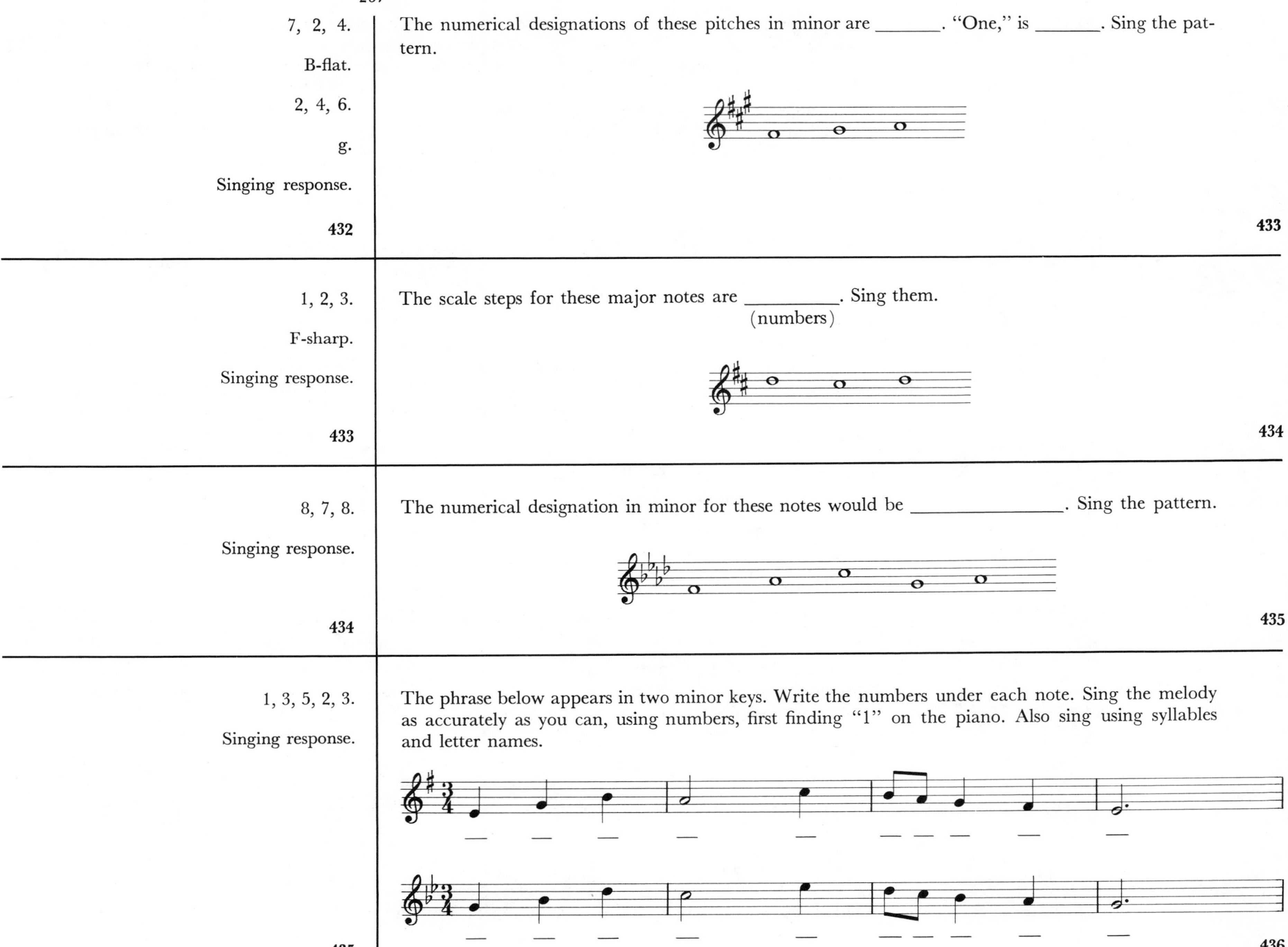

7, 2, 4.

B-flat.

2, 4, 6.

g.

Singing response.

432

The numerical designations of these pitches in minor are ______. "One," is ______. Sing the pattern.

433

1, 2, 3.

F-sharp.

Singing response.

433

The scale steps for these major notes are ________. Sing them.
(numbers)

434

8, 7, 8.

Singing response.

434

The numerical designation in minor for these notes would be ______________. Sing the pattern.

435

1, 3, 5, 2, 3.

Singing response.

435

The phrase below appears in two minor keys. Write the numbers under each note. Sing the melody as accurately as you can, using numbers, first finding "1" on the piano. Also sing using syllables and letter names.

436

Singing response.

Although the syllable system appears to have advantages for sight singing that letters and numbers do not have, it is sometimes difficult to learn well enough to be a help rather than a hindrance. To facilitate the learning of syllables by small children, Mary Helen Richards has adapted the Kodály system of hand signals. Each hand signal stands for a syllable. The children begin by recognizing two, then three hand signals. They progress to the five hand signals that stand for the five pitches of the pentatonic scales. Finally, they learn the signals for all seven pitches of the major scale; then they adapt these to minor.

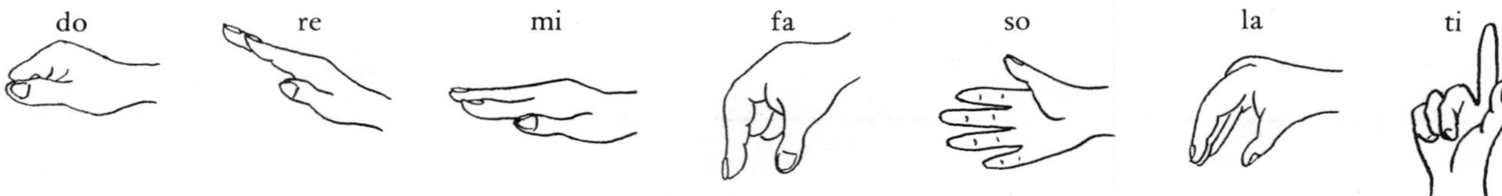

Practice the hand signals for the song "Button" in this frame. The ability to use hand signals in the classroom depends on sufficient practice on the part of the teacher to develop some skill. Several songs in this book should be used for practicing hand signals. Sing the song while using the signals in order to establish the correct rhythm and meter.

"Button" is in the key of _______________.

The number of pulses per measure is ______.

What kind of note gets one pulse? _______________ Clap the rhythm.

Practice singing the song with syllables, numbers, and letter names.

BUTTON

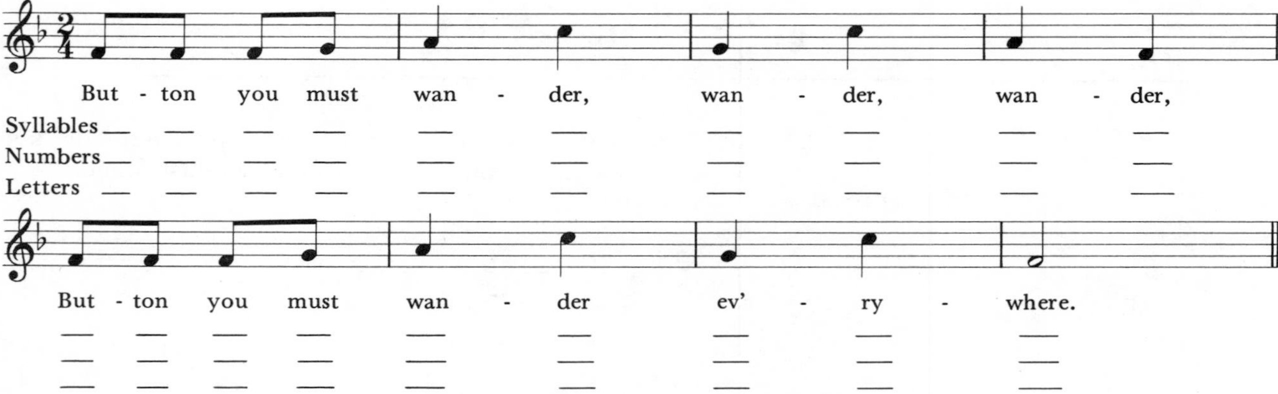

Write the syllables, numbers and letter names below the music.

F major.

2.

Quarter note.

Clapping and singing response.

437

What is the key for the song below? ______________

How many pulses in a measure? ______

What kind of note gets one pulse? ______________ Clap the rhythm.

What does the C♯ indicate? ______________

Practice singing the song with syllables, numbers, and letter names.

Write the syllables below the note.

438

d minor.

4.

Quarter note.

Raised 7th in harmonic minor.

Clapping and singing response.

438

APPLICATION: Sight Singing

Four songs are given. Learn each song by using the following method: 1. Examine the meter signature; then clap the rhythm of the entire song. 2. Examine the key signature; then write the numbers and syllables beneath the notes. Check with the answer. 3. Sing the song with letter names, numbers, and syllables, using correct rhythm. Check with the piano or other instrument for correct pitches. 4. When you have learned the four songs, listen to the recording to determine how accurately you learned them. Sing with the record.

Exercise 41: What is the meaning of the tempo mark in the following song? ______________

O CHRISTMAS TREE

Moderate speed.

5 1 1 1 2 3 3 3 3 2 3 4 7
so do do do re mi mi mi mi re mi fa ti
2 1 5 1 1 1 2 3 3 3 3
re do so do do do re mi mi mi mi
2 3 4 7 2 1 5 5 3 6 5
re mi fa ti re do so so mi la so
5 4 4 4 4 2 5 4 4 3 3 5
so fa fa fa fa re so fa fa mi mi so
1 1 1 2 3 3 3 3 2 3 4 7 2 1
do do do re mi mi mi mi re mi fa ti re do

Exercise 42:

MARCHING TO PRETORIA
Introduction:
Song:
I'm with you and you're with me and
so we are all to-geth-er, So we are all to-geth-er, So we are all to-geth-er,
Sing with me, I'll sing with you and so we shall sing to-geth-er as we march a - long.
What is the meaning of ₵ ? ________
How many counts does ♩. ♪ receive? ________

3 3 3 3 3 3 3 3 3 5 4
mi mi mi mi mi mi mi mi mi so fa
3 3 3 3 2 4 3 2 2 2 2
mi mi mi mi re fa mi re re re re
1 3 2 1 1 1 1 3 3 3 3
do mi re do do do do mi mi mi mi
3 3 3 3 3 5 4 3 3 3 3
mi mi mi mi mi so fa mi mi mi mi
2 4 3 2 1
re fa mi re do

Cut time, or "alla breve."

One count.

42

Exercise 43: What is the meaning of the tempo marking? ________________

FOUR IN A BOAT

Introduction:
Allegro
Song:
Four in a boat and the tide rolls high, Four in a boat and the tide rolls high,
Four in a boat and the tide rolls high, Wait-ing for a pret-ty girl to come by and by.

Fast.

1 3 3 1 3 3 1 6 5
do mi mi do mi mi do la so
1 3 3 1 3 3 5 5 2
do mi mi do mi mi so so re

Exercise 44:

SILVER BIRCH

Introduction:

43

What is the key? ________________

End of Band 3, Side 4 (A STOP BAND)
End of Application Section 4

g minor.

44

PRETEST for Chapters 23–24: Conducting and Advanced Concepts

1. Identify the meter for these conducting patterns.

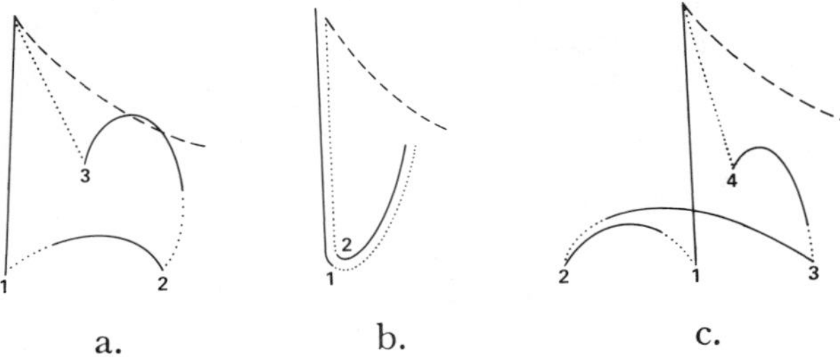

a. b. c.

2. Identify the whole-tone scale.

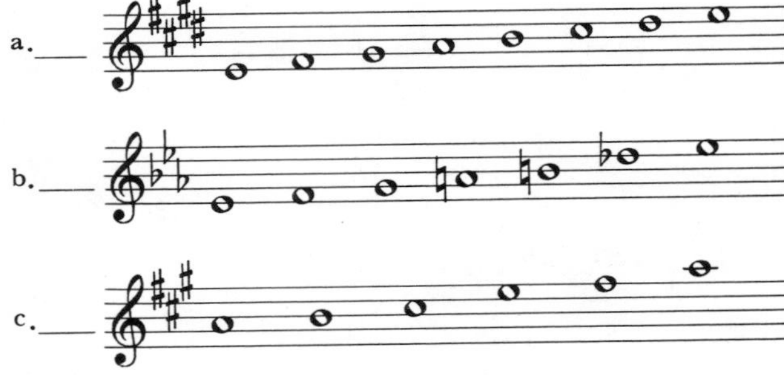

3. Which of these rhythm patterns is (are) syncopated?

4. In a song with polymeter:
   ___ a. the song has a rollicking meter
   ___ b. the soprano might be singing in $\frac{2}{4}$, the tenor in $\frac{3}{4}$
   ___ c. the first half of the song might be in $\frac{2}{4}$, the last half in $\frac{3}{4}$
   ___ d. Polynesian meters are used throughout the song.

5. Three notes on one beat is an example of:
   ___ a. cut time
   ___ b. triplets
   ___ c. polymeter
   ___ d. syncopation

6. These notes c, c♯, d, d♯, e, f, f♯, g, g♯, a, a♯, b form a:
   ___ a. chromatic scale
   ___ b. pentatonic scale
   ___ c. whole-tone scale
   ___ d. tone row

Answers

1. a. Triple; b. Duple; c. Quadruple.
2. b.
3. b.  c. 
4. b.
5. b.
6. a, d.

From your score determine if you can omit portions of the text.

265

CHAPTER 23 Conducting

As students develop skill in singing, the teacher may wish to use the standard conducting patterns when leading songs. The art of conducting requires a high level of skill, but the basic conducting patterns can be easily learned. When you have completed the exercises in this chapter, you should be able to (1) conduct simple songs in duple, triple, and quadruple meter; (2) identify and conduct pick-ups; (3) give a preparatory beat.

The first pulse of the measure, the accented pulse, is known as the downbeat; the hand or baton of the conductor always comes down on this beat. The final pulse of the measure is known as the upbeat because the hand or baton of the conductor comes up on this beat in preparation for the next downbeat.

In $\frac{3}{4}$ meter the upbeat would be on count ______; in $\frac{4}{4}$ meter, on count ______.

---

3. A meter that has only two beats, such as $\frac{2}{4}$ or $\frac{2}{8}$, would be conducted DOWN–UP, as the pattern

4. indicates. Notice a curve at the bottom of the downbeat; this is to create a slight feeling of bounce in the beat rather than a strict mechanical down and up.

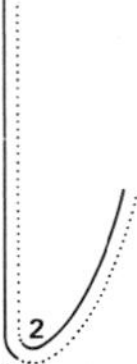

439

Draw the conducting pattern for two-beat meter. Practice conducting this pattern by counting "one-two." Use a mirror if possible. 440

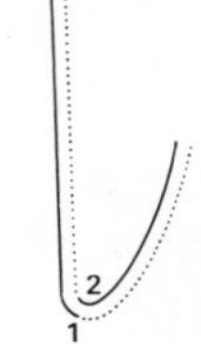

Conducting response.

440

Meters having more than two pulses use other motions inserted between the downbeat and the upbeat. Triple meter is conducted DOWN–RIGHT–UP. Left-handed conductors might use DOWN–LEFT–UP. Quadruple meter is conducted DOWN–LEFT–RIGHT–UP. A small feeling of bounce or accent is given on each beat. In the diagrams below the numbers indicate approximately where each beat is placed or accented. Notice that the last count of the measure—the upbeat—is not at the top of the upswing, but close to the bottom. The upbeat continues to rise after the pulse has been accented.

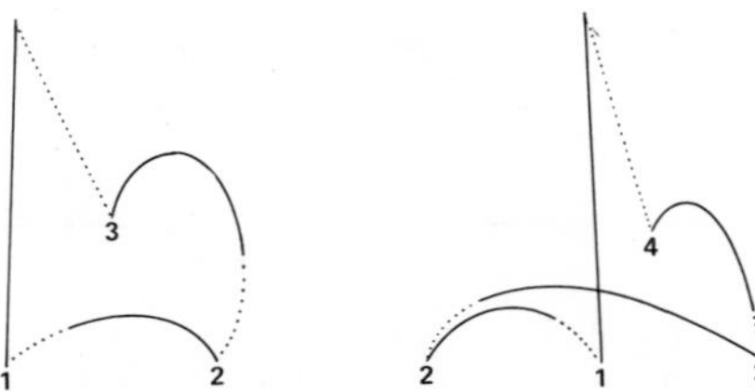

Draw the conducting patterns for triple and quadruple meter. Practice conducting these patterns. Give a small bounce on each beat. Use music or count aloud.

You can sing and conduct yourself. Use a mirror. Practice the motions in the air to music you know, but first determine the meter of the song. 441

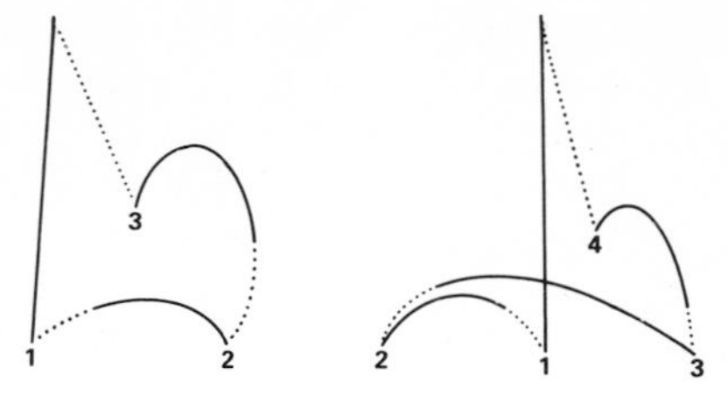

If the teacher simply gives a downbeat to begin the song, students will not be able to start together or start on time. A preparatory beat is needed to give singers (or players) the chance to breathe and come in together. The preparatory beat is usually an upbeat—the teacher conducts one pulse before the downbeat, where students are expected to begin. Below, the preparatory beats are indicated by the dashed line for the duple, triple, and quadruple patterns.

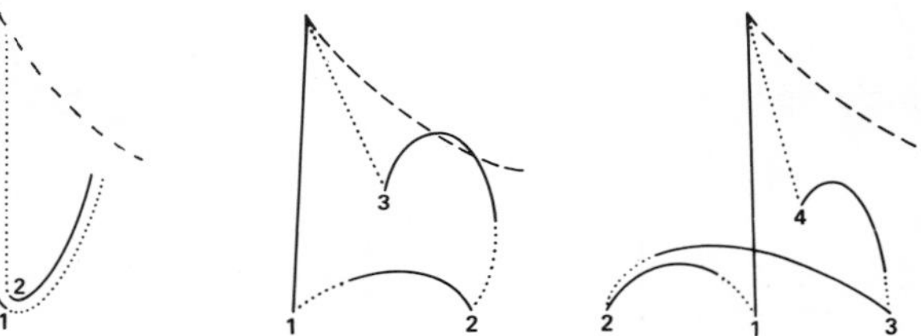

Draw the duple, triple, and quadruple conducting patterns with a preparatory upbeat (use a dashed line for the preparatory beat). Practice conducting these patterns. Take a breath on the preparatory beat.

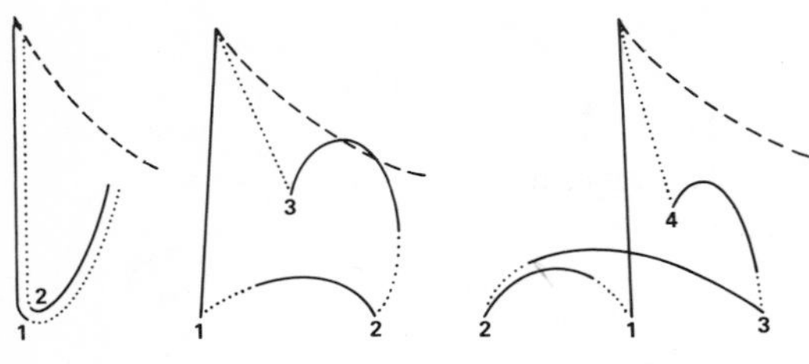
1
2
1
3
2
2
4
1
3

Conducting response.

Some music does not begin on the downbeat; the music has one or more pick-ups that occupy part of a measure. In this case, the preparatory beat must precede the pick-up beat(s). The arm motion used for a preparatory beat to a pick-up must match the normal conducting motion for that beat in the measure.

"The Star-Spangled Banner": triple meter, pick-up on count 3, preparatory beat on count 2.

"Oh, *say* can you see": Downbeat is on "say."

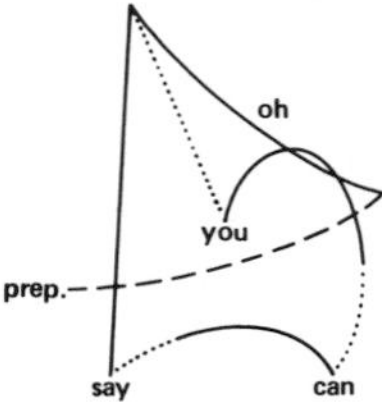
oh
you
prep.
say
can

"Annie Laurie": quadruple meter, pick-up on count 4, preparatory beat on count 3.

"Max*well*ton's braes are bonnie." Downbeat is on "well."

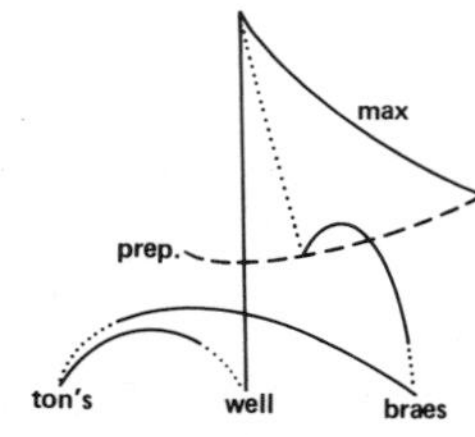
max
prep.
ton's
well
braes

THE STAR-SPANGLED BANNER

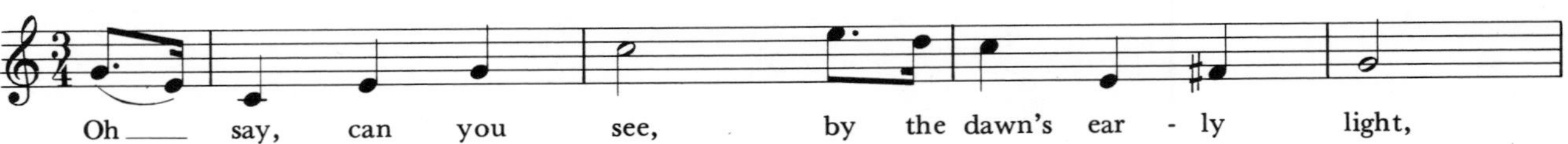
Oh say, can you see, by the dawn's ear - ly light,

ANNIE LAURIE

Max well - ton's braes are bon - nie, where ear - ly falls the dew,

Conducting response.

Sing "My Bonnie Lies Over the Ocean." What is the meter? _______

On which count does "My" (the pick-up) fall? _______

Which count will be the preparatory beat? _______

Conduct "My Bonnie" while you sing it.

MY BONNIE

443

444

$\frac{3}{4}$ or triple meter.

3.

2.

Singing and conducting response.

444

APPLICATION: Conducting

The four conducting exercises will use the songs you learned in the sight singing application. The sight-singing portion of the record is to be used for conducting. Look at the meter signature for each song and draw the appropriate conducting pattern. Six beats will be given before each song to set the tempo. Count the first five beats, give the preparatory beat on count six, and conduct with the record as you follow the notation in the exercise.

Exercise 45: Draw the appropriate conducting pattern.

The music begins on the upbeat, or third count of the measure. Draw the preparatory beat and upbeat that are needed to begin the music correctly.

O CHRISTMAS TREE

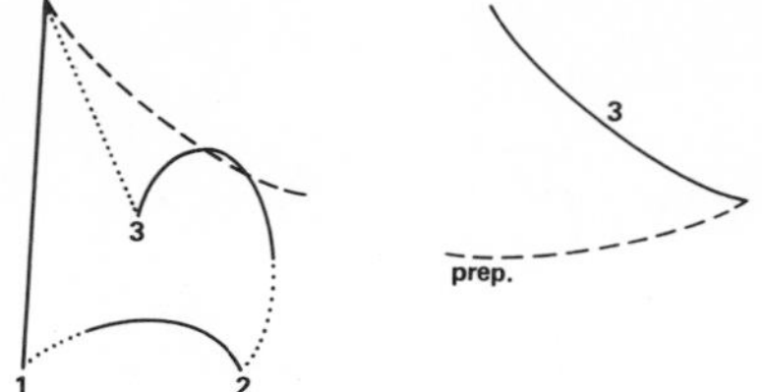
3
1
2
3
prep.

Exercise 46: Draw the appropriate conducting pattern.

MARCHING TO PRETORIA
Introduction:
Song:
I'm with you and you're with me and
so we are all to-geth-er, So we are all to-geth-er, So we are all to-geth-er,
Sing with me, I'll sing with you and so we shall sing to-geth-er as we march a - long.

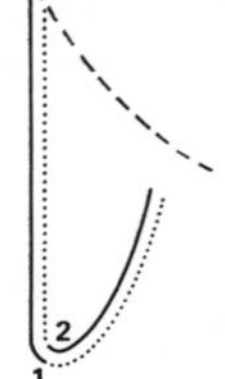

Exercise 47: Draw the appropriate conducting pattern.

What is the meaning of the tempo marking? ________________

Make your conducting pattern small so that you can keep the tempo easily.

FOUR IN A BOAT

Introduction:
Allegro

Song:

Four in a boat and the tide rolls high, Four in a boat and the tide rolls high,

Four in a boat and the tide rolls high, Wait-ing for a pret-ty girl to come by and by.

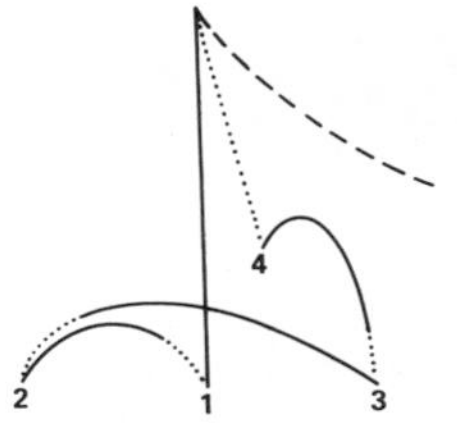
4
2
1
3

Fast.

47

Exercise 48: Draw the appropriate conducting pattern.

SILVER BIRCH

Introduction:
Song:
Sil - ver birch a - lone in a mead - ow Stand-ing all a - lone in a mead - ow
Soon a shep-herd boy comes strol - ling, With his sheep and goats he's strol - ling.

End of Band 3, Side 4 (A STOP BAND)
End of Application Section 5

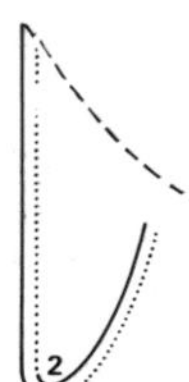
2
1

48

CHAPTER 24 Advanced Durational and Pitch Concepts

Several items pertaining to duration have been thus far omitted because they are more difficult than those discussed at the beginning of this book. The objectives of this chapter include the ability to (1) recognize syncopation and polymeter in music and (2) understand the whole-tone scale and the twelve-tone row. *Syncopation* occurs whenever an accent falls in an unexpected place in the music. Syncopation is created by placing a rest or the end of a tie on the strong beat so that no new pulse is sounded there. Syncopation is also created by stressing weak pulses on the last half of divided beats. Syncopation is sometimes defined as displaced accent, or irregular accent.

Syncopation occurs when the accent is temporarily ______________.

445

Displaced.

445

In quadruple meter the usual accent is on the first beat of the measure with a secondary accent on the third beat. Note regular accent and syncopation in the example.

POMP AND CIRCUMSTANCE

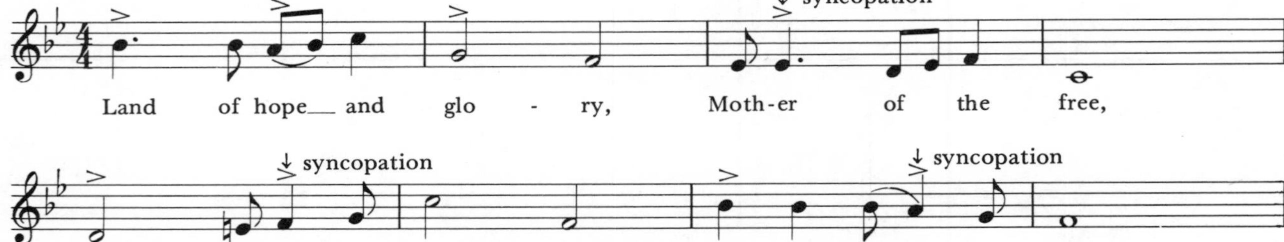
syncopation
Land of hope__ and glo - ry, Moth-er of the free,
syncopation
syncopation
How shall we ex - toll thee, Who are born__ of thee?

Sing the song to obtain a better idea of regular and irregular accents.

446

Singing response.

446

Syncopation is an important part of Latin-American rhythms, American folk music, Afro-American folk music, and jazz. In "The Erie Canal" examples of syncopation can be found in almost every measure.

ERIE CANAL

Notice that "got a," "name is," and "Fif-teen" all have this rhythm: the short note on the beat, followed by a longer note beginning off the beat, creating syncopation. Notice that "Erie canal" ends, not on count 3, but one eighth note before count 3, creating a displaced accent.

In the song below find four examples of syncopation. Circle the notes where the syncopation occurs. Counting the beat aloud or writing out the beat can help in recognizing the syncopation.

LITTLE DAVID

447

447

Circle the syncopated patterns in this song.

CANOE SONG

My pad- dle keen and bright, Flashing with sil - ver, Fol-low the wild goose flight, Dip, dip, and swing.

448

448

Another means of adding variety to musical rhythm is to make an unusual subdivision of the beat. The triplet was mentioned earlier: 3 , three notes played where two are normally found. Other unusual subdivisions of the beat may be found, but mostly in contemporary music. Five or six notes are sometimes played on a pulse: 5 or 6 ; these are also labeled by the number and connected by a bar whenever possible.

Another item to be mentioned is *polyrhythm.* Music written in two or more parts may have passages in which one part contains a rhythmic pattern strongly contrasting with the rhythmic pattern of another part. For example, one part may move in two pulses per beat or per measure while another part moves in three pulses per beat or measure:

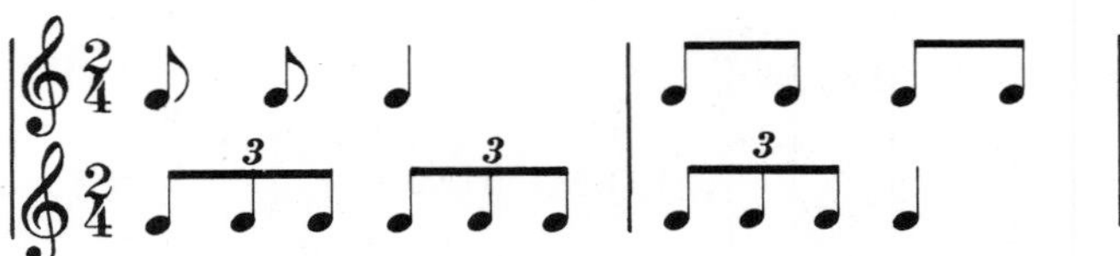

This is called polyrhythm or *cross-rhythm.* Cross-rhythms, or polyrhythms, are found in all music but especially in contemporary music.

In the rhythm pattern below find at least two places where polyrhythm occurs. Circle the notes included in the polyrhythm. Clap each pattern.

449

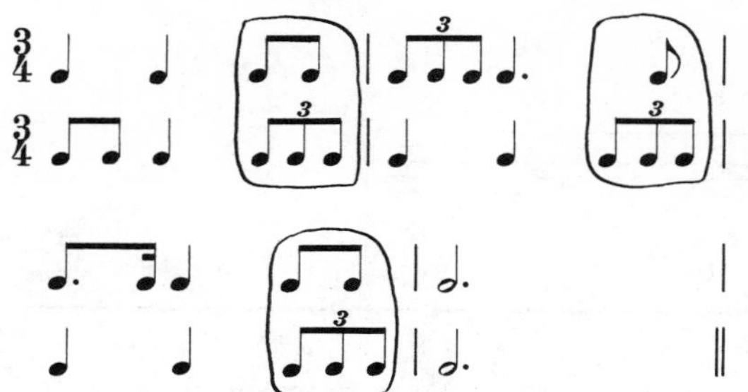

Clapping response.

449

Occasionally, music has passages in which two or more meters are being used at once. This is called *polymeter*. One instrument (or group of instruments) plays in one meter; another instrument (or group) plays in another.

RUMANIAN CHRISTMAS CAROL

Determine the meter for each line in the rhythm pattern below. Indicate this by writing the meter signature in the appropriate place. The quarter note is the unit beat.

Tap the pattern, two hands together (one hand for the upper line, one for the lower).

450

Tapping response.

450

ADVANCED PITCH CONCEPTS

In the earlier discussion of pitch, four kinds of scales were described: the chromatic, the major, the minor, and the pentatonic. One additional scale important in the music of the Western world is the *whole-tone scale*. As its name implies, the whole-tone scale has no half steps. It consists of six tones and the octave, each a whole step above the preceding tone. Whole-tone scales can begin on any pitch.

Play these two scales on the piano. Sing them if possible.

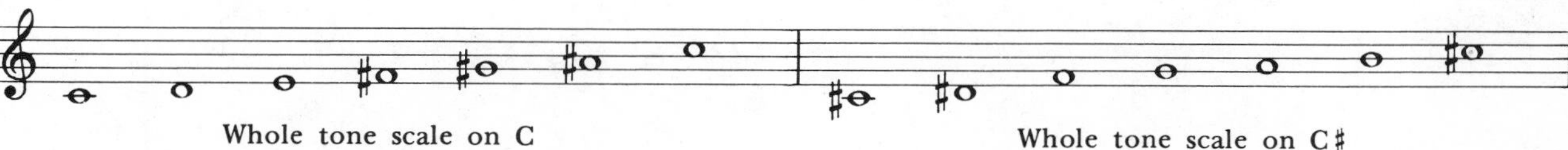

451

Playing response.

451

Write a whole-tone scale beginning on D. Play and sing it.

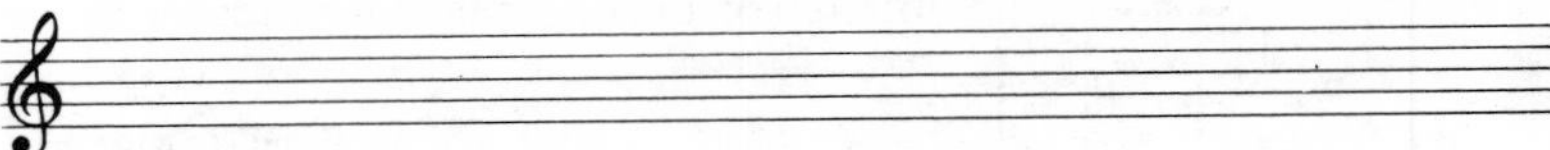

452

Singing response.

452

Some contemporary music uses the *twelve-tone row*. The row consists of the twelve notes of the chromatic scale (without the octave repetition) arranged in any order the composer desires.

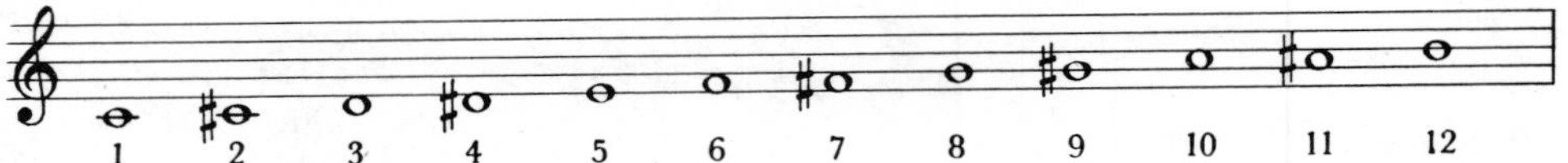

Each pitch of the row must be used in order throughout the piece. No note in the row can be repeated until all have been used. For example, the tone row for the "Webern symphony" is as follows:

The composer transposes this row to nearly every possible pitch level, inverts it (turns it upside down), and plays it backward to make both his melodies and harmonies.

PRETEST for Chapters 25–26: Melody and Form

Mark the correct answer or *answers.*

1. Draw the contour line for:

THE DUCKLINGS

2. Number the phrases. Indicate those that are similar.

REVOLUTIONARY WAR SONG

3. One might describe this melody as:

THE DUCKLINGS

—— a. conjunct

—— b. disjunct

—— c. scalewise

—— d. jagged

4. Mark the high point in the following song:

5. Form in music depends on:

—— a. repetition

—— b. contrast

—— c. phrases

—— d. sentences

6. Repetition in music can be:

—— a. exact

—— b. sequential

—— c. similar

—— d. contrasting

7. If someone were to describe form in music as A A B, you would know he was talking about:

—— a. three-part form

—— b. two-part form

—— c. modified form

—— d. exact form

8. The song "Yankee Doodle" is in:

—— a. three-part form

—— b. four-part form

—— c. binary form

—— d. two-part form

9. The sign D. C. means:

—— a. end of a period

—— b. return to the beginning

—— c. return to the sign

—— d. end of a phrase

10. If one wishes to transpose, he plays a melody:

—— a. with a different instrument

—— b. in a different key

—— c. with variations

—— d. with accompaniment

Answers

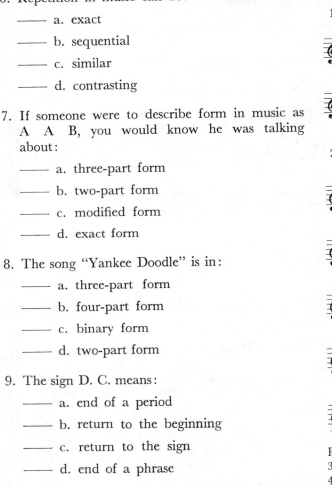

Phrases 1, 2, and 4 are similar.

3. a, c.

4.

5. a, b.
6. a, b, c.
7. b.
8. c, d.
9. b.
10. b.

From your score determine whether you can omit portions of the text.

CHAPTER 25 The Concept of Melody

Almost all music depends on melody. Melody is a basic concept of music. Although the word "melody" has not been mentioned, you have already looked at and sung many melodies in the preceding pages. Much that you have done so far—learning rhythm symbols and pitch symbols, learning to find the correct note on the keyboard, and so forth—will be useful in learning about melody.

Almost all people can recognize some melodies by ear, but if asked, they could not say how they are able to identify the tunes. Thus, discussing melodies without hearing them is meaningless. It is important that you use the record or perform the melodies discussed in this chapter. The objectives for this chapter include (1) ability to draw the contour line for a melody, and (2) ability to describe a melody by some of its characteristics.

Melody is often thought of as a tuneful group of notes. This definition is true enough, but it does not tell us everything we need to know about melody. Melody is made up of pitches, but it is more than pitch; each pitch has duration, and the varying durations fit together to make rhythm so that melody has rhythm. Melody will also have movement or direction; it will sound as if it is going somewhere. Finally, melody makes musical sense, that is, it is expressive.

A melody can be described by its direction: (1) A melody may rise, that is, its pitches may get higher as it moves from beginning to end. A rising melody usually creates tension just as climbing stairs or a mountain path takes effort. (2) Conversely, a melody may descend, giving the feeling of relaxation.

Sing the two melodies.

1.
Joy to the world, the Lord is come.
2.
Lift up your voice, re - joice, a - gain I say re - joice.

Which melody creates the more relaxed feeling? ______

Singing response.

Number 1. (Either answer may be correct depending on how it is sung.)

453

Which of these melodies *generally* ascend? _______Which *generally* descend? _______

TRIO NO. 1 IN D MINOR, OP. 49, 2ND MVMT.

SYMPHONY NO. 1 IN C, OP. 21, 3RD MVMT.

OVERTURE TO MIDSUMMER NIGHT'S DREAM, OP. 21

454

2, 3.

1.

454

Melodies rarely move in only one direction; they tend to turn around after a high or low note and move in the opposite direction. Such melodies can be described by their high or low point. In these melodies, mark the high points with * and the low points with X.

SIMPLE GIFTS

THE STAR-SPANGLED BANNER

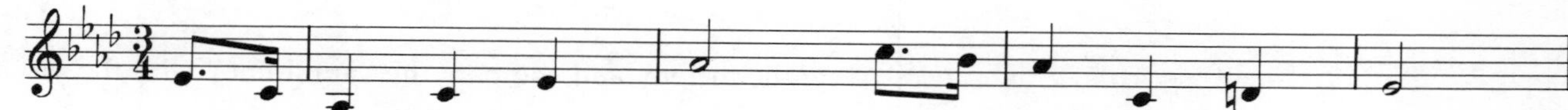

455

*High
1.
x Low
*High
2.
x Low

When we look for the high and low points of a melody, we become conscious of its shape. Shape is a word borrowed from art. Although shape in painting actually exists, in music shape is what is retained in the memory after the melody is performed. Thus, musical memory is important in the understanding of melody. In this example the shape of the melody is graphically represented by the contour line drawn beneath it.

DOWN IN THE VALLEY

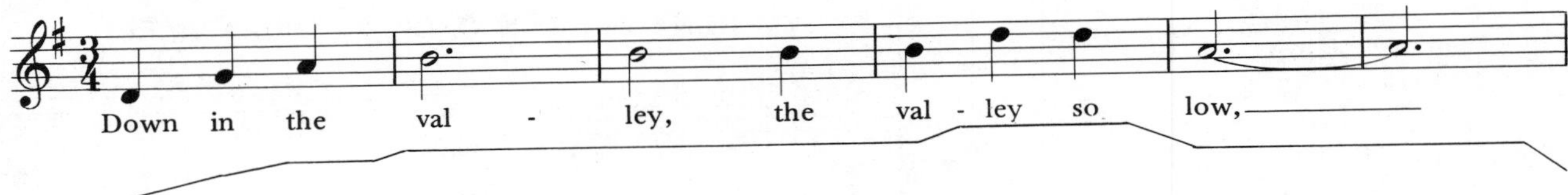
Down in the val - ley, the val - ley so low,

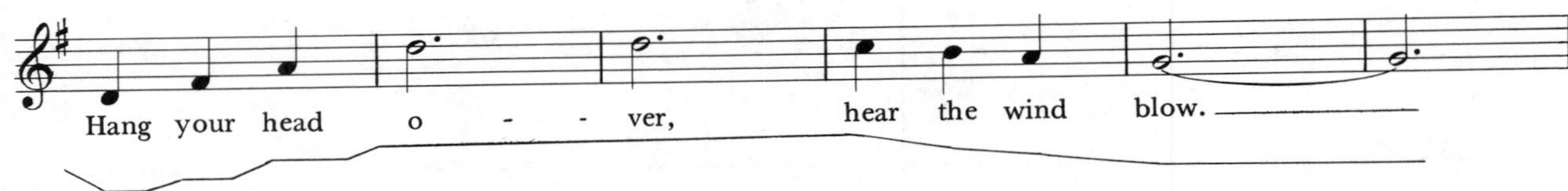
Hang your head o - - ver, hear the wind blow.

Draw the contour line for this melody.

JOY TO THE WORLD

Joy to the world, the Lord is come, Let earth re - ceive her king.

Sing the melody and compare the "aural line" with the visual line.

Singing response.

456

This melody consists of four sections, or phrases. Notice how the contours of phrases 1 and 3 match, as do those of 2 and 4.

MY HAT

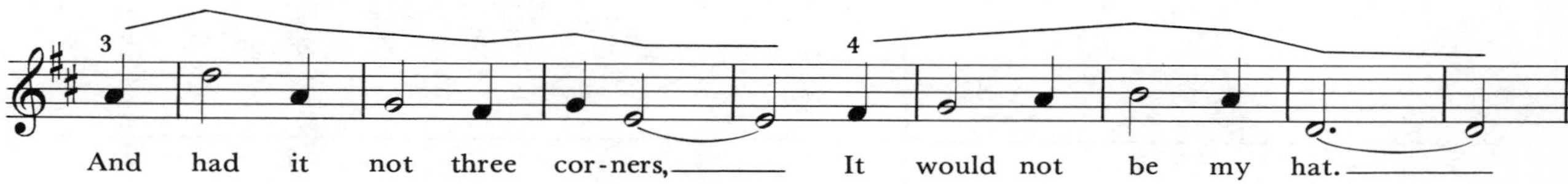

Which two phrases are largely descending? ______

457

1, 3.

457

Other melodic traits can be discovered. Melodies may move along the scale, that is, they are scalewise or *conjunct*. The opposite trait would be a *disjunct,* or skipping, melody, meaning that almost all of the intervals in the melody are larger than a whole step.

This Hungarian folk song is a good example of a melody that moves scalewise, or conjunctly. There are only three places where the melody leaps or skips. Between which measures do the leaps occur?

______ ______ ______

LILY STALK SO SLENDER

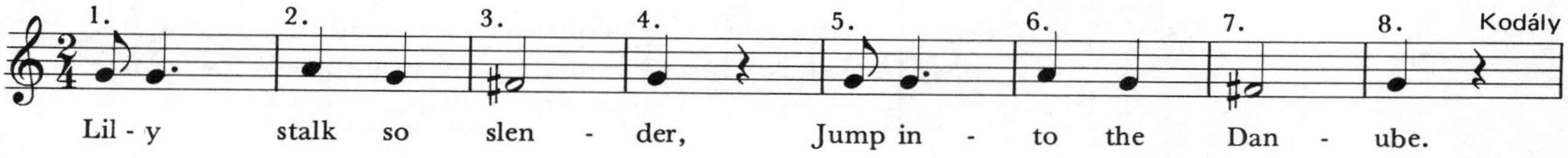

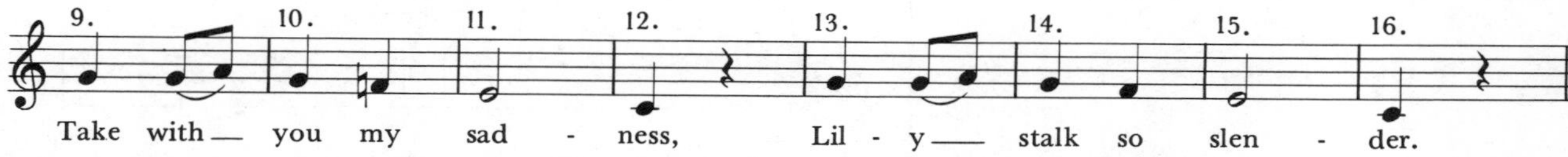

From Bicinia Hungarica, *Vol. I. Copyright 1941 by Zoltan Kodály; Renewed 1969. Copyright assigned 1957 to Boosey & Co., Ltd. English edition © 1962, 1968 by Boosey & Co., Ltd. Used by permission of Boosey & Hawkes (New York and London) and Editio Musica Budapest.*

458

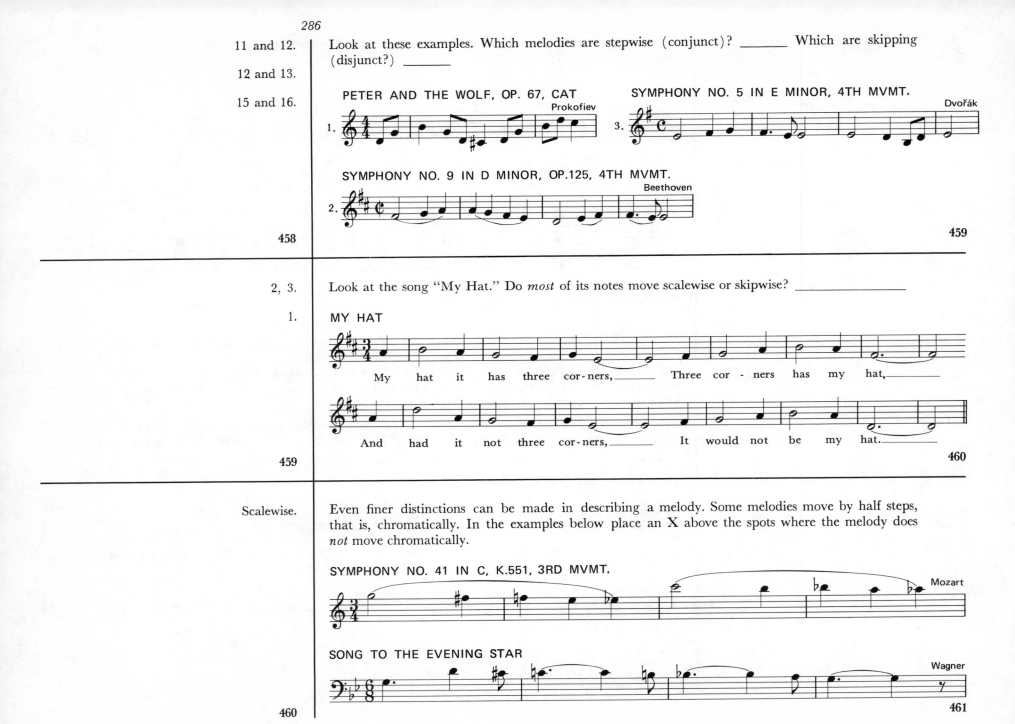

11 and 12.

12 and 13.

15 and 16.

458

Look at these examples. Which melodies are stepwise (conjunct)? ______ Which are skipping (disjunct?) ______

PETER AND THE WOLF, OP. 67, CAT
Prokofiev

1.

SYMPHONY NO. 5 IN E MINOR, 4TH MVMT.
Dvořák

3.

SYMPHONY NO. 9 IN D MINOR, OP.125, 4TH MVMT.
Beethoven

2.

459

2, 3.

1.

459

Look at the song "My Hat." Do *most* of its notes move scalewise or skipwise? ______________

MY HAT

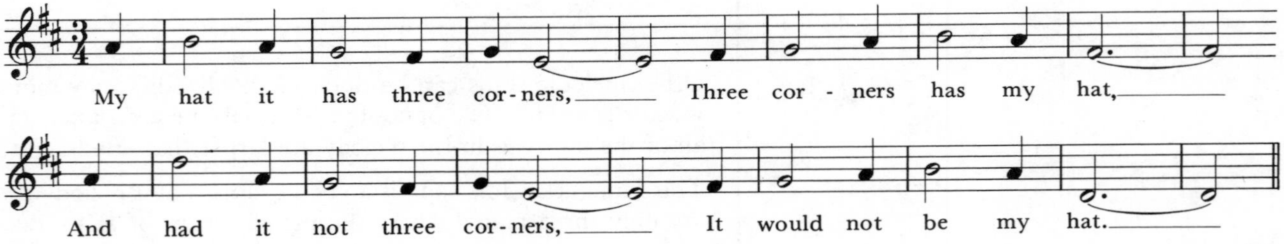

My hat it has three cor-ners,_____ Three cor - ners has my hat,_____

And had it not three cor-ners,_____ It would not be my hat._____

460

Scalewise.

460

Even finer distinctions can be made in describing a melody. Some melodies move by half steps, that is, chromatically. In the examples below place an X above the spots where the melody does *not* move chromatically.

SYMPHONY NO. 41 IN C, K.551, 3RD MVMT.
Mozart

SONG TO THE EVENING STAR
Wagner

461

461

Another identifying feature of melody is its dimensions. Melody has two dimensions; length and range. Some melodies are very short; others are quite long. Usually, length applies to the number of measures rather than to the number of notes.

FUGUE IN G MINOR

Bach

FUGUE NO. 9, W.T.C. NO. 2

Bach

A melody also has a *range*. A narrow range means that there is a short distance from the lowest note to the highest note in the melody. A wide range means that the lowest note and the highest note are far apart. "My Hat" (frame 460) has a rather narrow range because *most* of the song uses the pitches from D up to B, a range of six notes. The actual highest note is the D on "were" (making the real range an octave), but it is used only once. Vocal music can be distinguished from instrumental music by its range; instrumental music has greater range possibility.

Range means the distance from the __________ ________ of a melody to the __________ ________.

There is no dividing line on what is a narrow and what is a wide range. Many elementary songs are similar in range. More extreme range is indicated in one of the instrumental pieces in the next frame.

462

Lowest note; highest note.

462

Which melody has a wide range? ______________ A narrow range? ______________

EIN HELDENLEBEN, OP. 40

Strauss

VARIATION ON A THEME BY HAYDN, OP. 56a

Brahms

463

1. *Ein Heldenleben.*
2. *Variation on a Theme by Haydn.*

Register is another characteristic of melody. Two melodies can be similar in shape, rhythm, and dimensions but different in *register*. Some melodies are meant to be played (and heard) in the high register, for example, while others are written to be played and heard in the low register (see the next two melodies).

CLASSICAL SYMPHONY, OP. 25, 2ND MVMT.

Copyright 1926 by Edition Russe de Musique. Copyright assigned to Boosey & Hawkes, Inc., for the world. Reprinted by permission.

PETER AND THE WOLF, OP. 67, THE GRANDFATHER

Rhythm is still another distinguishing element. In many melodies the rhythm is the most interesting aspect. For example, the syncopation of "Erie Canal" is the quality that makes the melody attractive.

ERIE CANAL

Some melodies are decorated, embellished, or given added notes around the main notes in a melody.

PIANO SONATA IN A, K. 331, 3RD MVMT.

The melody notes are A, C, E, A, C (notes of the a triad). The melody is embellished by repeating these notes for emphasis and using a note above and a note below.

Another example of adding notes to "decorate or embellish" the melody is "Greensleeves."

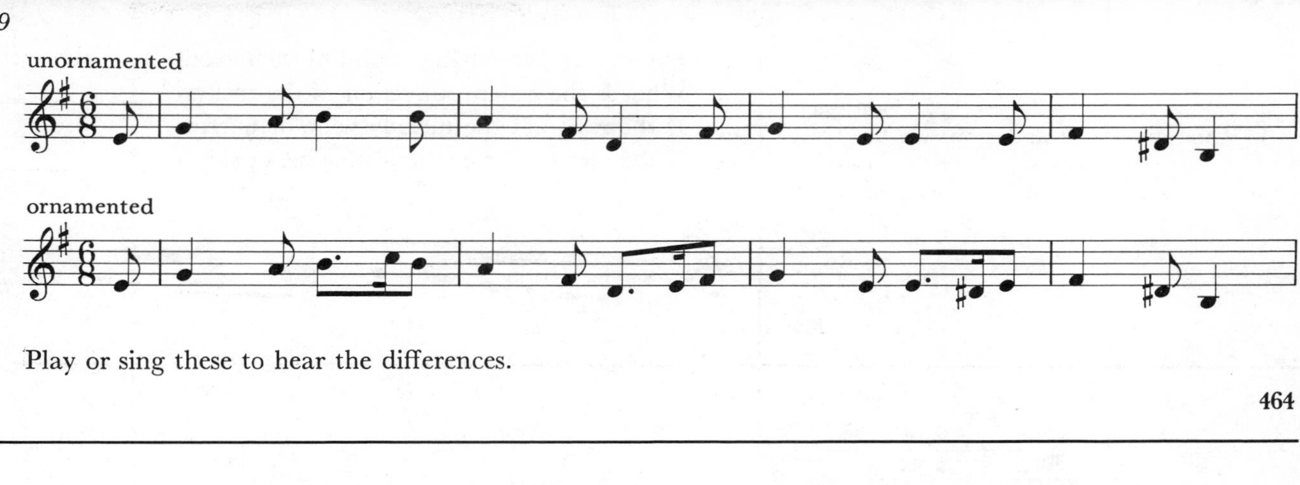

Play or sing these to hear the differences.

464

Playing or singing response.

464

Rhythmic flow is still another descriptor. Some melodies seem to move smoothly along without pause, while others go in spurts and bursts. "Greensleeves" has a smooth rhythmic flow.

Contrast this with the Webern Quartet #22, 2d mvmt.

QUARTET NO.22, 2ND MVMT.

Webern

© *copyright 1932 Universal Edition. Used by permission of the publisher. Theodore Presser Company Sole representative U.S.A., Canada and Mexico.*

1. Draw the contour of the melody below.
2. Is the melody primarily conjunct or disjunct? ________________
3. What is the key of the music? ________________ Which note would be the tonal center? ________________
4. Write the rhythm pattern that is repeated several times. ________________

LONG LONG AGO

Tell me the tales that to me were so dear, long long a - go, long long a - go

465

1. 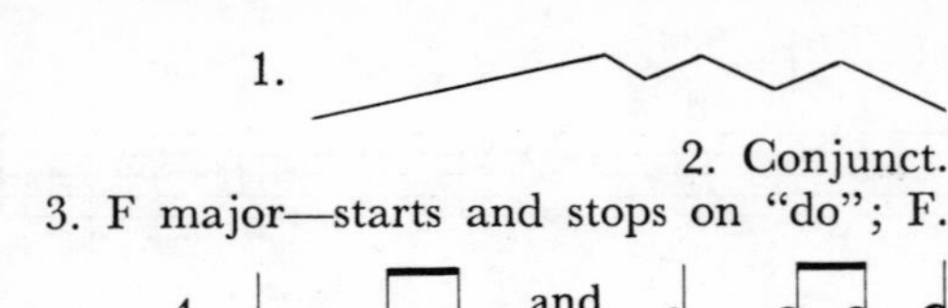

2. Conjunct.

3. F major—starts and stops on "do"; F.

4. ♩ ♫ and ♩ ♫ 𝅗𝅥

465

1. Put an x above the high point of the melody, a √ above its low point.
2. What is the general direction of the melody? ________________
3. Is the range of the melody wide or narrow? ________________
4. Is the motion chromatic, scalewise, or skipping? ________________

466

1. 

2. Rising, upward

3. Wide.

4. Scalewise.

466

CHAPTER 26 Form

At the beginning of this book we said that music depended on organization. Without organization musical sounds are meaningless. One aspect of organization is *form*. Form is found not only in music, but in other art including painting, sculpture, literature, and drama. In fact, these are called "art forms." When we can recognize a melody by its contour, its rhythm, its range, register, length, and tonality, we are ready to perceive musical form. The objectives for this chapter include (1) understanding of musical phrase; (2) recognition of repetition and contrast; and (3) acquaintance with simple two- and three-part form.

Besides those listed above, what other areas of the arts use form? ______________________

____

467

Architecture, dance, poetry, film, photography. All of the arts use form.

A small unit of musical form is the phrase. Like language, music is divided into phrases. The musical phrase is similar to that in language: a group of notes that fit together but may not necessarily be complete. Phrase may also be defined as "a natural break in the melodic line." These breaks or pauses are indicated by longer note values, rests, use of the tonal center, and other devices that provide a feeling of relaxation or pause in music. Look at "My Hat." It contains four sections, or phrases. Any one of these phrases by itself would make sense, but none would sound complete if sung or played alone.

MY HAT

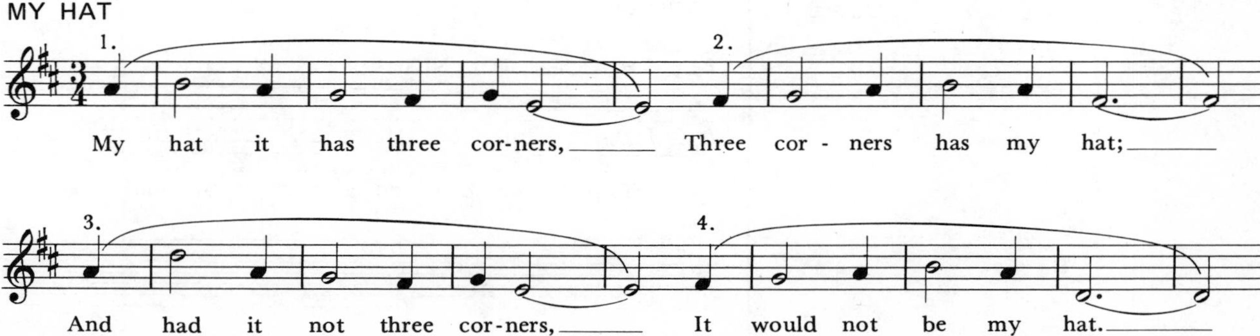
1.
My hat it has three cor-ners,
2.
Three cor - ners has my hat;
3.
And had it not three cor-ners,
4.
It would not be my hat.

467

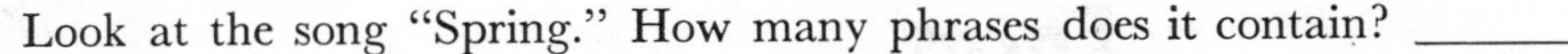

Look at the song "Spring." How many phrases does it contain? _______

SPRING

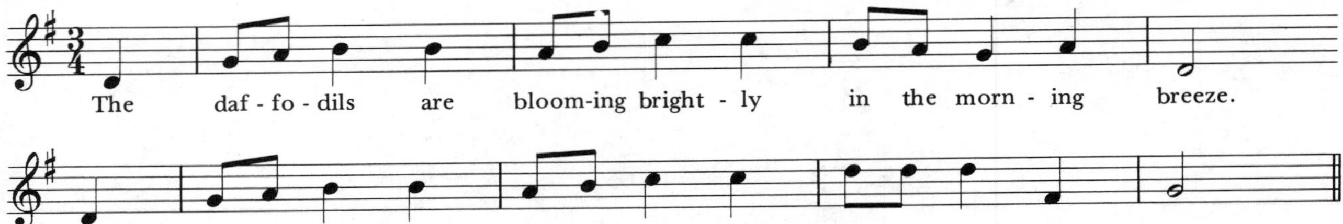

The daf - fo - dils are bloom-ing bright - ly in the morn - ing breeze.
The rob - ins all are sing - ing sweet - ly in the cher - ry trees.

What devices were used to help indicate a pause in the melodic line? ________________________

____

468

Two.

Long notes at pause points; use of tonal center at end; use of D, an important note in the I and V chords at the end of the first phrase.

468

The words help us to identify the end of the phrase. Even if there were no words, however, we would still know where the phrases end in the song in the previous frame. Note the repetition, the downward relaxing feeling, ending on a chord tone, and similar clues to identify the phrases.

Draw a curved line over each phrase of music in "Spring" to signify its beginning and ending. (See "My Hat" in frame 468 for how to draw the curved line.)

469

469

Although a piece of music may have a very complicated form, the concept of form is a simple one. Basically, form is built on two ideas: *repetition* and *contrast.*

Repetition in music appears several ways; some are obvious and some are "disguised." The simplest kind of repetition is exact repetition—the melody is presented exactly as it originally appeared. Examine the two phrases.

ALL THROUGH THE NIGHT

Sleep, my child, and peace at - tend thee, All thru the night.

Guard - ian an - gels God will lend thee, All thru the night.

Is the second phrase exact repetition of the first? ______

Play the two phrases on the piano to hear the similarity.

470

Yes.

Playing response.

470

Exact repetition is not very interesting, however, for we know just what is coming. The composer, therefore, may vary his musical ideas while keeping enough of the original idea to make it recognizable.

Use of the musical idea exactly as it was first presented is called ____________________.

471

Exact repetition.

471

Compare phrases 1 and 2 with phrases 3 and 4.

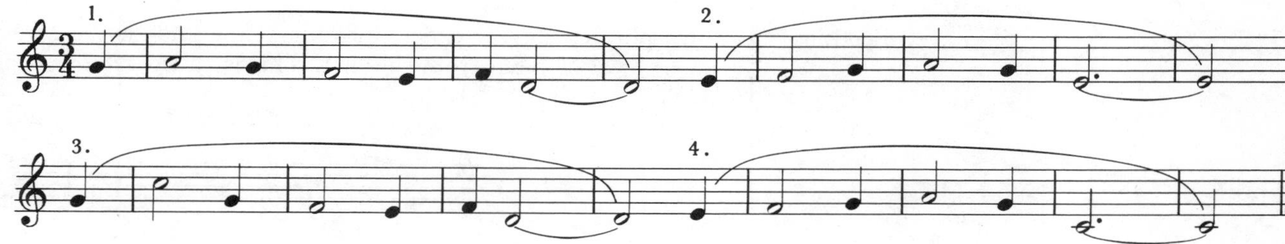

Are the final two phrases exact repetition of the first two? ______

If you find differences, put an X over the spots in 3 and 4 that differ from 1 and 2.

472

No.

472

Frame 472 was an example of what is called *varied repetition*. In the song "Spring," is phrase 2 exact repetition of phrase 1 or is it varied repetition? ____________________

SPRING

473

Varied repetition.

"Spring" and "My Hat" are good examples of *similar* phrases, or varied repetition. Two phrases may begin alike but be different at the end. Two phrases may be similar in rhythm but be different in pitch. Or two phrases may be alike throughout except for a few pitch or rhythmic changes.

Does this example have varied or exact repetition? ____________________

REVOLUTIONARY WAR SONG

473

474

Exact repetition.

Two phrases may be exactly alike in shape and rhythm, but the second one will lie at a higher or lower level of pitch from the first. This is called *sequence,* another method of varying melody.

Measure 2 is just like measure 1, but a step higher in pitch.

The following kinds of repetition have been explained: (1) exact repetition, in which the music is the same both in rhythm and pitch; (2) varied, or similar repetition, in which the music may start out the same but change or in which the rhythm is similar but the pitches are different; (3) sequential repetition, in which melodic and rhythmic patterns are repeated at a different pitch level.

In addition to repetition, another aspect of form is *contrast.* If a musical composition were made up only of repetitions, it would not be very interesting. Contrasting musical material is used in even the simplest piece in order to make an interesting form.

In music, repetition is used to give unity; contrast is used to give ____________________.

474

475

Variety or interest.

475

One way the composer can create music different from what he used at the beginning of his piece is to use a new melody, one different in its pitch, its shape, its rhythm, its duration, key, and so forth.

In the two phrases from "Erie Canal," notice how phrase 2 contrasts with phrase 1 in pitch, contour, and rhythm.

ERIE CANAL

1.
I got a mule, her name is Sal,
2.
Fif-teen miles on the Er-ie Ca-nal.

Draw the contour line for each phrase.

476

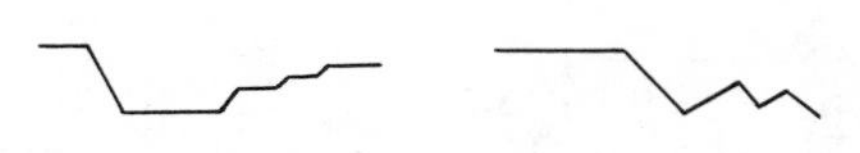

476

SWEETLY SINGS THE DONKEY (ROUND)

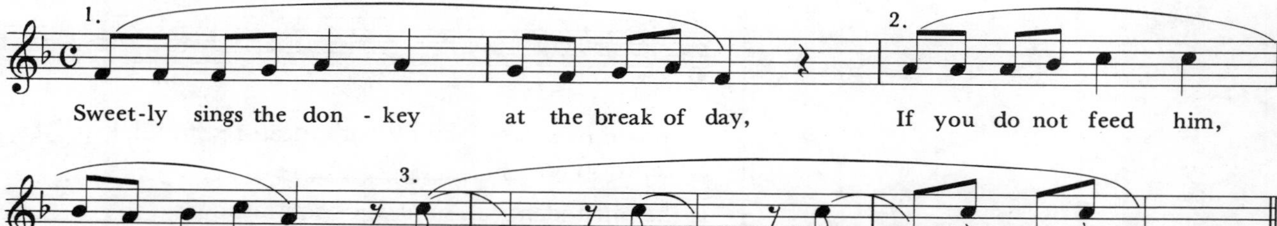
1.
Sweet-ly sings the don - key at the break of day,
2.
If you do not feed him, this is what he'll say,
3.
Hee haw! Hee haw! Hee haw! Hee haw! Hee haw!

In terms of exact repetition, varied repetition, sequence or contrast, describe the phrases in "Sweetly Sings the Donkey." ______________________________

____

477

Phrase 2 is a higher sequence of 1. Phrase 3 contrasts with 1 and 2.

477

When the composer states a melody and then uses contrasting material, we have *two-part form:* the first melody (A) and the contrasting section (B) make up the musical form. Sometimes A will be repeated (exact, varied, or sequence), and the form is indicated this way: AAB. If B is repeated, the form is: ABB. These are all two-part form because the form consists of two musical ideas, one following the other.

Using A for the first musical idea and B for the second, give three versions of two-part form.

1. _______ 2. _______ 3. _______

478

AB, AAB, ABB, AABB. (ABA is incorrect; see frame 485.)

478

Look at the first six measures of "America." Measures 3 and 4 are a varied repetition of measures 1 and 2; then measures 5 and 6 are different both in shape and rhythm. This phrase is a small two-part form: AAB.

AMERICA

A 1. 2. A 3. 4. B 5. 6.

Compare measures 1 and 2 with measures 3 and 4 in "America." Is the rhythm identical, similar, or contrasting? _______________

Is the pitch identical, similar, or contrasting? _______________

479

Identical.

Measures 1 and 3: sequence. Measures 2 and 4: contrast in pitch.

479

Another term for two-part form is *binary form.* Many familiar songs (popular, rock, and folk) are written in binary form. A song that has a chorus is two-part form, the verse being A, the chorus B.

Notice in "Yankee Doodle" that the verse (A) seems to consistently use and to center around F. The chorus (B) uses as well as , and centers around D and C. B contrasts with A both rhythmically and melodically.

YANKEE DOODLE

There are numerous examples in which binary form is the form for the complete composition. The two-part idea also occurs over and over *within* most pieces, no matter what their overall form may be. Often a phrase of music is incomplete by itself and seems to require another phrase to finish it. We may think of this as question–answer. It is really a very small two-part form. Below is the musical question (A). Can you sing the music that provides the answer (B)?

480

Singing response.

480

Sing the first phrase of "My Hat." Although it is an entity, it does not sound complete by itself. Sing the second phrase. Note the more complete effect.

MY HAT

481

Singing response.

481

When you sang the first two phrases of "My Hat" or of "The Star-Spangled Banner," you sang a small binary form, AB, in which B "answered" A. Phrase A is called the *antecedent phrase* and phrase B the *consequent phrase.*

The antecedent phrase and the consequent phrase together constitute a musical period. In music, a period is usually two phrases.

How many periods are there in the song "My Hat?" ______

MY HAT

My hat it has three cor-ners,
Three cor - ners has my hat,
And had it not three cor-ners,
It would not be my hat.

482

Two.

482

A period *may* consist of more than two phrases, although two is the most common. Look at "Sweetly Sings the Donkey." There are only three phrases in the entire song. The song is one period in length, made up of three phrases.

What is the form of the song? ______ (use letters)

SWEETLY SINGS THE DONKEY

Sweet-ly sings the don - key at the break of day.
If you do not feed him,
this is what he'll say.
Hee haw! Hee haw! Hee haw! Hee haw! Hee haw!

483

AAB, which is two-part or binary.

483

Are phrases 1 and 2 of "Sweetly Sings the Donkey" repetition or contrast? ______________

484

Repetition (sequence).

Another widely used musical form is *three-part form* or ternary form: ABA. The letters tell you what the form contains—the first music (A) followed by a contrasting section (B) and then a return to the first music (A). The first section is often repeated: AABA. Sometimes the second section is repeated as well as the first: AABBA. The final A is rarely repeated because the listener does not need to hear it more than once after having heard it earlier in the piece.

Remember, two-part form has two ideas, one following the other: AB, AAB, AABB. By definition, three-part form has only two ideas, A and B, but the first idea is always repeated *after* the second is presented: ABA, AABA, AABBA.

This song is in ternary form. Which phrase or phrases make up the B section? ______
The B section is different from A in what two ways? 1. ______________ 2. ______________

COME ROWING WITH ME

484

485

Phrase 3.

Rhythm; shape of melody (pitch).

Look again at the song. Phrases 1 and 2 are considered to be AA. (Phrase 3 is B; phrase 4 is A. Thus, we have AABA). Compare phrase 2 with phrase 1. What kind of repetition is used? ______________ Compare phrase 4 with phrase 1. What kind of repetition is used? ______________

COME ROWING WITH ME

485

486

1–2 sequential or sequence.

1–4 exact.

Several symbols are used to make the form of the music more easily understood when seen on the musical page.

The double bar (‖) indicates the end of the piece, and in longer works it is also used to indicate the end of a section.

The repeat sign (:‖) is a double bar with two dots. It indicates that the entire piece is repeated.

When a section of music is enclosed by repeat signs at both ends (‖: :‖), only that section is repeated.

The Italian term "Da Capo" (Abbreviated D.C.) means to return to the beginning of the piece. The piece is then performed as far as the "Fine," or finish, where a double bar occurs along with the term "Fine."*

A slightly different direction is given by the term "Dal Segno" (D.S.), which means return to the sign and perform the music from there to the "Fine."

D.C. al Fine = from the beginning to the Fine.

D.S. al Fine = from the sign to the Fine. The sign looks like this: 𝄋

Define each numbered item in the song below.

SHORT'NIN' BREAD

1. ________ 2. ________________ 3. ________________________

* Pronounce "fine" as fēē–nāy.

1. End.

2. Repeat.

3. Go to the beginning and stop at the Fine.

487

Our examples of form have been brief songs suitable for grade-school children. The most complex and lengthy compositions, however, such as symphonies, are built on the same principles of repetition and contrast as those in these simple tunes.

APPLICATION: Melody

Exercise 49: Listen to three melodies. Decide if each is a rising or falling melody and if each is scalewise (conjunct) or skips (disjunct).

Melody 1: Rising, falling or mixed? ________________ Conjunct or disjunct? ________________
Melody 2: Rising, falling or mixed? ________________ Conjunct or disjunct? ________________
Melody 3: Rising, falling or mixed? ________________ Conjunct or disjunct? ________________

End of Band 4, Side 4

Melody 1: Rising, conjunct.

Melody 2: Falling, conjunct.

Melody 3: Mixed, disjunct.

49

Exercise 50: Listen to a sixteenth-century song. The unornamented version is played first, followed by a version with added notes "ornamenting" the melody.

DALLE PIU ALTE SFERE - ARCHILEI — Sixteenth Century

End of Band 5, Side 4

No response.

50

Glossary

Tempo Terms (Italian)

Prestissimo: as fast as possible.
Presto: very fast.
Allegro: quick; cheerful.
Allegretto: a tempo between andante and allegro; cheerful.
Moderato: moderate.
Andante: walking.
Adagio: slow; at ease.
Lento: slow.
Largo: broad.
Ritard, ritardando: slow down gradually.
Accelerando: gradually quicken the tempo.
Rallentando: gradually slacken the tempo.
A tempo: return to the original tempo.
Rubato: unsteady tempo; free.
Ad lib.: vary the tempo as the performer desires.

Dynamic Marks (Italian)

Pianissimo (pp): very soft.
Piano (p): soft.
Mezzo piano (mp): medium soft.
Mezzo forte (mf): medium loud.
Forte (f): loud.
Fortissimo (ff): very loud.
Crescendo (cresc.): gradually get louder.
Decrescendo (decres.): gradually get softer.
Diminuendo (dim.): gradually get softer.
Sforzando (sf.): sudden, strong accent.
Forte-piano (fp): loud followed by soft.

Syllables

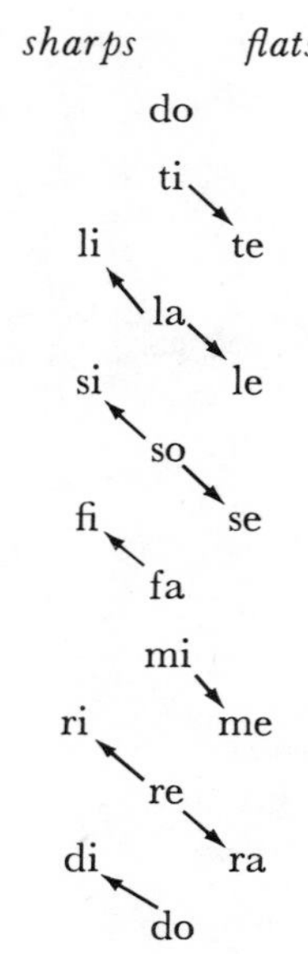

Scales

The chromatic scale consists of twelve pitches, each one-half step from the next, arranged in ascending or descending order. For example, C, C♯, D, D♯, E, F, F♯, G, G♯, A, A♯, B. The upper C completes the ascending scale and is the octave repetition of the starting pitch.

The diatonic scale consists of seven pitches, one for each letter degree, arranged in ascending or descending order, separated by half step or whole-step intervals. The eighth pitch is the octave repetition of the first pitch. The white notes on the piano keyboard, played in order, represent a diatonic arrangement.

The major scale is a diatonic scale consisting of the following intervals: whole step, whole step, half step, whole step, whole step, whole, step, half step; or two whole steps, a half step, three whole steps, a half step. For example, the white notes on the piano keyboard played from C to C: C, D, E, F, G, A, B, C.

Three forms of the *minor scale* are commonly used. *Natural minor:* a diatonic scale with the half steps falling between pitches 2 and 3, and pitches 5 and 6; for example, the minor scale played on the white keys of the piano from A to A. *Harmonic minor:* differs from natural minor in that the seventh pitch of the scale is raised one half step, creating an interval of a step and a half or three half steps between pitches 6 and 7 and an interval of a half step between pitches 7 and 8. *Melodic minor:* the ascending scale is similar to the major scale except that the third pitch is lowered one half step, making the interval between pitches 2 and 3 a half step and the interval between 3 and 4 a whole step. Some teachers explain the ascending scale as the natural minor with a raised sixth and seventh. The descending melodic minor scale is identical with natural minor.

The whole-tone scale consists of six pitches, each a whole step interval from the next. The seventh pitch is the octave repetition of the starting pitch. For example C, D, E, F♯, G♯, A♯, C.

The pentatonic scale consists of five pitches, the sixth pitch being the octave. The more common forms of the pentatonic scale may be illustrated by using only the black keys of the piano, the two most frequently used being exemplified by the pattern C♯, D♯, F♯, G♯, A♯, C♯ and the pattern F♯, G♯, A♯, C♯, D♯, F♯. These are *tonal* pentatonic scales that have only whole steps (whole-tones) or larger and no half step intervals. Tonal pentatonic scales may be built on any of the five pitches represented by the black notes of the keyboard. *Semitonal* pentatonic scales also exist that use half steps, whole steps, and larger intervals such as the major third.

Intervals

Major intervals (the second, third, sixth, and seventh intervals) are those in which the higher pitch fits into the major scale of the lower pitch. A major second consists of one whole step or two half steps; a major third consists of two whole steps; a major sixth consists of four whole steps and one half step; a major seventh consists of five whole steps and one half step, or one half step less than the octave.

Perfect intervals (the unison, fourth, fifth, and octave intervals) are those in which the higher pitch fits into the major scale of the lower pitch. A unison is two notes of the same pitch; a perfect fourth consists of two whole steps and one half step; the perfect fifth consists of three whole steps and one half step; the octave consists of six whole steps, the upper pitch having the same letter name as the lower pitch.

The major intervals (second, third, sixth, and seventh) are made *minor intervals* by lessening their size one half step by lowering the upper pitch or raising the lower pitch.

The minor intervals (second, third, sixth, and seventh) become *diminished intervals* by lessening their size one half step. The perfect intervals (fourths, fifths, octaves) become diminished intervals by lessening their size one half step.

All major and perfect intervals may be made *augmented intervals* by enlarging their size one half step. This may be done either by lowering the lower pitch one half step or by raising the upper pitch one half step.

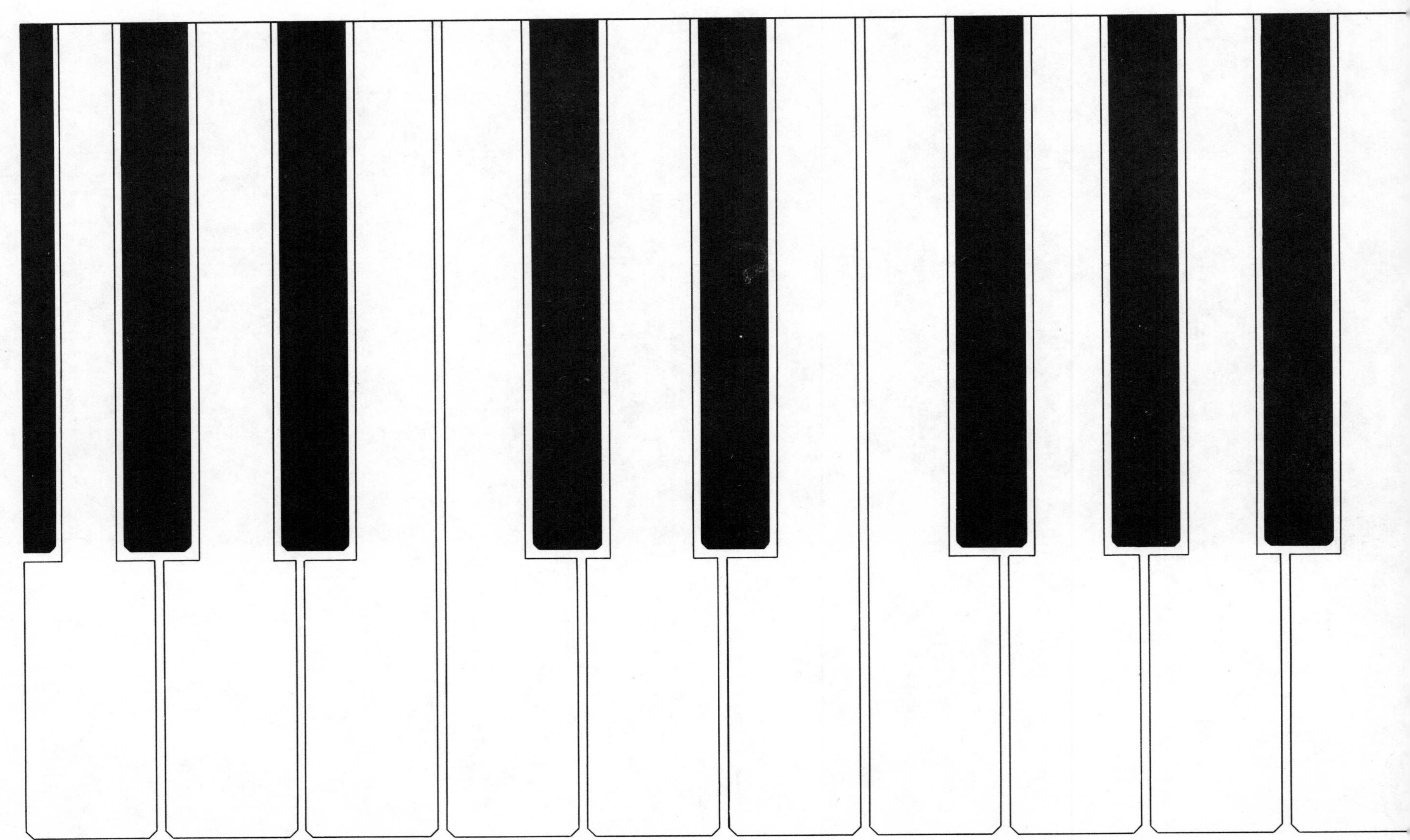

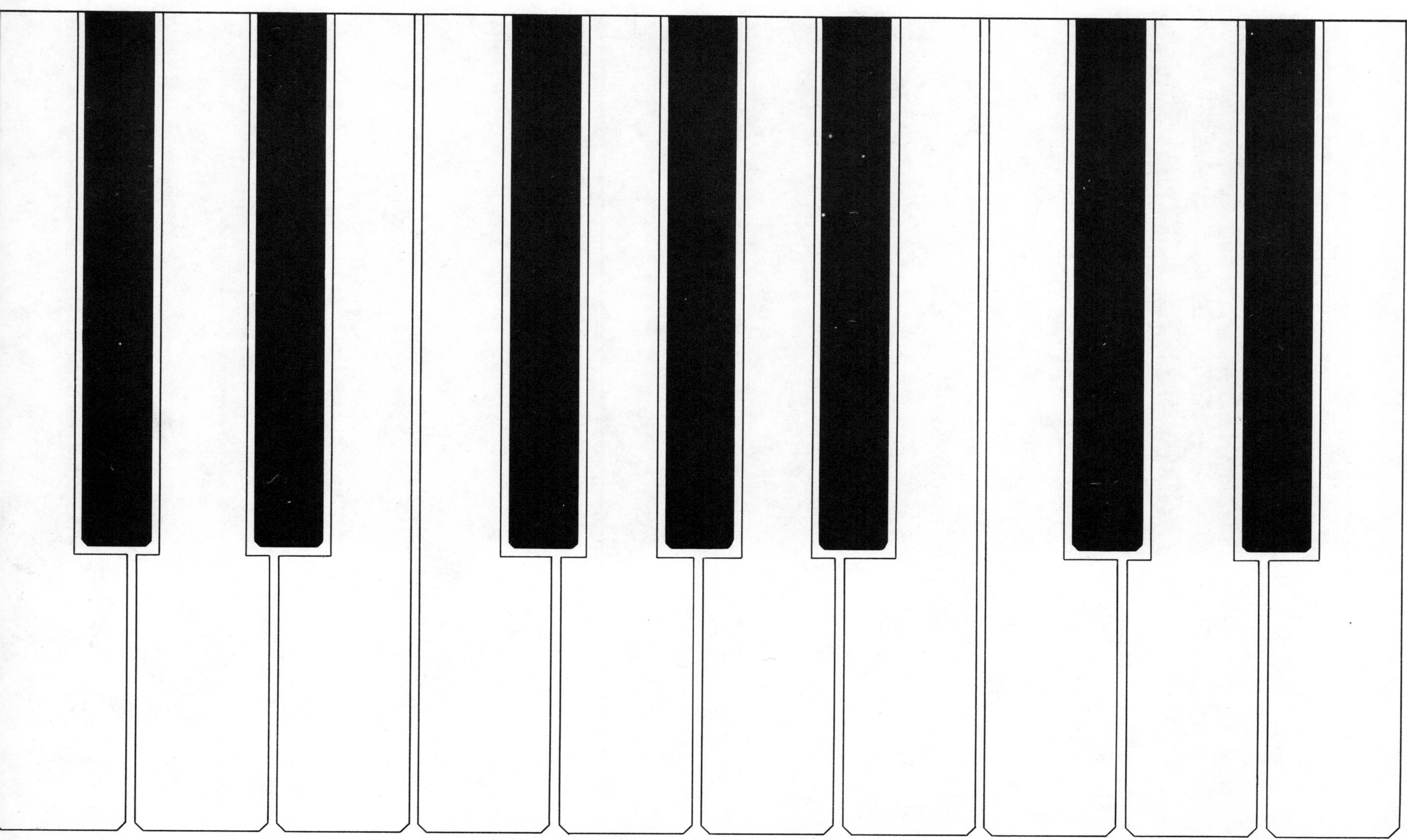